IMPERIAL FROM THE BEGINNING

IMPERIAL FROM THE BEGINNING

THE CONSTITUTION

OF THE

ORIGINAL EXECUTIVE

Saikrishna Bangalore Prakash

Yale
UNIVERSITY PRESS

New Haven and London

Published with assistance from the foundation established
in memory of Amasa Stone Mather of the Class of 1907,
Yale College.

Yale University Press books may be purchased in quantity for
educational, business, or promotional use. For information, please e-
mail sales.press@yale.edu (U.S. office) or sales@yaleup.co.uk (U.K.
office).

Set in MT Baskerville and Bulmer types by IDS Infotech Ltd.
Printed in the United States of America.

Library of Congress Cataloging-in-Publication Data
Prakash, Saikrishna Bangalore, author.
Imperial from the beginning: the constitution of the original
executive / Saikrishna Bangalore Prakash.
pages   cm
Includes bibliographical references and index.
ISBN 978-0-300-19456-2 (alk. paper)
1. Executive power—United States—History—18th century.
2. Legislative power—United States—History—18th century.
3. Presidents—United States—History—18th century. 4. Judges—
United States—History—18th century. 5. Republicanism—United
States—History—18th century.
6. Political leadership—United States—History—18th century.
7. Constitutional history—United States. 8. United States—Politics
and government—History—18th century. I. Title.
KF5053.P725 2015
342.73'062—dc23   2014030083

A catalogue record for this book is available from the
British Library.

This paper meets the requirements of
ANSI/NISO Z39.48–1992 (Permanence of Paper).

10 9 8 7 6 5 4 3 2 1

To my parents, B. K. Prakash and Subbalaxmi B. Prakash

CONTENTS

CONTENTS

ACKNOWLEDGMENTS

I owe thanks to many.

Gratitude to colleagues and mentors who have educated me on the presidency: Larry Alexander, Akhil Amar, Steve Calabresi, Neal Devins, John Harrison, Harold Koh, Gary Lawson, Caleb Nelson, Michael Paulsen, Eric Posner, Michael Ramsey, Michael Rappaport, Steve Smith, Kate Stith, Adrian Vermeule, Steve Walt, and John Yoo.

Thanks to the generous support offered by Deans Daniel Rodriguez and Kevin Cole of the University of San Diego and Paul Mahoney of the University of Virginia. Thanks to Robert George and Bradford Wilson of the James Madison Program at Princeton University for supplying a congenial place to begin writing. Thanks to excellent research support from the wonderful librarians at the University of San Diego and the University of Virginia.

I also owe much to a phalanx of research assistants: Ryan Baasch, Michael Baker, Lucas Beirne, Andrew Bentz, Simon Cataldo, Devin DeBacker, Bernadette Donovan, Andrew Ferguson, Thomas Feiter, Franchesca Fitch, Nicole Frazer, Russel Henderson, Alexander Krueger-Wyman, Carolyn Kuduk, Michael Lough, April Russo, Maria Slater, and Brian Stephan.

Thanks also to Lynn Chu, Glen Hartley, Kip Keller, Phillip King, Jaya Chatterjee and William Frucht for helping me navigate the new (to me) world of book publishing.

Finally, thanks to the patience of my loving wife, Rashmi, and my three girls, Gayathri, Gauri, and Aditi Lakshmi.

Endarō Mahānubhāvulu. Andarikī Vandanamulu.

INTRODUCTION

We live in turbulent times: a sputtering economy, an interminable war, and Kulturkampf over gay marriage and immigration. Hoping to satisfy public expectations for vigorous action, recent presidents have been energetic and ever grasping, recognizing that their legacy rests on how well they navigate the crises that periodically buffet the nation. This continues a pattern of hyperactivity in which chief executives have channeled Abraham Lincoln and Franklin Roosevelt. No modern president wants to be the next James Buchanan, a man who clung to a modest conception of his office while the Union disintegrated around him.

When chief executives emulate Lincoln and Roosevelt, delicate constitutional questions come to the fore. President George W. Bush claimed the right to ignore statutes and asserted that he was the "decider" on all military matters. His predecessor claimed a power to postpone civil suits brought against him and the power to bomb other nations. The current president seems no less enamored of the idea that the Constitution cedes him vast powers over foreign affairs, the military, and the execution of federal law. In the process, he has forsaken campaign pledges meant to demonstrate that his was a less regal conception of the office, proving once again that a politician's stance on presidential powers often turns on whether he or she occupies the Oval Office.

Has the reach of contemporary presidents exceeded their constitutional grasp? Some who favor the idea of a living Constitution, and believe that practice makes the Constitution, suppose that recent patterns are especially probative. For instance, if recent presidents regularly have settled the foreign claims of American nationals, then this practice establishes the legitimacy of that power, whatever may have been true a hundred or two hundred years ago. For other living constitutionalists, the Constitution is (or should be) whatever generates the best policies, suggesting that whether the executive has particular authority depends on whether we think, all things considered, a president ought to have it. Under this functional approach, the content of the Constitution rests on our refined sense of the optimal allocation of power among the branches.

Notwithstanding the appeal of the living Constitution in other areas, founding conceptions of the presidency remain at the forefront of conversations about the office. Unsurprisingly, scholars favoring the original Constitution apply their methodology (originalism) to Article II. But other scholars, even those dismissive of originalism, nonetheless make claims about the presidency the Founding Fathers constructed.[1] For whatever reason, many proponents of a living Constitution have a soft spot for the presidency ordained and established by the original Constitution.[2] Hence, there is something of a convergence with respect to presidential power and duties: almost everyone supposes that the Constitution's original meaning matters in some unusual way.

The widespread sense that the original presidency remains relevant has not eliminated sharp disagreements about the kind of president the original Constitution established. The dominant approach believes that the office has metastasized into what Arthur Schlesinger called an "imperial presidency," with modern chief executives amassing powers beyond the wildest nightmares of the Founders.[3] Centuries later, modern presidents are habitually compared to George III, often unfavorably. While we may no longer have Richard Nixon to kick around, George III has been immortalized as a "tyrant."[4]

A prominent minority scoffs at the notion of an imperial presidency, insisting that the nation suffers from a "fettered presidency."[5] The most visible of these contrarians is former vice president Dick Cheney. Cheney and other supporters of a robust presidency believe that the Founders established a mighty, energetic, and almost unrestrained executive. Yet on their account, modern presidents more closely resemble pitiful Lemuel Gulliver, struggling under scores of ill-advised restraints imposed by skittish Lilliputians in Congress and the courts.[6]

Whose depiction of the original presidency is better grounded in early history? In recapturing original conceptions of the Constitution's presidency, this book argues that the modern presidency is both imperial and imperiled. In some respects, contemporary chief executives claim and exercise powers that properly belong to other branches, making the label "imperial" seem especially appropriate. For instance, when presidents exercise the right to decide whether the United States will wage war, they act contrary to the original Constitution. Yet in other areas, presidents have far less authority than the original scheme envisioned. When it comes to the execution of laws and control of the executive branch, the modern presidency is a shadow of its robust 1789 counterpart.

If the vision of the original presidency sketched out above is true, why are we bedeviled by erroneous conceptions of the original presidency? Opponents of a strong presidency pay little attention to the period immediately predating the creation of the Constitution. Those votaries of a weak presidency imagine that the Constitution was ratified against the backdrop of a revolutionary revulsion toward all things smacking of monarchy. This is too simplistic. Though antipathy toward absolute monarchy was widespread, a surprising number thought limited monarchy was the cure to what ailed postrevolutionary America. While a constitutional monarch was the anti-archetype during the creation of the state constitutions, the resulting feeble state executives became, in turn, the very examples of what those at the Constitutional Convention sought to avoid. Those favoring a muscular executive mostly prevailed at Philadelphia, causing many of the Constitution's proponents and opponents to describe the presidency as an elective monarchy.

On the other hand, supporters of a relatively unbound presidency pay too little attention to the many explicit and implicit constraints on presidential power. The Constitution grants many traditional executive powers to Congress, such as the power to decide to wage war. It grants other executive powers to the president subject to a meaningful Senate "advice and consent" check. Furthermore, executive privileges and immunities, while fitting in more thoroughly regal systems, are best seen as foreign to the Constitution's republican monarchy.

Finally, a distorted sense of the original presidency arises from the failure to offer a holistic picture of constitutional text. Some scholars obsess over lesser clauses, such as the Opinions and Reception Clauses, imagining that they reveal subtle truths about the scope of presidential power.[7] Yet reading these provisions as if they were the most vital parts of Article II yields anachronistic conceptions of the original presidency. Many scholars downplay or wholly ignore Article II's central clause, the one that inaugurates the presidency—the Executive Power Clause. If we do not pay attention to all the Article II pieces and how they fit together, we will fail to appreciate that the Constitution established a complete mosaic and that its presidency is more than just the sum of a few narrow clauses.

Besides refuting some misguided conceptions of the original presidency, this book also offers a Washingtonian conception of the chief executive, one that provides a striking contrast with the more familiar conceptions offered by Theodore Roosevelt and William Howard Taft. Roosevelt advanced the "stewardship theory," claiming that the president could do whatever he wished for the benefit of the nation, except in cases where the Constitution expressly limited presidential power.[8] Rejecting the stewardship theory, Taft argued that the president had only the powers specifically or implicitly granted to him.[9] Reflecting the views of our first president, this book presents a more complicated theory, namely, that the president enjoys a bundle of traditional executive powers subject to the Constitution's many qualifications and restraints. From the beginning, many (but not all) people recognized that the opening grant of executive power is a grant of *all* executive power, subject to many, many exceptions. Consistent with this reading, early presidents routinely exercised powers not traceable to particular enumerations in Article II, sections 2 and 3, as Taft himself recognized.[10] At the same time, the Executive Power (or Vesting) Clause was clearly not seen as a grant of all power that the president (or the nation) might find useful. The claim that the president can do whatever is best for the nation, subject only to express constitutional or statutory constraints, has no basis in the original Constitution.

Because constitutional originalism is much disputed and criticized, some brief methodological comments seem necessary. The originalist inquiry seems related to the traditional historical inquiry, except that the former is focused on what some document meant when it was written or made law. Like historical inquiry generally, the originalist enterprise is fraught with difficulties. Determining the meaning of an old document is a complex task, particularly so when it is the product of numerous people acting at different times. There is also the thorny question whether one should search for the subjective intentions of those who made it law or try to piece together its public meaning.

Those hoping for either a justification of originalism or a defense of a particular originalist methodology must look elsewhere. Given the widespread interest in the kind of presidency that the original Constitution created, no justification seems necessary. Many seem fascinated by the question, and a considerable number of those believe that originalist readings of the Constitution are relevant (even dispositive) to shaping the Constitution's modern meaning. Moreover, on questions about Article II, competing originalist methodologies yield convergent meanings. Disputes between followers of original meaning and those favoring original intent are immaterial in this area, or so I argue.

This book's claims about the meaning of constitutional phrases rest on eighteenth-century usage. It recounts what people of that era said about the meaning of various words, phrases, and clauses found in the Constitution. It rejects the notion that words and phrases have inherent or essential meanings that do not vary over time. For example, the common meaning of "executive power" likely was broader in the mid–seventeenth century than at the close of the eighteenth. Hence a constitution created in the mid–seventeenth century that used the phrase would grant its executive more power than a constitution from the late eighteenth century would.

Some might object that materials from the founding era yield no definite conclusions about presidential power and duty. Justice Robert H. Jackson, formerly Franklin Roosevelt's attorney general, lamented the equivocal nature of the available evidence: "A judge, like an executive adviser, may be surprised at the poverty of really useful and unambiguous authority applicable to concrete problems of executive power as they actually present themselves. Just what our forefathers did envision, or would have envisioned had they foreseen modern conditions, must be divined from materials almost as enigmatic as the dreams Joseph was called upon to interpret for Pharaoh. A century and a half of partisan debate and scholarly speculation yields no net result but only supplies more or less apt quotations from respected sources on each side of any question. They largely cancel each other."[11] Though Jackson made this observation while considering the president's wartime powers, one might suppose that his claim applies to most questions of presidential power. Indeed, a wag might suppose that attempting to discern the original contours of Article II from the available founding materials is akin to predicting divine will by studying animal entrails, in the manner of the Etruscans and Romans. While "answers" of some sort will be found if one insists on finding them, many will view the process as unedifying.

Justice Jackson threw up his hands too soon. If one knows where to look—at English, colonial, and state antecedents, the debates preceding the Constitution's creation, and early practices—there are plenty of founding materials on presidential power. Moreover, the sources do not merely cancel each other out, as if there was equal evidence on both (or all) sides of a question. Often, the evidence points rather strongly in a particular direction, making the originalist answer rather clear. As a Supreme Court justice and an attorney general before that, Jackson lacked the time (and perhaps the inclination) to unearth and sift through these materials to discern whether the president enjoyed emergency powers. Academics are in a position to conduct the research necessary to make (and substantiate) claims about the original presidency.

Justice Antonin Scalia highlighted the opposite problem: the originalist method sometimes yields too much information. Scalia admitted that if "done perfectly it might well take thirty years and 7,000 pages" to discern whether the Constitution granted the president a power to remove executive officers.[12] If prodigious preparation and prose might be necessary for one question—removal—one cannot imagine the years and pages necessary for all the numerous constitutional questions about the original presidency.

This life is too short to spend thirty years and 7,000 pages on a single question of presidential power. As Justice Scalia later noted, we have to make do with the imperfections that arise when we write scholarship in shorter periods and of shorter length. A 7,000-page book might never be read in its entirety, and spending thirty years on one subject to the exclusion of all else is too much to ask of anyone. This slimmer volume, the product of scholarship stretching back a decade or so, will have to suffice.

Stating what is beyond the book's scope may prove useful. The book does not espouse the "literary theory" of the presidency, whereby the president's powers are narrowly construed and wholly dependent upon a lawyerly reading of the Constitution. Obviously, many factors affect presidential power—partisan control of congressional chambers, the incumbent's popularity and persuasiveness, the media, and so forth. Indeed, the nonconstitutional factors are often more important in predicting the president's sway. The only claim made is that if one wants to understand the original presidency's formal powers and duties, one must conduct an examination along the lines found in this book.

Moreover, though many claims made herein have implications for the modern assertions of presidents (and their critics), this book does not exhaustively consider contemporary controversies in light of the original meaning of Article II. Readers are free to draw their own conclusions about the constitutionality of modern presidential actions.

Each chapter centers on a theme. Chapter 1 recounts how a robust executive both attracted and repulsed the Framers at the Philadelphia Convention. Though some opposed particular proposals on the grounds that the resulting executive would be a monarch, others were less fearful of the idea. Delegates favoring a strong executive were relentless and aided by the sense that George Washington would be the first chief. That expectation caused many to lower their guard and approve proposals that yielded what one European ruler called "a king, under the title of President."[13]

Chapter 2 discusses the English, colonial, state, and federal precursors to the president. These antecedents help us better grasp the original executive's powers, duties, and constraints. Some presidential features drew from the English and colonial experiences. Other traits reflected a rejection of the weak state executives. By the same token, the dismal experience with a plural federal executive (the Continental Congress) propelled the creation of a singular executive relatively independent of the legislature.

Subsequent chapters build on this material. Chapter 3 discusses structural features, including tenure, salary, reeligibility, and selection. Congress cannot normally select the president, which helps ensure that he is not beholden to legislators. Additionally, the president has a relatively long term and is eligible for reelection. The former insulates him from transient political winds; the latter helps ensure that he feels some measure of responsibility, and also makes continuity in office possible. But the most important feature is that there is but one chief executive. Delegates toyed with a plural executive and a generic executive council. They rejected both, fearful that either would generate confusion and paralysis within the executive. One cannot overstate the significance of creating a single executive rather than a plural one.

Chapter 4 considers the vesting of executive power. The Executive Power Clause is Article II's most important provision. It is a grant of all power commonly regarded as executive; the rest of Article II amplifies, clarifies, and constrains the grant. Many resist this reading, arguing that the grant of executive power is a nullity or something of a redundancy. But alternative readings, besides lacking a firm grounding in history, render the presidency a mere shadow of its familiar self.

The grant of executive power principally was, as the phrase strongly suggests, a grant of the power to execute the law. In the common parlance of the eighteenth century, someone vested with the executive power could execute the law. Chapter 5 discusses this law enforcement sense of executive power and shows how the pardon power complements the president's control over law execution. The chapter also considers the president's obligation to faithfully execute federal law.

Most of the president's authority over foreign affairs arises from the grant of the executive power and not from the particular, narrow foreign relations clauses found in the rest of Article II, or so Chapter 6 argues. The president's abilities to formulate and announce generic foreign policy, control U.S. diplomats, and send foreign diplomats packing stem from the grant of executive power. With respect to treaties, the chapter recounts early practice and how the Senate was to serve as an executive council.

Chapter 7 addresses the president's power as commander in chief. Though the president may command the military as commander in chief, Congress has almost complete authority over war and military matters. Only Congress may declare war, meaning that it decides whether the nation will wage war. Moreover, Congress may regulate the armed forces, meaning that it may establish a system of military discipline and may determine how to use the armed forces in wartime or otherwise. In particular, Congress may decide where armies will patrol, where ships will sail, and which targets to attack. As commander in chief, the president has no constitutionally protected sphere of autonomy, for congressional powers are so extensive that Congress may make any decision that ordinarily might be left to military commanders. But whatever military discretion Congress chooses not to exercise, it must leave for the president. Because the president is the commander in chief of the entire military, Congress cannot cede autonomy to lesser generals or admirals.

The next chapter considers the president's power over offices and officers. Congress creates and funds offices; the president can do neither. After the creation of offices, the president nominates and appoints to them, and the Senate again plays the role of executive council by providing its advice and consent to appointments. Once in office, executive officers serve at the chief executive's pleasure, meaning that the president can remove them at will. Moreover, because they help execute presidential powers and satisfy presidential duties, the president may direct these officers. Hence, while executive officers are creatures of Congress in that laws establish their offices, salaries, and responsibilities, they are also the creatures of the president in that they help exercise his constitutional powers at his sufferance.

Chapter 9 briefly discusses the many significant powers that do not rest with the president. Many prerogatives of the English Crown have no place in the U.S. system. Moreover, the president lacks a generic crisis power to take whatever measures he deems necessary in emergencies, such as suspending habeas corpus or imposing martial law. Finally, despite his office's semblance to monarchy, the president lacks constitutional privileges and immunities. He lacks a constitutional right to shield his branch's communications. He is subject to judicial process and may be sued in the courts. And he may even be prosecuted while in office. Congress, via statute, may ameliorate problems arising from the absence of executive privileges and immunities, for it may grant protections the Constitution never bestows.

The final three chapters focus on the presidency's relationship to other institutions. Chapter 10 focuses on Congress. The Constitution envisions an active presidential role in legislation. Sometimes the president must act as a facilitator of legislation, providing information about the state of the union and proposing topics or measures. At other times, the president can prevent legislation from taking effect. Finally, the chapter considers the extent to which Congress can regulate presidential power.

Chapter 11 argues that the president has an implicit duty to execute judicial judgments. The judicial power is the power to decide cases finally, to determine which party prevails and the relief to be awarded. Though the president may disagree with the relief awarded and the underlying opinion, he cannot ignore the judgments. To the contrary, he must take care to faithfully execute them. His duty to execute judgments means not only must he honor judgments against the government, but he and his branch also must execute judgments awarded in suits in which the government is not a party.

The states have had a vexed relationship with the federal executive. Before Eisenhower sent in the army to enforce *Brown v. Board of Education*,[14] Lincoln waged a war against secessionists. But relations were not meant to be so acrimonious, or so Chapter 12 claims. State executives must treat federal law as their own, meaning that they must stand ready to enforce it. In times of crisis, this may be done via state militias. In more pacific times, civilian state officers may be called upon to enforce federal law. Whenever state officials enforce federal law, they must do so in subordination to the federal chief executive. Because the president has the federal executive power, all those who help execute federal law must heed his orders.

Chapter 13 discusses how the president's constitutional duty to "preserve, protect, and defend" the Constitution makes him a constitutional protector. The Presidential Oath not only forbids presidential violation of the Constitution—a duty of avoidance—but also imposes a duty of action. He must defend the Constitution against the violations of others. He must veto unconstitutional congressional legislation and must disregard (rather than faithfully execute) unconstitutional federal statutes. Vis-à-vis the judiciary, he must criticize their constitutional misconstructions. And with respect to the states and private parties, he must likewise hinder and obstruct their unconstitutional designs and measures.

The picture that emerges from the founding era is of an elective monarch, constitutionally limited in a number of significant ways. The president controls law execution but needs Congress to create and fund the offices and the Senate's consent before he appoints officers. The president is commander in chief, but is utterly reliant upon Congress to create, fund, and discipline the armed forces. The president is the nation's chief diplomat, but cannot make treaties without the Senate's consent and can never take the nation to war or regulate foreign commerce, those powers resting with Congress. While nothing like an absolute sovereign, the Constitution's original presidency rivaled, and in some cases exceeded, several European monarchies in the scope of its powers.

CHAPTER ONE

"A KING, UNDER THE TITLE OF PRESIDENT"

A familiar and longstanding narrative insists that if one thing is clear about the constitution of the executive, it is that the Constitution's authors detested anything that smacked of monarchy. Given this loathing, there was no way that the revolutionaries turned Founding Fathers could have erected a regal Constitution wholly alien to their republican sensibilities.

This account seems to cohere with what preceded the Constitution. After all, the nation only recently had rebelled against George III. The Declaration had charged him with a litany of abuses: blocking beneficial legislation, ousting independent judges, and siccing hoards of taxmen.[1] Americans had deposed the symbols of kingly authority, too, the colonial governors. In their stead, state constitutions erected diminished executives, usually legislatively appointed to short terms and barred from reappointment. Even more telling, executive powers often did not rest solely with a governor, but were often checked by a council, sometimes vested in a council, or granted to the state assembly. Meanwhile, continental executives were the docile servants of Congress, with no chief executive to direct them. Perhaps Tom Paine spoke for many. After first asserting that the king of America "reigns above," he went on to claim "that in

America[,] the law is king."[2] Given the general mistrust and fear of strong executives, the Philadelphia Convention was incapable of erecting an executive that bore any resemblance to a king.

This common account is reasonable enough but mistaken nonetheless. While many Framers did not seek a monarchy, many also sought to avoid repeating the mistakes of the revolutionary state constitutions, with their frail executives. Eventually, the deeply felt need to avoid a federal cipher, coupled with the confidence fostered by the conviction that George Washington would serve as the first president, led to the creation of an executive that rivaled (and in many cases exceeded) European monarchs in power. The Constitution created nothing like an absolute monarchy. Rather, it ushered in a limited monarchy, or a monarchical republic, of the sort that England enjoyed and that France would have under its 1791 Constitution.

In the states, Anti-Federalists were quick to criticize the proposed presidency's considerable powers, claiming that the executive was, or soon would be, a monarch. This was not hyperbole, designed to sink a Constitution opposed for other reasons. We know this because those who took little or no part in the debate over the Constitution concluded the same. Europeans and Americans spoke of the document as establishing an elective, mixed, or republican monarchy. Such claims were credible because the Constitution's presidency was redolent of monarchy. As recounted in subsequent chapters, the Constitution's early years witnessed repeated attempts to make the regal Article II executive even more kingly.

The Imprecise Contours of Monarchy

Monarchy may seem a rather definite concept. The word conjures up several images and impressions. For some, golden thrones and crowns, resplendent carriages, purple robes, and magnificent scepters are the familiar trappings. Those of a more scholarly bent may recall authorities long associated with monarchs, such as the powers to declare war and appoint to offices. For many, monarchy implies life tenure, with heirs succeeding to the throne. Finally, monarchy implies singularity; where authority is split among many, one is tempted to say that there is no monarch.

Yet most of these traits are not necessary conditions of a monarchy, certainly not today. The so-called bicycle monarchs of Continental

Europe have pared back the pomp.³ Other modern crowns enjoy very limited powers, serving as figurehead chiefs of state, such as the king of Sweden.⁴ A few are elected to short terms of office, with successors likewise chosen by ballot. For instance, the office of the king of Malaysia rotates every five years among provincial royals.⁵ Finally, many modern monarchs reign over countries where sovereignty is divided among many institutions.

Eighteenth-century monarchs more closely resembled the familiar picture. One shared trait was grand living. The French Constitution of 1791 required that the Assembly provide for the "splendor of the throne."⁶ Another commonality was immunity from judicial process. The same French Constitution declared the "person of the king [to be] sacred and inviolable,"⁷ and the English Crown enjoyed a similar status.⁸ Finally, monarchs served for life and could not be easily ousted.

Beyond these similarities, however, eighteenth-century monarchies greatly varied. Though "monarch" comes from "mono," meaning "one" or "single," and "arch," derived from "archon," meaning ruler,⁹ not every monarch from the era enjoyed absolute rule, retaining all powers of government in their hands. Besides generally lacking the power to make law or adjudicate disputes, English kings and queens were hemmed in by a number of statutory and common law constraints. Similarly, monarchs in Sweden, Denmark, and Poland were constrained.¹⁰ Even limited monarchical regimes might have a diarchy, as when William and Mary jointly reigned over England.¹¹

Within the class of limited, constitutional monarchies, we find great variation. Though certain powers, such as granting pardons and stewarding foreign affairs, were long associated with monarchies, their allocation varied across limited regimes. Under the 1791 French Constitution, the king could not declare war or make treaties.¹² While English monarchs could declare war, they typically first secured Parliament's approval, for they knew that wars would fail without the necessary funds.¹³ Parliament even limited when the Crown might declare war, as when it decreed that without prior parliamentary approval, England would not defend the continental territories of the English monarch.¹⁴ Before the 1707 Acts of Union, the Scottish Parliament went further, barring executive war making unless the Scottish monarch first received Parliament's consent.¹⁵

Though hereditary succession was the norm, some monarchs were elected. For a time, the Holy Roman emperor was meaningfully elected. Gradually, the election became something of a formality as the office essentially became hereditary.[16] The Polish king was selected from among nobles, and the electorate at one time reached forty thousand.[17] The pope, who ruled over portions of Italy, was elected by the much smaller College of Cardinals.[18] And in England, Parliament occasionally selected monarchs, as when one chose William and Mary to serve as coregents after James II fled.[19]

Just as the precise boundaries of monarchy were less than clear, there also was a certain fuzziness associated with the concept of a republic. In particular, it was common to speak of republics with monarchical features and monarchies with republican traits. Montesquieu said that England was a "republic, disguised under the form of monarchy," a claim that assumed imprecision in both terms.[20] Maximilien Robespierre confirmed that the two were not wholly distinct: "[F]or many people the words 'republic' and 'monarchy' are entirely without meaning. The word 'republic' does not signify any particular form of government. . . . What is the present [1791] French constitution? It is a republic with a monarch. It is therefore neither monarchy nor republic, it is both one and the other."[21]

Robespierre went too far in saying that the terms were meaningless, for his last sentence used the terms as if they had accepted senses. But the imprecision of the terms (and their potential overlap) was clear. As one English writer noted in 1796, Sparta and the Greek states had kings even though they were republics. More generally, many so-called mixed monarchies of the eighteenth century were republics, including Poland, Bohemia, and Hungary.[22]

The Founding of America's Elective Monarchy

In the wake of the Declaration of Independence, there were many Americans who agreed that there should be, in the words of one popular children's song from the 1970s, "no more kings." George III went from venerated to detested. Tom Paine's immensely popular *Common Sense* was a full-throated denunciation of monarchy.

But one must not overstate the opposition to monarchy. Though the Declaration denounced the king, Parliament was to blame for many of the wounds that led to the rupture. Moreover, the Declaration did not denounce all monarchs, just George. The praise showered upon Louis XVI once France entered the war[23] suggested that attitudes toward monarchs turned in part on whether they were friend or foe.

Perhaps because state and continental executives were so weak (more on this in the next chapter), a few Americans believed that a federal monarch was necessary.[24] During the war, one military officer proposed to Washington the establishment of a monarch in the western territory, albeit with "some title apparently more moderate" than king.[25] Another disgruntled officer argued that only "absolute Monarchy, or a military State" would save the nation from ruin.[26] Some historians also believe that in 1786, the president of the Continental Congress wrote a letter asking Prince Henry of Prussia to serve as king of America.[27] Lending a bit of credence to the story, an agent of the Canadian governor hyperbolically claimed in 1787 that there "is not a gentleman in the States from New Hampshire to Georgia . . . who is not desirous of changing it for a monarchy."[28] One class supposedly favored a hereditary monarchy, while another favored a merely elective one. The agent asserted that George III's sons were the favorites of some, while others thought that France or America itself might supply a monarch.[29]

George Washington, the man whom many supposed could be king if he desired, was aware of such sentiments. In 1786, he was amazed "that even respectable characters speak of a monarchical form of government without horror." He added that "[f]rom thinking proceeds speaking, thence to acting is often but a single step."[30] A few weeks before the Constitutional Convention, Washington wrote a letter to James Madison: "I am fully of opinion that those who lean to a Monarchical governmt have either not consulted the public mind, or that they live in a region where the levelling principles in which they were bred, being entirely irradicated, is much more productive of Monarchical ideas than are to be found in the Southern States. . . . I also am clear, that even admitting the utility; nay, necessity of the form—yet that the period is not arrived for adopting the change without shaking the Peace of this Country to its foundation."[31]

Judging by some of the comments at the Philadelphia Convention, Washington was not alone in thinking that the people could not stomach a king. Virginia governor Edmund Randolph said, "[T]he permanent temper of the people was adverse to the very semblance of Monarchy."[32] Massachusetts delegate Elbridge Gerry declared that fewer than one in one thousand Americans favored any move toward the institution.[33] Citing the popular distaste of monarchy, some delegates opposed a unitary executive, instead favoring a plural one. Randolph predicted that a single executive would be the "foetus of a monarchy."[34] Another opponent, Hugh Williamson of North Carolina, said that "a single Magistrate . . . will be an elective King, and will feel the spirit of one."[35] It seems fair to say that although a majority opposed the creation a king, some feared that a monarchy was inevitable in any event because of, as Benjamin Franklin put it, a "natural inclination in mankind to Kingly Government."[36]

Perhaps because of this proclivity, others had kinder words for the institution. While admitting that the people could not stomach a king, James Wilson claimed that the size of America argued for "the vigour of [a] monarchy" and that the "people of Amer[ica] did not oppose the British King but the parliament . . . not . . . Unity but a corrupt multitude."[37] Another delegate deemed a limited monarchy "*one* of the best Governments in the world," since "equal blessings had never yet been derived from any of the republican form." Nonetheless, he added: "[A] limited monarchy . . . was out of the question. The spirit of the times—the state of our affairs, forbade the experiment, if it were desirable."[38] Others perhaps differed with his assessment. One delegate said he "was not so much afraid of the shadow of monarchy as to be unwilling to approach it."[39] Another praised the "vigorous minds" that had advocated a "high toned Monarchy" in the convention.[40] Monarchical sentiments might have been surprisingly common, especially if we credit the story that one delegate had compiled a list of more than twenty who favored monarchy.[41]

Again, there was uncertainty about what features made for a monarchy. Delegates sometimes opposed proposals on the grounds that they would create a king. Certain powers—war, veto, and appointments—were said to make a single executive a monarch.[42] Other features—like good-behavior tenure or a long term of office—were thought to have the same effect.[43] Some delegates tried to counteract such claims, arguing that if the convention constrained the executive—say, by making him impeachable—the executive, by definition, could not be a monarch.[44]

Alexander Hamilton sought to hide behind the ambiguity of "monarchy." When proposing a life term for the chief executive, he anticipated that some would object that he was proposing "an *elective Monarch*."[45] He responded to the expected charge by arguing "that *Monarch* . . . marks not either the degree or duration of power." If his proposed executive would "be a monarch for life," the existing proposal would "be a monarch for seven years."[46] He also asserted that state governors might be considered monarchs.[47] Though Hamilton had a point, he overstated the imprecision. The more powerful, independent, and securely tenured a single executive is, the more it resembles a monarch. The more weak, dependent, and transient, the fainter the semblance.[48]

The gradual emergence of a unitary, powerful, and independent executive triggered apprehension. Outside the convention, some whispered that delegates wished to crown the second son of George III king of America.[49] Letters to the delegates poured in, leading some to slip an item into the press.[50] The note acknowledged the "reports idly circulating" of an attempt to "establish a monarchical government, to send for the bishop of Osnaburgh," the second son of King George. The anonymous delegates assured the public that "we never once thought of a king."[51] But this assertion was beside the point, for even if many had not once thought of a king, the convention had proposed an executive whose powers rivaled those of the crowned heads of Europe. Edmund Randolph predicted that when the people beheld the president, they would find "the form at least of a little monarch."[52]

Given the claim that the people would not stomach a monarchy, and the apparent need to reassure members of the public that no monarch was intended, why did the executive's powers mushroom over the summer and reach kingly proportions? First, there had always been a sizable faction favoring a strong executive. Undoubtedly, these delegates believed that executive vigor would serve the nation well. Others might suspect that some delegates retained a lingering attachment to monarchy. As Thomas Jefferson put it in 1789, Americans "were educated in royalism: no wonder if some . . . retain that idolatry still."[53] Whatever the reason for their preference for a vigorous executive, on issue after issue the coalition held fast. Second, as a spur to their proposals, Madison and his allies darkly predicted that if the executive were not made powerful, the nation might "have something worse than a limited Monarchy."[54] Third, when advocates of a robust executive lost, they often refused to concede. They repackaged their losing proposals, adjusting them here and there. This strategy meant that when it came to the executive's features—its size, powers, selection, and tenure—the delegates had to endure what James Madison termed "tedious and reiterated discussions."[55]

Finally, one cannot underestimate the effect of taciturn George Washington on the proceedings. When it became clear that there would be but one chief executive, the sanguine prospect of the former commander in chief lent confidence to those favoring a strong executive and caused others to drop their guard. One delegate said, after the fact, "I [do not] believe they [the executive powers] would have been so great had not many of the members cast their eyes towards General Washington as President; and shaped their Ideas of the Powers to be given to a President, by their opinions of his Virtue."[56] In a sense, the office was tailor-made. As Thomas Paine put it years later, "[T]he Executive part of the Federal government was made for a man, and those who consented, against their judgment, to place Executive Power in the hands of a single individual, reposed more on the supposed moderation of the person they had in view, than on the wisdom of the measure itself."[57]

When the scene shifted from Philadelphia to the ratifying conventions, Edmund Randolph's prediction proved prophetic, since many beheld a monarch in the chief executive. Anti-Federalists present at the framing minced no words. Luther Martin of Maryland, who had left Philadelphia in protest, objected that the president was "so constituted as to differ from a monarch scarcely but in name" and that because he could be re-elected without limit, the president was "nearly . . . the same thing" as an elective king.[58] His fellow dissenter, Virginia's George Mason, agreed that the presidency "will be an elective monarchy."[59]

Anti-Federalists not privy to the framing debates drew the same connection. "Cato" noted that the president possessed "the powers of a monarch" and rhetorically asked, "[W]herein does this president, invested with his powers and prerogatives, essentially differ from the king of Great-Britain (save as to name, [and] the creation of nobility . . .)[?]"[60]

Patrick Henry observed, "[The] Constitution is said to have beautiful features; but when I come to examine these features, sir, they appear to me horribly frightful. Among other deformities, it has an awful squinting; it squints towards monarchy."[61]

Others beheld the system of electors and drew sneering parallels to the Papal States and Poland. "Philadelphiensis" asserted that he had "clearly proven, that the president is a King to all intents and purposes, and at the same time one of the most dangerous kind too—an *elective King.*" Then he resorted to hyperbole, "I challenge the politicians of the whole continent to find in any period of history a monarch more absolute."[62] "Old Whig" similarly groused that the president was "in reality to be a KING as much *a King as the King of Great Britain,* and a King too of the worst kind;—an elective King."[63]

Those outside the ratification fray saw the resemblance as well. From France, Thomas Jefferson said that the president "seems a bad edition of a Polish king."[64] This was unflattering, for the Polish monarch was said to be the stooge of foreign powers who used intrigue and corruption to sway regal elections.[65] William Short, Jefferson's aide in France, said the Constitution would "convert[] the thirteen republics into one mixed monarchy—for notwithstanding the humble title of President . . . he will have greater powers than several monarchs have."[66] One American commentator, in an account of the Swedish revolution, claimed that though Sweden was commonly called a monarchy, it really was a republic, one in which the "nominal king" had less power than the proposed president.[67] And those with no stake in the debate also noticed the Constitution's monarchical features. William V, the Dutch stadtholder, told John Adams in 1788 that Americans would have "a king, under the title of President."[68] According to Adams, the stadtholder's conclusion "would be confirmed by every Civilian in Europe, who should read our Constitution."[69]

Supporters of the Constitution denied that it would erect a monarchy. But as the historian Max Farrand put it, "[T]he supporters of the new order were at a loss to defend their contention that no monarchy had been established."[70] Some Federalists tried to utterly deny any resemblance. John Marshall insisted that Federalists "idolize democracy" and "prefer this system to any monarchy."[71] Others appeared to concede the resemblance. One said that the system would not trigger problems related to an elective monarchy.[72] Another supposedly remarked that the president had to be respectable in the eyes of foreign nations and was to be powerful, but that everyone nonetheless wished to prevent despotism and "*absolute* monarchy."[73]

As "Publius," Hamilton denied that the president would be the equal of the English Crown. But his comparison left much to be desired. To diminish the president, Hamilton systematically inflated the Crown's powers.[74] Moreover, he did not compare the president to weaker monarchs, like the Polish king. Relatedly, he never denied that the president would have some powers that certain monarchs lacked.[75] Even if the president would have less authority than the English Crown, that hardly refuted those who saw the distinct outlines of a monarchy in Article II.

Hamilton's speech in the New York Convention was more honest because it was not predicated on an unblinking denial of the resemblance to monarchy. Citing England and Poland, he noted that while some imagined that republics and monarchies were always distinct, some nations deemed republics had monarchs.[76] This observation, which echoed his claim at Philadelphia, naturally raised questions about the nature of the proposed Constitution. While Benjamin Franklin reportedly said at the close of the Philadelphia Convention that the Constitution had established a republic rather than a monarchy, the truth was that it had elements of both.[77] And because it had elements of both, it was not wholly satisfactory to many. As one American said of the Constitution, "I doubt whether it has monarchy enough in it for some of our Massachusetts men, nor democracy enough for others."[78]

Contested Features of the Elective Monarchy

After the Constitution was set in motion, the comparisons continued. Clear-eyed foreigners could see that the president was a "limited monarch."[79] One who observed that "the President . . . is invested with monarchical prerogatives" predicted that the "Crown of America" would eventually move from an elective system to a hereditary one.[80] Another said that the Polish king had less executive power than "the king of England and the officer who without the name discharges the functions of a king in America."[81] And a third said that both Poland and America were, "strictly speaking," elective monarchies, albeit with different ten-ures.[82] A particularly republican Englishman, who denounced monarchy in all its forms, warned against the idea of "a President with regal pow-ers."[83] He went on to list the powers of a king, claiming that each rested with the U.S. president.[84] A fan of the Constitution praised the "elective King of America" because the burden on the taxpayers was so modest.[85] Finally, an author attempting to refute Thomas Paine noted that "in real-ity" America was "under a sort of limited monarchy," since "General Washington has been to them all the king which the character and condi-tion of their nation has yet required."[86]

Some Americans also persisted in noting the resemblance. John Jay, the holdover secretary of foreign affairs, explained to a U.S. consul that the president "possesses Power and Prerogatives in many Respects similar to those which are enjoyed by the Kings of England."[87] Writing in 1789, New York chancellor Robert Livingston said that the powers of limited monarchs did not "greatly exceed those of the president."[88] That same year, Vice President John Adams insisted that America had a "monarchi-cal republic, or, if you will, a limited monarchy" and pointed out that the president's authority was not unduly constrained: "[H]is power during those four years is much greater . . . than a king of Poland; nay, than a king of Sparta. I know of no first magistrate in any republican govern-ment, excepting England and Neuchatel, who possesses a constitutional dignity, authority, and power comparable to his."[89] Adams further claimed that the president's "rights and duties . . . are so transcendent that they must naturally and necessarily excite in the nation all the jeal-ousy, envy, fears, apprehensions, and opposition, that are so constantly observed in England against the crown."[90] When someone denied the Constitution's monarchical aspects, Adams insisted that the "general sense of mankind differs from you in opinion, and clearly sees, and fully believes, that our president's office" resembled a monarchy.[91] Writing in 1794, a detractor of Washington's treatment of Revolutionary France said the following of the president: "That we have given him the power of a monarch, is undeniable, tho' our's is a limited monarchy."[92] A more caus-tic critic said the president approached "in some views to terrestrial omnipotence" and that the Constitution had "its formation before the United States had sufficiently un-monarchized their ideas and habits."

Americans, he claimed, "had dismissed the name of king, but they retained a prejudice for his authority"[93]

Others noted that the Constitution demonstrated that Americans had come to favor monarchy. Samuel Chase lamented that "our Governments and the principles of the people, are changed, and are monarchical."[94] Similarly, William Short claimed that the Constitution's executive showed that the people had made "larger strides towards a toleration of monarchical principles" since the Revolution.[95] What Jefferson had described as "idolatry"—affinity for monarchy—Adams saw as normal, as if the era of weak executives had been an aberration: "[E]very Part of the Conduct and feelings of the Americans tends to that Species of Republick called a limited Monarchy. . . . They were born and brought up in it . . . but their Heads are most miserably bewildered about it."[96]

Still, once the Constitution became the supreme law of the land, it became less common for Americans to mention its monarchical aspects. Americans were stuck with the presidency, and while it may have been necessary to create a strong executive, it was impolitic to dwell on features that might discomfit some. When Noah Webster observed in 1794 that the French monarch under the 1791 Constitution had less authority than the American president, his comment was appropriate largely because he was criticizing the Jacobins.[97] For some, a frank comparison to monarchy was possible only when another executive was the focal point.

Instead of debating whether or how the Constitution created a monarchy, the focus shifted to whether the nation should adopt regal customs. Controversies erupted over presidential addresses to Congress, executive pomp, and executive privileges. In practice, these struggles consisted of a fight between those who wished to make a high-toned Constitution higher-toned still and those who wished to draw the line. Later chapters say more about these disputes, but a short discussion is merited here.

To emphasize the importance of the office (and by extension, the dignity of the new government), the president held fancy levees at his home, parties that led critics to say that the president held "court."[98] They featured elaborate garb, deep bows, stilted conversations, and awkward silences. One senator grumbled that the practice, "considered as a feature of Royalty, is certainly Antirepublican; this certainly escapes Nobody." He added that some did not bother trying to hide their approval: "The Royalists glory in it as a point gained."⁹⁹ Along the same lines, the president acquired a luxurious coach with a number of attendees.¹⁰⁰ The aping of royal practices was meant to awe Americans and garner the respect of foreigners used to such pageantry.

Congress and the courts also drew on English regal customs. The president's annual address to Congress, complete with responses from both chambers, was said by critics to mimic the English Crown's annual address.¹⁰¹ One senator objected to referring to the president's speech as "His [m]ost gracious [s]peech," saying that it aped British practice.¹⁰² But the fact that both chambers drafted responses suggested the general appeal of the regal custom.

The Senate considered or passed measures that would have further underscored the presidency's regal aspects. Senators debated a committee's recommendation that the president should be styled "His Highness the President of the United States of America and Protector of the Rights of the Same."¹⁰³ This title, and other variations, were opposed precisely because they smacked of monarchy. Similarly, some senators wished to have the enacting clause that prefaces all bills include the president and not, as today, merely mention the two chambers. This suggestion, which aped English traditions, never came to a vote.¹⁰⁴ Finally, the Senate unsuccessfully sought to have judicial process issued in the president's name, just as it was issued in the monarch's name in England.¹⁰⁵

Though legislative attempts to further elevate the presidency generally failed, attempts outside Congress often prevailed. After the House refused to adopt a bill providing that judicial writs would be issued in the president's name, the Supreme Court unilaterally imposed that practice on federal courts. So the president's name was used to summon people, order courts, and so forth, even though he had no share or control over the judicial power.¹⁰⁶

These attempts to further ennoble the executive were hardly aberrational. After all, these proposals were made repeatedly in the context of a Constitution that had many regal features. Though Thomas Jefferson railed at times against "monocrats," he once, in a moment of candor, wrote that a constitution "like ours, wears a mixed aspect of monarchy and republicanism": "Some will consider it as an elective monarchy" and "[o]thers will view it as an energetic republic."[107] Naturally, said Jefferson, some were inclined to "strengthen either the monarchical or the republican features of the Constitution."[108]

The Textual Foundations of the Elective Monarchy

When we read the Constitution today, the semblance to monarchy is difficult, almost impossible to perceive. The text seems wholly republican in nature. Article IV guarantees each state a republican form of government, suggesting that the Constitution likewise created a republic at the federal level, for who would erect a federal monarchy over a series of republics? Moreover, in the same article the Constitution speaks of republican "citizens" rather than regal "subjects." Finally, the Constitution requires various elections, the hallmark of republican government.

Yet once we recognize that monarchy and republic existed along a continuum and that there was an intermediate category of mixed monarchies (what John Adams called "monarchical republics"), we should perceive that certain republican features or code words could not wholly counter or mask the Constitution's monarchical attributes. And once we realize that some European monarchs were elected, we should understand that elections do not necessarily signal a pure republic. The Constitution's many republican elements hardly establish that it lacks monarchical flourishes as well.

For a number of reasons, eighteenth-century Americans were better at perceiving the Constitution's monarchical aspects. The standard narrative of implacable opposition to kings had not yet fully crystallized and colored perceptions. Without a long tradition of rhetorical opposition to a strong executive clouding people's judgments of the presidency, its features naturally brought to mind regal authority. Moreover, with the memory of kingly sway still fresh, eighteenth-century Americans had an easier time identifying royal traits in the Constitution. A single executive alone predictably triggered comparisons to monarchy. When coupled with electors, a feature associated with elective monarchies, the resemblance grew stronger still. Finally, by giving the president command of the military, treaty authority, and powers to appoint to office and dispense mercy, the Constitution guaranteed comparisons to European monarchs. All the ingredients necessary for making the comparison to kingly government were found within the Constitution itself.

One might even cite the executive's title. "President" seems like a rather modest label. As Senator Oliver Ellsworth sneered when arguing for a loftier title, "there were Presidents of Fire Companies & of a Cricket Club."[109] But if we delve into Samuel Johnson's *Dictionary*, we find a (somewhat) surprising entry. He defined "monarch" as "A governor invested with absolute authority; a king; one superior to the rest of the same kind; *president*."[110] Citing Shakespeare for the usage, Johnson considered "president" a synonym for "monarch."[111] Though many clearly did not equate a "president" with a "monarch"—recall those who remarked on the former's supposed innocuousness—a handful might have considered that moniker, alongside the office's unity, powers, and manner of election, as fairly proving that the Constitution had created an elective, mixed monarchy.

Conclusion

Many saw the president as a monarch, with powers rivaling, and in some cases exceeding, the powers granted to European sovereigns. What implications does this have for the scope of presidential power at the founding? While subsequent chapters discuss presidential power in greater detail, at this point it seems appropriate to say that the ramifications are rather modest. As discussed later, the president was not said to enjoy additional powers or privileges just because many regarded the presidency as a monarchy. For instance, no one said that the president could remove executive officers because he was a king. Rather than some freestanding monarchical status serving as a basis for contending that the presidency enjoyed a host of implied executive powers, Article II's various features generated the sense that the Constitution had created a republican monarchy.

Having said this, the founding-era perception of the president as a monarch undermines the cliché that the president should not be understood to have particular powers because the Framers were opposed to a monarchy and obviously did not create one. The Constitution's presidency resulted from a confluence of voices and votes; some tried to create a weak executive, and others were just as intent on establishing a powerful executive. Even though many wished to avoid an absolute monarchy, many others sought an efficient, vigorous, and responsible executive. Just as there is no freestanding monarchical status that one can use as a basis for grafting a host of monarchical powers to the presidency, there likewise is no independent "weak executive" template that one may rely upon to twist constitutional text in a bid to minimize presidential powers. Whether the president has a power or privilege turns on a reading of the Constitution's text and structure and not on a generic aversion to monarchy that motivated only some of the Framers. Sometimes the Constitution granted the president the powers that some monarchs enjoyed, and other times it did not.

Given the presidency's resemblance to monarchy, the original Constitution established the underpinnings of what Arthur Schlesinger would later decry as "an imperial presidency." J. G. A. Pocock has written: "If we seek a *modern equivalent and successor* to [George III's] monarchy, it is clearly the American Presidency: a monarchy elected for a limited term, *but required to establish personal* relations with a legislature, while functioning surrounded by both a court and a palace."[112] As we have seen, this equivalency was noted before the Constitution went into effect and has been recognized ever since. George Washington—America's Cincinnatus—was maligned as an "embryo-Caesar," a Cromwell, and a King George IV.[113] Such rebukes were common because the Constitution lent them credence, ensuring that they were (and are) part of political discourse. Of George W. Bush, it was said that he acted as a monarch. It is said of Barack H. Obama. And it will be said of future chief executives.

CHAPTER TWO

"ENGLISH WHIGS, CORDIAL IN THEIR . . . JEALOUSIES OF THEIR EXECUTIVE MAGISTRATE"

While the presidency could be said to have many antecedents, the Anglo-American executives who preceded it exerted the greatest influence: the British monarch, British colonial governors, state governors and councils, and the Continental Congress and its officers, boards, and departments. Most of Article II descends, in some way, from these institutions. One cannot fathom the presidency unless one has a sense of these precursors, for their story is part of its story.

The English Crown and Its Colonial Governors

The Crown's principal executive power was the power to execute the law. William Blackstone imagined that society had ceded the "execution of the laws" to "one visible magistrate."[1] As "*pater-familias*," the king had to protect individuals from "injurious violence, by executing those laws, which the people themselves in conjunction with him have enacted."[2] Because the Crown was "injured by every infraction of the public rights belonging to [the] community," it was "in all cases the proper prosecutor for every public offence."[3] For some, it seemed to follow that the Crown should be able to forgive public offenses. As one observer put it, the Crown could "pardon offences, that is, remit the punishment that has been awarded in consequence of his prosecution."[4]

Extensive foreign affairs and military prerogatives also rested with the Crown. Blackstone noted that the king had "the sole power of sending embassadors to foreign states, and receiving embassadors at home";[5] could "make treaties, leagues, and alliances with foreign states and princes";[6] could issue letters of marque and reprisal when his subjects suffered injury overseas;[7] and had "the sole prerogative of making war and peace."[8] As part of its war power, the Crown could decide whether to wage war, the type of war to wage, and the rights of enemy aliens residing in England.[9] Additionally, the Crown had "the sole power of raising . . . fleets and armies"[10] and the "sole supream government, command and disposition of the militia."[11] Finally, the Crown could create a code of military justice and had rather limited authority to enforce the code using courts-martial.[12]

An individual, acting alone, could not meaningfully exercise all these powers. Kings and queens needed executive officers, civil and military. The Crown had means of self-help. It not only was the "fountain" and "parent" of offices, able to create and set each office's duties and powers,[13] but also could appoint.[14] Moreover, in its commissions laying out an office's metes and bounds, the Crown had some latitude to set tenure, determining whether an officer served at the Crown's whim ("at pleasure"), for a set period (say, four years), or during "good behavior." Because most executives served at pleasure, the Crown could remove most officers without cause.[15]

George III's predecessors were weak, so much so that his father, George II, grumbled that "ministers were kings in this country."[16] George III, however, insisted upon and maintained his primacy.[17] Unlike his father and grandfather, George III spoke fluent, unaccented English and hence was more comfortable asserting himself. Moreover, he had grown up reading Blackstone's *Commentaries*.[18] Blackstone had stressed the Crown's personal exercise of executive power, writing that the Crown was not only the "chief, but properly the sole, magistrate of the nation; all others acting by commission from, and in due subordination to him."[19] This appeared to be George III's creed, for he made all manner of executive decisions, both major and minor. One historian claims that George exercised "important

29

and often decisive influence on every act of the administration."[20] Ministers, no longer the vital players they had been during the reigns of his father and grandfather, were "insignificant and powerless,"[21] reflecting George III's assessment that they were but his "tools" and "instruments."[22]

Although the powers to create, appoint, and direct officers were vital to the Crown, no less crucial was the "civil list."[23] The civil list annuity, fixed by Parliament at the outset of a monarch's reign, was a permanent appropriation meant to fund all civil officers. It originally was conceived as a means of ensuring the Crown's independence, preventing Parliament from using appropriations as a weapon.[24] Ministers insisted that Parliament had no right even to inquire how the Crown distributed the civil list funds, much less to control their expenditure. Some legislators agreed, with one admitting that "the King was the only judge of what officers were necessary to carry on the executive business of government."[25]

The Crown had other powers worthy of mention. First, because the Crown's consent was necessary before any bill could become law, the Crown was considered a constituent part—a third branch—of the British legislature.[26] This power was vital, for it generally prevented Parliament from altering or abridging executive prerogatives without the Crown's assent.[27] The king had a number of associated powers, including the power to convene, adjourn, prorogue, and dissolve Parliament.[28] In a measure that guaranteed the Crown some level of parliamentary influence, it could create peers within the House of Lords[29] and could rely upon certain "rotten boroughs" to elect members who would be the "king's friends" in the House of Commons.[30] Second, the Crown enjoyed several commercial powers, including the power to regulate commerce, establish markets, coin money, and fix weights and measures.[31] Third, the Crown could grant special privileges and benefits, including monopolies and the immunities that accompanied corporate status.[32] Fourth, English monarchs headed the Anglican Church,[33] created and appointed bishops, and served as the court of last resort in ecclesiastical disputes.[34] Finally, after the Act of Settlement, English monarchs perceived the need to work closely with the majority in Parliament. Select members of that majority typically became ministers of the Crown, thereby ensuring a good deal of harmony between the two institutions. By working with the legislative majority, the Crown could help shape English laws.

Many of the powers vested in the Crown were deemed "executive" because they were closely associated with the chief executive, that is, the officer charged with superintending law execution. Because supreme executives in other countries had a similar basket of powers, it became common to speak of an "executive power" that encompassed an array of powers commonly wielded by monarchs.

A single-minded focus on the Crown's powers can leave a mistaken impression, for it neglects the constraints imposed on executive power over centuries. Such constraints are worth mentioning now, with more commentary later. The Crown could not adjudicate criminal and civil cases,[35] suspend statutes, grant individualized dispensations from the applicability of the law,[36] or remove high-ranking judges at pleasure.[37] Even when it came to war powers, Parliament sometimes constrained the executive. It prohibited the Crown from sending the militia overseas[38] and barred its monarchs from making war in defense of their non-English dominions.[39] Finally, the need for war appropriations led the Crown to seek parliamentary approval for its wars in advance of their initiation,[40] meaning that the war power was shared in practice.

Colonial governors had similar authority. Using powers granted by royal commissions and instructions, governors executed the law and prosecuted offenders; exercised minimal foreign affairs authority (with Indian tribes); commanded the militia; appointed, controlled, and removed most executives; erected courts; pardoned offenders; granted commercial privileges; vetoed legislation; and convened and prorogued colonial legislatures.[41] Many of these powers were subject to structural and practical restraints. The Crown sometimes provided that governors had to exercise certain powers only with the consent of an executive council, thus limiting the chief executive's latitude.[42] Moreover, the assemblies wielded considerable leverage arising from their power over the purse.[43] In sum, the colonial governors were akin to princelings, limited by their instructions and constrained by assemblies in much the same way that Parliament curbed the Crown.

The State Executives

With the Revolution, the states wrested the executive power away from the Crown and its colonial minions. Initially, state conventions and congresses assumed legislative and executive authority,[44] often forming "committees of safety" to exercise executive functions.[45] Eventually, state constitutions created a separate executive.[46]

Notwithstanding demands that the three powers (legislative, executive, and judicial) be kept separate, distrust of the executive was far too ingrained to ensure their adequate separation. For many, executives brought to mind the unloved agents of the Crown, who had long battled local assemblies.[47] A Delaware Whig reflected the lingering suspicions: "The executive power is ever restless, ambitious, and ever grasping at encrease of power."[48] These "vicious traditions" of distrust yielded constitutions meant to ensure executive subordination to the legislature.[49] As Gordon Wood put it, "[T]he gubernatorial magistrate [was] a new kind of creature, a very pale reflection indeed of his regal ancestor."[50]

Several features typified the weakest of these executives. First, though all were vested with the "executive power" or its equivalent, in many states the power was exercised at the sufferance of the legislature. Specifically, many constitutions provided for executive authority to be exercised "according to the laws."[51] As Charles Thach observed, "Language like this fairly invited legislative interference" for it suggested that the legislature could modify executive powers by statute.[52] Under such constitutions, the executive exercised default powers that could be regulated or reallocated at will. Not surprisingly, assemblies frequently dictated to the executive and occasionally stripped away powers.

Legislatures dominated for a second reason, namely, the absence of a veto. Without a veto to curb them, grasping assemblies could eviscerate executive prerogatives. The few chief executives with a veto benefitted tremendously because it helped shield their constitutional powers.[53] As the drafters of the Massachusetts Constitution noted, a veto ensured that there was "a due balance . . . in the three capital powers of Government" and that no body of men would "enact, interpret and execute the Laws."[54]

Third, a host of structural features ensured executive subservience. Under seven state constitutions, legislatures selected the chief executive.[55] Surely, docility was a prime criterion. Most chiefs had a one-year term[56] and effectively could not serve again.[57] Furthermore, many states splintered executive authority. Nominal chief executives often lacked appointment and removal authority and thus found it difficult to direct other executive officers.[58] Just as importantly, some constitutions created a plural executive, whereby the chief executive was compelled to seek the advice or approval of an executive council before making certain decisions.[59] In at least two states, the executive *was* a council, meaning that a council majority decided how to exercise all or almost all executive powers.[60] With executive power constrained and divided in numerous ways, executives could not stand firm against imperious assemblies.

New York's governorship was far more robust than most of its counterparts. Vested with the "supreme executive power," the popularly elected chief executive had a share in appointing officers and vetoing bills. As Charles Thach put it, "[A]ll the isolated principles of executive strength in other constitutions were here brought into a new whole."[61] Because the New York chief executive was seen as well constructed, some treated it as a template during the Constitutional Convention.[62]

The Massachusetts governor was another exemplar of strength. Under the 1780 state constitution, the governor had a unilateral veto power; served as commander in chief of the state's army, navy, and militia; and could appoint and pardon with the consent of a council.[63] The drafters of the Massachusetts Constitution learned much from the drawbacks of weak executives in the other states. Indeed, a proposed constitution was defeated in part because its executive was considered too feeble.[64]

Americans drew lessons from the early state constitutions. Jefferson wrote that because no adequate barriers separated the three powers and because the other branches were dependent on the legislature for reappointment and salary, in Virginia "[a]ll the powers of government, legislative, executive, and judiciary, result to the legislative body."[65] A Pennsylvania constitutional council claimed that despite the fact that its constitution had by a "most marked and decided distribution" separated the powers of "making laws, and carrying those laws into execution," the legislature repeatedly had usurped the executive power.[66] At the Constitutional Convention, James Madison spoke for many when he deplored this tendency: "Experience had proved a tendency in our governments to throw all power into the Legislative vortex. The Executives of the States are in general little more than Cyphers; the legislatures omnipotent."[67]

Such observers supposed that the state charters reflected naïveté and bias. Thomas Jefferson remarked that the 1776 Virginia Constitution was formed "when we were new and unexperienced in the science of government."[68] He also recalled that before the Revolution, all were "good English Whigs, cordial in their ... jealousies of their executive Magistrate."[69] James Wilson of Pennsylvania noted that the revolutionaries had treated the executive and judiciary as "stepmothers" because of their association with the Crown.[70]

The Continental Executives

During the Revolutionary War and until the inauguration of President Washington, Congress created and controlled national executives, both civil and military. Even before the Declaration of Independence, the Continental Congress established ad hoc committees to oversee the execution of its resolves.[71] After experiencing difficulties with this arrangement, Congress adopted standing committees to superintend the execution of its orders.[72] The problems continued, however, because members were overwhelmed with legislative and executive tasks.[73] The "want of method and energy in the administration"[74] stemmed from "the want of a proper executive,"[75] said Alexander Hamilton. Congress was a "deliberative corps" and should not "play the executive."[76] His solution consisted of creating a "single man in each [executive] department" who could give administration "more knowledge, more activity, more responsibility, and, of course, more zeal and attention."[77] General Washington agreed, advising that there must be "more responsibility and permanency in the executive bodies."[78]

By 1781, most congressional delegates had come to agree as well.[79] After creating a foreign affairs department headed by a secretary,[80] Congress established three more "civil executive departments"—Treasury, Marine, and War—as well as a superintendent of finance, and secretaries of marine and war.[81] Yet Congress continued to micromanage. In truth, congressional delegates served as the real chiefs of the executive departments.[82]

That was so because the Continental Congress was the nation's plural, proto–chief executive. Congress served in that capacity both before and after the Articles of Confederation's ratification, with the Articles creating no distinct, much less independent, continental executive that could implement continental laws or direct administrative officials. The commanders in chief, of both the army and the navy, were wholly subordinate to Congress, and any discretion or deference came from the respect they earned. Neither had any legal discretion that Congress was bound to honor.

Conclusion

For many, the need for an independent, energetic national executive was evident. A plural, fluctuating, and often-absent executive could never be vigorous. Thomas Jefferson, who had served in Congress, observed that it would be best "to separate . . . the Executive & Legislative powers" because the "want of [separation] has been the source of more evil than we have experienced from any other cause."[83] Another reformer remarked that if the "power of the whole" was vested in one man, "the execution of laws will be vigorous and decisive."[84] A third averred that law execution should be entrusted to one "great and fearful executive officer." His power "must be greater than that which is hereditary in the house of Orange [the Dutch], and as nearly like the head of that power we are contending with [England] as can well be imagined, the name only excepted."[85]

As discussed in ensuing chapters, Article II reflected the 1787 consensus that a weak executive, so common in the states, would not do for the new national government. No longer as inexperienced in making constitutions or as biased against offices linked to the Crown, many Americans had come to eschew the executive-as-cipher model. A single, superintending chief executive was thought to be more accountable and more capable of taking swift, energetic action than any of the recent state or continental models. As Hamilton wrote in July 1787, there had been an "astonishing revolution" in the minds of people, for they had come to recognize the utility of "something not very remote from that which they have lately quitted."[86]

CHAPTER THREE

CONSTITUTING "HIS HIGHNESS" THE PRESIDENT

The introductory section of Article II erects the foundation of an energetic and powerful office. In an attempt to avoid the dawdling and dissension that often typifies plural entities, the first section enshrines unity. It also hopes to grant the president a measure of independence from Congress by generally leaving his selection to an electoral college. Finally, the section guarantees a fixed salary, preventing legislators from drawing the purse strings closed as a means of purchasing the president's complaisance.

Even though many sought a strong executive, these features were scarcely preordained. Some at the Philadelphia Convention pushed for a triumvirate or an executive council, with an eye to erecting an internal check on executive power. A handful hoped that Congress would select the executive or that he would serve at its pleasure, thereby making him something of a beholden, at-will employee. Had such schemes prevailed, the president might have been something of a prime minister dependent upon Congress. Or he might have been much like the state ciphers that James Madison derided.

The Need for a Meaningfully Separate Executive

The appeal of an executive distinct from the legislature may seem obvious today. But before the Constitution, the attraction was lost on many. As noted in the previous chapter, the Articles of Confederation did not establish a distinct chief executive. Instead, the Continental Congress served as a plural executive, with authority over foreign affairs, the execution of its resolves, and the appointment and removal of executive officers. While some inflated the influence of the departmental secretaries that Congress created in 1781—one called the superintendent of finance the "Premier, the King, or Grand Monarch of America"[1]—these officers were but creatures of Congress, subject to continual direction. For instance, the secretary of foreign affairs was treated as "little better than a congressional clerk."[2] The departmental secretaries had "the arduous task before them to govern without power"[3] because they were the servants of a relatively weak Congress.

While the states nominally separated the executive and legislative powers, in practice the formal division was somewhat irrelevant. Legislatures were too potent and coveted still more power, while executives were incapable of defending whatever authority they had. By 1787, there was something of a consensus that most states had dysfunctional distributions of power.

Reflecting this consensus, each of the main Philadelphia Convention proposals sought the creation of a distinct executive.[4] No longer would the executive power be exercised at the sole discretion of Congress. Left unclear was whether the separation would be more real than nominal. As the state experience proved, a distinct executive was a necessary but not sufficient condition for a proper separation of powers. If the federal legislature was too potent and could encroach with ease, the establishment of a separate chief executive would matter little. Delegates favoring a measure of executive independence understood that the federal executive would need many other features to ensure that the separation was meaningful.

The Unitary Executive as a "Foetus of a Monarchy"

Another executive feature that seems natural, almost inevitable, is singularity. Indeed, some perhaps cannot even conceive of a plural executive council or how it would function. Yet the decision to have a single chief executive was hardly obvious. Some states, such as Pennsylvania, vested executive authority in a council. Majorities made executive decisions, with a "president" having a single vote.[5] Other states, such as Virginia, created a chief executive but granted a council a check on most decisions.[6] While the chief might set the agenda, others helped make final decisions.

At the Constitutional Convention, delegates faced two related questions: Should there be a single rather than plural chief executive? And if delegates proposed a unitary chief executive, would a council serve as a constraint? On the first question, though two plans—the Pinckney and Hamilton proposals—contemplated a single chief executive, neither plan received much consideration.[7] The two more prominent plans, the Virginia and New Jersey Plans, left the matter up for debate. The Virginia Plan proposed a "national executive," saying nothing about the number of chief executives. When the Virginia Plan's executive came up for discussion, James Wilson of Pennsylvania proposed a single executive.[8] Delegates fell silent,[9] perhaps realizing that because George Washington likely would serve as the first chief magistrate, any comments could be seen as reflecting the speaker's views about the presiding chair.

Addressing the merits, one delegate favored vesting the "Executive power in a single person" because a "single man would feel the greatest responsibility and administer the public affairs best."[10] James Wilson similarly observed that a "single magistrate" would supply the "most energy dispatch and responsibility."[11] Others disagreed. One delegate wished to leave the matter to Congress, since in his view the executive was but the former's instrument.[12] A strenuous opponent, Virginia governor Edmund Randolph, decried unity as a "foetus of monarchy."[13] He argued that the British example was not a proper "prototype" and that a triumvirate could supply energy, dispatch, and responsibility.[14]

Proponents of executive unity scoffed. One predicted that each triumvir would favor local interests, something especially troubling in wartime.[15] James Wilson claimed that a triumvirate was highly unusual, erroneously insisting that all thirteen states had placed a single magistrate "at the head of the [government]."[16] Perhaps thinking of ancient Rome, he said that a triumvirate would trigger "uncontrouled, continued, & violent animosities."[17] He added that because not all choices were binary, each triumvir might favor a different course and trigger an impasse.

In a preliminary vote, delegations voted 7–3 in favor of a single executive.[18]

Notwithstanding this vote, the New Jersey Plan, introduced later, pointedly left open the question, proposing a "federal Executive to consist of _____ persons."[19] Likewise, some delegates lobbied for a plural chief executive, usually in the context of other matters, such as the veto.[20] Yet with the passage of time, the idea seemed to lose ground, for the state delegations unanimously approved a unitary executive.[21]

Outside the Philadelphia Convention, many felt the need to defend the choice, probably because singularity raised the specter of a king. James Wilson reiterated his claim that executive authority in the hands of one person ensured vigor, decision, and responsibility.[22] Alexander Hamilton agreed with the maxim that "the executive power is more easily confined when it is one."[23] He asserted as well that plural executives would sow discord. Finally, he claimed that unity made possible "[d]ecision, activity, secrecy, and dispatch."[24] Other Federalists sang from the same hymnal.[25]

While some Anti-Federalists condemned executive unity as establishing a monarchy, others praised it. The "Federal Farmer" observed that "[i]n every large collection of people there must be a visible point serving as a common centre in the government, towards which to draw their eyes and attachments."[26] He added that even supporters of a plural executive admitted that it would be slow and unaccountable.[27] The Federal Farmer might have had someone like Edmund Randolph in mind. The Virginia governor, who had vowed opposition to a unitary executive till the end of his days and who had refused to sign the Constitution, reversed course. During his state's convention, Randolph not only supported ratification but also claimed that "[i]t cannot be objected . . . that the power is executed by one man." Despite his previous support for a plural executive, he confidently asserted that "[a]ll the enlightened part of mankind agree that" one man can act with "superior dispatch, secrecy, and energy."[28] Perhaps Randolph had swallowed hard, making the best case for unity.

Though there would be no plural apex, a council might check the unitary executive, as was true in England and the states. In ancient times, the Crown had a council known as Curia Regis (royal council), which eventually became Parliament. "With the advice and consent" of the Lords and Commons, the Crown enacted laws. Sometimes, however, the Crown

would enact laws using a much smaller privy council. Over time, the
Privy Council's consent became necessary for the exercise of certain
Crown powers, while the Parliament's consent was necessary to pass laws.
When the Privy Council grew too large, English monarchs formed an
inner cabinet of their most trusted advisers. Decisions were often made in
the cabinet and then formally approved by the Privy Council. Hence, by
the eighteenth century, the Crown had a privy council recognized by statutes and an efficient, powerful cabinet.[29]

Colonial governors also had councils that advised and checked them.[30]
Consent typically was needed to call the assembly, make appointments,
and erect courts.[31] Councils also might opine about vetoes and the scope
of gubernatorial power. Although often subservient, councils occasionally
rejected measures and successfully secured the ouster of governors.[32]

State constitutions continued the conciliar tradition, providing that exercises of power required the "advice," the "consent," or the "advice and
consent" of a council. In Virginia, the "advice" of a "Council of State"
checked almost all gubernatorial powers, including the "executive powers
of government."[33] Similarly, the Delaware governor exercised a few powers in conjunction with a council. Summoning the militia required "advice
and consent," while convening the legislature, laying embargoes, or imposing export bans merely required "advice," perhaps hinting that the governor could exercise these powers without consent.[34] Such councils were
purely executive, serving solely to advise and check the chief executive.

Other councils had nonexecutive functions. Councils in Georgia and
Vermont served as upper legislative chambers.[35] Councils in New Jersey,
Massachusetts, and elsewhere exercised judicial powers, such as hearing
impeachments, deciding ordinary cases, or serving as the state supreme
court.[36] The mixed nature of some executive councils likely paved the
way for the Senate's split personality (a mixture of legislative, executive,
and judicial authority).

The familiarity and perceived utility of executive councils undeniably
influenced some Philadelphia delegates. One noted that in "all the States
there was a Council of advice, without which the first magistrate could not
act," and that this was likewise the case in England, where "the King has a
council; and though he appoints it himself, its advice has its weight with
him, and attracts the Confidence of the people."[37] Another spoke of the

benefit of a council (composed of executive officers, the Senate president, and the chief justice) that "should advise but not conclude the President."[38] Late in the convention, two delegates proposed a "Council of State" composed of six secretaries and a chief justice. The president might submit any matter to the council for "discussion" and seek the written opinion of any of its members. "[I]n all cases" the president was to "exercise his own judgment, and either conform to such opinions or not as he may think proper."[39]

Committees shrank this proposal to the point that it became unrecognizable. One suggested a "Privy Council" of officers that would advise the president in "the execution of his Office," but only at his behest.[40] Their advice was not to "conclude him, nor affect his responsibility for the measures which he shall adopt."[41] Another committee eliminated the idea of a distinct executive council. Instead, the Senate would check appointments and treaty making, and the president could seek the written opinions of the "principal officers" of the executive departments upon any subject relating to their respective duties.[42]

Many objected when the Convention took up this truncated, councilless Opinions Clause. George Mason said that without an executive council, the nation would embark on an experiment unknown in even "despotic Governments."[43] He suggested a six-person council of state, two each from the northern, middle, and southern regions.[44] James Madison and Benjamin Franklin agreed, the latter lamenting that many were too worried about cabals and placed too much confidence in a single executive.[45] Another delegate thought it odd that the president could make decisions without some consultation.[46] James Wilson, who had earlier opposed a council, now favored a distinct council in lieu of the Senate's appointment role.[47] Gouverneur Morris explained that the committee had rejected the familiar council because it believed that the president would persuade it to agree with his misguided measures and thereby "acquire their protection for them."[48] Despite the apparent support, the motion to create a generic executive council lost by a lopsided vote.[49]

When the scene shifted to the states, there were some misunderstandings and many protests. Some erroneously regarded the Senate as a generic executive council.[50] Others claimed that because there was no "constitutional Council," something "unknown in any safe & regular Government," the president would lack "proper Information & Advice."[51] Courtiers might lead the president astray; he might become a "Tool to the Senate"; or worst of all, the secretaries might form "a Council of State" and screen their "dangerous or oppressive measures."[52]

Future Supreme Court justice James Iredell of North Carolina tried to rebut such criticisms. He argued that a council would shield the executive from the consequences of bad decisions because the president would blame the council for supplying bad advice. Without a council, however, the president would be responsible for any decision taken because he would "follow advice at his peril."[53] Later, Iredell took up the matter again. In England, a council was necessary because while the king himself could *"do no wrong,"* councilors could be held accountable for their misguided advice.[54] Under the Constitution, however, the president could be removed from office and criminally punished. Because the chief magistrate would be fully responsible for his own decisions, an advisory council was unnecessary.[55]

As Publius, Alexander Hamilton argued that a council would "tincture the exercise of the executive authority with a spirit of habitual feebleness and dilatoriness."[56] It also would "conceal faults[] and destroy responsibility" because multiple actors would make it "impossible, amidst mutual accusations, to determine on whom the blame or the punishment of a pernicious measure ... ought really to fall."[57] To make his point, he cited "[s]candalous appointments" in New York, where the governor and appointments council faulted each other.[58] A council would be a "clog upon [the executive's] good intentions" and the "instruments and accomplices of his bad."[59]

One suspects that at least some Federalists were insincere and defended a structure that they favored for other reasons. In any event, an extraconstitutional council subsequently developed, as Chapter 8 recounts. This practice of consultation with multiple department heads did not detract from presidential responsibility because, as the Opinions Clause suggests, the president received "opinions" of his subordinate and then decided how best to exercise his executive powers.

Dignifying Titles

Recall that one definition of "monarch" in Samuel Johnson's *Dictionary* was "president."[60] When we turn to his entry for the latter word, we find the following: "One placed with authority over others; one at the head of others. Governor; prefect. A tutelary power."[61] So "president" denoted, among other things, a person with authority over others. While subsequent chapters consider the extent of presidential authority, it must be noted that not all presidents have meaningful authority. The Constitution proves as much. The vice president serves as the Senate's "president," meaning that he may chair its meetings. Additionally, he may break ties in Senate votes.[62] If the president presided in the manner of the president of the Senate, the Article II presidency would be more about procedures and ceremony than about the exercise of power.

The nation's first "presidents" had more in common with our vice president. As early as 1774, the Continental Congress appointed a delegate to serve as "president." He presided over deliberations, handled official communications, received and entertained foreign ambassadors, and took ceremonial precedence over other delegates.[63] Despite the office's narrow scope of authority, the Articles imposed term limits. No delegate could serve as president for more than one year in every three, a curb that likely reflected an acute (and excessive) concern with monarchy.[64]

Most state constitutions labeled their chief executives "governors," bringing to mind the colonial executives. Three states—Delaware,[65] South Carolina,[66] and New Hampshire[67]—had a "president" as chief magistrate.[68] Pennsylvania's "president" presided over a plural executive council and was but the first among equals, having little independent authority.[69] For some, perhaps any title other than "governor" was preferable, since the latter had royal connotations.[70]

At the Convention, "governor" and "president" were obvious choices. But there were other possibilities. Jefferson had once proposed an "administrator" for Virginia;[71] in a different era, Benjamin Franklin had suggested a national "president general."[72] On the eve of the Convention, some spoke of a "governor generl."[73] And, as Chapter 1 recounts, a few favored a "king."

The most important comprehensive proposals—the Virginia and New Jersey Plans—never specified a title, perhaps because each had left open whether the supreme executive would be singular or plural. Alexander Hamilton's plan anticipated a "governor."[74] Charles Pinckney of South Carolina may have had the most influence on the executive's title. His plan, perhaps borrowing from the South Carolina Constitution of 1776, envisioned a "president."[75] A committee eventually drafted the Article II Vesting Clause, granting "[t]he Executive Power" to a "President of the United States of America."[76] After one committee proposed an additional title—"His Excellency"[77]—another eliminated it;[78] neither of these decisions apparently elicited floor debate.

These events raised the question whether other titles (beyond those merely descriptive, such as "chief executive" or "supreme magistrate") were implicitly forbidden. Or might the president also be called "His Excellency," alongside other honorifics?[79] Some state constitutions had supplementary titles, such as "honorable"[80] and "His Excellency."[81] Moreover, "Excellency" had served as a title for the commander in chief of the Continental Army and for state governors.[82]

The matter came to a head in the first year of Washington's presidency. Some senators wished to refer to the president's oration as "His most gracious speech," aping an English custom. A Senate committee charged with examining how to address the president suggested "His Highness, the President of the United States of America, and Protector of their Liberties."[83] Vice President John Adams supposedly derided "president" as too pedestrian: "[W]hat will the Common People of Foreign Countries, what will the Sailors and Soldiers say, George Washington, President of the United States, they will despise him *to all eternity*."[84] Adams eventually settled on "His Majesty," apparently believing that "Highness was not high enough."[85] Foes responded that the Constitution permitted no title other than "president."[86] Though the Senate pressed, the House stood firm, refusing to use anything but "president" in its address.[87] The Senate eventually agreed to use "president" temporarily.[88] Yet the question was never formally revisited.

One reason for the Senate's defeat was that "His Highness" had come to oppose the title. Although Washington agreed that a title would be "useful and proper," he believed that there would be a popular clamor against it.[89] Madison, supposedly acting on Washington's behalf, opposed the title for the same reasons.[90] A controversial title would have inflicted "a deep wound to our infant government."[91]

Following the title debate, the French ambassador reported that some Americans thought "President of the United States was grand enough by itself."[92] He noted that other Americans prophesized that "soon the more lofty title will be the name of Washington which will become the title of the Presidents of the United States as the name of *Caesar* became that of Emperors."[93] The forecast proved wrong.

In retrospect, the clash over the constitutionality of titles, which lasted for weeks, seems trivial. The Constitution does not explicitly bar additional titles for the president. The bar against "titles of nobility" certainly did not prevent honorifics; notwithstanding the Articles' express bar on titles of nobility,[94] delegates to each Continental Congress called their presidents "His Excellency."[95] Moreover, the Constitution does not dictate how citizens should address federal officers. Even if the People's House could not bring itself to use "His Excellency," the people were free to do so. Indeed, some early Americans addressed the president in a manner befitting a monarch. One office seeker told Washington that he was the "Father and protector of [the] People."[96] A prisoner spoke of Washington as the nation's "protector & ornament."[97] And in the first two years of Washington's presidency, some addressed him as "your Highness."[98] Over time, "Excellency" held sway among those who sought to ingratiate themselves or underscore the president's high station.[99]

Though supplementary titles for the president have varied across time, what remains unchanged is America's partiality for titles. After the debate about the president's title, the French ambassador observed that "Americans love" them.[100] Indeed, Americans have long supposed that those in high stations merit high titles. Delegates to the Constitutional Convention—the ones who incorporated the Constitution's bar on titles of nobility—referred to their presiding officer, George Washington, as "His Excellency," going so far as to stand while addressing him and when he left the building.[101] Even those senators who opposed a flowery presidential title nonetheless addressed their colleagues as "the Honorable."[102] The title lingers on, for Americans use "honorable" to address many sorts of federal officials, including the president.[103]

Qualifications

The eighteenth-century English monarch faced a host of qualifications for office. By statute, Parliament reserved the Crown for Protestants[104] and provided that a regent would rule in the place of any monarch younger than eighteen years.[105] Though Parliament barred the foreign born from serving in the legislature or as officers, it expressly permitted them to serve as monarch.[106] Both George I and George II were foreign born.

While some state constitutions had little or no restrictions on who might serve as chief executive,[107] many more imposed age, residency, property, and religious restrictions. Maryland limited the office of governor to those who owned £5,000 in property, had resided in the state for five years, and had attained the ripe age of twenty-five.[108] New Hampshire had the most requirements, which related to residency, age, property, and religion.[109] South Carolina's 1778 Constitution was perhaps the most demanding, requiring £10,000 in state property, ten years residency, and professed Protestantism.[110] Finally, some imposed rather precise religious tests for their officers, including the executive. Delaware required a belief "in God the Father, and in Jesus Christ His only son, and in the Holy Ghost."[111]

The Constitution contains its own set of qualifications: "No Person except a natural born Citizen, or a Citizen of the United States, at the time of the Adoption of this Constitution, shall be eligible to the Office of President; neither shall any Person be eligible to that Office who shall not have attained to the Age of thirty five Years, and been fourteen Years a Resident within the United States."[112] The citizenship test was stricter than the one imposed on representatives and senators, for while those naturalized after the Constitution's adoption could serve in the House and Senate, they could not serve as chief executive. Only natural-born citizens and those naturalized before the Constitution's ratification were eligible. Such a provision was perhaps necessary to quiet speculation about the possibility of a foreign chief executive. As discussed in Chapter 1, in 1786 the president of the Continental Congress supposedly inquired whether a younger brother of Frederick the Great might serve as king.[113] During the Convention itself, reports surfaced that the delegates sought to crown the second son of George III.[114]

Perhaps in response to such rumors, John Jay suggested to George Washington that it might be wise "to provide a strong check to the admission of Foreigners into the administration of our national Government; and to declare expressly that the Command in chief of the american army shall not be given to, nor devolve on, any but a naturally *born*

Citizen."[115] Washington thanked Jay for the suggestion,[116] and two days later the natural-born limitation was before the Convention,[117] suggesting that the future president might have been the impetus behind it. Delegates perhaps realized that the best way to squelch the rumored desire for a foreign executive was to bar aliens from serving. The citizenship requirement made clear that neither siblings of the Prussian king nor George III's offspring could be president.

Questions recur about what constitutes a natural-born citizen. It seems clear that those born within the United States are "natural born" citizens, certainly after the Fourteenth Amendment. Less clear is whether children of U.S. citizens, when born outside the United States, are natural born. A 1790 statute declared that such children are "natural born citizens."[118] This statute likely reflected the original sense of the constitutional qualification. Alternatively, perhaps members of Congress supposed that they could create citizenship rules and decree that people who were U.S. citizens at birth were natural born, even if they were born elsewhere.

The fourteen-year residency requirement (reduced from a twenty-one-year period)[119] barred U.S. citizens who had spent much time abroad. Though they might otherwise be qualified, these onetime emigrants might have grown unfamiliar with American society. The residency rule has several ambiguities, including what counts as being "resident" and whether that period must immediately precede a candidate's ascension to the presidency.[120]

The age threshold (thirty-five years) ensured that presidents were worldly wise. It was more limiting than constraints imposed upon state governors and far more confining than English statutes, which allowed monarchs to rule at eighteen. Evidently, delegates believed that presidents required extra ripening, since the qualifications for representatives (twenty-five) and senators (thirty) are less restrictive. In *Federalist* 64, John Jay argued that the constraint ensured that citizens would select only experienced men with known backgrounds.[121]

Missing from the list of qualifications is any reference to property, religion, or multiple-office holding. After toying with the idea of property qualification, the convention abandoned the idea because it proved difficult to establish a uniform property requirement and because of concerns that any such test would become obsolete.[122] But there may have been an antielitist impulse too. Benjamin Franklin argued that Europeans would pay close attention, "and if [the Constitution] should betray a great partiality to the rich," the nation would lose the goodwill of the enlightened in Europe and also discourage its common folk from settling in America.[123] This was perhaps the germ of the populist adage that any man might become president. On religion, the Constitution contains a general ban on religious tests or qualifications. Hence, the office was open to Christian and non-Christian alike, including atheists.[124] Finally, although one delegate had proposed that the president not hold any other office under the United States or any of them,[125] this provision never emerged from committee. Perhaps the delegate wanted to bar presidents from serving as state officers, as had occurred under the Articles with several presidents of the Continental Congress.[126] Accordingly, while a president may not simultaneously sit in Congress, the Constitution left open the possibility that a president also could serve as state governor or as a Supreme Court justice.

Election

If, in retrospect, some features of Article II seem obvious, the electoral system appears rather suspect. Though the Twelfth Amendment improved matters, calls for reform continued unabated. Since 1789, federal legislators have introduced almost 700 presidential election amendments.[127]

The matter was just as controversial in the beginning. At the Constitutional Convention, no issue occupied as much time or remained so much in flux. Delegates sifted through almost a dozen proposals.[128] James Wilson confided that delegates "were perplexed with no part of [the Constitution] so much as with the mode of choosing the President."[129]

William Blackstone had conceded the theoretical superiority of elective monarchy. But in practice it would occasion "periodical bloodshed and misery."[130] Blackstone specifically mentioned the difficulties with the Polish system. The election of Polish monarchs became ridden with intrigue as nations schemed for their favorite.[131] The desire to avoid intrigue, plus the suspicion of anything smacking of monarchy, may help explain why most states relied upon legislatures to select the executive.[132]

Given the prevalence of legislative appointment in the states, it was natural that most Constitutional Convention plans adopted that model. When the matter first came up for debate, however, James Wilson hesitantly advanced the "chimerical" idea of popular election.[133] One delegate responded that independence from the legislature was "the very essence of tyranny."[134] Hence, the executive should be "absolutely dependent" upon Congress.[135] After the matter was deferred, Wilson refined his proposal, suggesting that voters should choose electors, who would then select the president.[136] Delegations lopsidedly rejected his proposal and endorsed legislative selection.[137]

Over several weeks, the convention heard many alternatives. One delegate suggested that state executives select their federal counterpart.[138] Another proposed that state legislators appoint electors.[139] Days later, a similar plan garnered a majority, only to have the coalition fracture over details.[140] Hoping to limit the executive's incentive to curry favor with federal legislators, James Wilson proposed that randomly chosen members of Congress elect the executive.[141] Another proposal envisioned that each state's voters could propose a "best Citizen," and that another entity could choose from the resulting pool.[142] Or maybe a bifurcated system was best: Congress would select new presidents, and reelection would be left to state-appointed electors.[143] The delegates eventually returned to legislative selection.[144]

Yet even if they could not coalesce around one alternative, a nascent majority opposed routine legislative selection. Some opponents argued that the legislature might choose a servile president or that the executive might try to corrupt the legislature in order to secure reelection.[145] Others feared that legislative selection might grant larger states too much influence in the selection of a president.[146]

The entire issue was sent to a committee, which eventually proposed that each state would have a number of electors equal to the sum of its representatives and senators; the Senate would choose the president when no candidate received a majority of the electors.[147] This proposal ensured that small states had disproportionate influence at the initial stage and an even larger voice in who would be president in cases when a candidate failed to muster a majority. In the convention's waning days, delegates weakened the Senate's "aristocratic influence" and allowed the House to select the president when no candidate secured an electoral majority, with each state getting one vote.[148] As compared with a popular vote for electing the president, the Constitution's unique mechanism secured the small states outsized influence, in the primary electoral method, and especially in the secondary House mode. So unstable were the coalitions and so controversial was the issue that one suspects that had there been more time there would have been more tinkering.

Outside the convention, the system drew praise, even from some Anti-Federalists.[149] Hamilton extolled it as "excellent" because it curbed "cabal, intrigue and corruption."[150] The transience of presidential electors would make it more difficult for scheming foreign powers to influence an election. Similarly, having separate state conclaves would insulate the electors from popular "heats and ferments."[151] Finally, the system helped ensure that the president would be independent, for the legislature would play only a limited, backup role. Hamilton claimed that the election process was the only constitutional feature "which has escaped without severe censure, or which has received the slightest mark of approbation from its opponents."[152]

During the ratification process, many imagined that the system somehow ensured that ordinary voters would select the electors. Hamilton said as much,[153] as did some speakers in the state conventions.[154] Others asserted that state legislatures might select electors.[155] This sparked disagreement, since some reasoned that because the legislatures supposedly could only "direct the manner" of selecting electors, they could not actually appoint them.[156] A few seem puzzled, unsure whether state legislatures could appoint electors or had to authorize their popular selection.[157]

The Constitution states that "[e]ach State shall appoint, in such Manner as the Legislature thereof may direct," the electors.[158] This text fairly invited legislatures to direct by law that they would appoint electors. For the first election, only four states used a popular vote to select electors.[159] States that had yet to ratify the Constitution by early 1789 had no electors, and even one that had, New York, never directed the selection of its electors and hence had no say in what would be the unanimous election of George Washington.[160]

Although people today commonly speak of an "electoral college," the Constitution never uses the term. An electoral college consists of a single group of voters (electors) who gather together in a single college (from the Latin *collegium*—a group of colleagues, a society). Because presidential electors meet in every state, the Constitution requires many "electoral *colleges*," which is how early Americans referred to these conclaves.[161]

From the beginning, people foresaw problems with the original system. Because each elector had to vote for two candidates as president, Alexander Hamilton worried that machinations might throw the first election to John Adams rather than George Washington. If Adams got the maximum number of votes, while a few were diverted from Washington, Adams would become the first president. Hamilton plotted to have some electors vote for someone other than Adams to ensure that Washington became president.[162] His fears proved unwarranted: Washington was a unanimous choice, and Adams received far fewer votes.

Yet Hamilton was prescient. In the 1796 election, Thomas Pinckney of South Carolina might have garnered the second-most number of votes and become vice president to President John Adams had not northern Federalists diverted votes from their copartisan Pinckney. These northern Federalists, who wanted to ensure that Adams became president, were concerned that Hamilton was attempting to sway Federalists toward Pinckney. Enough New England Federalist votes were siphoned away from Pinckney—a number of them voting for dark-horse candidates— that Jefferson slipped in with the second-highest vote tally and became vice president.[163]

Resolving not to let the same problem strike them in the 1800 election, the Democratic-Republicans ensured that all their electors voted for the same two candidates.[164] But this created a different problem. Because Thomas Jefferson and Aaron Burr received the same number of electoral votes, the election went to the House. After thirty-six separate votes occurring over a week, Jefferson finally received a majority of the state delegations.[165] To prevent further such embarrassments, Democratic-Republicans backed the Twelfth Amendment, which required that electors vote separately for president and vice president.[166] Though this section of the Constitution has been amended more times than any other, one suspects that a few more may be in the offing.

Tenure and Reeligibility—At Pleasure, During Good Behavior, or Something in Between

Monarchs of the era served for life. As a practical matter, this tenure was a little less secure than it might seem upon first impression. The English tried and executed Charles I, thus highlighting a somewhat underappreciated dimension of life tenure.[167] Although the French Constitution of 1791 declared that the king was inviolable, it also provided means of violating him. The French king would be deemed an abdicator if he led an army against the people, fled the kingdom, or retracted his constitutional oath.[168] After abdication, he might be punished as an ordinary citizen, meaning that he might face criminal prosecution for undermining the Constitution. Colonial governors in America had a far less secure tenure because they served at the Crown's pleasure.[169] Though colonials had no formal power to dismiss their governors, popular or legislative pressure could sway the Crown to oust a subordinate.[170]

State executives were on extremely short leashes, generally appointed to one-year terms. Only New York, Delaware, and South Carolina permitted slightly longer terms.[171] Most also faced term limits, thereby preventing much continuity.[172] Such restrictions reflected a severe mistrust of executive power and the fear that if chief executives were not periodically rotated out of office, incumbents might seize power permanently. Many Americans had come to believe that "where annual elections end, tyranny begins."[173]

States that lacked term limits had a rather different experience. New York's George Clinton, enjoying a long term (three years) and unimpeded by term limits, won reelection five times and served a total of eighteen years.[174] In New Jersey, William Livingston served fourteen one-year terms.[175] John Hancock successfully ran for reelection in Massachusetts every year until poor health forced him from office.[176] It must have seemed that in the absence of term limits, governors might govern indefinitely.[177]

At the Convention, proposals ranged from legislative pleasure to tenure during good behavior.[178] When the latter proposal was put to a vote, many favored it as necessary to secure the executive's independence,[179] so much so that it failed only narrowly.[180] Though the proposed terms ran the gamut, most delegates opposed short terms as inconsistent with the need for a strong executive. For much of the convention, the term was seven years, with delegates eventually moving to six and then reverting to seven.[181]

Delegates proposed two types of term limits. Some sought a one-term limit. The Virginia Plan proposed that the executive be ineligible after serving a single term.[182] Later, delegates removed the reelection bar.[183] With the move to six years, however, some attempted to introduce another sort of rotational rule. One moved that no one could serve as president for more than six years in a twelve-year period.[184] This would ensure rotation, but still permit reelection after six years. Delegates eventually settled on four-year terms without any term limits.[185]

Outside the convention, critics agreed with Jefferson that "[e]xperience concurs with reason in concluding that the first magistrate will always be re-elected if the constitution permits it."[186] "Cato," quoting Montesquieu, argued that "the greatness of the power must be compensated by the brevity of the duration."[187] Yet the Constitution ignored this wisdom, ceding the president the "power and time sufficient to ruin his country."[188] Federalists responded that a short term would make the office unappealing to the most talented. They argued too that the chance of reelection allowed the people to maintain stability and retain the competent.[189]

The fear that the Constitution permitted life tenure led state conventions, including those in Virginia, New York, and North Carolina, to suggest term limits.[190] When George Washington stepped down after two terms, he created a de facto term limit that his successors adhered to for almost a century and a half. After the death of the only president (Franklin D. Roosevelt) to serve more than two terms, the nation acted on the recommendation of a bipartisan commission and barred presidents from serving more than two elected terms.[191]

A Guaranteed Salary but No Civil List

Though the English monarch received no salary, he (and occasionally she) needed money to run the government. To fund officers and expenses, monarchs long drew from eighteen sources of "ordinary revenue," coming from custom or statutes.[192] At some point, because such revenue proved insufficient, the Crown relied upon "extraordinary revenue"—supplemental "aids, subsidies, and supplies" ceded by Parliament.[193] Upon his ascension,

George III yielded some of his hereditary revenue in return for a fixed annual subsidy of £800,000.[194] This "civil list" defrayed the cost of salaries and expenses, including executive, judicial, and household costs.[195]

The Crown instructed colonial governors to secure a guaranteed salary for themselves and a civil list annuity. The assemblies resisted, fearing the loss of leverage. Funds usually flowed only after a governor assented to particular bills. According to Benjamin Franklin, public monies were well spent on "the Purchase of Good laws."[196] This practice became so common that when one legislature gave an annual salary rather than a biannual one, it did so as a "Mark of Confidence" in the executive's continued cooperation.[197] Because governors depended on the assemblies, they had "two Masters; one who gives him his Commission, and one who gives him his Pay."[198]

State constitutions were a mixed bag. Some said nothing, leaving the salaries of executives to legislative discretion. Others dictated that all officers be paid "reasonable"[199] or "adequate" salaries.[200] And still others required as much for the chief executive in particular.[201] South Carolina experimented with a set salary of £9,000 before its second constitution adopted a standard.[202] The Massachusetts Constitution was unique, listing four reasons for an "honorable stated salary, of a fixed" value: to prevent the legislature's "undue influence"; to allow the executive to "act with freedom" for the public's benefit; to prevent a focus on his "private concerns"; and to "maintain the dignity of the commonwealth in the character of its chief magistrate."[203] So crucial was the matter that fixing executive pay was to be "among the first acts" of the legislature.[204]

At the Constitutional Convention, the Virginia and New Jersey Plans provided that the executive would receive a fixed compensation, thereby barring the legislature from increasing or decreasing the salary during the executive's term.[205] Yet some opposed any salary. Benjamin Franklin argued that a salary would attract the wrong sort of men. He cited officials who took no salary, including the Continental Army's commander in chief.[206] He was in the minority, for the delegations unanimously voted for a guaranteed salary.[207]

As finalized, Article II, section 1, clause 7 provides that "[t]he President shall, at stated Times, receive for his Services, a Compensation, which shall neither be increased nor diminished during the Period for which he shall have been elected, and he shall not receive within that Period any other Emolument from the United States, or any of them." The clause does not cap compensation so much as it bars in-term modifications. Congress cannot grant new compensation, salary or otherwise (such as fine stallions or property), to a sitting president, even if the aim is to express gratitude for his stewardship. In addition, clause 7 seems to bar the states from compensating the president. While the second part of the clause prohibits states from granting any new compensation once the president is in office, the first part seems to assume that only Congress will set presidential compensation. It speaks of "a Compensation" and not "compensations." Though states no less than Congress might compensate "at stated times," it seems unlikely that the Constitution envisions that the president might be compensated from different sources at different stated times.

Before the first Congress could set his pay, Washington grandly declined any salary. In his inaugural address, the president said that he had long ago resolved to serve the nation without compensation, and so he declined "any share in the personal emoluments, which may be indispensably included in a permanent provision for the Executive Department." He wished that his expenses be reimbursed and nothing more.[208]

Congress rebuffed Washington, out of a sense that the Constitution obliged it to grant a salary.[209] "[T]he [C]onstitution requires that he shall receive a compensation, and it is our duty to provide it,"[210] said one representative. As the constitutional scholar David Currie noted, this was a powerful argument because the guarantee was not meant for the president's protection alone; it also was meant to safeguard the public's interest in an independent executive who might resist Congress and could decline bribes without risking penury.[211] Any president who declined a salary might later meet some hardship and find himself in need.

The Constitution does not require an "adequate" or "reasonable" salary, only that it be fixed. At the same time, it does not limit the salary to a "modest" amount, as was true in Virginia.[212] Legislators followed the provision's spirit, initially proposing a generous $20,000 salary and such sums as were necessary for furniture and carriages.[213] Some lawmakers objected that an expense account amounted to an unconstitutional emolument. Others replied that it did not matter whether compensation was fixed in one line or two, for as long as they were set in one bill, the legislation would be constitutional.[214] Still others thought that if Congress covered expenses, an expense account might serve as a backdoor means of improperly increasing pay within a term. Eventually, Congress settled on $25,000, with no mention of expenses.[215] Washington accepted it, perhaps recognizing that he had no choice in the matter.

Twenty-five thousand dollars was a princely sum, meant to allow the president to live in majestic style and thereby reflect the dignity of the entire nation. The relative size becomes clear if we compare it to the size of the diplomatic budget ($40,000),[216] the vice president's salary ($5,000),[217] or the secretary of state's pay ($3,500).[218]

The Vice Presidency—"The Most Insignificant Office that Ever the Invention of Man Contrived"

In modern elections, the vice presidency is mostly an afterthought. And so it was at Philadelphia. The convention initially made the president of the Senate the president's successor, with the Senate selecting its own president. In September, a committee, perhaps using the New York Constitution as a template, proposed a vice president, who would succeed the president if necessary as well as preside over, and break ties in, the Senate.[219] The committee provided that the candidate with the second-most electoral votes would become vice president.[220]

The most divisive proposal was the vice president's role as Senate president. Virginian George Mason claimed that vice presidency encroached "on the rights of the Senate; and that it mixed too much the Legislative & Executive."[221] Elbridge Gerry of Massachusetts said that because of the "close intimacy that must subsist between the President & vice-president," the convention "might as well put the President himself at the head of the Legislature."[222] Pennsylvanian Gouverneur Morris drolly responded that the fears supposed that the vice president would be "the first heir apparent that ever loved his father."[223]

Delegates such as Mason and Gerry must have been confused by the superficial resemblance of the vice president to the president, arising from the ability to succeed the latter and from the somewhat similar title. In truth, the vice president is not an executive officer at all because he has no share of any executive power. He has no constitutional authority to

56

execute the laws, conduct foreign affairs, superintend executive officials, and so forth. The vice president has less executive sway than a senator, for the latter routinely votes on appointments and treaties, whereas the former votes on appointments only to break a tie.[224] The vice president becomes a true executive only if the president leaves office or becomes disabled in some way. But until such an event, he or she is but a high legislative official with precious little authority over executive matters.

The 1796 presidential election exploded the idea of a necessary intimacy between the two offices. Thomas Jefferson, a Democratic-Republican, became vice president to the Federalist John Adams. Given the rule that the candidate with the second-most electoral votes would become vice president, there was always a possibility that persons with dissimilar outlooks might occupy these offices. The Twelfth Amendment made this possibility more remote by requiring electors to cast one vote for each office.[225] After that amendment, a political party could propose a ticket and partisan presidential electors could vote for both members of it. But even with this change, the vice president owes no obedience to the president. Any deference to the president arises from shared policy stances and an intense desire to be the party's candidate in the next election.

There remains the question of the vice president's legislative authority. Was his a ceremonial position, or did it give him real power? Under the Articles, the president of the Continental Congress presided over its proceedings and could cast a vote, but could not cast an additional tie-breaking vote, serve on committees, or participate in debates.[226] In some respects, the president of the Senate seems weaker. Whereas the former president of the Continental Congress always had a vote, the Constitution granted the president of the Senate a vote only when there is a tie. Yet in other respects, the Constitution's failure to bar certain functions suggests a change. For instance, the silence on whether the president of the Senate may participate in debates suggests that he or she may speak freely.

The first vice president, John Adams, vacillated about the office's importance. In an early letter, Adams boasted that "[t]he Constitution has instituted two great offices, of equal rank . . .: one who is the first of the two . . . is placed at the Head of the Executive, the other at the Head of the Legislature."[227] Adams was mistaken, for the vice president does not lead Congress; he merely presides over the Senate. With experience,

Adams accurately observed that vice president "is totally detached from the executive authority and confined to the legislative."[228] Later still, he despaired that he occupied "the most insignificant office that ever the invention of man contrived or his imagination conceived."[229]

The last comment went too far. The vice president may play an influential, occasionally pivotal role, as Adams himself demonstrated. Adams frequently lectured from the chair, attempting to influence votes. On the question of designating a grand title for the president, he supposedly "harrange[d]" senators.[230] Adams may have been quite persuasive on whether the president may remove executives (discussed in Chapter 8), for he is said to have convinced one or two senators to support a statute that assumed the president had a constitutional removal power. One senator said that all regarded Adams as "the great converter."[231] With the conversion of one or two senators to his point of view on removal, the vote stood at 9–9, enabling him to cast the deciding vote. In all, he cast thirty-one tie-breaking votes, a record perhaps impossible to exceed.[232]

By his second term, Adams had grown more reserved.[233] Today, Senate rules implicitly bar vice presidents from participating in debate.[234] This makes vice presidents less inclined to preside over the Senate, leaving that task to the president pro tempore or some other senator serving as chair. This gag is dubious. If the Senate can muzzle the vice president, someone whom the Constitution makes clear is a participant in Senate proceedings, what is to prevent the Senate from stifling disfavored senators? Legislatures are places of debate, and while there must be some ability to place limits on endless monologues, such limitations cannot go so far as to utterly silence participants. By making the vice president the president of the Senate, the Constitution contemplates that he will have a meaningful role in its proceedings and perhaps hints that he must be able to address matters before that body.

Substitution and Succession

Because the Virginia and New Jersey Plans contemplated legislative selection of the executive, there was perhaps no need for any further discussion of succession. If the office became vacant, Congress would select a new president. Hamilton's plan, which proposed a more complex electoral system, provided that upon the president's removal or death, the president of the Senate would temporarily assume the office until a successor was chosen.[235] This idea became part of a committee proposal.[236]

When the matter came up for discussion, one delegate argued that the chief justice would be a more fitting temporary successor, another warned that the Senate might delay in choosing a permanent successor if their president became the interim chief executive, and a third suggested that the entire legislature should select a temporary chief executive.[237] As noted, a committee proposed the election of a vice president who would serve as president of the Senate and would succeed the president upon removal, death, absence, resignation, or disability.[238] In many respects, this text mirrored language found in the New York Constitution.[239] Late in the convention, a delegate successfully moved that the legislature would select which officer would succeed the president should the vice president die, resign, or become disabled.[240]

Delegates said nothing about what counted as a disability, even though the issue surfaced repeatedly. When Benjamin Franklin asked who would "conduct the Public Affairs" if the single chief executive became sick,[241] apparently no one responded. Later, George Mason argued that a triumvirate would function better precisely because "casual disability by sickness or otherwise" would not arrest the executive.[242] One delegate objected to the proposal that the Senate's president would take over when the president had a "disability to discharge the [office's] powers and duties,"[243] not only because "disability" was "too vague" but also because he was unsure who would decide the matter.[244]

As finalized, the Constitution provides that "[i]n Case of the Removal of the President from Office, or of his Death, Resignation, or Inability to discharge the Powers and Duties of the said Office, the Same shall devolve on the Vice President, and the Congress may by Law provide for the Case of Removal, Death, Resignation or Inability, both of the President and Vice President, declaring what Officer shall then act as President, and such Officer shall act accordingly, until the Disability be removed, or a President shall be elected." Though the clause initially discusses "inability," it provides that the president can resume his office after the "disability" vanishes. "Disability" might cover only mental or physical disabilities, while "inability" might extend further, covering any situation in which the president could not execute the office, whatever the reason. The New York Constitution had a similar list of conditions that would permit the lieutenant governor to assume the governorship, except that it never mentioned "inability" but included the governor's "absence from the state." Was "inability" meant to cover absence from the nation's capital? If so, what if the president left to command the army in person? In that case, would someone else serve as the civilian president? Moreover, would the vice president take charge whenever the president had a severe flu, that is, whenever the chief executive was unable to effectively function, even if only for a short period?[245]

The question of a president's absence from the (temporary) capital came to the fore in 1791. In that year, Washington toured the southern states. He instructed the department heads that "if any serious and important cases should arise during my absence (of which the probability is but too strong)," the secretaries should meet to determine "whether they are of such a nature as to require my personal attendance at the seat of government." If they determined that his immediate action was unnecessary, the president would later "approve and ratify the measures" they took. Washington also asked that the vice president be consulted if the latter was in town.[246] Using this authority, the secretaries, acting with the vice president, agreed to borrow funds overseas, send commissioners to certain Indian tribes, and complain to the British about their supply of arms to some tribes.[247] On another occasion, the secretaries (without the vice president) came close to ordering cannons fired upon a disputed vessel, a move that would have risked war with France. Had not Thomas Jefferson, the secretary of state, opposed the attack for reasons unrelated to Washington's absence, the secretaries might have triggered a war.[248]

Apparently, Washington's absences were not treated as instances of an "inability to discharge the Power and Duties" because Adams did not become the acting president in Washington's absence. Yet while the latter was on tour, the cabinet "essentially ran the government."[249] Perhaps Washington, his cabinet, and Adams concluded that the president could discharge the office through the agency of his principal executive officers. But if that were so, there might be few, if any, occasions of presidential "inability" that would result in the vice president assuming office. Presidents always might be said to be acting via their alter egos within the departments, even when they were deathly ill for a prolonged period. Perhaps it is better to suppose that these officers concluded that an absence from the nation's capital, standing alone, was not an inability, even though the president could not make all the decisions that he would have made had he remained in the capital.

Besides the question of what constituted "inability," there was the separate question of who would decide the matter. Would it be a president who had come to recognize that his disability impaired him? Would it be a vice president, who might too easily conclude that a president was incapacitated? Or would it be some more neutral (but hardly disinterested) entity, like Congress or federal judges? The Twenty-Fifth Amendment, enacted almost two centuries after the Constitution's ratification, laid out rules related to presidential incapacity. Either the president acting alone or the vice president plus a majority of the heads of the executive departments may declare the president incapacitated, at which time the vice president becomes "acting President." Should the elected president claim that he is no longer incapacitated, he can resume his functions. Yet he may be ousted again. Within four days of the president's resumption of power, the vice president *and* a majority of the heads of the executive departments may conclude that the president is incapacitated and oust the president. At that point, Congress must decide. Two-thirds of both chambers must find the president disabled in order for the vice president to continue to serve as acting president. Otherwise, the president resumes office.[250]

Conclusion

When lawyers consider presidential authority, what comes to mind is authority to make treaties, command the troops, and direct officers. Yet in the presidential power equation, the structure of the executive is just as meaningful. Article II, section 1 begins by establishing executive unity. Though some Founders favored a triumvirate, unity won the day because many more delegates believed that a single executive would be more accountable, powerful, and decisive. Just as importantly, section 1 does not establish a generic executive council, a committee that would likely impede the energetic exercise of most executive powers. Section 1 also guarantees the president a salary and establishes a selection process, both of which were meant to give the executive a measure of independence from Congress. The president need not constantly curry favor with the legislature, bending to its preferences, in order to secure a salary or reelection. Considered together, section 1's provisions make meaningful the separation of the executive from the legislature, implicit in the very establishment of Article II, and create the conditions necessary for a robust, active branch under the president's control.

CHAPTER FOUR

THE EXECUTIVE POWER AS THE "ACTIVE PRINCIPLE IN ALL GOVERNMENTS"

Article II, section 1 does more than establish the executive's superstructure. Before Article II details how the nation will select a president and lists derivative powers and duties, it opens with a terse clause—"[t]he executive power shall be vested in a President of the United States"—that grants power. Or at least that is what the clause seems to do. Contrary to the conclusions that ordinary readers might draw, some scholars (and some Supreme Court justices) regard the clause—the Executive Power or Vesting Clause—as something of a nullity. For them, the clause is surplusage. It either grants the president those powers awarded elsewhere in Article II, or it does nothing more than signify that there shall be a single executive called the president.

These readings are mistaken, at least as a matter of the original Constitution. Late-eighteenth-century usage reveals that the phrase "executive power" referred to a set of "active" governmental powers: execution of federal law, management of foreign affairs, and direction of executive officers. By granting "executive power," section 1 of Article II marks the president as the supreme executive magistrate of the federal government. Without the grant of executive power, presidents would lack constitutional powers they have exercised for over two centuries, and the presidency would be a pale reflection of the familiar, energetic office.

To understand why the president has generic executive powers, we first take a short detour into eighteenth-century separation-of-powers theory.[1] Three principles frame our consideration. First, many of the era's writers on government believed that one could classify all governmental powers into one of three categories: legislative, executive, and judicial. Second, each category consisted of strands of authorities. Third, the categorization of powers did not turn on the characteristics of the entity exercising such powers. The power to make criminal laws was legislative whether exercised by one or many. The same was true of the various strands of executive power. Though disputes arose about the proper classification of some powers (such as treaty making), there was a consensus on the tripartite division and on the core powers of each category, namely, lawmaking, law execution, and adjudication.

Categories of Governmental Power

Writers have long sorted governmental powers into categories. In the seventeenth century, John Locke claimed that there were three powers: legislative, executive, and federative (relating to foreign relations).[2] In conformance with late-eighteenth-century categories, baron de Montesquieu saw three powers as well: legislative, executive, and judicial.[3] Some, such as John Adams, supposed that the latter classification rested on an "unalterable foundation in nature" and existed "in every society natural and artificial."[4] While the division was hardly natural—after all, Locke's writings proved that one might categorize governmental powers in various ways—many agreed with Adams.

Deliberation and openness were thought to characterize the legislative power because sound lawmaking required frank debate. When vested in a plural assembly (a legislature), the power was seen as transient, because eighteenth-century legislatures were often out of session. In contrast, exercises of executive power were associated with energy and action. A New Hampshire constitutional convention noted that the executive power was "the active principle in all governments; it is the soul, and without it the body politic is but a dead corpse."[5] A French minister observed that the "executive power is the moving force of a government," uniting "action to the will."[6] For good reason, the second entry for "executive" in an eighteenth-century dictionary was "active."[7]

The Multifaceted Executive Power

Why was the executive power unavoidably active? Because the exercise of its constitutive powers demanded movement. Executive power was most closely associated with the power to execute the law. In fact, the executive "gets its name from *one* of its major functions, that of putting the law into effect."[8] Writers such as Montesquieu and William Blackstone noted that the power also extended to foreign affairs and direction of executive officers.[9] One dictionary of the period said the power encompassed, among other things, making treaties and war, appointing officers, commanding forces, and spending appropriations.[10]

Americans shared this sense of executive power. Sometimes they drew upon the broad scope of the phrase even as they sought to fetter the executive. As mentioned, Thomas Jefferson in 1776 proposed an "administrator" for Virginia, one vested with "executive powers"[11] "formerly held by king."[12] And yet Jefferson sheared the office of the kingly powers to declare war, grant pardons, veto bills, and grant titles.[13]

The Essex Result, a 1778 critique of a proposed constitution for Massachusetts, confirmed the many facets of executive power: "The executive power is sometimes divided into the external executive, and internal executive. The former comprehends war, peace, the sending and receiving ambassadors, and whatever concerns the transactions of the state with any other independent state. . . . [T]he internal executive power . . . is employed in the peace, security and protection of the subject and his property, and in the defence of the state. The executive power is to marshal and command her militia and armies for her defence, to enforce the law, and to carry into execution all the others of the legislative powers."[14] In 1787, Alexander Hamilton said much the same, noting that "the objects of executive power are of three kinds, to make treaties with foreign nations, to make war and peace, to execute and interpret the laws."[15] A year later, writing as "Publius," he observed that "executive authority" included expending funds, directing the military, and conducting foreign negotiations.[16]

Because "executive power" had a familiar content, it was common to speak of entities exercising "executive power" without further explanation. Despite the fact that John Adams's "Thoughts on Government" discussed the proper distribution of powers, including the "executive power," without any elaboration of what he meant by the phrase,[17] it influenced the shape of state constitutions. A contemporaneous letter from a southerner to a New Yorker recommended, with little elaboration, that when a state "abounds with Rascals," one should "vest the executive powers of Government in an individual that they may have Vigor."[18] Numerous Americans noted that the Continental Congress exercised "executive power,"[19] even though the Articles of Confederation never expressly granted it that power. Americans could use the shorthand "executive power" because the phrase was widely understood to encompass law execution, oversight of foreign affairs, and direction of executive officers.

Of course, there were disagreements about the scope of executive power. As we shall see, there were (and would continue to be) differences of opinion about the peripheries of the power. Moreover, across governments, the executive powers granted to the principal executive varied. Colonial governors had very few foreign affairs powers, limited primarily to conducting relations with Indian tribes.[20] State constitutions hemmed in executives with constraints relating to military force, pardons, and appointments.[21] Finally, chief executives across nations enjoyed more or less authority over war declarations.[22] In each case, polities allocated a familiar set of powers in different ways in order to suit their particular needs and preferences.

Allocating Executive Power

Separate from the contours of executive power was the distinct question of who should wield it. Though certain traits were thought necessary for the proper exercise of executive power, the concept of executive power did not necessarily imply anything about the wielder of such power. While the phrase "executive power" might conjure up images of a single person, nothing prevented a triumvirate, council, or large assembly from wielding the power. That is to say, however the executive power was allocated, it was no less "executive" when vested in a council or assembly. Indeed, people in a state of nature might wield executive power and execute the laws of nature, punish criminals, and defend themselves, or so Locke claimed.[23] Proponents of a unitary executive had to justify their preference, because even if the category of executive power seemed a natural fact, no one imagined that only a single person could exercise the power.

In practice, there typically was a loose correspondence between a branch's designation and its assorted powers. What made an entity the executive branch of a particular government was its exercise of most powers deemed executive. Likewise, what made an entity legislative was its control of most legislative powers. Sometimes a legislature might have some executive and judicial powers—say, the powers to appoint and to sit as a court. Other times, the executive branch might enjoy some legislative power, such as the power to participate in lawmaking. In short, branches and powers were usually not perfectly aligned, meaning that the executive branch did not exercise only executive powers and the legislative branch only legislative powers.

Because "executive power" referred to a set of powers and because those powers might be divided among two or more entities, a government might have more than one executive. If one entity had the power to execute the laws and another the power to make treaties, that government had two executives. Or if one entity's ability to appoint was checked by another, both entities were executive, because each had executive functions. Moreover, because entities might exercise more than one governmental power, an institution could be described as both legislative and executive. The Senate was seen as legislative and executive because of its authority over lawmaking, appointments, and treaties. While natural objects cannot simultaneously be animal, vegetable, and mineral, an institution that exercised all three types of governmental power, like the Continental Congress, was legislative, executive, and judicial.

How to allocate executive power was a question of considerable complexity and controversy. One author averred that the "constitution of the executive power forms the essential and perhaps sole difficulty of every system of government."[24] Two extremes had their able advocates at Philadelphia. As Chapter 3 recounted, some delegates favored a unitary executive. Men such as James Wilson and John Rutledge claimed that unity would generate energy, dispatch, and responsibility.[25] Publius agreed, arguing that energy was "a leading character in the definition of good government" because it was "essential" to protecting a nation against "foreign attacks," to the "steady administration of the laws, to the protection of property," and to "the security of liberty against the enterprises and assaults of ambition, of faction and of anarchy."[26]

Another faction dreaded a unitary executive, so much so that it favored a triumvirate or a conciliar executive. Its members argued that unity would end in despotism because a unitary executive would be more apt to suspend civil liberties and the Constitution in a bid to maintain or increase his powers.[27] Ever since, their intellectual descendants have sought to minimize and contain the presidency. Reflecting this fear of a unitary executive, Daniel Webster once said that in "the contest for liberty, executive power has been regarded as a lion which must be caged."[28]

A third strategy was to make some aspects of the executive unitary and others plural. Early American state constitutions did this to a remarkable degree. As seen in Chapter 2, sometimes a constitution vested authority in one person; at other times the same constitution gave the initiative to one person, but checked final decisions via the use of an executive council; and executive power occasionally rested with a large, plural body, with no chief magistrate.[29]

In sum, in the eighteenth century there was a category of powers called "executive power," the proper exercise of which required energy, vigilance, secrecy, and responsibility. This bundle of powers—over law execution, foreign affairs, and the military—could be vested in one person, increasing the likelihood of energy and vigilance at the risk of a descent into despotism. Alternatively, the powers could be vested in a council or assembly, decreasing the likelihood of tyranny, but at the risk of inaction and discord. A third possibility was that some executive powers could be vested solely in one person's hands, others granted to a plural entity, and a few vested in one person's hands but subject to various checks. As we shall see, the Framers embraced the last strategy of concentrating some executive powers and scattering others.

The Generic Grant Theory and Its Critics

Read against the backdrop of writings on government and the familiar category of executive power, the Vesting Clause grants the president those powers deemed executive in the late eighteenth century. This seem-

ingly broad grant is greatly constrained because it is subject to the excep-
tions and qualifications, explicit and implicit, found in Articles I and
II. Two examples: the Constitution requires the president to secure the
Senate's consent to make appointments and treaties, and despite his
executive power, the president cannot take the nation to war, because
Congress enjoys that power.

From the Constitution's inception, this generic grant theory has had its
critics. In a debate about whether the president had a constitutional
power to remove executive officers, some members of the first Congress
insisted that the Vesting Clause vested nothing.[30] In a later controversy
about removal authority—the issue proved quite durable and vexing—
Daniel Webster made a forceful case against the generic grant theory:

> Executive power is not a thing so well known, and so accurately defined, as
> that the written constitution of a limited government can be supposed to
> have conferred it in the lump. What *is* executive power? What are its
> boundaries? What model or example had the framers of the Constitution
> in their minds, when they spoke of "executive power"? Did they mean ex-
> ecutive power as known in England, or as known in France, or as known in
> Russia? Did they take it as defined by Montesquieu, by Burlamaqui, or by
> De Lolme? All these differ from one another as to the extent of the execu-
> tive power of government.[31]

Webster never denied that one might sensibly speak of a category of
"executive power." Rather, he claimed that the only executive powers
that mattered were the ones listed in the remainder of Article II, for only
they actually were vested in the president.[32]

Webster's claim has adherents in the courts[33] and the academy.[34]
Proponents argue that if the Executive Power Clause actually vested
power, the remainder of Article II would be redundant. After all, why
separately grant the powers to pardon and demand written opinions if
these also were components of a generic grant of executive power? To
avoid rendering much of Article II superfluous, we must read something
like "herein granted" into the Vesting Clause, or so proponents argue.[35]

This claim—call it the herein-granted theory—has four flaws. First, it is
contrary to the text. Ordinarily, one does not read a straightforward
grant of power as if it did no more than refer to a list of subsequently

enumerated powers. No one reads Article I, section 8, clause 1, a clause that grants Congress the power to lay and collect taxes, as merely granting the powers subsequently enumerated. Likewise, no one interprets Article III, section 1—the grant of judicial power—as if it merely referred to powers granted in the rest of Article III. If we so read the vesting clause of Article III, we would be in a bit of a bind, because the rest of Article III grants no powers to the federal courts.

Admittedly, with the right text, a clause might do no more than confirm powers granted elsewhere. Article I, section 1 does exactly that. "All legislative powers herein granted shall be vested in a Congress of the United States, which shall consist of a Senate and House of Representatives," it says. This clause evidently does not grant Congress any power not enumerated elsewhere. It implicitly declares that Congress lacks a generic "legislative power"—a power to make laws on all subjects.

To read the Executive Power Clause as if it paralleled Article I, section 1 is to read the clause as if it contained the "herein granted" found in the latter. Yet Article II does not have this phrase or any limitation that resembles it. There is no textual warrant for uprooting a phrase found elsewhere in the Constitution and grafting it onto Article II.

Second, Webster's herein-granted theory was premised on the idea that the powers found in the rest of Article II are executive, but that premise undermines his principal claim that "executive power" has no common meaning. If the power to direct the military is an executive power, as Webster was quick to admit,[36] how can it be that "executive power" has no generic meaning? To acknowledge that the commander-in-chief power (or direction of the military) is an executive power is to concede that "executive power" actually *has* a well-known meaning that encompasses military command. Yet this was a concession that perhaps had to be made. After all, the Vesting Clause could have provided that "[T]he powers herein granted shall be vested in a President," a provision making no assertion about the type of the powers later mentioned. Had the clause left out "executive," Webster's claim would have enjoyed an internal coherence.

Third, as noted earlier, it was common to speak of "executive power" without specifying a particular conception. If Webster was right about the utter indeterminacy of "executive power," no one ought to have ever used it without further explication. After all, no one would know whether the writer was referring to Montesquieu's conception as opposed to Blackstone's or France's. References to "executive power" were not followed by a definition because it was understood that the phrase had a core related to law execution, foreign affairs, military command, and direction of executive officers.

Finally, proponents of the herein-granted theory imagine a redundancy where none exists, for the generic-grant reading does not render the rest of Article II superfluous. Rather than reiterating powers already given to the president by the Vesting Clause, the remainder of Article II cabins and refines the otherwise broad grant of executive power.[37] Despite Article II, section 1, the pardon power is not as robust as it might be. The president can pardon federal, but not state, offenses. Moreover, he cannot shield officials from the effects of impeachment.[38] Notwithstanding the Executive Power Clause, the president cannot unilaterally make a treaty or appoint officers. For both, he must first secure the Senate's consent.[39]

Some may object that interpreting sections 2 and 3 as refining the generic grant yields an implausibly inelegant structure for Article II. Why grant a generic power and then refine it with other provisions? Why not instead list all the powers separately and dispense with the generic grant? Would not that structure have been as convenient and less susceptible to misinterpretation?

In fact, Article II's structure was efficient and ordinary. To begin with, listing all the individual powers separately would have been inconvenient. For instance, separately granting the powers to go to war, establish the rights of enemy aliens, and declare the status of treaties is unnecessary when one could simply vest the "declare war" power, knowing that these subpowers are part of the more generic power.[40] The generic grant of executive power was similarly well suited. As "Pacificus" (Alexander Hamilton) said of the Vesting Clause, "the difficulty of a complete and perfect specification of all the cases of executive authority would naturally dictate the use of general terms."[41]

Nor was there anything unusual about coupling a general grant with limiting particulars. When Hamilton cautioned that it "would not consist with the rules of sound construction to consider this enumeration of particular authorities as derogating from the more comprehensive grant in the general clause,"[42] he meant that it would be a mistake to read the

Vesting Clause as if it did not grant generic executive power. Madison, writing as "Publius," went further, claiming that "[n]othing is more natural or common than first to use a general phrase, and then to explain and qualify it by a recital of particulars."[43] The generic grant theory is wholly consistent with founding-era drafting principles.

Others who oppose the generic grant theory argue that the Vesting Clause merely establishes that there shall be a single entity, dubbed the "president," who holds the powers listed in Article II. Under this "title and number" reading of Article II, the Vesting Clause merely establishes the name and number of the executive apex.

If the introduction of Article II merely provided that "[t]here shall be a President," the Vesting Clause likely would do no more than establish a title and number. Had the Framers wanted to draft such a clause, they might have borrowed from the New Hampshire and Massachusetts Constitutions.[44] But the Executive Power Clause contains more. It provides that "[t]he executive Power shall be vested in a President of the United States." A clause that expressly "vests" a power in an entity should be read as granting that power. As Steve Calabresi has argued, that is what it means to *vest* power.[45] Recall that the Article III vesting clause, which "vests" the "judicial power," is universally seen as granting the federal courts the power to adjudicate cases. Other constitutional provisions, such as the Necessary and Proper Clause, likewise speak of "vesting" power as a means of conveying authority. What is true for these clauses is no less true for the Executive Power Clause.

Like the herein-granted theory, the title-and-number theory raises the question why the Vesting Clause mentions *executive* power. If the Vesting Clause did no more than establish a title and number, there would be no reason for the adjective "executive." The clause might well have read, "[T]here shall be a President with various powers." Once again, "executive" indicates that a category is being described. In this case, "executive" describes the type of power that the Vesting Clause conveys.

If redundancy avoidance is a cardinal rule of constitutional interpretation, the title-and-number theory noticeably suffers by comparison. Even if one struck out Article II's first clause, it would be crystal clear that one person, dubbed the "president," would enjoy the prerogatives specified elsewhere in Article II. Each of the other Article II powers and duties begins with either the "president" or "he," indicating that the Constitution established a single officer with the title "president."[46] Moreover, Article I requires Congress to present bills to a "president" and provides that "he" may sign or return them with "his" objections.[47]

Relatedly, if the Executive Power Clause merely confirmed that the president would enjoy those powers found in Article II, then the phrase "herein granted" in Article I, section 1 would be superfluous for a grant of "legislative power" to Congress; without more, it likewise would have been understood as an obvious reference to only those powers specifically enumerated. If one imagines that the Constitution meant to eschew any redundancies, one ought to reject the generic grant theory's rivals because each yields superfluities.

The generic grant theory offers the best reading of Article II, section 1. It takes the text seriously, is consistent with the era's drafting and interpretive conventions, and does not generate a host of redundancies. As discussed in succeeding chapters, it is also consistent with what was said of the Constitution and with early practice. The Founders, early presidents, and early Congresses understood that presidents had powers beyond those specifically listed in the Constitution by virtue of the grant of executive power.

Generic Grants of Executive Power in the States

When James Madison observed that "nothing is more natural or common" than to grant a generic power and then tinker with its facets,[48] perhaps he had in mind the state constitutions and their grants of executive power. Because the state constitutions supply a context, enabling us to make better sense of the Constitution's grant of executive power, a close examination is indispensible.[49]

Five state charters granted "supreme executive power" or some variant to the executive. Four of these—the Pennsylvania, New Jersey, and two Vermont Constitutions—granted the "supreme executive power" to the executive.[50] The last, the New York Constitution, granted the state's "supreme executive power and authority."[51] The constitutions of Virginia and Georgia granted "executive powers."[52] The constitutions of Delaware, Maryland, and North Carolina granted "other executive powers."[53] Finally, the two South Carolina Constitutions vested "executive authority,"[54] equivalent to "executive power."

For a number of reasons, these constitutions are inconsistent with the herein-granted theory. To begin with, many conveyed a generic grant and then qualified it with exceptions, a strategy indicating that the grants of executive power were meant to convey power. The Georgia Constitution of 1777 provided that "[t]he governor shall . . . exercise the executive powers of government . . . save only in the case of pardons and remission of fines."[55] If the generic grant referred only to the powers specifically enumerated, there would have been no need to expressly bar a pardon power. The governor would lack such power precisely because a power to pardon was not specifically granted. The exception was necessary because the authors understood that the governor otherwise would have the pardon power pursuant to the grant of executive powers of government.

The South Carolina Constitutions had the same structure of a grant coupled with exceptions. Though the 1776 version granted "executive authority" to a "president," he could not "make war or peace, or enter into any final treaty, without the consent of the general assembly and legislative council."[56] The bar on making war and peace is revealing enough, for it signals the breadth of executive authority. But note also that the president was prohibited from making "final" treaties without legislative consent.[57] This locution suggests that he could negotiate treaties. The only source of such authority had to be his executive authority, for neither the prohibition on final treaties nor anything else in the constitution allowed him to negotiate them. Along the same lines, the constitution said he could not adjourn, prorogue, or dissolve the assembly or legislative council.[58] If we suppose that the president only had specifically enumerated powers, those exceptions were gratuitous, for no one should have supposed he had such powers.[59]

The Virginia governor could "exercise the executive powers of government" with the advice and consent of the council of state.[60] The state constitution provided immediately thereafter that he "sh[ould] not, under any presence [sic], exercise any power or prerogative, by virtue of any law, statute or custom of England."[61] Yet there was an exception to this exception. The next sentence reads, "But he shall, with the advice of the Council of State, have the power of granting reprieves or pardons."[62]

The conjunction "but" suggests that the grant of "executive powers" encompassed the pardon power, something traceable to England. Relatedly, the constitution declared that the governor "shall not prorogue or adjourn the Assembly."[63] If the governor was limited to only those powers specifically enumerated—if the grant of "the executive powers" did not cede any authority—there was no need to bar him from proroguing or adjourning the legislature, for nothing else in the constitution could be construed as permitting him to do either.

Besides the presence of exceptions to generic grants, constitutions contained structural clues that their grants of executive authority were not merely references to specifically enumerated powers. Sometimes the grant of executive power was located at the end of a list of powers, suggesting that it was a catchall, vesting all other executive powers not previously mentioned. Constitutions from South and North Carolina had this structure.[64] While Madison confirmed that it was "natural [and] common" to grant generic authority and then refine it, it hardly could have been common to enumerate a series of authorities to be vested in a governor and then to obliquely refer to them again at the end. If the grants of executive power in these constitutions merely applied to powers already granted, then they served no purpose, other than to confound.

One constitution granted executive power in the middle of a list of authorities, a structure no more consistent with the herein-granted theory than the others discussed above. Article 33 of the Maryland Constitution granted the powers to summon the militia and to control the military. The former power could be exercised only with the consent of an executive council.[65] Following these grants was the statement that the governor "may alone exercise all other the [sic] executive powers of government."[66] Article 33 ended by vesting the governor with the powers to pardon and to embargo.[67] Subsequent articles granted the governor some authority over appointment and removal, the former exercisable only with the council's consent.[68] There was no reason to list various powers, some of which required the consent of the council and some which did not, and then note, in the middle of the list, that the governor "may alone exercise all other the [sic] executive powers of government," unless one sought to grant generic executive powers to the governor alone.[69]

Similarly, Article 7 of the Delaware Constitution listed two specific powers for its "president"—the unilateral power to grant pardons and, with the consent of the Privy Council, the power to lay embargoes—and then provided that the president could "exercise all the other executive powers of government."[70] Later articles mentioned one power that the Delaware president could exercise unilaterally—the power to appoint to certain civil offices—and two others that needed the Privy Council's consent, namely, the powers to appoint to the military, convene the legislature, and summon the militia.[71] If the phrase "exercise all the other executive powers of government" was meant to refer to powers granted elsewhere, the only two he could exercise unilaterally were the pardon power and the power to appoint to some civil offices. It is hard to fathom why constitution makers would refer to these two powers listed separately as "all the other executive powers of government." It seems more likely that the reference to "all the other executive powers of government" was intended to incorporate those powers commonly considered executive but not previously listed.

The New Jersey Constitution is particularly illuminating because in one short article it granted its governor the "supreme executive power" and made him chancellor and commander in chief.[72] It granted no other executive powers to the governor alone. If the grant of "supreme executive power" referred only to the subsequently listed executive powers, the governor would have had only the commander-in-chief power. The designation of the governor as "chancellor" did not convey any executive power; it ceded him a share of the judicial power, allowing him to serve on the state supreme court. It is implausible that the grant of the "supreme executive power" gave the governor only the power to serve as commander in chief.

Sometimes the generic grants, considered in isolation, cast doubt on the herein-granted theory. Five state constitutions granted "supreme executive power." Under the herein-granted theory, this phrase was merely a reference to the powers subsequently listed, such as the powers to appoint to office and to convene the legislature. But there was nothing "supreme" about such subsequently listed powers. The powers to appoint and to convene the legislature are ordinarily not considered "supreme" powers. Supremacy implies a position of dominance or superiority and brings to mind a hierarchy, such as the Supreme Court and its relationship to lower courts. When these constitutions referred to "supreme" executive power, they encompassed executive powers that implied supremacy, such as control over law execution and executive officers.

Consider, in this regard, the structure of the New York Constitution. As noted, one article granted "the supreme executive power and authority of this State" to the governor.[73] The next article listed unilateral powers: commander-in-chief authority, powers to convene and prorogue the assembly, and authority to grant reprieves and pardons.[74] The grant of "supreme executive power and authority" could not have related to the powers over legislative sessions and pardons. The governor is not "supreme" over the legislature merely because he has some authority over its sessions and because he may pardon some violations of its laws. Moreover, it makes little sense to imagine that the phrase referred to nothing more than the commander-in-chief power, a power ceded immediately after the grant of "supreme executive power and authority."

Finally, there is the matter of law execution. As noted in the next chapter, each state executive executed the laws. Yet most constitutions never granted any such power in particular terms. Indeed, some said nothing specifically about the subject at all, at least as it related to the executive.[75] The only way that many state constitutions could have granted a law execution power was via the generic grants of executive power.[76] And if constitutions conveyed powers beyond those particularly enumerated, they must have ceded more than the power to execute the law, because some grants referred to "executive powers" or "other executive powers," thereby indicating they conveyed more than one sort of executive power.

Other Uses of "Executive" in the Constitutions

States employed the adjective "executive" in their declarations of rights, usages that shed light on whether the adjective "executive" had a shared, commonly understood meaning. First, these declarations often contained a provision that, echoing Montesquieu, provided that the executive powers must be kept separate from the legislative and judicial powers.[77] Typical of these provisions was language found in the North Carolina Constitution: "That the legislative, executive, and supreme judicial powers of government, ought to be forever separate and distinct from each other."[78] Second, declarations occasionally identified those invested with "executive powers" as public trustees. Consider the Maryland Declaration of Rights, which provided that "all persons invested with the legislative or executive powers of government are the trustees of the public, and, as such, accountable for their conduct."[79] Third, declarations sometimes noted that executives should periodically return to private life. For instance, the Virginia Constitution recommended that to keep executive officers "restrained from oppression, by feeling and participating the burdens of the people, they should, at fixed periods, be reduced to a private station, return into that body from which they were originally taken."[80]

Those who drafted the state constitutions must have had some sense of what "executive power" meant and who was an "executive" officer. It would be odd to declare that "executive power" must be kept separate from legislative and judicial powers without some sense of what constituted that power. Likewise, one cannot meaningfully declare that executive officials are trustees and require that they should periodically return to private life without some sense that certain officials are executive and others are not. Finally, it seems likely that constitutions that expressly incorporated Montesquieu's separation maxim likely borrowed his multifaceted definition of the executive power.

Grants of Generic Legislative Power

The grants of executive power were not the only generic grants. Clauses that vested legislative power likewise vested generic authority. Some constitutions ceded generic legislative power without any enumeration. The 1776 South Carolina Constitution declared that the "legislative authority [shall] be vested in the president and commander-in-chief, the general assembly and legislative council."[81] The 1778 version excluded the executive's participation, vesting the "legislative authority" in the general assembly.[82] In neither case did the constitutions grant any additional power to make laws, meaning that these generic grants were the sole sources of lawmaking authority.

Other constitutions granted generic legislative power while also vesting other specific powers. For example, the New York Constitution provided at the outset that the "supreme legislative power . . . shall be vested" in the two chambers of the legislature, and then went on to grant other powers to the legislature.[83] If we imagine that the "supreme legislative power" referred only to specifically enumerated powers, then the legislature lacked the power to enact criminal, property, and tax laws; it would have had only such powers as directing the census, creating legislative districts, and apportioning legislators among them.[84]

Clearly, grants of generic power were not uncommon in the state constitutions, at least with respect to legislative power. The fact that we must read some grants of legislative power as grants of generic lawmaking power tells us something about the generic grants of executive power.

Lessons from the State Constitutions

Summing up, state constitutions written before the U.S. Constitution are best read as granting generic executive authority. First, some constitutions contained exceptions, denying certain authority to the executive. These provisions were necessary because of the broad authority ceded by the grants of generic executive power. Second, some constitutions granted "other executive powers" (or a variant) at the end of a list, indicating that the phrase was meant to be a catchall. Third, unless we read references to executive power as generic grants, state governors had no constitutional power to execute the law, even though this was the principal function of executives. Finally, constitutions regularly used generic grants to empower their legislatures, suggesting that similar grants to the executive would hardly have been unusual.

State executives certainly believed that they enjoyed generic executive power and not merely those powers specifically enumerated. A survey of practice across several states indicates that state executives, whether singular or plural, exercised numerous powers not traceable to any clause other than the grants of executive power. More will be said about this in subsequent chapters, where these particular powers are discussed in greater detail. For present purposes, we should note that state executives controlled law execution, repeatedly ordering the apprehension and prosecution of alleged scofflaws. They also appointed treaty commissioners, negotiated treaties with Indian tribes, and served as the organs of communication between their states and other sovereigns.

The claim that state constitutions granted generic executive power coheres with the conclusions of those who have studied the matter closely. The preeminent scholar on state executive power before the Constitution, Margaret Burnham MacMillan, noted that "[n]early all the constitutions contained some phrase bestowing general executive authority."[85] Likewise, Charles Thach, in his celebrated book *The Creation of the Presidency*, noted that these constitutions granted a "field of unenumerated [executive] powers."[86]

As with any generic grant, there were disputes about its scope, for the convenience of using a broad phrase came at the cost of precision. In New Jersey, people debated whether the grant of executive power enabled its executive to grant charters of incorporation.[87] There also were questions about whether state grants of executive power included pardon authority.[88] Yet these disputes involved the fringes of executive power; no one contested that executive power encompassed authority over law execution, foreign affairs, and executive officers.

Admittedly, demonstrating that grants of executive power in the states vested generic executive powers does not tell us how we ought to understand the U.S. Constitution. Still, this analysis answers scholars who assert that the state constitutions never granted generic executive powers to their executives.[89] And it demonstrates that reading the Vesting Clause in the Constitution as if it granted power could hardly have been unusual or uncommon. To learn more about the grant of federal executive power, we must turn to the creation and ratification of the Constitution.

The Creation of Federal Executive Power

Three proposals before the Constitutional Convention ceded generic executive power or the equivalent. The Virginia Plan proposed that a national executive enjoy the "Executive rights vested in Congress by the Confederation."[90] Alexander Hamilton's "governor" would have "[t]he supreme Executive authority of the United States."[91] Finally, Charles Pinckney envisioned a "president" with "[t]he Executive Power of the United States."[92] The Virginia Plan clearly relied upon a defined category of executive power, referring as it did to the executive authority conveyed by the Articles of Confederation to the Continental Congress.

Initially, the delegates did not adopt any of these variants. By July, the Convention had agreed to nothing more than veto, appointment, and law execution powers.[93] These provisions, along with the Pinckney plan, were sent to the Committee of Detail, charged with drafting a constitution.[94] James Wilson drafted the committee's final report,[95] in which the president would enjoy the "Executive Power of the United States."[96] Charles Thach speculated that Wilson borrowed from Pinckney's plan, which in turn supposedly was influenced by the New York Constitution.[97] But one might suppose that Wilson had looked to the constitution of his own state (Pennsylvania), which granted "supreme executive power."[98] Likewise, perhaps Pinckney found a closer inspiration; his state constitution (South Carolina's) had the exact phrase ("executive authority") found in his proposal.[99]

In late August, the convention adopted the Vesting Clause. Madison notes that "on the question for vesting the power in a *single person*,"[100] there was no dissent. He seemed not to regard the clause as merely establishing the title and number, else he would not have spoken of the clause as "vesting the [executive] power."

The Committee of Style, charged with "revising the style" of the Constitution, added a phrase to the Legislative Power Clause. Whereas previously Congress was to have the "legislative power," it would now have all "the legislative powers 'herein granted.'"[101] Although some see the change as designed to strengthen the executive by implication,[102] the amendment did nothing more than clarify the legislative power. Gouverneur Morris, a member of the Committee of Style, likely made this revision to reflect the prevailing understanding regarding federal legislative powers. The alteration helped clarify that Congress, unlike the state legislatures,[103] would lack generic legislative power. No such limitation was added to Article II.

By replicating the structure of some state generic grants, Article II drew upon a tradition of conveying a general power and then qualifying it in various ways. While there were some who later argued that the president had only the specific powers found in Article II,[104] the far more common claim was that the president had generic power arising from the

Vesting Clause. Moreover, as we shall see in subsequent chapters, only the generic grant theory explains the many powers that early presidents exercised.

In the wake of the Constitution's creation, it became common to say that the president had the executive power, without elaborating on any specific powers. For instance, Madison stated in a letter to Jefferson no more than that there would be a "President cloathed with Executive power."[105] Madison knew that his unadorned assertion conveyed something about the scope of that power. His description was crude, as summaries must be. Nonetheless, the reference confirmed that people at the time recognized that the president had a generic executive power. To say that someone would have the "executive power" was to confirm that the phrase had a common meaning.

Conclusion

Charles Thach called the Executive Power Clause a "joker" because of its potential to legitimate claims of broad power.[106] That very possibility likely causes some to recoil from the best reading of the text. They worry that the Executive Power Clause might grant the president all powers ever regarded as executive and thereby cede alarming powers over life, liberty, and property. To avoid the possibility of a monarchical president, some subtract text and wish away the grant of executive power, reading the Vesting Clause as a title-and-number clause instead. Others add constraints ("herein granted"), rectifying the Constitution's perceived flaw. Either way, the executive lion is more securely caged.

As the succeeding chapters argue, there is little to fear from the Constitution's grant of executive power. Though executive power brings to mind a set of connected concepts—secrecy, energy, vigilance—and though it is most associated with vigorous action, it is not a grant of absolute authority, allowing the president to do whatever he thinks is best for the nation. The power includes executing laws, stewarding foreign relations, commanding the military, and directing executive officers. But the Constitution tempers these powers by granting Congress control over the military and over many crucial areas of foreign affairs. It also grants Congress authority over the structure of the executive branch. Finally, the Vesting Clause does not authorize the president to indefinitely detain prisoners without trial, confer titles of nobility, or adjudicate religious disputes. The clause was qualified by relatively defined limits and was incapable of legitimating anything and everything the president might wish to do. Charles Thach was mistaken; the Constitution's Vesting Clause bears little resemblance to a wild card.

Another reason why fear of the Vesting Clause's generic grant is unwarranted is that the Constitution splinters the eighteenth-century category of executive power in three ways. First, most powers deemed executive rest with the president, so much so that we continue to regard him as the executive. Second, the Senate checks the exercise of some executive powers, namely, the powers to appoint and make treaties. The Senate's association with treaties and appointments has long marked it as an executive institution. To this day, the Senate conducts "executive" business in its "executive" sessions. Third, the Constitution grants some eighteenth-century executive powers—such as the powers over war and foreign commerce—to Congress. Though Congress has such powers, it (unlike the Continental Congress) has never been seen as an executive institution, in part because some at the founding believed that its executive powers were better classified as legislative and because its legislative powers predominate.

CHAPTER FIVE

"THE CONSTITUTIONAL EXECUTOR OF THE LAWS"

The primary executive power is law execution, the function that gives the executive its name.[1] One founding-era dictionary defined "executive" as "having the power to put in act the laws."[2] Because the president possesses the executive power, he is the one "who is to execute the laws."[3] Apart from the grant of executive power, Article II repeatedly signals as much. When Congress approves, the commander in chief may use the militia to help execute the law. The Faithful Execution Clause obliges him to take care that the laws are faithfully executed, a duty that assumes he has power to execute. And the president may pardon those who violate the laws committed to his care.

For many, the fact that the president has the power to execute the law seems elementary, so basic it is taught in grade school. Yet some scholars are certain that the original Constitution granted the president little or no law enforcement authority. Indeed, the modern administrative state may rest (in part) on the belief that the president has no constitutional authority to direct the execution of federal law. The lingering and persistent doubts about whether law execution and enforcement are presidential powers make an in-depth treatment of the topic vital. Those who question the president's authority over execution miss the principal facet of executive power. If we are to better understand the original presidency, we must heed a founding-era grammar book that observed that the *"Executiv*[e] *power"* is "that power which puts the laws in force."[4]

The Executive Power of the Laws in Europe and America

Europeans well understood that executive power and law execution were closely linked. John Locke noted the executive power "see[s] to the execution of the laws that are made."[5] Montesquieu's separation maxim assumed the same: "When the legislative and executive powers are united in the same person . . . apprehensions may arise, lest the same monarch or senate should enact tyrannical laws, to execute them in a tyrannical manner."[6] In his *Commentaries,* William Blackstone observed that the Crown had the "executive power of the laws" and was the "proper person to prosecute for all public offences."[7] A French minister counseled that "laws would in effect be nothing more than counsels . . . without this active and vigilant authority, which assures their empire."[8]

The English bequeathed this sense of executive power to America. Before shots were fired in the Revolution, Thomas Jefferson noted that though the king "possesses . . . the executive power of the laws," he could not administer the laws of one colony in another.[9] An American Tory observed that the king had the "executive power" to see that the "laws are duly carried into execution,"[10] and protested that many had betrayed the Crown, who was "to superintend the execution of the laws."[11] When the focus shifted toward crafting colonial and state constitutions, many noted that the executive power implemented the laws.[12]

Later American writings reflected the same understanding. *The Essex Result,* discussed in Chapter 4, notes that one branch of "[t]he executive power is to . . . enforce the law."[13] Specifically, it is "to arrest offenders, to bring them to trial."[14] The executive "should be able to execute the laws without opposition. . . . If the laws are not obeyed, the legislative power is vain, and the judicial is mere pageantry."[15] In neighboring New Hampshire, a convention declared that the executive was "to put in execution all the laws enacted by the legislative body."[16] Noah Webster, writing in 1785, argued that when the "executive power" is vested in many, the laws will be poorly executed. But when the executive power rests with one, "the execution of laws will be vigorous and decisive."[17]

Besides the typical grants of executive power discussed in the previous chapter, some state constitutions contained other signals that their executives were to execute the laws. A few obliged the executive to ensure the faithful execution of the laws.[18] One imposed an oath that explicitly referred to the law execution function.[19] Chief executives understood that under state constitutions, they had a power to execute the laws.[20] Although the outer reaches of the executive power were uncertain,[21] no one gainsaid the executives' law enforcement role.[22]

As noted in Chapter 2, the Continental Congress served as a plural chief executive for the nation. Sometimes it leaned on state executives, calling upon them to relay information about the enemy and to superintend federal officers.[23] At other times, it directed its own corps of national executives. In 1787, Jefferson complained of its micromanagement: "Nothing is . . . so mischievous in a great assembly as the details of execution. The smallest trifle of that kind occupies as long as the most important act of legislation."[24] He hoped that the Constitutional Convention would separate national powers, thereby invigorating them. Around the same time, John Adams insisted upon the desirability of having truly separate branches and confirmed the nexus between executives and law execution: "The executive power is properly the government; the laws are a dead letter until an administration begins to carry them into execution."[25]

The President's Executive Power to Execute the Law

Each of the principal plans presented to the Constitutional Convention vested law execution authority with the executive. Virginians proposed "a National Executive" with "general authority to execute the National laws."[26] The New Jersey Plan sought an executive with the "general authority to execute the federal acts."[27] South Carolinian Charles Pinckney sought a president who would "attend to the Execution of the Laws."[28] Alexander Hamilton proposed vesting "[t]he supreme Executive authority . . . in a Governour" charged with "the execution of all laws passed."[29] Eventually, the convention unanimously resolved that the "national Executive" should "carry into execution the national Laws."[30] A committee took up this resolution and reported out the Executive Power Clause,[31] thus codifying the power to execute the law.

Throughout the proceedings, delegates supposed that the executive would execute. "[E]xecuting the laws" was "strictly Executive," observed James Wilson.[32] Madison agreed: "certain powers were in their nature Executive, and must be given to that depart[ment]," including the "power to carry into effect the national laws."[33] Some thought that Congress should select the executive precisely because he would be executing its laws.[34] Others warned that if Congress chose the executive, it would be "the Executor as well as the maker of laws; & then . . . tyrannical laws may be made that they may be executed in a tyrannical manner."[35] One delegate argued that vesting veto authority in a council comprising the judiciary and the president improperly united "the expounder" and "the Executor of the Laws."[36]

Outside what would come to be known as Independence Hall, participants in the ratification debates used the standard sense of "executive power." James Wilson claimed that the government must enjoy all three powers: "For what purpose give the power to make laws, unless they are to be executed? and if they are to be executed, the executive and judicial powers will necessarily be engaged in the business."[37] Similarly, "A Jerseyman" praised the creation of an executive, saying it would be "highly ridiculous to send representatives . . . to make laws for us, if we did not give power to some person or persons to see them duly executed."[38] One state delegate referred to the active connotation of "executive": "Is not this government a nerveless mass, a dead carcase, without the executive power? . . . By whom are [federal] laws and projects to be executed? By the President."[39]

The president's power to execute featured prominently in debates about the veto. One opponent of the Constitution grumbled that there could be no liberty because the "supreme continental executive power"[40] also enjoyed legislative authority in the form of a veto, and hence the president would "exercise the combined authority of legislation, and execution."[41] Others disagreed, arguing that the president should have "a share in making the laws, which he must execute."[42] The Massachusetts governor noted that a veto helped preserve uniformity in the laws that the president was to administer.[43] Some Anti-Federalists favored the veto, for Congress would be little constrained without it. Even with a veto, however, the president faced meaningful restraints, as "A Federal Republican" noted: "[T]o execute [laws] when made, is limited by their existence."[44]

Law execution played a central role in debates about selection and tenure. Charles Pinckney claimed that while the people would select the president, the proposed Constitution had infused the chief magistracy with sufficient vigor so that "the President [could] execute the laws with energy and despatch."[45] Another Federalist asserted that annual election of executives yielded "a negligent, partial and corrupt administration" and a "lax execution of the laws."[46] But because the president was popularly selected and served a four-year term, he could "execute any law, however unpopular, without hazarding his person or office."[47] An Anti-Federalist agreed that the "first executive magistrate ought to remain in office so long as to avoid instability in the execution of the laws."[48] Another noted that "[i]f the executive is changeable, he can never oppose large decided majorities of influential individuals—or enforce on those powerful men . . . the rigor of equal law, which is the grand and only object of human society."[49] Only "a *properly constituted and independent executive,*—a vindex injuriarum—an avenger of public wrongs . . . [could] enforce the rigor of equal law."[50] The Virginia governor, Edmund Randolph, catalogued the president's powers, beginning with the most obvious: "What are his powers? To see the laws executed. Every executive in America has that power."[51]

In the Constitution's early years, the consensus—that the executive power included the power to execute the law and that the Constitution granted the president such authority—held firm. Defending Washington's 1793 Neutrality Proclamation, an edict admonishing Americans not to assist any of the warring European powers,[52] Alexander Hamilton observed that "[t]he President is the constitutional EXECUTOR of the laws."[53] It was the executive's "province" and "duty to enforce the laws incident" to neutrality because "[t]he Executive is charged with the execution of all laws, the laws of Nations as well as the Municipal law."[54] The proclamation's opponents "will readily admit that it is the right and duty of the Executive to judge of . . . those articles of our treaties which give to France particular privileges, in order to the enforcement of those privileges."[55] As he predicted, adversaries agreed. Though Madison opposed many of Hamilton's claims, he acknowledged that "[t]he natural province of the executive magistrate is to execute laws."[56] Other notables, including James Wilson, John Marshall, and Thomas Paine, agreed that the president was to execute the laws and superintend those officers who did the same.[57]

Prosecution and the President

Some scholars maintain that the claim that the president has constitutional authority over execution is a "myth" lacking a foundation in the original Constitution.[58] An element of their argument is the assertion that prosecution was not an executive function at the founding.[59] Revisionist scholars note that no statute granted anyone in the executive branch control over district attorneys.[60] They further claim that early presidential control of these prosecutors was nonexistent.[61] The absence of such control suggests that prosecution could not have been an executive function. And if prosecution was not executive, that circumstance casts grave doubt on the general claim that law execution was subject to presidential control.

This tale of founding-era independent prosecutors is mistaken. Early practice decisively established the opposite, since presidents repeatedly directed attorneys. Using their constitutional authority, chief executives directed attorneys in tax controversies, cases with foreign affairs implications, and even cases involving the political opposition.

In the wake of the Whiskey Rebellion—a revolt in western Pennsylvania against the federal excise on liquor[62]—Washington directed attorneys. In October 1792, he ordered the U.S. attorney general to supervise indictments.[63] In a subsequent speech to Congress, Washington noted these prosecutions and declared "that nothing within Constitutional and legal limits, which may depend on me, shall be wanting to assert and maintain the just authority of the laws."[64] In the next year, concluding that two indictees were not rioters, Washington "instruct[ed]" the attorney to halt their prosecutions.[65]

Given that the nation was in its infancy, Washington was particularly concerned that Americans might draw the nation into wars. In 1791, Washington promised rigorous prosecution of violators of the Indian Intercourse Act.[66] Two years later, his annual address to Congress noted with satisfaction that his administration had prosecuted Americans who had murdered some Cherokees.[67] In his Neutrality Proclamation, Washington announced that he had "given instructions to those officers to whom it belongs, to cause prosecutions to be instituted against all persons, who shall . . . violate the law of nations."[68] Washington similarly warned aggressive settlers against antagonizing Indian tribes at peace with the United States.[69]

The president's direction of district attorneys was not limited to the criminal context. When it appeared that a suit against a former governmental employee was properly regarded as a civil suit against the United States, Washington—on the advice of the secretaries of state and treasury and the attorney general—directed a district attorney to represent the United States and defend the former employee.[70]

Washington also commanded his attorneys general.[71] So deeply rooted was the sense that the attorney general was the president's subordinate that the Supreme Court, on a divided vote, refused to grant a writ of mandamus sought by Attorney General Edmund Randolph, because certain justices were unsure whether the president had authorized the suit.[72] The justices who concluded that presidential approval was necessary evidently believed that the president had constitutional authority over the attorney general, for no statute authorized the president to direct the attorney general in his work before the Supreme Court. Indeed, Justice James Iredell declared that the Constitution's grant of "executive power" gave the president an unquestionable "general superintendence over all" attorneys and officers.[73]

Prosecutors understood as much. One district attorney noted that he always "honored . . . the directions of the Chief Executive Magistrate."[74] His language was telling. Washington was not petitioning district attorneys, in the manner of a private citizen. He was directing them, as a superior commands a subordinate.

Washington's successors exercised the same control. John Adams directed prosecutions under the Sedition Act, gathering evidence and forwarding it to attorneys with directions to prosecute.[75] Because he thought the act unconstitutional, Thomas Jefferson commanded attorneys to terminate those prosecutions.[76] On other occasions, he instructed prosecutors about how they ought to handle cases.[77]

Members of Congress recognized the constitutionality of such control. Though presidents publicized their commands to prosecutors, lawmakers never protested. On the contrary, the Senate requested John Adams to order a prosecution, an appeal premised on the propriety of presidential control.[78] In the House, John Marshall likely voiced the consensus view. While debating a controversial extradition, he noted: "[T]he nation may at will stop [a] prosecution. In this respect the President expresses constitutionally the will of the nation; and may rightfully as was done . . . enter a *nolle prosequi*, or direct that the criminal be prosecuted no farther. . . . It is the exercise of an indubitable and a Constitutional power."[79]

In sum, presidential control of federal prosecutors was absolute and generated no opposition, at least on legal grounds. Such authority arose from the Constitution itself, for no federal statute authorized the president to direct either the district attorneys or the attorney general. If we use early conceptions of executive power as a yardstick, the longstanding orthodoxy that prosecution is an executive function measures up quite well.

The Commander in Chief as Executor

Sometimes civil means of enforcement are inadequate because opposition to the law or to the government is too extensive and potent. Recognizing this, the Constitution expressly authorizes more vigorous means in Article I. Congress may "provide for calling forth the Militia to execute the Laws of the Union, suppress Insurrections and repel Invasions."[80] In essence, Congress determines when the militias may be summoned; the commander in chief directs their execution of laws when called into federal service.[81]

Legislative history confirms as much. At the Constitutional Convention, one delegate questioned whether the executive would be able to use the army or the militias to execute the laws.[82] Perhaps borrowing from the New Jersey Plan,[83] the Constitution eventually declared that the president would be commander in chief of the militias and that Congress could provide when they might assist in law execution.

The prospect that the president might use the militias to enforce the law led some to ask whether he might call upon the army for the same purpose. The Anti-Federalist "Philadelphiensis" asked whether the president would be "a king elected to command a standing army?" and then provided his own answer: "Thus our laws are to be administered by this tyrant."[84] Patrick Henry cleverly argued that Congress could use the

Necessary and Proper Clause to allow the president to use the army to execute federal laws.[85] Both protests assumed that the president would implement the laws.

The first federal use of the militias occurred in the wake of the Neutrality Proclamation. Washington ordered governors to use their militias to enforce his rules against arming vessels in American ports.[86] In a sense, the president circumvented the Calling Forth Act of 1792.[87] While the act required a judge or justice to certify that the use of a militia was necessary to execute the law,[88] the administration, by directly instructing the governors to use their militias to help enforce the law of neutrality, evaded that requirement. Washington evidently thought that he could order governors to use state resources, including militias, to enforce federal law.[89]

The Neutrality Act of 1794 authorized the president to use the army, navy, and militias to stop the arming of foreign ships and to halt military expeditions emanating from the United States.[90] Congress must have thought the use of the armed forces might be necessary to enforce the law, as when the state militias were unequal to the task. Whatever the case, the act suggested that members of Congress did not regard the Constitution as implying that the regular military could not be used to enforce federal laws. Just as the army might repel invasions, so too might it enforce laws and suppress insurrections.

The first substantial use of the militias occurred in the wake of the Whiskey Rebellion. In 1794, after Justice James Wilson certified that the ordinary means of enforcing the excise laws were inadequate, Washington summoned more than 15,000 militiamen from four states.[91] The president briefly led the militias in person before returning to the capital.[92] Despite his departure, the commander in chief continued to enforce the laws via his agents, ordering prosecutions and generally directing the militias.[93] Washington was zealous in his efforts, fearing that if the rebels were not subdued, hostility to federal law would spread "until all Laws are prostrate."[94]

The Faithful Execution Clause

Why would prostration of the laws have troubled Washington so? As he put it, he had a "duty to see the Laws executed: to permit them to be trampled upon with impunity would be repugnant to it."[95] He was referring to the Faithful Execution Clause, which requires the president to "take Care that the Laws be faithfully executed."[96]

This seemingly simple injunction poses something of a conundrum, for distinguishing faithful execution from its opposite can be difficult. Hoping to tether the Faithful Execution Clause to a more concrete standard, some have claimed that it was meant to bar suspensions and dispensations.[97] Suspensions were executive declarations that an otherwise valid law would no longer be enforced or honored. Until the suspension was lifted, no one had to honor the suspended law.[98] Dispensations were licenses granting individuals the right to ignore some provision of law in the future. Because dispensations might go only to some, others still had to obey the law.[99] By imposing the faithful execution duty, the Constitution bars all suspensions and dispensations, or so the argument goes.

This entirely reasonable claim seems mistaken. The English statutory bars on dispensations and suspensions arose in 1689,[100] *after* the Faithful Execution Clause's precursor appeared in Pennsylvania.[101] Unless one supposes that William Penn banned suspensions and dispensations without specifically mentioning either and did so before the Crown agreed in unambiguous terms to abandon such powers, it seems likely that the 1682 Pennsylvania precursor had nothing to do with suspensions and dispensations.

As late as the founding, the obligation of faithful execution seemed not designed to bar suspensions and dispensations. First, delegates in three state ratifying conventions proposed that no one should suspend the laws, except with consent of Congress.[102] If the Faithful Execution Clause was principally meant to prohibit suspensions and dispensations, then such proposals were puzzling. Second, the 1786 Vermont Constitution had an express bar on suspensions and dispensations *and* a proto–Faithful Execution Clause.[103] The presence of both the bar and the duty suggests that the latter had little to do with the former.

Whether or not the Faithful Execution Clause bars suspensions and dispensations, it is clear that the president has no such authority. By the late eighteenth century, few would have thought that chief executives could exercise such powers without a statutory delegation or a specific grant of constitutional authority. After all, the Crown had lacked these powers for almost a century. To be sure, some state constitutions contained express bars on these powers.[104] But these bars likely were added out of an abundance of caution. In any event, no state executive seems to have asserted a power to suspend or dispense with the laws, even in those states lacking bars on those actions. With respect to the Constitution, everything that we know about its creation and implementation suggests that it was not read to authorize suspensions or dispensations. Though a few delegates at Philadelphia favored giving the president the power to temporarily suspend laws, the state delegations unanimously rejected the idea.[105] Implicit in the proposal was the sense that the executive power did not include a generic power to suspend execution—hence the need for a specific suspending provision.

In retirement, George Washington denied that presidents could dispense with a treaty's provisions, claiming that do so was an impeachable offense.[106] But he was a little quick to claim that impeachment might follow, for sometimes the legislature might favor a suspension of its laws.

As president, Washington suspended a provision of law. A federal statute required the executive to construct warships, but provided that the construction should stop should the nation make peace with Algiers.[107] Essentially, Congress had agreed to raise a navy only so long as Algiers continued to prey on American shipping. After ratifying a peace treaty with Algiers, Washington told Congress that he would continue construction until it considered the issue. Washington justified his suspension of the statute requiring a construction stoppage because of the considerable "loss which the Publick would incur" from the departure of laborers and the halt of work.[108] His letter and justification were necessary because he was acting contrary to law, as he admitted. Because Congress wanted the ships built (it passed a new law to that effect),[109] it made no move to punish the president for his refusal to enforce the preexisting law. Of course, there would have been no need for Congress to authorize the continuing construction of the vessels had the president enjoyed a generic constitutional power to suspend statutes.

If the Faithful Execution Clause was not meant to forbid suspensions and dispensations, we are left with a relatively opaque obligation. More than any of his contemporaries, one Anti-Federalist saw the clause's ambiguities: "Can we exactly say . . . what may be called or comprehended in a faithful execution?" Could the president plead a mistake in interpreting the law but nonetheless be acting faithfully? If "the legislature direct[ed] the mode of executing the laws, or any particular law, is he obliged to comply, if he does not think it will amount to a faithful execution?"[110] Neither this Anti-Federalist nor anyone else during the ratification process addressed such questions.

Some modern-era scholars seize on one supposed ambiguity, claiming that the clause indicates that the president is *not* the constitutional executor of the laws. The clause's use of the passive voice purportedly suggests that others will execute the law—he must "take care that the Laws be faithfully executed" *by others.*[111] When Congress empowers officers to enforce the law without regard to presidential direction, the president must honor such laws, or so these scholars claim. Any presidential attempt to control departments and officers to whom Congress has ceded autonomy would constitute unfaithful execution. In making such claims, scholars rely upon James Monroe's attorney general, William Wirt. Wirt argued that the president could not revise the decisions of accounting officers: "[I]t could never have been the intention of the constitution, in assigning this general power to the President to take care that the laws be executed, that he should in person execute the laws himself. . . . If the laws, then, require a particular officer by name to perform a duty . . . no other officer can perform it without a violation of the laws; and were the President to perform it, he would not only be not taking care that the laws, were faithfully executed, but he would be violating them himself."[112]

Wirt's reading of the Constitution is flawed. As a matter of syntax, the wording of the Faithful Execution Clause implies only that someone— the president, others, or the president and others—execute the laws. Moreover, the Wirt reading discounts the grant of executive power. Repeatedly and across time, Americans understood the executive power as the power to execute the law. Because the president has the power to execute the law, he may execute any federal law himself. A doubtful reading of the Faithful Execution Clause should not be used to nullify the clear import of the grant of executive power. To be sure, Congress has long enacted laws that authorize executive officers to execute the laws. But to say that particular officers will execute the laws and that the president must ensure the faithful execution of the laws hardly implies that the president cannot execute the laws himself or control others as they execute. Put another way, neither the Faithful Execution Clause nor

Congress's power to create executive officers refutes the notion that the president may execute the laws and direct other law enforcement officers.

Wirt's reading also is ahistorical. The clause's state antecedents were never read as undermining grants of the power to execute. As noted, the clause's origins go back at least as far as 1682, when William Penn adopted a precursor.[113] The 1776 Pennsylvania Constitution simplified the provision, requiring its Executive Council "to take care that the laws be faithfully executed."[114] New York perhaps borrowed from its neighbor; its governor was "to take care that the laws are faithfully executed to the best of his ability."[115]

By granting the "supreme executive power"[116] and imposing a duty of faithful execution, both constitutions required their executives to administer the laws. Neither state executive read the clause as somehow detracting from its law execution power. To the contrary, each noted that it was "to execute."[117] The Pennsylvania Executive Council was especially insistent on this point, repeatedly claiming as much.[118] When the Assembly created commissioners to spend money, the council objected that the statute "plainly encroaches on the rights of the people, who have elected you for the purpose of devising measures, and us for that of executing them."[119]

The clause's legislative history in the Constitutional Convention contains nothing suggesting that it permits the creation of independent executive officers. Based on a resolution that the executive would execute the laws,[120] a committee drafted the Executive Power Clause, with language resembling the New York Constitution's Faithful Execution Clause: the president "shall take care that the laws of the United States be duly and faithfully executed."[121] After the clause took this form, delegates continued to note that the executive would execute.[122] No one at the convention read the clause as signaling that the president had been (or could be) deprived of his executive power to execute the law.

What little was said about the Faithful Execution Clause during the ratification debates confirmed that the president could execute the laws. In *Federalist* 77, Alexander Hamilton noted that the "power[]" of "faithfully executing the laws" was unobjectionable.[123] More importantly, as discussed earlier, people repeatedly noted that the Constitution empowered the president to execute the law.[124]

Occasionally, Washington referred to the clause and his central role in law execution. During the Whiskey Rebellion, he ordered civil officers to bring the rebels to justice, citing his "particular duty" to take care that the laws be faithfully executed.[125] When those measures proved ineffective, Washington summoned the militias, citing his "high and irresistible duty, consigned . . . by the Constitution, 'to take care that the laws be faithfully executed.'"[126] In pursuance of this duty, he "resolved . . . to reduce the refractory to a due subordination to the laws."[127] Finally, in a proclamation addressed to those bent on invading foreign territory, he noted, "[I]t is the duty of the Executive to take care that such criminal proceedings should be suppressed [and] the offenders brought to justice." He further cautioned, "[A]ll lawful means will be strictly put in execution for securing obedience to the laws and for punishing such dangerous and daring violations thereof."[128] The president understood that the clause required him to faithfully execute the laws, obliging him to exercise his executive power to direct executive officers and to deploy his resources to ensure the vindication of federal law.

The clause is best seen as imposing a flexible (but meaningful) obligation to enforce the law. Should the executive concentrate on tax cheats or those who pilfer the mail? Should he focus on repeat offenders or first timers? Should the president go after kingpins or their many minions? In a world with constrained resources and so many laws and scofflaws, the Faithful Execution Clause supplies no easy answers to such questions. The pardon power—discussed later—further complicates matters, for it suggests that the Constitution does not require the unyielding execution of all laws.

What should be clear by now is that the clause casts no doubt either on the prevailing view that the executive power included a power to execute the law or on the consensus that the president could execute and direct the execution of others. Again, a dubious reading of a clause in section 3 of Article II should not be exploited to undermine the grant of power in the first sentence of the Article. To quote Hamilton, "It would not consist with the rules of sound construction to consider this enumeration of particular authorities as derogating from the more comprehensive grant contained in the general clause."[129]

Washingtonian Execution

Did President Washington execute the law? Or did he merely take care that others did so faithfully, leaving them at liberty to exercise statutory discretion as they saw fit so long as they were faithful executors? Washington did not collect taxes from individuals, withdraw funds from the treasury, or arrest and prosecute the accused. Yet he did execute the law, via his own actions and his command of officers. Though Chapter 8 considers presidential direction in detail, a few comments are necessary here.

Some laws demanded that the president himself make a decision. Washington regularly asked his attorney general to give him a list of statutes that required the "*special* agency of the President,"[130] recognizing that there were some statutes that *only* the president could execute. More often, laws specified that they were to be executed by some other officer or officers. But these statutes were almost never understood as barring presidential direction. Rather, they designated the instruments the president could use to exercise his executive power and ensure faithful execution of the laws. That is, the president executed the law via these officers and departments, directing them in their functions.

For instance, on one occasion, Washington warned Americans that it had become "peculiarly necessary" to "enforce [an] Act" and treaty regulating trade and intercourse with Indian tribes. What followed were orders to all officers, military and civil, and an admonition to citizens to honor the act and treaty.[131] Similarly, upon learning of a delay in the construction of a naval vessel, Washington agitatedly laid down rules for "executive officers": "In all important matters, to deliberate maturely, but to execute promptly and vigorously. And not to put things off until the morrow which can be done, and require to be done, to day. Without an adherence to these rules, business never will be *well* done, or done in an easy manner, but will always be in arrear."[132] Leonard White, the author of an exhaustive treatment of administrative practices under the Federalists, concluded that "[a]ll major decisions in matters of administration . . . were made by the President."[133] By issuing orders to officers, Washington was executing the laws no less than his secretaries were, each of whom likewise typically acted via their aides.

When circumstances warranted, the president became quite intimately involved in minute administrative matters. On one occasion, when all the secretaries were away from the capital, all departmental matters were transmitted to the president for his decision, meaning that he executed federal laws and otherwise governed without the assistance of his absent secretaries.[134] In a sense, Washington served as the secretary for all three principal executive departments because the Constitution authorized as much. During the Whiskey Rebellion, Washington marched with the militia to execute the excise laws. Had he chosen to remain with the militia, he might have arrested the ringleaders. Instead, he directed subordinates, executing the tax laws from afar.

Congress recognized that the president executed the law. The Senate advised the president "to execute and enjoin an observance of" a treaty with Indian tribes.[135] Much later, the House praised the president's efforts to end the Whiskey Rebellion peaceably. It gushed that Washington's "laudable and successful endeavors to render lenity in executing the laws . . . and to convert tumult into order" inspired public confidence.[136]

The first president's executive assistants generally were obedient; he ousted the few that were insubordinate or remiss. Had Washington chosen (for whatever reason) to retain unruly or inadequate officers, he could have intervened directly and assumed their functions, as he did when his secretaries were absent. Similarly, he could have exercised his executive power and assumed direct control of the authority wielded by inferior officers, such as the statutory powers of customs officers and district attorneys. Because the federal executive power was his, there was no area of federal law execution outside Washington's domain.

The Pardon Power, "Naturally Vested in the President"

The pardon power extends the president's command of law execution across time. If predecessors secured punishments that seem unwise, unjust, or unconstitutional, the incumbent may wipe them away with pardons. Likewise, the president may revisit his own administration's successful prosecutions and modify or efface them. Finally, if the president grants pardons for acts before any successful governmental prosecution, he extends his control of law execution into the future. No successor may prosecute someone for pardoned offenses.

Despite the fact that the pardon power magnifies the president's power over law execution, some scholars maintain that the Pardon Clause intimates that the chief executive lacks power to execute the law generally and control prosecution in particular.[137] Under this view, the pardon power enables him to mitigate or efface the effects of prosecutions undertaken by independent prosecutors. Hence, although the Constitution authorizes the president to halt prosecutions and terminate the effects of successful prosecutions, it never authorizes him to direct prosecutors.

Early practice refutes this claim, for, as we have seen, early presidents routinely directed prosecutions without any statutory warrant and without anyone doubting the propriety of such commands. Moreover, simultaneous power over prosecutors and pardons was not seen as incongruous. To the contrary, the powers were understood as complementary. As William Blackstone put it, violations of the law are affronts to the chief magistrate because "the public . . . has delegated all it's power and rights, with regard to the execution of the laws" to him.[138] The king is "therefore the proper person to prosecute for all public offences and breaches of the peace, being the person injured in the eye of the law."[139] Because a public offense injured the Crown, "it is reasonable that he only who is injured should have the power of forgiving."[140]

The Founders likewise believed it made a good deal of sense to cede the pardon power to the one empowered to execute the law. James Iredell at the North Carolina ratifying convention observed how pardons could help with law enforcement: "This [pardon] power is naturally vested in the President, because it is his duty to watch over the public safety; and as that may frequently require the evidence of accomplices to bring great offenders to justice, he ought to be intrusted with the most effectual means of procuring it."[141] Alexander Hamilton discussed how pardons would be useful during insurrections, with a "well timed" amnesty perhaps yielding peace.[142] Much later, Chief Justice John Marshall, on behalf of the Supreme Court, acknowledged that the pardon authority rested with the nation's chief law enforcer, without a nod to the supposed incongruity: "A pardon is an act of grace, proceeding from the power entrusted with the execution of the laws."[143]

Because the pardon power significantly augments the president's power over law execution, a more detailed consideration of it is in order. Its antecedents and text reveal a breathtakingly broad grant of authority and a host of implied limits.

Antecedents

The English Crown's use of pardons dates to the sixteenth century.[144] Besides being a means of dispensing mercy, pardons helped secure soldiers, exile miscreants, and fill the Crown's coffers.[145] Pardons also facilitated parliamentary appropriations and cultivated the public's gratitude and fealty. The Crown even granted pardons as a means of bestowing favors on courtiers who charged fees in exchange for their influence.[146]

The Crown made general offers of pardon in conjunction with coronations and at the end of rebellions and wars.[147] Those wishing to take advantage of a general pardon had to prove they qualified and usually pay a fee for an individual copy. To be useful, the copy would have to be produced in court during a later prosecution.[148] Sometimes the Crown would ask Parliament to codify the pardon in a statute as a means of publicizing the offer. One potential advantage of statutory pardons was that individuals could plead the act of indemnity itself, without having to pay a fee for an individual pardon.[149]

In the colonies, governors enjoyed a power to pardon offenses and remit fines, subject to a host of constraints. Some needed the advice of a council before pardoning (sometimes an executive council itself enjoyed the power); some could pardon only after conviction; and some could not pardon treason or willful murder at all.[150]

Although Blackstone claimed that the pardon power was incompatible with democracy,[151] Americans disagreed. New York, Delaware, Maryland, and North Carolina expressly granted their chief executives the sole power to pardon.[152] In New Hampshire, Massachusetts, New Jersey, and Virginia, the chief executive could pardon with a council's participation;[153] in Pennsylvania and Vermont, executive councils had the pardon power.[154] In South Carolina, neither the 1776 nor the 1778 Constitutions contained a pardon clause. Nonetheless, the grant of "executive authority"[155] ceded a pardon power. One of that government's first acts was a gubernatorial pardon.[156] South Carolina's governors offered numerous amnesties as a means of turning Tories.[157]

In the states, the pardon power was quite constrained. Some barred the executive from pardoning offenses prosecuted by the Assembly.[158] Others authorized the legislature to restrain or bar pardons.[159] Massachusetts and New Hampshire authorized only postconviction pardons.[160] New York and others forbade their executives from pardoning treason or murder; they could only offer a reprieve (a postponement of the punishment) to persons convicted of those offenses, pardons being left to the legislature.[161]

Georgia was rather distrustful of executive pardons, granting only a power to "reprieve . . . or suspend" sentences. All pardons were left to the legislature.[162]

As in England, pardons in America served many purposes. Besides serving as a means of mitigating harsh punishments,[163] pardons made it possible for Tories to switch sides during the Revolution without fear of punishment.[164] Similarly, pardons helped reconcile secessionists.[165] Finally, pardons helped the executive gather information about the enemy, as when a spy received three reprieves for spilling secrets.[166]

At the national level, the Continental Congress pardoned offenses against the United States.[167] Recognizing that the power might be of better use in the hands of others, it delegated pardon authority to its two principal commanders in chief.[168] Sometimes General Washington granted amnesties to celebrate an event, as when he commemorated the French alliance.[169] At other times, pardons were used to pacify mutinies.[170] Most remarkably, Washington sometimes used his authority to strike terror in the hearts of his men. After soldiers were convicted by court-martial, Washington would have nooses tied around their necks. At the last minute, he would pardon or reprieve them, the message dramatically conveyed by galloping horsemen. But a pardon or reprieve sometimes would go to only nine of ten poor souls, with the unlucky one serving as a vivid example.[171] His practice brings to mind the Roman custom of decimation.

The Creation of the Pardon Power

Delegates at the Constitutional Convention said little about the pardon power. The Virginia Plan would have granted the new executive "the executive Rights vested in Congress by the Confederation,"[172] a phrase that presumably included a pardon power. Hamilton's plan expressly mentioned pardons, specifying that pardons for treason required the Senate's consent.[173] No more detailed discussion took place until late August, when the convention took up a committee proposal. One delegate wished to limit the president to reprieves, and to require the Senate's consent for pardons.[174] Another successfully proposed that pardons be barred "in cases of impeachment."[175] By a close vote, delegates rejected the idea that no pardon would be "pleadable in bar" of an impeachment, perhaps because it was redundant.[176] Later proposals to bar pardons before conviction or for treason failed.[177] The last idea generated discussion when some argued that the legislature also should be able to pardon treason.[178]

In the states, Anti-Federalists complained that the president could pardon treason, grant clemency before conviction, dispense mercy without proper advice, and use pardons to shield his own illegal measures.[179] Supporters of the Constitution countered that impeachment would uncover malfeasance and that pardons granted before conviction might defuse rebellions.[180] They noted too that pardons could mitigate harsh punishments and permit a tailoring of consequences to actions that would be otherwise impossible in a system of general law.[181]

Given the generic grant of executive power, why does the Constitution contain a separate Pardon Clause? It seems likely to have been added as a means of constraining the pardon power. As discussed below, the president can pardon only *federal* offenses. Moreover, he cannot halt impeachment proceedings or preclude the removal of convicted officers. Finally, it is possible that the clause was added out of an abundance of caution. In the absence of a Pardon Clause, some might cavil that the president lacked a pardon power. That sort of (mis)reading is not possible when the power is made express.

"Reprieves and Pardons"

The new president enjoyed the "power to grant reprieves and pardons for offenses against the United States, except in cases of impeachment."[182] As noted, a reprieve is a temporary suspension of a judicial sentence.[183] It allows the executive time to consider a pardon application either before the onset of a sentence or before the imposition of a punishment that cannot be undone, such as execution. The pardon power is more potent than the reprieve power and encompasses several types of pardons: full, partial, and conditional. A full pardon completely "blots out" the legal guilt of an offender, thus leaving him, in the eyes of the federal government at least, as if he had never committed any offense—a "new man" in effect.[184] A partial pardon or commutation releases an offender from part of the consequences of a sentence. For example, the president might release someone from jail before completion of her sentence, but not efface the conviction or restore her civil rights (such as the right to vote). A conditional pardon's effectiveness depends upon the offender's subsequent acts. The president might ask a rebel to renounce her disloyalty in order to secure a pardon. Alternatively, the executive might pardon a person under the condition that he cease violating the law. Should the offender subsequently breach the conditions, the pardon would be null and void.

Armed with the pardon power, the president can take judicial judgments favoring the United States and either moderate their severity or eliminate them. In light of the pardon power, legislatively adopted and judicially imposed punishments are maximums that the president may moderate or eliminate. Under the Constitution, there are no mandatory minimums, at least not ones the president must honor.

"Offenses Against the United States"

The phrase "Offenses against the United States" makes clear that the executive's pardon power extends to federal, but not state, offenses. Many also imagine that this language limits the pardon power to crimes, enabling the president to pardon or reprieve criminal punishments and remit criminal fines only.[185] In this view, violations of federal law that trigger civil fines and forfeitures are not "offenses against the United States." One reason for so reading the phrase is that the Fifth Amendment's Double Jeopardy Clause clearly uses "offense" to cover criminal offenses—after all, jeopardy of life and limb could come only from being tried for crimes. If "offense" in the Fifth Amendment refers to crimes, it likely means the same thing in the Pardon Clause, or so some suppose.

The word "offenses" often connotes crimes; yet it also often connotes nothing more than transgressions of the law.[186] That the Fifth Amendment applies only to criminal offenses does not mean that "offenses" should be so read in Article II. The Fifth Amendment was ratified at a different time, raising the possibility that these different provisions might use the same word in different ways.[187] More importantly, the amendment does not actually indicate that the word "offenses" should be read to cover crimes only. While the Double Jeopardy Clause covers offenses threatening life and limb, it nowhere dictates that *only* criminal acts are offenses against the United States. Instead, it merely provides that within the category of "offenses" (however broad or narrow), only those that jeopardize life and limb are subject to the double-jeopardy bar.

"Offenses against the United States" should be understood as encompassing any violation of federal law in which public interests predominate—that is, in instances where Congress has authorized governmental prosecution of the offenses. Where Congress determines that some official may prosecute to vindicate the law, Congress has provided that violations of the underlying law constitute offenses against the United States. Obviously, criminal offenses prosecutable by the government fit within that category.

And so do civil offenses prosecutable by the government. When the government sues to collect fines and forfeitures, it prosecutes to redress offenses against the United States. In these situations, the president may pardon any such fines and forfeitures. Put another way, it does not matter whether Congress designates some penalty, fine, or forfeiture as "civil" rather than "criminal." The president can remit any fine or forfeiture due the United States; the fact that such a penalty accrues to the United States indicates that someone has committed an offense against the nation.[188]

The pardon power might seem to resemble the powers to dispense with the law or suspend it, two powers that the president lacks. But even though there is a resemblance, the second and third powers are analytically distinct from the first. The suspending power makes legal that which was illegal. The dispensing power does the same, but on an individualized basis. Both may be issued before the commission of any act. In contrast, a pardon may be issued only after the completion of the act and does not make the underlying act legal. It merely provides that the pardoned individual will suffer little or no consequences for having violated the law.[189] To see the differences, imagine a statute that required all federal tax collectors to be college graduates. A suspension or dispensation of the law would permit the executive to appoint those who lack college degrees. In contrast, the power to pardon does not permit the president to circumvent the college qualification. Because the power to pardon does not absolve the president of his general obligation to abide by the law and its restrictions, the ability to issue general pardons is not the equivalent of a suspending or dispensing power.

Executive Amnesties

May the president grant amnesties (a general pardon to all people who meet particular criteria)? In the wake of the Civil War, some senators opposed to the rehabilitation of rebels denied that the president could grant amnesties, claiming that they were technically different from pardons.[190] Because the Constitution does not specifically grant power over "amnesties," the president could not issue them.

Text and history indicate otherwise. As a matter of text, nothing in the Constitution suggests a limit to the numbers of pardons the president may grant.[191] Nor does the text contain any constraint requiring the president to grant individualized pardons as opposed to a blanket pardon covering groups. As a matter of history, executives had offered and issued general pardons for centuries. The Crown had done so numerous times,[192] perhaps most vividly (to Americans, at least) when it offered pardons (via its agents) to all rebels who reconciled themselves to England.[193] The Crown also offered what we might call celebratory pardons. For example, coronation pardons forgave thousands.[194] Under the state constitutions, executives likewise issued general pardons, as when New York governor George Clinton pardoned secessionists.[195] As noted, the commander in chief of the Continental Army granted general pardons to commemorate anniversaries, including that of the French alliance.[196]

During the Constitution's creation, many spoke of the president's ability to grant amnesties, praising it as necessary to pacify rebellions.[197] They understood that no less than his predecessors, the president might issue general pardons. Washington pardoned "all persons" who participated in the 1794 Whiskey Rebellion, providing that they met certain conditions.[198] In 1800, John Adams granted a full pardon "to all and every person" who participated in Fries's Rebellion, excepting some crimes.[199] And in 1815, James Madison granted a general pardon to a band of pirates in gratitude for their assistance in defending New Orleans.[200]

"Except in Cases of Impeachment"

The pardon power proved controversial in England, and Parliament periodically attempted to constrain it. By the eighteenth century, Parliament had barred the Crown from pardoning those who sent imprisoned subjects overseas,[201] and provided that "no pardon . . . shall be pleadable to an impeachment by the Commons in Parliament."[202]

Though the former constraint has no application in America, the latter lives on in slightly broader form. Reacting to Charles II's pardon of an English earl, and resolving a long simmering dispute, Parliament passed the Act of Settlement.[203] The act stated that "no Pardon . . . [shall] be pleadable to an Impeachment by the Commons in Parliament."[204] The language barred the use of pardons to halt impeachments, thereby safe-guarding Parliament's role as "grand inquest." The Constitution's impeachment exception serves the same function, meaning that the president cannot preempt impeachments.

But the Constitution's impeachment exception goes beyond English practice, preempting more of the pardon power. The Act of Settlement did not preclude pardons after an impeachment conviction. Indeed, in 1715 George I pardoned three Scottish lords whom the House of Lords had sentenced to death.[205] Under the Constitution, however, the president may not pardon the effects of a Senate conviction. The broader exception—"in cases of impeachment" rather than "pleadable to an impeachment"—strongly suggests that the president cannot shield federal officers from the effects of an impeachment conviction (removal and potential bar on future office holding).

This broader limitation on the pardon power makes a good deal of sense. Given the narrow sanctions that the Senate may impose, the pardon power seems unnecessary in impeachment cases. More importantly, because the House has the right to prosecute impeachments, it (rather than the president) represents the public's interest in such cases. In a real sense, the House has a share of the executive power of prosecution over high crimes and misdemeanors. Just as the president cannot pardon private wrongs done by one person to another, he or she likewise cannot eliminate the House's interest in prosecuting impeachments.

Self-Pardons

May the president pardon himself? This question could never arise in England, for as a legal matter the Crown could do no wrong and hence could not be convicted in its own courts. In our system, no one doubts that a president eventually might face a judge and jury. Rogue presidents might find it very useful to self-pardon, thus escaping punishment for their misdeeds. One scholar has made a respectable argument that the president cannot pardon himself.[206] The president should not be a judge in his own case, and it seems odd for a constitution to grant an executive a power to forgive his own transgressions. Under this view, any self-pardon would be a nullity.

On balance, the slightly better view is that the president may pardon himself. As a matter of text, the Constitution grants the president the power to pardon all offenses against the United States. If the president commits an offense against the United States, he may pardon himself, just as he may pardon anyone else who commits an offense against the United States. Consistent with this grim view of the Constitution, some objected that the president might use his pardon power "to Screen himself and other offenders," perhaps suggesting that a president might pardon himself.[207] As far as the structural argument is concerned, the Constitution repeatedly violates the self-judging prohibition. Members of Congress determine their own pay; judges decide cases that effect their salaries and jurisdiction; and the president may forbid executives from investigating and prosecuting him.

There is at least one federal self-pardoning precedent. After Isaac Stevens, the governor of the Washington territory, declared martial law in 1856, he ordered the arrest of a judge. The judge later held the governor in contempt, fining him $50. The governor subsequently issued a reprieve to "Isaac I. Stevens" for his contempt of court conviction.[208] The federal statute under which the governor issued his pardon gave him authority to "grant pardons and . . . remit fines and forfeitures for offenses against the laws of the said Territory,"[209] text that largely parallels the Pardon Clause. Though this episode hardly establishes that self-pardons were constitutionally permissible at the founding, it does confirm that the Constitution's text arguably authorizes self-pardons.

Conclusion

At the founding, the executive power principally consisted of the power to execute the law. The Constitution's conspicuous grant of executive power makes the president the nation's chief law enforcement officer. Other provisions modify this authority, some augmenting his control (the Commander in Chief and Pardon Clauses) and others constraining him (the Faithful Execution Clause). Wielding their constitutional grant of executive power, early presidents routinely executed the law by directing federal executives, usually without any statutory warrant for doing so.

The Pardon Clause enables the president to control the prosecutorial successes of his predecessors and to limit the prosecutorial latitude of his successors. Additionally, the clause allows the president to limit the effect of any sentences issued while he is in office. In other words, the pardon power essentially ensures that while Congress can set statutory maximums, the president may determine what lesser penalty criminals and civil offenders will actually suffer.

CHAPTER SIX

THE "TRANSACTION OF BUSINESS WITH FOREIGN NATIONS IS EXECUTIVE ALTOGETHER"

One might suppose that the Executive Power Clause conveys a single power—the power to execute the law. The clause does not vest the "executive Powers," as some state frameworks did.[1] Yet a solitary grant of constitutional power can be disaggregated into its components. For instance, one can divide the foreign-commerce power into authority over the means of commerce, the terms of trade, and tariffs.

In the eighteenth century, executive power was often thought to have an internal component—law execution—and an external component— foreign relations. From this usage, two insights emerge. First, the Constitution is not incomplete or full of gaps on the subject of foreign affairs, as some imagine. Rather, the Constitution explicitly grants the federal government the full spectrum of foreign-relations authorities. Congress has specific foreign affairs powers related to war, foreign commerce, and the law of nations; the president must act with the Senate's consent in two areas, treaties and appointments; and the president enjoys all other foreign-relations powers by virtue of his executive power. Second and relatedly, the grant of executive power justifies the broad foreign affairs authority that early presidents routinely exercised. Though

Article II contains but three specific foreign-relations clauses—concerning appointing and receiving ambassadors and making treaties—the first president exercised a far broader foreign affairs jurisdiction. Among other things, he formulated foreign policy, essentially monopolized diplomatic communications, and controlled America's diplomats. Washington exercised these powers (and others) because they were uncontroversial elements of his generic grant of executive power.[2]

The Constitution's Framework for Foreign Affairs

We can better grasp how the Constitution's text completely vests foreign affairs powers with the federal government if we keep in mind four principles. First, the president's grant of "executive Power"[3] included a general foreign affairs power. As discussed below, Locke, Montesquieu, Blackstone, and others noted that foreign affairs powers were components of the "executive power." Americans likewise voiced this understanding before, during, and after the Constitution's ratification. When the Constitution conferred the "executive Power," that grant meant that the president not only could execute the laws, but also had power over international relations.

Second, the Constitution incorporates broad exceptions to its grant of executive power. Many at the founding believed that the English Constitution ceded too much foreign affairs power to the Crown and that some aspects of foreign affairs had legislative overtones (such as the war power).[4] Acting on this belief, the delegates to the Philadelphia Convention created exceptions to the executive power. Sometimes the president would have but a veto over foreign affairs, and Congress would have the primary role (for example, in matters of war, foreign commerce, and the law of nations). At other times, the president might have the initiative, with final action requiring Senate consent (treaty making and diplomatic appointments). These exceptions to the grant of executive power ensured that the president would have fewer foreign affairs powers than the English monarch.

Third, the president cannot make foreign-relations law, that is, law that regulates individuals. With limited exceptions, the Crown relied on Parliament for funds and legislation to implement its foreign policy, including treaties.[5] Because the Constitution evinces a more thoroughgoing distrust of executive lawmaking, the president generally lacks authority to make foreign-relations law.[6] The one exception—treaty making—is express and requires the Senate's supermajority consent.

Fourth, Congress lacks a generic foreign affairs authority. To be sure, it enjoys significant foreign affairs powers, most prominently the powers to regulate foreign commerce and declare war. These powers can be exercised even in the face of fierce executive opposition by overriding a presidential veto. Yet even when considered in the aggregate, the powers to declare war, regulate commerce, and define and punish violations of international law, along with the authority to enact laws necessary and proper for the implementation of federal powers, do not convey a generic foreign affairs power. Hence, Congress has no claim on the foreign affairs powers not specifically mentioned in the Constitution.

A Secondary Feature of Executive Power

The first principle discussed above rests on the claim that the "executive power" was understood to have a foreign affairs component, making an examination of usage necessary. Before the late seventeenth century, the executive power consisted of the present-day categories of executive power and judicial power.[7] Both of these subcategories involved law execution, the primary executive function.[8] By the end of the eighteenth century, the executive power had taken on an additional feature, a foreign affairs aspect.

John Locke discussed why the executive power had an external component.[9] In the state of nature, each individual could interact with others. When individuals created civil society, however, things stood differently. The government assumed the "federative power," or the power over "war and peace, leagues and alliances, and all the transactions with all persons and communities" outside the state.[10] Though the executive and federative powers were distinct in theory, they "are always almost united" in fact. They were "hardly to be separated, and placed . . . in the hands of distinct Persons," because both required the command of the "force of the society."[11] To vest these authorities in different hands would be to invite "disorder and ruin."[12] So tight was the link that Locke occasionally used "executive power" as a synonym for "federative power."[13]

In *The Spirit of the Laws* (1748), Montesquieu claimed that "[i]n every government there are three sorts of power: the legislative; the executive in respect to things dependent on the law of nations; and the executive in regard to matters that depend on the civil law."[14] The first category of executive power included making war and peace, sending or receiving embassies, establishing public security, and protecting against invasions.[15] His taxonomy reflected the mid-eighteenth-century view that the executive power had domestic and foreign affairs components.[16]

Blackstone seemed to borrow from Montesquieu.[17] His enumeration of those prerogatives, "the exertion whereof consists the executive part of government,"[18] began with a discussion of "foreign concerns."[19] The king "has the sole power of sending embassadors to foreign states, and receiving embassadors at home;"[20] he may "make treaties, leagues, and alliances with foreign states and princes;"[21] and he has "the sole prerogative of making war and peace."[22] The executive "is the delegate or representative of his people" who transacts with "another community," because individuals in one society practically cannot transact "the affairs of that state" with those in another.[23]

Besides Blackstone and Montesquieu, other eighteenth-century writers identified foreign affairs as a strand of executive power. One international law expert wrote that "[t]he second branch of executive power, which is called external executive power," included the power "of making war or peace, the power of engaging alliances . . . [and] the power of entering into treaties."[24] An observer of the English Constitution noted that the Crown's executive power enabled it to serve as "the representative . . . of all the power and collective majesty of the nation; [the Crown] sends and receives ambassadors; he contracts alliances; and has the prerogative of declaring war, and of making peace."[25]

Politicians had the same understanding. In 1780, a member of the House of Commons claimed that the Crown could recognize the American colonies as independent because it had the executive power.[26] A French politician noted that the "executive power" could make treaties and was charged with "foreign connections."[27] Another criticized the 1791

French Constitution for containing a "contradiction" because though it granted the king the executive power, it denied him the peace and war powers, a complaint resting on the view that the executive power encompassed foreign relations.[28]

The Executive Power over Foreign Affairs in Early America

On this side of the Atlantic, Americans understood that executive power had an external branch. As Chapter 4 recounted, *The Essex Result* observed: "[The] executive power is sometimes divided into the external executive, and internal executive. The former comprehends war, peace, the sending and receiving ambassadors, and whatever concerns the transactions of the state with any other independent state."[29] John Adams warned that whenever "executive power" rested with plural bodies, "disputes forever arise concerning every step in foreign affairs."[30] Finally, recall Alexander Hamilton's observation that the executive power included authority over treaties, war, and peace.[31]

Apart from usage, American executives enjoyed foreign affairs powers. Colonial governors were the "natural representative[s] of the colony in its external relations,"[32] with limited powers to declare war against, and make treaties with, Indian tribes.[33] Similarly, state executives corresponded with other nations.[34] Foreign emissaries were told to present their credentials to state executives on the theory that failure to do so might cast doubt on their diplomatic status.[35] State constitutions never specifically granted such authority to their executives. Rather, the generic state grants of executive power sanctioned such actions. When a state was said to lack a "proper Executive power," it lacked someone whose "Duty" it was to "[r]eceive & answer all letters sent to the State,"[36] a reference to authority over communications.

Jefferson's proposed Virginia constitution confirms the connection between executive power and foreign relations. He proposed an "Administrator" armed with the "executive powers . . . in manner following."[37] What followed was a list of powers denied to the administrator, including the powers to declare war, grant letters of marque and reprisal, and lay long-term embargoes.[38] Such exceptions were necessary because without them, the grant of executive power would have conveyed such authorities. Given the omissions from the list of forbidden powers, Jefferson's administrator could have imposed short-term embargoes, made treaties, and served as the state's organ of foreign communication.

The South Carolina Constitutions similarly assumed that grants of "executive authority" included foreign affairs authority. Recall that the 1776 Constitution denied its executive any power "to make war or peace, or enter into any final treaty, without the consent of the general assembly and legislative council."[39] Again, there would have been no need to deny the powers to make treaties, war, and peace unless "executive authority" was typically understood to include them. Moreover, the Constitution allowed the executive to negotiate treaties because that power, along with others, was left as an unrestrained feature of "executive authority."[40]

Under the Articles of Confederation, the Continental Congress could make treaties, war, and peace and could send and receive ambassadors. Even though the articles never specifically granted Congress "executive power," it was widely seen as enjoying executive power over foreign affairs.[41] *The Essex Result* asserted that the articles had "lopped off this [external] branch of the executive" and granted it to Congress.[42] Madison observed that "all the great powers which are properly executive" were granted to Congress and not state governors, a statement that evidently referred to foreign affairs powers.[43] Many others (including John Jay, James Wilson, Jefferson, and some foreigners) described Congress as enjoying the executive power.[44]

By lodging executive power in the hands of many, those who crafted the articles were reacting to the perceived excesses of the English monarchy. Yet the cure for excessive executive vigor was worse than the disease, for a plural, part-time executive proved far from ideal. In a reform measure, Congress created a Department of Foreign Affairs, headed by a single officer. The secretary could communicate with foreign and domestic envoys, transmit congressional messages, and report applications to Congress.[45]

Because the secretary was a "clerk" and Congress micromanaged everything,[46] the reform was something of a failure. The clerk himself complained. Decrying the plight of American hostages, John Jay pronounced Congress "unequal" to the task of wielding the executive power.[47] In a letter to Washington, Jay lamented that Congress could never act with vigor and dispatch: "The Executive Business of Sovereignty depending on so many wills" and moved by "contradictory motives," would be "feebly done."[48] Contemporaries agreed.[49]

More sweeping reform was necessary. Foreign affairs often required confidentiality, swiftness, and consistency, qualities in short supply in a plural, fluctuating executive. When delegates gathered in Philadelphia, they had to thread a needle, invigorating the executive power without facilitating the ability to make hasty, ill-advised decisions that might endanger the nation. In a move to introduce secrecy, speed, and stability to foreign affairs, the Constitution assigned some executive authority to a unitary, independent executive. In key foreign affairs areas, a plural, deliberative executive would continue to hold sway.

Splintering the Executive Power over Foreign Affairs

Three of the four plans presented to the Convention would have granted generic foreign affairs powers to the executive. The Virginia Plan ceded the "Executive rights vested in Congress by the Confederation."[50] By ceding "Executive rights," the Virginia Plan vested the executive power over foreign affairs with the national executive. Alexander Hamilton's plan would have ceded less authority. Though his "Governor" would enjoy the "supreme Executive authority of the United States" and therefore would have had generic foreign affairs authority, the Senate had a check on treaties and diplomatic appointments and had the "sole power of declaring war."[51] South Carolinian Charles Pinckney sought a president with "the executive Authority of the U.S."[52]

Some objected to the Virginia Plan's grant of "Executive rights," arguing that the new executive should not enjoy some powers commonly regarded as executive. One opposed ceding the "Executive powers of (the existing) Congress" because such powers "might extend to peace & war &c which would render the Executive a Monarchy."[53] James Wilson of Pennsylvania "did not consider the Prerogatives of the British Monarch as a proper guide in defining the Executive powers," since some "were of a Legislative nature," including "that of war & peace &c."[54] Madison agreed, arguing that "executive powers ex vi termini [from the force of the term], do not include the Rights of war & peace &c."[55] He successfully moved that the "Executive rights" provision be struck.[56] Because the substituted list of powers did not contain a generic grant of executive power, the executive contemplated at this stage would have lacked any foreign affairs powers.

Criticisms of the Virginia Plan confirmed that executive rights included foreign affairs authorities. To be sure, some did not believe that certain foreign affairs powers should be regarded as executive or, more importantly, concentrated in the hands of a single or handful of magistrates. Yet these delegates also understood that the common definition of executive power included foreign affairs. Unless one believes that these delegates were quite aware of the widespread sense of executive power, their opposition to the vesting of the "Executive rights" of the Continental Congress makes little sense.

A number of convention resolutions and proposals eventually were sent to the Committee of Detail. That committee's final report ceded Congress the "legislative power," along with specific foreign affairs authority: the powers to make war, regulate captures, punish piracy and offenses against the law of nations, raise armies, and build fleets.[57] The Senate would make treaties and appoint ambassadors.[58] The president was obliged to receive ambassadors, and reacquired a generic foreign affairs power via a conspicuous grant of the "Executive Power of the United States."[59]

With the change in wording, delegates voiced support for (and assumed) a significant presidential role in foreign affairs. Charles Pinckney and Gouverneur Morris jointly proposed an Executive Council of State presided over by the secretary for foreign affairs, who would serve during the president's pleasure, correspond with all foreign ministers, prepare draft treaties, and generally attend to the foreign relations of the United States.[60] Their scheme presupposed that the president had generic foreign affairs powers, for the president could direct the secretary. Other delegates deemed the treaty[61] and war powers[62] to be executive, comments consistent with the notion that the grant of executive power conveyed generic foreign-relations powers.

Eventually, delegates tinkered with the Senate's role and proposed a more complicated allocation of the executive power over foreign relations. Certain foreign affairs powers would rest with a unitary executive capable of supplying stable, experienced stewardship, thereby solving many of the problems that had plagued the Continental Congress' direction of foreign affairs. Other foreign affairs powers were split across two branches, thereby mollifying opponents of a unitary executive in foreign affairs. Congress would make certain foreign-relations decisions related to war and commerce, subject to a presidential veto. The Senate would serve as an executive council on treaties and diplomatic appointments. By ceding significant executive powers to Congress, a deliberate and bicameral body, and by requiring the Senate's participation in other foreign affairs matters, delegates tamed those executive powers. A single executive could not unilaterally declare war, raise armies, make treaties, or appoint ambassadors; over such matters, the executive was plural. At the same time, a unitary executive would possess an interstitial foreign affairs authority as a result of the reintroduction of the grant of executive power. He could superintend U.S. diplomats, control foreign communications, and craft foreign policy.

In the states, people noted that the president enjoyed generic foreign affairs powers. Addressing the North Carolina ratifying convention, James Iredell observed that the president would "regulate all intercourse with foreign powers."[63] Though the Senate had an executive role, the president was still the "primary agent," the Senate being but a council designed to preclude improper decisions.[64] "Publius" knew that "a great part of the business" that kept Congress sitting through the year "will be managed by the president." The "management of foreign negociations will naturally devolve" upon the president, subject to the Senate's ultimate concurrence.[65] Others assumed that the president, as the principal executive, would enjoy foreign affairs power. After observing that the president's powers naturally belonged to the executive branch and could not be properly vested elsewhere, a Virginian noted that the Constitution had "lessened" the president's power by granting the Senate a role in treaties.[66] The writer regarded the Senate's role as a derogation of authority that would otherwise have been part of the president's executive power.

Though the president's interstitial foreign-relations power was circumscribed and uncontroversial, the Senate's executive powers over foreign affairs raised hackles. One Anti-Federalist said that because of their treaty role, senators had "an alarming share of the executive."[67] Other opponents groused that the Senate had "various and great executive powers, viz.: in concurrence with the president general, they form treaties with foreign nations."[68] One insisted that because of the Treaty and

Supremacy Clauses, the president and Senate enjoyed a perilous mix of legislative and executive powers.[69]

Federalists generally agreed that treaty making was an executive power. "Cassius" noted that treaty making had always been considered "part of the executive" because it had been "safely exercised in other countries, by the executive authority alone."[70] A South Carolina delegate observed that the making of treaties "properly belongs to the executive part of government" because only that branch could act with secrecy and dispatch.[71] In North Carolina, one delegate observed that when the president made treaties, he acted "in his executive capacity."[72] Though "Publius" contested the view that treaty making was executive, his efforts were unconvincing and contradictory.[73]

Washington Exercises the Executive Power over Foreign Affairs

After ratification, politicians consistently read the Constitution as granting the president generic foreign affairs powers. In 1789, the new president explained to the Moroccan emperor that after a "peaceable . . . Revolution," he now enjoyed "the supreme executive Authority."[74] The transformation meant that Washington (rather than Congress) could respond to the emperor's letter.

Others agreed. John Adams claimed that the president had "the whole executive power," including the power of "managing the . . . external affairs of the nation."[75] The holdover secretary of foreign affairs, John Jay, wrote to a U.S. agent overseas, observing that the president had the "great executive Powers" previously granted to the Continental Congress.[76] The new secretary, Thomas Jefferson, claimed that though the Senate had to approve diplomatic appointments, it could not set either destination or grade. Citing the Vesting Clause, Jefferson noted that the "transaction of business with foreign nations is Executive altogether," belonging "to the head of that department" except where the Constitution created exceptions.[77] According to Washington's diary, Madison and Jay agreed with Jefferson that setting destination and grade were "Executive and vested in the President by the Constitution."[78] In 1793, John Quincy Adams wrote that by virtue of the Constitution, the president had both branches of executive power, foreign and law enforcement, and hence had authority over all executive acts relating to foreign affairs, including the delivery and re-vocation of consular credentials.[79] Speaking at the close of the eighteenth century, John Marshall said that the executive department is entrusted "with the whole foreign intercourse of the nation," and that the president is the nation's "sole representative with foreign nations. . . . He possesses the whole executive power." Marshall added that the Constitution "name[s]" the president as he who "conducts the foreign intercourse,"[80] likely referring to the Vesting Clause. Finally, Alexander Hamilton fa-mously defended the Neutrality Proclamation by arguing that the execu-tive power was "the *organ* of intercourse between the [United States] and foreign nations."[81] The executive powers vested with Congress or shared with the Senate were but exceptions from "the more comprehensive grant contained in the general clause."[82]

The president's institutional rival held the conventional view of execu-tive power. In 1789, Congress created an "executive" Department of Foreign Affairs and recognized that its officials—including the secretary of foreign affairs—were executives.[83] Moreover, Congress admitted that the president's executive power authorized him to remove the secretary.[84] Finally, Congress provided that the secretary would enjoy whatever for-eign affairs jurisdiction the president ceded him, a provision that assumed that the latter had generic foreign affairs powers.[85] As one legislator ex-plained, foreign affairs pertained "to the department of the Executive Magistrate."[86]

The Principal Organ of Communication

One power that the Constitution never specifically enumerates is the power to serve as the nation's voice in the international arena. Nonetheless, early statesmen believed that the president enjoyed a communications monopoly and that it arose from his grant of executive power. Though John Marshall's comment that the president was the "sole organ of the nation in its external relations"[87] is well known, he was hardly alone. Recall Washington's claims that he was empowered to receive, and respond to, all foreign communications addressed to the United States and that these pow-ers flowed from his "supreme executive Authority."[88] Senator Oliver Ellsworth noted that "correspondence with foreign nations" was "positively placed in the hands of the Executive. . . . The Constitution left the whole business in his breast."[89] When the French emissary to the United States, Edmond Genêt, threatened to bypass the president and appeal to Congress or the people, Jefferson supplied a constitutional lesson. The president was "the only channel of communication between this country and foreign nations . . . whatever he communicates as [the will of the nation]" must be considered as such.[90] Such was the belief in executive control of communications that it sometimes led to inflated claims of presidential power. After the House debated whether to ask the president to convey its sentiments to another nation, Washington alleged that the House was "invad[ing] the Executive."[91] His concern fairly proves that foreign communication was, for him at least, an undisputed component of the executive power.

Early Congresses had the same understanding. As noted, members occasionally wished to congratulate other nations. Despite the unremarkable nature of such messages, neither chamber corresponded directly with foreign heads of state. Whenever a chamber wished to felicitate, it invariably appealed to the president to convey the sense of the chamber.[92] These were marked departures from prior practice for, as Michael Ramsey observes, the Continental Congress held a tight grip on communications with nations.[93]

Control of Diplomats and the State Department

Upon assuming office, Washington took control of the existing Department of Foreign Affairs, which was created by, and formerly under the direction of, the Continental Congress.[94] Washington relied upon his executive power for the authority to do this, for neither statute nor any other constitutional text authorized his control of the department.

After Congress created a new department of foreign affairs, Washington continued to direct all instruments of foreign relations. Though the organic statute expressly required the new secretary to conform to the president's commands,[95] it did not grant the president any authority over overseas diplomats and consuls. And no specific foreign affairs provision in the Constitution ceded the president control over such personnel. Nonetheless, Washington assumed such authority, issuing orders to,[96] and occasionally removing,[97] diplomats. Equally important, he decided where to station U.S. diplomats and their rank.[98] While Congress had to fund such missions and the Senate had to confirm officers, the president dominated the foreign affairs bureaucracy.

Recognition of Foreign Governments and Diplomats

The first president also determined which governments to recognize and which emissaries to credential. One early question was whether the nation would receive the revolutionary French government's emissary and thereby recognize his government. After seeking advice, Washington unilaterally decided to receive the emissary.[99] He also accredited foreign consuls, even though there was no specific textual warrant for his actions.[100] On one occasion, he pointedly denied consuls the ability to function within the United States when their letters of introduction were addressed to Congress.[101] Jefferson explained that while commissions addressed to Congress were appropriate under the Articles of Confederation, because Congress was "then the Executive as well as . . . Legislative," the Constitution required a change in practice.[102]

Formulating Foreign Policy

Nations make foreign policy in a host of circumstances. Because the Constitution does not grant Congress a monopoly on the generation of foreign policy, Washington utilized his executive power to make decisions not textually committed to Congress. For instance, he unilaterally considered whether British troops should be allowed to traverse a portion of the United States.[103] Similarly, he decided that the Treaty of Alliance with France did not oblige America to wage war against England in order to protect France's West Indian possessions.[104]

Of greatest significance, he famously issued the Neutrality Proclamation and a number of subsidiary rules designed to ensure that the United States remained rigorously neutral.[105] In that era, the obligations of a neutral nation were hardly obvious, meaning that the United States had a good deal of discretion about the type of neutrality to adopt.[106] For instance, Washington's rules could have sanctioned a "benevolent neutrality" toward France, a policy that many Republicans favored.[107]

Over the course of the crisis, the president made rather consequential foreign policy decisions without any congressional input. After deciding how far off the coast the sovereignty of the United States ran, and thereafter concluding that the French had captured a ship within American territory, he directed the French to relinquish it.[108] He also told the French that they could neither fit out privateers nor convene capture courts in the United States.[109]

Seeking to defend the president from the slings and arrows of distraught Republicans, Hamilton's "Pacificus" claimed that the president could declare neutrality. To Jefferson, it seemed that Hamilton had distorted the president's proclamation. Though the proclamation (as a sop to Jefferson) had omitted the word "neutrality," Pacificus claimed that the president had declared neutrality. He also argued that the president could have suspended or voided the French treaties, something Jefferson opposed in the cabinet. Angered, Jefferson asked Madison (as "Helvidius") to respond: "[T]ake up your pen, select the most striking heresies, and cut him [Hamilton] to peices in the face of the public."[110]

The exhortation exaggerated the disagreement. Though Jefferson objected to the use of the word "neutrality" and any claim that the president might declare it, he admitted the propriety of an executive declaration that the nation was at peace.[111] Jefferson seemed to believe that a formal neutrality declaration constituted a definitive judgment that the nation would not wage war,[112] as if neutrality were a semipermanent state that ruled out war or a later decision to tilt toward one side. Yet neither Washington nor Pacificus had argued that the executive could preclude Congress from either declaring war or favoring one side. Even if the president had used the word "neutrality" in his proclamation, Congress might have declared war or enacted laws favoring a belligerent. Jefferson's objections were based on an inflated sense of the consequences of using the word "neutrality."

In any event, Jefferson never denied that the grant of executive power included authority over foreign affairs; he merely insisted that declarations of neutrality were part of Congress's exclusive power to declare war, a claim about the scope of an obvious exception to the executive power. His general agreement with the notion that the grant of executive power conveyed foreign affairs powers becomes clear when we consider comments bracketing the proclamation. In 1792, Jefferson wrote a draft presidential message to the Senate, one protesting the implication that the Senate could decide where to send diplomats. Jefferson suggested that Washington claim the Senate had "no executive act but the single one of giving or withholding their consent" to a nomination, a statement indicating that the president could decide other foreign affairs matters, including where to station diplomats.[113] In late 1793, after the Pacificus-Helvidius exchange, a question arose whether a foreign ship had been captured within the United States. In a letter, Jefferson claimed that if the judiciary could not decide the matter, the executive could resolve it, charged as it was with "the conduct of [the nation's] affairs with foreign nations."[114] Such comments reflected the secretary of state's general views about the executive's wide authority in foreign affairs.[115]

As Helvidius, Madison proved more aggressive than his instigator. Helvidius discussed whether the executive could interpret the Treaty of Alliance with France and determine that it permitted the United States to remain neutral. He insisted that the president could not decide whether the treaty either permitted neutrality or required America to declare war against France's enemies. Those sorts of decisions were for Congress to make under the declare-war power.[116] In the course of making this argument, he admitted that the grant of executive power included authority to execute the law and direct and remove executive officials.[117] He further admitted that English writers had classified foreign affairs authority as executive.[118] Nonetheless, Helvidius vigorously denied that the Vesting Clause ceded the president any foreign affairs powers.

Helvidius's arguments were rather unsatisfactory.[119] He could not explain how other foreign affairs powers were allocated, such as the powers to craft foreign policy and serve as organ of foreign intercourse. He could not stitch congressional foreign affairs authorities into a generic foreign affairs power and thereby demonstrate that Congress had residual foreign affairs powers. His reading of the foreign affairs provisions of the Constitution left gaping holes, none of which he acknowledged.[120]

His claims about the scope of the executive power also ran contrary to his alter ego's claims in less partisan contexts. In the debate over the Department of Foreign Affairs, Representative Madison championed language that not only contemplated a constitutional power to remove departmental officers, but also assumed that the president had constitutional authority over foreign affairs beyond those specifically enumerated in Article II. As noted earlier, the organic act conveyed no foreign affairs powers to the president. Instead, it allowed him to delegate certain powers to the secretary. Specifically, it said that the president could allow the secretary to direct U.S. diplomats, to receive memorials from foreign emissaries, and to control negotiations with foreign nations. Additionally, the act authorized the president to delegate other foreign affairs authorities to the secretary.[121] If the president could receive ambassadors and make treaties only, as Helvidius insisted, then why had the act creating the Department of Foreign Affairs *assumed* that he could instruct U.S. diplomats, receive foreign petitions, direct all foreign negotiations (whether related to treaties or not), and exercise still other foreign-relations powers? This statutory authority to delegate foreign affairs powers neither granted by statute nor specified by constitutional provisions made sense only under the theory that the executive power conveyed generic foreign affairs powers.

Helvidius's argument also was inconsistent with the advice that Madison gave the president about the executive's power to decide the grade and destination of diplomats. Recall that Madison had agreed with Jay and Jefferson that the Senate had no say on either because both decisions rested with the executive.[122] Nothing in the Constitution, other than the grant of executive power, could support this conclusion.

Troubling gaps and inconsistencies were not his only difficulties. As William Casto notes, Madison "systematically refuse[d] to grapple with Pacificus."[123] Madison argued points unrelated to his principal argument denying the executive's ability to determine whether the United States, under the Treaty of Alliance, had to declare war on France's enemies. What could have been a plausible argument about the scope of the war power instead became an untenable assertion about the grant of executive power. For good reason, many have deemed Helvidius the loser of the debate. Madison perhaps agreed. Years later, he confessed that had come to "regret" the "polemic," which had been written in haste and under pressure from friends. He admitted that Helvidius reflected "a spirit which was of no advantage either to the subject, or to the Author."[124]

Limits of the President's Executive Power over Foreign Affairs

The Washington administration prosecuted those who ignored the Neutrality Proclamation and enlisted in France's cause. But juries refused to convict these Americans.[125] This led Washington to seek an act that would lay down penalties for neutrality violations,[126] a move suggesting that the acquittals stemmed not from jury nullification but from the sense that Americans fighting for France had violated no law. In requesting legislation, Washington perhaps recognized that only Congress could authorize the punishment of Americans. Despite his executive power, the president could not criminalize actions inconsistent with U.S. foreign policy or the law of nations.

This limitation arose from a sense that the executive branch could not exercise any lawmaking power. Though Washington initially failed to apply this principle in the context of neutrality, he understood it from the outset in other situations. For instance, when the Senate suggested that Washington withdraw treasury funds to implement a treaty, Washington demurred,[127] perhaps recognizing that using funds without a regular appropriation would have been contrary to the requirement that Congress (and not the president) authorize treasury withdrawals.[128] More generally, the Neutrality Act, the act creating the Foreign Affairs Department, and the many funding statutes demonstrated that outside the treaty context, foreign affairs lawmaking rested with Congress.

Other related constraints on the executive power over foreign affairs, such as the bar on presidential regulation of foreign commerce, were implicit in the Constitution's design. Unlike those governors who had state constitutional authority to impose short-term embargoes either to prevent trade with an enemy or to preserve goods for domestic use,[129] the president lacked such powers.[130] In the nation's second embargo act, Congress authorized the president to impose an embargo for fifteen days, but only when Congress was not in session.[131] The act's structure fairly proved that neither the president nor Congress believed that the president enjoyed any constitutional power to lay an embargo.

Shared Executive Power over Foreign Affairs

Recall that Montesquieu had stressed the need to separate the three governmental powers. Reflecting his influence, some state constitutions included declarations about the need to keep the powers separate.[132] Though the Constitution contains no similar admonition, Montesquieu's advice shaped not only its features but also its reception, since critics claimed that it blended powers inappropriately.[133] The separationist milieu, coupled with the tendency to read express grants as exclusive, led many to conclude that whenever the Constitution vested a power with Congress, it provided that only Congress could exercise the power. People applied the same logic to presidential powers.

Notwithstanding this tendency, some powers clearly were shared. They were shared in two ways. First, some powers were shared because more than one branch had the same power. Consider legal interpretation. Every branch may assert, and in many cases act on, its understanding of the law. Congress must interpret statutes in the course of its functions, particularly those related to oversight and impeachment. The executive and the judiciary likewise must interpret laws as a condition of enforcing them. Similarly, each branch must interpret treaties. The president must interpret them as a means of understanding U.S. obligations. Congress must interpret them for the same purpose, since it might need to enact implementing legislation. And the judiciary might be called upon to interpret and enforce a treaty's terms in cases before it.[134]

Though Helvidius mocked the idea that the executive could judge the meaning of the Treaty of Alliance, he was clearly wrong. The president might believe that the treaty obligated the United States to declare war against France's enemies. If so, execution of the treaty arguably required him to urge Congress to declare war. Congress would then have to read the treaty and come to its own conclusion about the nation's obligations. The fact that only Congress could declare war did not imply that the president lacked authority to interpret the treaty and judge whether the nation could be neutral until Congress provided otherwise. What Madison once said of constitutional interpretation—that no one branch had superior or exclusive authority over it[135]—applied equally to treaty interpretation.

Second, a power might be shared in the sense that the Constitution might divide it, assigning some aspects to the control of one branch and the rest to another. Three shared foreign affairs authorities are discussed below: ambassadorial dismissal, the power to communicate for the United States, and treaty withdrawal and violation.

Dismissing Foreign Emissaries

Dismissal of foreign emissaries might seem like an indivisible authority that must be ceded to one branch alone. But under the original Constitution, it was a shared power. The president may dismiss in certain cases, and Congress in others.

The executive power included authority to dismiss emissaries in peaceful contexts. When the French emissary, Edmond Genêt, proved to be obnoxious, Washington resolved to dismiss him. America's emissary to France was to notify that country of the insults offered by its emissary. He was to say that if the French diplomat continued much longer, the administration might "be forced even to suspend his functions."[136] Jefferson in fact told Genêt that the president could "interdict" emissaries, a not-so-veiled warning about his continued status.[137]

Washington reported to Congress the difficulties with the French representative, the request for recall, and the ultimate French acquiescence.[138] Congress understood that whether Genêt would continue to function in this context was a matter for the executive, for no member seems to have raised doubts about Washington's authority to, as Jefferson put it, "require the recall" of the French minister.[139] The ouster of a foreign emissary based on displeasure with his conduct was part of the executive power.[140]

Other ousters were in the domain of Congress. It had authority because certain dismissals were seen as informal declarations of war, left solely to Congress's discretion. In particular, if a nation had severe differences with another, sending that nation's emissary packing was a declaration of war; it signaled that the time for peaceful discussion was over.[141] Certain treaties expressly regarded dismissals as informal declarations of war.[142] Recognizing that certain dismissals might be ambiguous, John Quincy Adams suggested that Congress ought to clarify when the president could dismiss a foreign emissary and when Congress could via its declare-war power.[143]

The Shared "Sole" Organ Power

As discussed earlier, the president ordinarily served as the organ of the United States, no other entity having a generic power to speak on behalf of the nation. Moreover, nations came to address their messages to the executive, recognizing that the executive branch served, by virtue of the executive power, as the focal point for diplomatic messages. Consistent with these claims, many (including Jefferson, Hamilton, and Marshall) claimed that communications with governments was an executive prerogative.

But the president was not truly the *sole* organ of communication, because Congress had its own, albeit limited foreign affairs voice. It could "declare war," a phrase that resounds with the language of communication. It could pass laws regulating commerce, and it could define and punish violations of the law of nations, laws containing preambles and substantive text that would communicate to foreign nations just as a letter from the president might. When Congress declares war and regulates commerce, it generates written materials that speak not just for itself but also for the whole nation. Nothing would be amiss if Congress (rather than the president) summoned a foreign ambassador and conveyed a U.S. declaration of war. Were the rule otherwise, Congress would be obliged to keep its declarations of war and regulations of commerce secret until such time as the president conveyed them to foreign nations, lest those nations hear of them from other sources, such as a newspaper or members of Congress. Helvidius made this point when he said that with respect to declarations of war, Congress was the "organ of the will of the nation."[144] Madison clearly was speaking of Congress as the war decision maker, but seems also to have meant that Congress served as an instrument of communication too when it came to declarations.

Contrary to Representative John Marshall's claim, the president is but the primary organ of communication, for while he has constitutional authority over the vast majority of diplomatic messages, Congress can communicate in limited circumstances. The Constitution's division of foreign affairs authority requires as much.

Treaty Withdrawals and Violations

Though the Constitution specifies how treaties are to be made, it says nothing specifically about who may withdraw from, or violate, them. There seems to have been no consensus on these matters, leaving us the text and structure of the document, and scattered claims about treaty withdrawals and violations.

Madison considered treaty withdrawal as early as 1791, outlining some possibilities but drawing no firm conclusions. He asked who could decide to use a breach by the other party as a reason for declaring a treaty null and void. He suggested the answer might be either the president acting in concert with the Senate (based on its power over treaty making) or Congress (based on its power over lawmaking).[145]

The role that Madison imagined for the Senate is unclear. Perhaps he supposed that the Senate and the president jointly could withdraw from a treaty if the president proposed withdrawal and the Senate agreed (via supermajority or otherwise). Or maybe the Senate's participation might come in the formation of a new treaty that expressly or implicitly superseded the previous treaty.

Congress likely had authority over treaty withdrawal, for certain congressional powers convey the right to renounce voidable treaties. In particular, the power to declare war includes authority to decide whether to renounce voidable treaties. During the administration of John Adams, Congress withdrew from a treaty. It declared that treaties with France should not be "regarded as legally obligatory" on the government or citizens of the United States because repeated French violations of the treaties made it clear to Congress that the United States is "of right freed and exonerated" from the treaties.[146] This declaration was issued pursuant to Congress's power to declare war.[147]

There was a third possibility, one that Madison left unmentioned. When a treaty provides that a signatory may withdraw, the president may exercise that right. Likewise, where general principles of international law permit withdrawal from a treaty, the president may make that decision. When the president withdraws from a voidable treaty, he executes the nation's legal option; he executes, in a manner of speaking, the discretion that the law (the treaty) supplies.

In 1793, Washington and his lieutenants apparently concluded that the president could withdraw from a voidable treaty. After the overthrow and execution of the French king and the establishment of the First Republic, the cabinet discussed whether the president should renounce or suspend treaties with France on the grounds that they had been made with a radically different government. Hamilton favored suspension, which Jefferson opposed on international law grounds. Though the question whether to suspend was the matter in dispute, no one, not even Jefferson, argued that the president utterly lacked the power to use international law principles to renounce or suspend treaties.[148] As "Pacificus," Hamilton specifically argued that international law gave nations the option to renounce treaties that threatened their safety and asserted that the president could exercise that option and withdraw from treaties that endangered the United States.[149]

There is the separate question of treaty violations, in which a treaty remains valid but the United States violates it nonetheless. Though the president has constitutional authority to withdraw from some treaties, does he have the distinct constitutional authority to violate them while they remain intact?[150] Given the confluence of the Supremacy and the Faithful Execution Clauses, the better view is that the president lacks constitutional authority to violate a treaty.[151] Washington concluded as much. In a 1790 Senate message, Washington said he felt "bound to exert the powers entrusted to me by the Constitution in order to carry into faithful execution the treaty of Hopewell."[152] Washington felt obliged to execute the treaty unless a new treaty, creating a new border between the Cherokee and the United States, was made. That duty to execute would have been meaningless if the president simultaneously had constitutional power to violate a treaty's terms.

Others also concluded that the president could not simply annul or violate otherwise valid, nonrenounceable treaties. In a 1796 letter to President Washington about potential French demands to annul English treaties without cause (and thereby violate them), Alexander Hamilton claimed that the executive was "not competent . . . it being of the province of Congress by a declaration of War or otherwise in the proper cases to annul the operation of treaties."[153] Similarly, while discussing terms of the Jay Treaty (which ended the War of Independence), John Marshall insisted that the Constitution's Faithful Execution Clause required the president to enforce the treaty, a claim that presumed he did not have the right to violate it.[154] During the Pacificus-Helvidius debates, both sides spoke of the president's duty toward existing treaties, implying that the president could not choose to transgress them at will.[155] When the president disapproves of a treaty that he cannot renounce, he should renegotiate[156] or seek the legislative modification of implementing laws.

Having said this, one might conclude that the president occasionally should be less than totally faithful to treaties. Lax enforcement or loose adherence would be useful when it better served the national interests. Speaking of the Jay Treaty, Marshall noted that because the "executive" was responsible for executing a "national contract," it was "accountable to the nation for the violation of . . . engagements with foreign nations."[157] At the same time, he recognized that strict execution was not always sound: "If, at any time, policy may temper the strict execution of the contract, where may that political discretion be placed so safely as in the department whose duty it is to understand precisely the state of the political intercourse and connexion between the United States and foreign nations, to understand the manner in which the particular stipulation is explained and performed by foreign nations, and to understand completely the state of the Union?"[158] In the international realm, where no nation remains forever true to its commitments, Marshall's pragmatism is sound. While the president should honor national contracts, he occasionally might choose to be less than punctilious when the interests of the United States, as he understands them, run contrary to a strict adherence to a treaty. This seemingly less than strictly faithful execution of treaties can be justified in much the same way that less than strict enforcement of the laws often can be justified as a sound exercise of prosecutorial discretion and resource allocation.

Modern Attempts to Marginalize the Executive Power

As noted in Chapter 4, many scholars dismiss the grant of executive power as redundant. According to some of these scholars, the grant of executive power played no role in early practice and was little cited as a source of authority in foreign affairs. To justify the range of powers Washington exercised, these scholars cite the Article II clauses related to receiving foreign ambassadors, making treaties, and appointing ambassadors.[159]

At many levels, this claim misfires. Consider the Reception Clause. To begin with, it seems a mistake to read the clause as a power at all. The "power" to receive ambassadors is found in a section of duties and reads like an obligation—"he shall receive Ambassadors and other public Ministers."[160] A duty to receive ambassadors does not seem to convey power; rather, the duty plausibly suggests that the president otherwise has foreign affairs authority. That is to say, the clause assumes that the president has a generic foreign affairs power and obliges him to use this power to greet emissaries.[161]

Why impose this duty? Because by receiving a nation's emissary, the president conveys the importance that the United States places on a relationship. The Romans believed that the law of nations required countries to receive ambassadors.[162] Similarly, Emmerich de Vattel, in his 1758 work on the law of nations, explained why ministers had to be received and why emissaries should be sent to foreign capitals.[163] As Benjamin Irvin notes, the elaborate "performative ceremony" accompanying reception underscored its importance in the eighteenth century.[164]

If one wishes to grasp reception's significance to the United States, look no further than the rules in place before the Constitution. In 1778, the Continental Congress prescribed an elaborate "ceremonial" for foreign envoys, involving, among other things, the delivery of credentials, the use of a coach, numerous bows, and a formal speech.[165] It altered these rules several times, underscoring their importance.[166] Polished formality and an aping of European customs conveyed the impression that a fledgling, rough-hewn nation was somewhat sophisticated and had taken its place on the world stage.[167] Americans had to learn rules about bowing, toasts, lowering swords, and doffing hats.[168] For a weak nation that had secured independence only with the assistance of others, paying attention to diplomatic niceties might pay off handsomely. Just as the president must take care that the laws are executed, so must he take care to receive diplomats with the dignity befitting their nations.

Even if one regards the Reception Clause as a power rather than as a duty, the clause cannot justify all or even most of Washington's foreign affairs actions. The clause clearly cannot legitimate his control of U.S. diplomats, for to receive foreign ambassadors hardly gives one control over *America's* diplomats, overseas or otherwise. Nor can the Reception Clause be used to rationalize the president's role as principal organ of communication, for foreign emissaries were hardly the only means by which the United States communicated. Though the president of the Continental Congress received foreign emissaries,[169] no one imagined that he had these other, far more significant powers.

Some read the Reception Clause as at least encompassing the authority to decide which governments and nations to recognize. Perhaps the president may decide, in the act of reception, which governments and nations to recognize. But this still reads much too much into a modest clause. Congress may declare war and regulate commerce with foreign nations. These powers more strongly imply a power to decide which people form a nation and which do not. After all, the power to make a law regulating commerce with a foreign nation perhaps implies that the entity making the law in question can decide which territories and assemblages of people constitute nations. It would hardly be inconsistent with an ambassadorial-reception power (assuming, for a moment, that the Reception Clause grants a power) for someone other than the president to decide with whom the United States would have diplomatic relations. As a matter of text, in a world where the president may (or must) receive ambassadors and lacks a generic foreign affairs power, and where Congress may declare war and regulate foreign commerce, the legislative branch has a far stronger claim on the recognition power.

But we live in a very different world, because the Constitution grants the president the executive power. This explains why no one objected to President Washington's recognition decisions. Given his executive power and the absence of any generic congressional recognition power, the president had a superior claim to the recognition power. Washington's uncontroversial assumption of the power to recognize governments can be defended only by resort to the generic grant of executive power. While the Senate might refuse to send an emissary (by refusing to consent to the appointment), and while Congress may not recognize a nation in its statutes, the president may establish and maintain diplomatic relations with whatever governments he chooses to recognize.

The president's specific grants of foreign affairs authority—the power to appoint ambassadors and make treaties—likewise cannot be stretched to encompass all the authority Washington exercised. The appointment power cannot grant the president his communications power, for the former clearly has but a tenuous relation to the latter. U.S. emissaries are hardly the only means of communicating between this nation and another one. But even if they were the sole means, the power to appoint hardly conveys the quite different power to direct. No one has ever imagined that the power to appoint cedes the president the power to direct appointees (consider the rather easy case of federal judges). Nor can the power to appoint ambassadors some-how grant the president the generic power to formulate the nation's foreign policy, a power often exercised without the aid of overseas diplomats. Most of the first administration's policies were formulated with little direct in-volvement of these officers, something necessitated by their distance.

The power to negotiate and make treaties does imply some control of communications and foreign policy. But treaties hardly exhaust the means by which nations communicate. To the contrary, such communications constitute but a tiny fraction of diplomacy. Similarly, though treaties em-body foreign policy, they are hardly the only, much less the primary, means of crafting foreign policy. Nations regularly make foreign policy outside the treaty process. When we look to early practices, Washington controlled almost all communications between foreign nations and the United States and decided numerous matters of foreign policy, the vast majority of which had nothing to do with making treaties.

The final difficulty with trying to stretch the Constitution's specific for-eign affairs powers to encompass all the authority that Washington exer-cised is that no contemporary regarded those specific powers as authorizing the president to assume all the powers he exercised. No one claimed that the chief executive could instruct and remove American diplomats because of his power to make treaties. Similarly, no one as-serted that because the president had to receive ambassadors that he could therefore make nonbinding foreign policy.[170] When people articu-lated constitutional rationales for the president's exercises of power, they relied upon the generic grant of executive power. The assertion by some scholars—that the grant of executive power played no role in early prac-tice and was little cited as a source of authority—turns a blind eye to what people of the era actually said. Luminaries, including Washington, Adams, Jefferson, Hamilton, and Marshall, explained that the executive power included generic foreign affairs powers.

The Senate's Share of the Executive Power: The Case of Treaties

The power to make treaties had long been an executive power, having been identified as such by numerous writers. The English Crown had this power, as did its representative in the colonies, the governor.[171] Publius observed that if the United States dissolved, "it would become a question, whether the executives of the several States were not solely invested with that delicate and important prerogative."[172]

Of the outlines presented to the Constitutional Convention, only Hamilton's specifically vested the treaty power, allowing his governor to make treaties with the Senate's advice.[173] The Virginia and Pinckney Plans would have vested executive authority with their executives, thereby ceding a treaty power. For most of the convention, delegates did not take up the power. Some, such as James Wilson, assumed that the Senate would make treaties.[174]

Late in the convention, a committee reported out a measure that granted the Senate the treaty-making power, perhaps recalling the executive powers associated with the Roman Senate.[175] Some opposed the proposal on the ground that the power of making treaties "belonged to the Executive department."[176] Madison asserted that "the President should be an agent in Treaties."[177] Another committee eventually adopted Hamilton's approach: the president would make treaties, subject to the Senate's advice and consent.[178] After the convention approved this without dissent,[179] discussions centered on the two-thirds requirement and whether the clause would apply to peace treaties.[180]

The Treaty Clause triggered a good deal of criticism in the states. Some complained of the Senate's role, arguing that the president should have had the sole power to make treaties.[181] Others protested that if there was to be a check on treaty making, a distinct executive council might have been created instead.[182]

Under the Constitution, the president may make treaties with the Senate's advice and consent. When may the Senate advise and consent? In the modern era, Senates have typically advised and consented to treaties after the president has negotiated with other nations. But the Constitution permits the Senate to give its advice before treaty negotiations begin. Securing advice in advance of any negotiations would be useful in deciding whether to negotiate a treaty and what instructions to give negotiators.

Washington believed that the Senate could give advice before any treaty negotiations. In August of 1789, he personally consulted with the Senate to receive advice on a number of propositions. When the Senate declined to immediately respond, Washington became ruffled, apparently saying, "This defeats every purpose of my coming here."[183] Others have claimed that Washington more colorfully remarked that "he would be damned if he ever went there [to the Senate] again."[184] Whatever Washington might have uttered in exasperation, he did return to the Senate to get answers to his seven questions. And, he continued to seek prenegotiation advice, though he ceased going in person.[185] Washington submitted the eventual treaty, apparently concluding that the Senate's previous advice was no substitute for consent on the final agreement.[186]

On another occasion, after acting upon the Senate's advice to negotiate certain amendments to a proposed treaty, Washington ratified the revised treaty without resubmitting it to the Senate for its consent, concluding that he did not need to resubmit the treaty to the Senate.[187] In doing so, he acted against Hamilton's advice. Edmund Randolph, the attorney general, asserted that so long as the amended treaty conformed to the Senate's initial advice-and-consent resolution, the president could ratify it. If it did not conform to their previous advice, it would not be a treaty and would not be law.[188] Perhaps Randolph had the better argument, for no one objected to Washington's ratification of the amended treaty.

This particular Washington-era practice suggests that when the president acts consistent with an advice-and-consent resolution (passed with the necessary supermajority), he need not resubmit the final treaty to the Senate, because their previous resolution may be all the consent he needs under the Constitution. Moreover, if the Senate enacts an advice-and-consent resolution before any foreign negotiations, there may not be any constitutional requirement that the text of the final treaty ever be submitted to the Senate. In essence, the Senate might be able to set the necessary conditions that the president must satisfy in order to make a treaty. If the negotiated treaty meets those conditions, the president can ratify it without further Senate input.

When presented with a negotiated treaty, the Senate has three choices: consent to ratification, deny such consent, or consent with conditions. President Washington suggested the last option when he unsuccessfully encouraged the Senate to amend a negotiated treaty.[189] On another occasion, the Senate provided that it consented to a treaty "on condition" that its terms be construed a particular way.[190] Of course, the president may reject such amendments and interpretive conditions. But should he object to any amendments or conditions, he cannot ratify any treaty that lacks them. After all, the Senate did not consent to a treaty that lacks the amendments or conditions.

The Senate's power to consent to a treaty different from the one submitted to it by the president stems from its general power to advise, a power that, as we have seen, encompasses both advice issued before any treaty negotiations and to unsolicited advice. The general power to advise the president would seem to permit the Senate to draft treaties on its own and to urge ("advise") him or her to convince other nations to agree to their provisions. The president would not be bound to honor this advice, of course. Though nothing quite like this occurred in the early years, senators were the impetus behind the Jay Treaty, suggesting the idea of a treaty and possible negotiators whom the president might nominate.[191]

While people often speak of the Senate "ratifying a treaty," the Senate can do no such thing. It supplies its "advice and consent" only to the making of treaties, that is, it consents to the president's ratification of them, an act that finalizes them as international contracts and the law of the land. The Senate recognized this when it passed the following resolution for the first proposed treaty: the Senate "do consent to the said convention, and advise the President of the United States to ratify the same."[192] Only the president may ratify treaties, something Washington understood.[193]

Early politicians faced a host of questions about treaty implementation. As noted, the first president seemed to believe that he lacked constitutional authority to withdraw funds to implement treaties.[194] Yet he believed that Congress was obliged to enact implementing legislation. In particular, Washington insisted that the House (and Congress) had to appropriate funds to implement the Jay Treaty, for failure to do so would violate the treaty.[195] The House eventually voted to appropriate the funds, all the while insisting that it had the constitutional right to decide whether to appropriate.[196] The House resolved that when a treaty had provisions "on any subjects submitted by the Constitution to the power of Congress, it must depend, for its execution . . . on a law or laws to be passed by Congress." In other words, the House concluded that if a treaty contained provisions that pertained to the Article I powers of Congress, those treaty provisions could not create or constitute domestic law;[197] congressional laws would be necessary. The question whether treaties can create federal law and supersede state law (the extent to which treaties can, or must, be "self-executing") remains contentious.

Hamilton and Madison, antagonists on whether the president could declare neutrality, agreed that the president had to interpret and execute treaties. Consistent with this view, the president, with the help of his advisers, usually determined the meaning of treaties without seeking senatorial advice. On one occasion, however, Washington sought the Senate's counsel on the meaning of a treaty. The French had complained that a federal statute violated the Treaty of Commerce. Washington asked whether the United States ought to insist that there was no violation or else concede a violation and modify American statutes.[198] The Senate advised that he take the former course.[199]

Washington was surely not obliged to seek the Senate's understanding of the treaty, any more than he would have been required to seek the opinion of Congress on the meaning of an ambiguous statutory provision. The Constitution contains nothing hinting that the president must seek the interpretive advice of those who help make laws and treaties. By the same token, the Constitution does not forbid the president from seeking the views of Congress and the Senate about the meaning of laws and treaties. On this occasion, Washington seemed to be seeking nonbinding advice. He "recommended" Senate consideration so that he would be able "to give to [the French complaint] such answer as may best comport with the justice and interests of the United States."[200] The Senate's resolution "advise[d]" the president, suggesting that the decision was his.[201]

The Status of Sole Executive Agreements

Treaties are important, long-term contracts between nations.[202] Because of their significance, the Constitution creates a high hurdle to their ratification. But nations also make more temporary and less significant international agreements. As Michael Ramsey has pointed out, the Constitution itself refers to such agreements, for while it bars states from making treaties, alliances, and confederations, it permits states to make agreements or compacts, with congressional consent.[203] Because there is no constitutional check on the making of agreements and compacts at the federal level, the president may use his executive power to make them. In finalizing these agreements, the president must take care that his agreements not serve as substitutes to treaties, lest he circumvent the Treaty Clause's strictures.[204] So while the Constitution makes it rather difficult to form some international compacts—those that are significant and durable—it leaves less consequential agreements far easier to make.

Conclusion

Once we understand that foreign affairs authorities were conceived of as part of the executive power and we read the Constitution with that knowledge, a number of lost understandings come to light. First, the Constitution's text grants the federal government the complete panoply of foreign affairs powers. Second, the president generally may exercise those foreign affairs powers not granted to Congress or shared with the Senate. Third, the president lacks a broad foreign affairs lawmaking authority; his legislative role is limited to his duty to make legislative proposals, his power to make treaties, and his power to veto bills. Fourth, Congress lacks a residual foreign affairs power, for though its powers in this area are considerable, none grant generic foreign affairs authority.

From the perspective of separation-of-powers theory, the Constitution fractured the executive power over foreign affairs, providing that it would be exercised via three mechanisms. First, Congress was a partial successor to the executive Continental Congress, able to declare war and regulate foreign commerce via statutes presented to the president. Second, the president could exercise the executive power to appoint emissaries and make treaties, but only after first securing the Senate's approval. The Senate's role somewhat mimicked the use of executive councils in the colonies and states. Finally, some lesser but still quite significant executive powers having to do with the creation, implementation, and enunciation of foreign policy and control over the instruments of foreign policy were granted to the president to be exercised at his discretion. In these areas, the executive was strictly unitary.

In this way, the Constitution energized certain aspects of the executive power, thus ameliorating problems associated with the Continental

Congress's exercise of executive power under the Articles. At the same time, the Constitution left the most consequential executive powers with Congress and made other vital powers exercisable only with the Senate's consent. With respect to the most significant executive powers, the Founders decided that it was better to divide and check the executive power, thereby obstructing hasty decisions. The nation might regret injudicious decisions to go to war and enter into ill-advised treaties.

CHAPTER SEVEN

"FIRST GENERAL AND ADMIRAL OF THE CONFEDERACY"

As a formal matter, the Constitution steers clear of ceding its unitary executive anything approaching unbridled command of the armed forces. As a practical matter, it avoids ceding complete control of the military to a fractious, sluggish executive committee. The result is a single executive who has sufficient authority over the military but is nonetheless checked by Congress and its laws, and hence is not potent enough to pose a continuous threat to the republic. The Constitution achieves this happy medium by re-creating a familiar, subordinate military office and by appending to it a number of nonmilitary authorities that typically enable the president to thwart or mitigate congressional micromanagement.

While the president occupies a powerful military office, the commander in chief has no right to direct the military free from legislative interference. No prior commander in chief, of whatever sort, had such autonomy. English and American commanders in chief always had been subject to direction, including during the Revolutionary War. Hence, in making the president "Commander in Chief," the Constitution used a phrase indicating command of the military, but not one implying autonomy. Just as importantly, the Constitution grants Congress sweeping authority over the armed forces. To be sure, Congress is not a collective commander in chief. Its members cannot even serve in the military, much less direct units from the battlefield. Yet subject to a few important constraints, the Constitution gives Congress plenary authority over the military. Only Congress may declare war, impose a system of military justice, and raise, fund, and equip the military; the commander in chief may do none of this. Additionally, under its power to create rules for the military's government and regulation, Congress may dictate how soldiers will train, where they will patrol, and what sorts of targets to attack during a war.

Despite its near-complete power over the military, Congress often regulates with a light touch. Members often will be (rightly) unwilling to micromanage such things as battlefield operations. Even when legislators wish to impose such regulation, bicameralism and the delays endemic to the legislative process will constrain them. And after a bill emerges from Congress, the president may veto it because he believes it too intrusive or unwise. These factors yield a commander in chief that lacks any constitutionally conferred military autonomy but nonetheless enjoys, in practice, considerable latitude on military matters.[1]

The Executive Power and the Use of Military Force

The executive power traditionally included power over the military. John Locke spoke of the executive power as "being possessed of the force of the commonwealth."[2] Montesquieu noted that the power encompassed the power to establish "the public security" and provide "against invasions."[3] A Cambridge professor claimed that the "second branch of executive power" acted with "the common strength or joynt force of the society to guard against such injuries, as threaten it from without . . . or to inflict punishment upon the authors and abettors of them."[4] In *The Federalist Papers*, Hamilton observed that the "power of directing and employing the common strength, forms an usual and essential part in the definition of the executive authority."[5] No doubt exaggerating to make his point, one Frenchman asked whether the executive power was "any thing else than the right of employing the public force?"[6]

It seemed relatively certain that the Constitution's executive would command the military. Delegates such as Gouverneur Morris observed that "[i]t is the duty of the Executive to appoint the officers & to command the forces of the Republic."[7] Given that the phrase "executive power" included command of the public force, what further purpose was served by the Commander in Chief Clause of Article II, section 2?

One answer lies in the need to counter possible implications of the many grants of executive power to Congress. Apart from the Commander in Chief Clause, the Constitution grants every war and military power to Congress. As noted, Congress may declare war, raise the army and navy, and fund, govern, and regulate the armed forces and the militia. Given the breadth of congressional power, there may have been no residue of military authority left to the president via the grant of executive power. In other words, in the absence of the Commander in Chief Clause, some might have supposed that the president had no power over the military, because the Constitution arguably granted Congress all such power.

Alternatively, the Commander in Chief Clause might limit the grant of executive power because it makes clear that though the president commands the military, he cannot control the militia until it is called into federal service. Under this reading, the Commander in Chief Clause establishes that unlike many state executives, the president has no constitutional right to call forth or employ the militia.

Whatever the precise relationship between the Executive Power and Commander in Chief Clauses, the scope of the president's military authority was well understood at the founding. To garner a better sense of that authority, it makes sense to begin with war and military powers that rest exclusively with Congress.

Exceptions to the Executive Power over the Public Force

Exceptions to, or limitations on, the president's executive power over the military arise in two ways. First, by conveying certain military authority to Congress, the Constitution creates implicit exceptions to the power to deploy the common force. For example, despite his executive power, the president can neither declare war nor raise an army. Second, certain military powers did not rest with the president not so much because the Constitution makes them exceptions to the executive power, but because they were not understood to be part of that power in the first place. In particular, the president cannot punish members of the military; neither chief executives nor commanders in chief enjoyed a unilateral power to fine, imprison, or execute soldiers for their military crimes.

Declaring War

All agree that because the Constitution grants Congress the power to declare war, only Congress may issue formal declarations of war. Most scholars also acknowledge that as a matter of eighteenth-century practice, nations often waged wars without first formally declaring them. Beyond these basics, the consensus fragments.

Many scholars suppose that because Congress may declare war, only it can decide whether the nation should wage war.[8] Their argument often eschews constitutional text, resting instead on the intent of the Framers. They admit that the declare-war power was obsolete in the eighteenth century because nations typically fought wars without first declaring their intent to do so. Nonetheless, because the Founders intended Congress to decide whether the nation should go to war, we ought to read the Constitution as if it granted Congress that power. In a sense, these scholars would have readers fix the Constitution's text via interpretation in a bid to better reflect what the drafters intended.[9]

Another group largely eschews the intent of the Framers, emphasizing constitutional text. According to these scholars, because nations could wage hostilities without first formally declaring war, the Declare War Clause does not speak to situations in which the nation wages war without a formal declaration. In other words, the Constitution does not grant Congress the power to decide whether to wage war, just the narrow power to issue formal declarations. Because the executive power includes the authority to decide whether to wage war, the president may elect to wage it. In sum, when the president orders troops and fleets to war, thereby exercising his executive power, he neither declares war nor usurps any congressional power.[10]

These modern perspectives misconstrue the declare-war power, reading it far too narrowly. That power went beyond the authority to issue formal war declarations and encompassed any decision to wage war, however made. Because a declaration of war was a signal evincing a decision to wage war, any formal or informal signal that revealed a choice to go to war was a war declaration and an exercise of the power to declare war.

Formal declarations are the most familiar ways that nations signal their intent to wage war, so much so that if a formal declaration does not mark the onset of modern hostilities, many regard it as an "undeclared war."[11] Though formal declarations of war existed in the eighteenth century, they hardly ever marked the onset of hostilities, and they were not issued in all wars.[12] But the absence of formal declarations did not mean that some or many eighteenth-century wars were undeclared.

Eighteenth-century statesmen adopted a functional approach to declarations in which both words and actions could constitute declarations of war.[13] What mattered was whether the words or actions reflected a decision to wage war. If they did, those words or actions were a declaration of war, no less so than a formal declaration. Sometimes a verbal or written statement dripping with enmity signified that a nation had chosen to wage war. For example, the Declaration of Independence's condemnation of the English Crown was an informal declaration of war.[14] Similarly, France's treaty of alliance with the United States (and the insolent notification of it) was seen as an informal declaration of war against England.[15] As noted in the previous chapter, disrespectful dismissals of emissaries also were war declarations.[16] One commentator even noted that it was "the common law of Europe" that when nations massed troops, gathered supplies, and baked biscuits, they had declared war, because it was obvious that they had resolved to wage it.[17]

The commencement of warfare was the "strongest declaration of war" because in fighting a war, a nation unmistakably had chosen to wage it.[18] For that reason, monarchs, legislators, and diplomats routinely described the commencement of hostilities as a war declaration.[19] For instance, John Adams noted that by attacking each other during the Revolutionary War, France and England had declared war.[20] Likewise, the English prime minister Robert Walpole noted in 1738 that informal declarations were commonplace, and wars typically were first declared via the "mouths of cannons."[21]

The declare-war power not only encompassed the authority to decide to start a war, but also included the power to decide whether to wage war in response to a war declaration. After one nation declared war, the victim faced a choice: wage war or sue for peace.[22] Because nations had a choice, the decision to wage war in response to a declaration of war was

quite meaningful. When nations chose to fight, some responded to a declaration of war by issuing a formal declaration of their own.[23] Others
waged war in response, thereby informally declaring war.[24]

Because Congress has power to declare war and not merely the power
to decide whether the United States will be the aggressor, it may decide
whether the nation will wage war in response to another nation's declaration. Though Alexander Hamilton mocked Thomas Jefferson's public en-
dorsement of this reading of the Constitution,[25] constitutional text and
early practice decisively favored Jefferson. As noted, the recipient of a
declaration chose whether to declare war in response, and nations that
chose to fight were seen as declaring war. Moreover, across several administrations, presidents and their staffs understood that if the nation was
to wage war, Congress had to authorize that warfare. When several
Indian tribes declared war against the United States, George Washington
observed (with Hamilton's concurrence) that because only Congress
could declare war, only it could decide whether to authorize offensive
measures against those tribes.[26] In the next administration, both John
Adams and Alexander Hamilton noted that France had implicitly declared a naval war against the United States. Nonetheless, Adams and
Hamilton understood that congressional authority for offensive operations was necessary.[27] Recognizing that it had to act, Congress, in a series
of statutes, declared a rather limited naval war against France.[28] As president, Thomas Jefferson repeatedly noted that he could not sanction offensive operations against aggressor nations because only Congress could
declare war.[29] Finally, the nation's first formal declaration of war was presaged by President James Madison publicly observing that while England
was in a state of war, America remained in a state of peace.[30] Congress
responded by issuing a formal declaration of war.[31] Like his three predecessors, the Father of the Constitution recognized that he could not wage
war until Congress declared it. In sum, because the power to declare war
included the power to decide to wage it, only Congress could determine
whether the nation would declare war, even when an aggressor had already declared war against the United States.

In theory, the declare-war power might have been a concurrent authority,
exercisable by either Congress or the president. Under such a scheme, the
nation could wage war if either entity declared it. Yet people understood

the power as exclusively vested in Congress. At the Philadelphia Convention, delegates suggested that the text meant that the president would not be able to declare war.[32] When the Constitution was presented to the people, James Wilson observed that "[i]t will not be in the power of a single man, or a single body of men, to involve us in [a war], for the important power of declaring war is vested in the legislature at large."[33] As president, Washington noted that "[t]he Constitution vests the power of declaring War with Congress, therefore no offensive expedition of importance can be undertaken until after [Congress] shall have deliberated upon the subject, and authorized such a measure,"[34] a claim premised on the notion that the president could not declare war. Treatise writers,[35] politicians,[36] and successive Congresses[37] agreed that presidents could not declare war. When Thomas Jefferson declared in 1789 that the Constitution had "one effectual check to the Dog of war[,] by transferring the power of [declaring war] from the Executive to" Congress,[38] he voiced the uniform view.

As noted in Chapter 4, the declare-war power encompasses more than the power to decide whether to go to war. Congress may determine whether its war declarations will serve a number of other functions traditionally associated with declarations. Besides ordering the use of military force, war declarations may command or authorize the civilian population's participation in the war, enumerate rules for trading with the enemy, impose restraints upon enemy residents, and declare the status of treaties with the enemy state.[39] In this way, the declare-war power resembles the Constitution's grant of generic executive power. Just as the Executive Power Clause grants a host of executive powers to the president, the Declare War Clause conveys a number of war powers to Congress.

Vesting Congress with the power to judge whether the nation ought to go to war replicated an arrangement from previous regimes. The Continental Congress had such authority, made express by the Articles of Confederation and its grant to Congress to "determin[e] on peace and war." But the Constitution's allocation was something of a continuation of British practice as well. While the Crown had the formal power to declare war, this power was almost always exercised after receiving Parliament's sanction. One reason was pragmatic; the Crown needed funds from Parliament to wage war and hence would seek its preapproval. Another reason arose from a desire to exercise discretion wisely.

On a matter of such grave import (whether to declare war), the Crown ought to receive the advice of its legislative council. Given the practice, members of Parliament and commentators argued that the Crown had to receive parliamentary approval before declaring war.[40] In a sense, the Constitution's allocation of the war power better reflected actual English practice as opposed to the formal allocations described in Blackstone and elsewhere.

Granting Letters of Marque and Reprisal

A closely related authority is the power to issue letters of marque and re-prisal. When executives declared war, they often simultaneously issued general letters of marque and reprisal, allowing any citizen to seize and convert enemy property. When executives favored narrow retaliation against another nation, they granted letters only to actual victims of an-other nation's depredations.[41] Had the Constitution not separately men-tioned this power, it would have been granted to Congress via the Declare War Clause.[42] Like the Declare War Clause, the Marque and Reprisal Clause creates an implied exception to the Executive Power Clause: only Congress may grant letters of marque and reprisal or autho-rize the president to do so.[43]

Raising and Funding the Military and Militia

Though the English Crown had the "sole power of raising . . . fleets and armies,"[44] it relied heavily on Parliament in exercising this power. The 1689 Bill of Rights provided that the Crown could not keep a standing army in England in peacetime without parliamentary consent.[45] So while the Crown might raise an army, it could not station it in peacetime England without Parliament's approval.[46] Lacking sufficient revenues of its own, the Crown relied on Parliament for army funds, too.[47] The Crown was so dependent that some Americans believed that Parliament had authority to "raise and keep up" the army.[48]

The Constitution expressly grants Congress the powers to raise and supply the military.[49] The first Congress established the maximum num-ber of soldiers; organized them into regiments, battalions, and compa-nies; and dictated their pay and rations.[50] As noted in Chapter 5, Congress in 1794 authorized the president to secure six ships to form a navy to protect commerce from Algerian corsairs.[51] The statute decreed the ships' firepower as well as the size, composition, pay, and rations of the crews.[52] Congress later ceded to the president the flexibility to vary crew size and composition, confirming that the 1794 law was obligatory.[53]

Under the Constitution, Congress may disband and defund the armed forces. Having created an army, it is under no obligation to continue it. In fact, the bar on army funding beyond two years[54] forces Congress periodically to reexamine the desirability of any existing army and, if need be, disband it via a cessation of funds. Consistent with the claim, an early statute provided that soldiers would be discharged after three years unless sooner discharged by law.[55] Similarly, the 1794 law creating the navy provided for its dissolution upon peace with Algiers.[56]

The clauses granting Congress the power to raise and equip the armed forces implicitly forbid the president's exercise of the same. The Constitution supplies several clues pointing to this conclusion. First, by providing that no army appropriation can last longer than two years, it strongly hints that only Congress can fund the army.[57] This is a limit on Congress, for as the Constitution elsewhere provides, laws must appropriate funds before the withdrawal of money from the treasury.[58] If one supposed that the president could fund the army as he saw fit, then the Constitution would have checked Congress's power to fund the army by limiting its appropriations to two-year periods while simultaneously leaving the president at liberty to finance the army for decades. Second, because the Constitution generally precludes the presidential creation of offices,[59] it implicitly bars his creation of an army or navy. If the president cannot create military offices, it seems quite likely that he cannot raise or expand the army and navy.

At the founding, commentators recognized that the power to raise and fund the armed forces rested exclusively with Congress. Alexander Hamilton, writing as Publius, noted that the "whole power of raising armies was lodged in the *legislature*, not in the *executive*."[60] Similar comments were made in the state conventions.[61] When President Washington assumed office, he understood that Congress would have to authorize the army[62] and the navy.[63] In addition, early statutes demonstrate that the president cannot raise or augment an army or navy. Statutes expressly authorized the president to accept naval vessels as gifts[64] and to accept "volunteers."[65] Such authorization would have been superfluous if the

Constitution had granted the president unilateral authority to raise and equip the armed forces.

English antecedents reveal that the commander in chief's power over the militia is subject to similar constraints. Before the English Civil War, the Crown could call out, organize, and discipline the militia.[66] Afterward, Parliament acquired and exercised considerable authority over it.[67] Parliament barred the militia's use outside the kingdom and imposed restrictions on the militia related to discipline and deployment.[68] It even specified the equipment that militia members needed to bear.[69]

By vesting Congress with the power to call out, fund, and equip the militia, the Constitution implicitly bars any concurrent presidential power. The Constitution hints at this when it provides that the president is the commander in chief of the militia only when it is "called into the actual Service of the United States."[70] If the president could use the militia as he saw fit, there would have been no need to speak of it being "called into" federal service. Consistent with this inference, Washington followed the militia statute to the letter when summoning state militias to suppress the Whiskey Rebellion.[71] Relatedly, only Congress may fund and equip the militia. Again, before the withdrawal of funds from the treasury, a law must first appropriate them, and only Congress may pass statutes.[72] Nor can the president finance and supply the militia by using his own wealth or that of private donors.

The most significant implication of the congressional monopoly on raising and funding the armed forces and summoning and equipping the militia is that although Article II, section 2 makes the president the commander in chief, the president may find that there are no soldiers, sailors, or militia members to order. Congress determines, via its statutes, whether the commander in chief has anyone to command.

Military Punishment

The Crown had limited punitive authority over its forces. Though it could enforce its "Articles of War" (rules of conduct and discipline) overseas, they were generally inoperable on soldiers within England.[73] On English soil, the articles functioned "as the rules of a private club," for during peacetime the Crown could only halt pay, suspend soldiers and sailors, or dismiss them.[74] Only in wartime could the Crown unilaterally subject soldiers in

England to military trial and punishment.[75] This regime was less than ideal, since the Crown could not punish deserters stationed in England during peacetime.[76] The threat of dismissal would not deter deserters.

Early in the seventeenth century, Parliament enacted articles of war for the navy.[77] Toward the end of that century, it passed annual Mutiny Acts for the army.[78] These laws proscribed a few acts, such as mutiny and desertion.[79] The acts also implied that the Crown could issue articles of war for the army, as it had done in the past.[80] Eventually, Parliament authorized the Crown to apply its articles of war and the court-martial system to all military offenses, wherever and whenever committed.[81] The Crown's dependence upon the Mutiny Acts became evident during lapses. Without an act of Parliament, the Crown again found that it could do no more than withhold pay, suspend, or remove.[82]

In America, the Continental Congress created articles of war for both the army and the navy.[83] Among other things, the rules punished mutiny, desertion, the destruction of enemy papers, and cowardice.[84] The Articles of Confederation regularized such rules by providing that Congress could "mak[e] rules for the government and regulation of the said land and naval forces."[85]

By granting the new Congress the same authority over the regulation and government of the armed forces, the Constitution continued the system in place under the Articles: only Congress can create a separate system of military justice. In the absence of articles of war authorizing the use of military courts and creating uniquely military crimes, military personnel may suffer loss of life, liberty, or property only via ordinary civilian courts using civilian law. As a matter of constitutional authority alone, the most the president can do is to cashier wayward soldiers and sailors. Fortunately, Congress always has supplied a system for military justice. In the earliest days under the Constitution, Congress created articles of war that established uniquely military rules and the court-martial system.[86]

Antecedents of the Constitution's Commander in Chief

Understanding the Constitution's many exceptions to the executive power over the public force gives us a sense of what the president cannot do. To go beyond this negative sense—to determine what he may do—

we must determine what a commander in chief is. Article II provides little help, for it confers the office without elaboration. The absence of an explanation of the office's contours suggests that the Framers drew upon prevailing conceptions of what it meant to be a commander in chief.

The office of commander in chief had many antecedents, English, state, and continental. Though the Crown could command the armed forces, monarchs were not regarded as commanders in chief.[87] Instead, commanders in chief were appointed by, and subordinate to, the Crown. The office originated in mid-seventeenth-century England,[88] when early commanders in chief of the English army served as generals of generals, able to direct all army officers.[89] But commanders in chief did not exist only at the army's highest echelon. *Any* officer was a commander in chief of his particular unit. A military dictionary of the era defined "General of an Army" as he "that commands [the army] in chief."[90] Similarly, a captain was "commander in chief of a company of foot" soldiers, horsemen, or dragoons.[91] A colonel was "commander in chief of a regiment, either horse, foot, or dragoons."[92] Evidently, "commander in chief" merely described an officer's control over particular units in an army or navy.[93]

There seems to have been no canonical definition of what authority commanders in chief enjoyed. Nonetheless, we can draw inferences from the definition of "general." Generals were to "regulate the march of the army, and their encampment, to visit the posts, to command parties for intelligence, to give out the orders . . . in day of battle, he chuses the most advantageous ground, makes the disposition of his army, posts the artillery, and sends his orders."[94] Commanders in chief of entire armies had such authority across all units, wherever stationed.

A further sense of what it meant to be a commander in chief comes from state constitutions. Several made their governors commanders in chief without specifying the office's contours.[95] The constitutions of Massachusetts and New Hampshire were more detailed. The Massachusetts governor was made "commander in chief" of the army, navy, and all military forces. The governor could "train, instruct, exercise, and govern the militia and navy."[96] He also could repel, pursue, and kill those attacking the state and seize their property.[97] Finally, he could exercise the "law-martial" over the armed forces and militia during war and when the legislature had declared the existence of a rebellion.[98] Though the Massachusetts Constitution ceded its commander in chief ample authority to fend off and attack intruders, it never granted him the power to start war.

The resolves of the Continental Congress are quite revealing. Washington's 1775 commission as the commander in chief of the Continental Army required all soldiers to obey his orders, vested him "with full power and authority to act as [he] shall think for the good and welfare of the service," and commanded him to "punctually . . . observe and follow such orders and directions, from time to time, as you shall receive from this, or a future Congress of these United Colonies, or committee of Congress."[99] Although this commission seemed to grant sweeping authority, it had a narrower compass than one might suppose. In late 1776, Congress made the commander in chief a "dictator," granting him a host of new powers. He was "vested with full, ample, and complete powers" to increase the size of the army; to apply for the aid of state militias as he judged necessary; to form military warehouses; to appoint and remove all officers under the rank of brigadier general; to seize property from private citizens, provided that reasonable compensation was paid them; and to arrest those disaffected from the American cause.[100] These powers were to last six months unless Congress rescinded them sooner. Evidently, Congress did not believe that its commander in chief previously enjoyed the powers to augment the size of the army, appoint and remove officers, erect warehouses, seize private property, or arrest Tories.

This quick survey of precursors yields a sense of a commander in chief's authority. To learn more about the Constitution's commander in chief in particular, we must focus on the authority and duties of the office and consider Congress's authority over the military and its commander.

Military Authority of the Constitution's Commander in Chief

The commander in chief enjoys extensive authority. Perhaps most importantly, he may order limited uses of military force. Moreover, like any general, the president may "regulate the march of the army [and] give out the orders . . . in day[s] of battle"[101] and "train, instruct, exercise, and govern" the military.[102] Further, the president may exercise all wartime discretion that Congress fails to exercise. Finally, he may assume command in the field.

Limited Uses of Force

As commander in chief, the president may order any use of force that does not encroach upon any exclusive congressional power over the military. Although only Congress may declare war, and though some uses of force constitute declarations of war and are exercises of the declare-war power, not all uses of the military constitute a declaration of war. When the military repels attacks, subdues pirates, or rescues imperiled citizens, such actions are not war declarations so long as they do not represent a decision to wage war.

REPELLING ATTACKS

From the beginning, Americans understood that executives could repel invasions or attacks. Recall that both the Massachusetts and New Hampshire Constitutions explicitly noted that their commanders in chief could fend off military attacks. Whether these commanders in chief would have lacked such authority in the absence of specification is unclear. Yet one imagines that chief executives and military commanders must defend themselves and their nations even without explicit authority, in the same way that firefighters created by a government must fight fires even when no law expressly imposes this obligation. In other words, while the office of commander in chief does not imply the authority to be the aggressor, surely it encompasses implied authority to defend oneself, one's troops, and one's nation.

At the Constitutional Convention, delegates understood that the new commander in chief could repel attacks. The proponents of the "declare war" language noted that the president could "repel sudden attacks."[103] Though one delegate believed that no amendment was necessary, he agreed that the president should "be able to repel and not to commence war."[104] Such comments suggest that delegates did not believe that either the original language or the amendment granted Congress a monopoly on the use of military force.

Members of the Washington administration certainly believed that the executive had constitutional authority to repel attacks or invasions. In 1791, some feared that the British might use force to evict U.S. settlers in disputed territory. With the approval of the commander in chief, Thomas

Jefferson advised that the Massachusetts government should "repel force by force" if the British attempted to dislodge settlements within the disputed territory.[105] Likewise, when certain Indian tribes declared war on the United States in 1792 and 1793, governors sought authority for offensive operations against them.[106] Washington and his cabinet agreed that though only Congress could authorize offensive measures, repelling attacks was entirely permissible.[107]

This narrow understanding of the president's ability to order uses of force against other sovereigns continued into the administrations of John Adams and Thomas Jefferson. Like Washington, each understood that though the commander in chief could not take the nation to war, he could order the armed forces to repel attacks.[108] When the president orders members of the military to defend themselves or U.S. territory, he neither declares war nor usurps any other war power that rests exclusively with Congress.

RESCUING CITIZENS

The commander in chief may order the military to rescue citizens located abroad.[109] A speedy rescue does not rise to the level of an informal declaration of war because such a mission does not evince any decision to wage war.[110] If U.S. troops take fire and hostilities become fierce, prolonged, and widespread, it may become necessary to secure legislative approval, since those military operations may constitute an informal declaration of war. The key question is how best to characterize the use of force. Has the United States gone to war against another nation, or has it merely engaged in a limited use of military force designed to rescue Americans?

The case of rescuing Americans highlights the complications of a general framework that is easily stated but sometimes difficult to apply. Though the president can command uses of military force, he must take care not to usurp the declare-war power. Hence, he cannot order any military force that would constitute an informal declaration of war against another nation. Though the dividing line between permissible defensive actions and impermissible informal declarations of war often will be unclear, it is a line the original Constitution required the president to respect.[111] Likewise, all soldiers and sailors, whatever their rank, must respect congressional power. No less than the commander in chief, they may not assume Congress's declare-war power by ordering or starting hostilities that constitute an informal declaration of war.[112]

SUBDUING PIRATES

Though the president cannot order offensive operations against a foreign power without a previous congressional declaration of war, he or she may order offensive measures against international criminals, like pirates and bandits. International law has long distinguished the predations of pirates and bandits from the military actions of nations. The Romans believed that because pirates were the common enemy of all, they could be attacked without any previous declaration of war.[113] Similarly, international law scholar Emmerich de Vattel claimed that nations could exact summary justice on pirates because they were "enemies of the human race."[114]

Early episodes confirmed that the commander in chief could use the military against pirates. In 1798, John Adams ordered the navy to seize attacking ships that sailed without the authority of governmental commissions, on the grounds that they were mere pirates.[115] Similarly, Thomas Jefferson twice approved attacks on pirates. On one occasion, Jefferson informed Congress that he had ordered the navy to capture pirates found within American waters.[116] Jefferson also retroactively approved the seizing of a pirate vessel.[117] There was no statutory authority for these uses of military force.[118] Apparently, both presidents believed that the Constitution authorized them to subdue pirates with whatever resources Congress supplied.[119]

Executive Regulation of the Armed Forces and Soft Discipline

The very title—*commander* in chief—denotes the ability to command. In the absence of any statutory articles of war, the commander in chief may issue general disciplinary orders.[120] Even where Congress has enacted such articles, the president may supplement congressional regulation with his own rules. For example, the commander in chief may regulate military training.[121] Should Congress fail to specify a training regimen, the president may impose one.[122] Even if Congress requires minimal training—mandating exercises three days a week, for example—the president may impose additional training. Consistent with these claims, the commander in chief of the Continental Army issued general orders touching on the use of guard codes, attendance at training exercises, and military preparedness.

The crucial difference between the presidential power to create military rules and the broader congressional power to provide rules for governing and regulating the armed forces is that the president lacks the unilateral power to fine, imprison, or execute personnel who violate his rules. Just as the English Crown had the power to withhold pay from soldiers, suspend them, or remove those who violated its articles of war,[123] the president can suspend or oust disobedient soldiers and sailors.[124] By the same token, just as the Crown lacked the unilateral power to punish soldiers on English soil, the president lacks such power in the United States. Though the Crown exercised legislative power over military personnel stationed overseas, the president stands on a different footing. He cannot unilaterally impose military justice, even on soldiers and sailors stationed abroad, because enacting laws and punishments rests wholly with Congress. If the president wants to do more than remove errant soldiers, Congress must authorize such punishments.

This modest power to discipline the armed forces mirrors what the president may do with respect to civilian executives. Under the Constitution, only Congress can establish punishments for civilian officers. The president cannot unilaterally impose fines or punishment on civilian executives, however useful they might be as a means of control. Nonetheless, as discussed in the next chapter, he can establish rules governing the conduct of these officers and remove disobedient ones.[125] The ability to remove is a useful (if limited) means of disciplining wayward or incompetent officers—civilian and military alike.

Wartime Discretion

Operating within the confines of the discretion afforded by a congressional declaration of war, the president may decide what type of war to fight, whether to escalate hostilities, and what objectives to pursue. The more open-ended the declaration of war and accompanying laws, the more authority Congress leaves for the president. The more detailed these laws, the less discretion the president enjoys.

If Congress does no more than declare war and authorize the general use of the armed forces, the president may judge which forces to use and how to deploy them. Congress took this approach in the War of 1812, delegating a large reservoir of wartime authority to President Madison.[126] He decided what type of war to fight—land, naval, or both.

Should Congress authorize a general naval war and do no more than indicate that protection of commerce is the goal, as it did in the wars against Tripoli and Algeria,[127] the president may decide how best to deploy the navy to secure this limited objective. Though the commander in chief cannot use the army or militia to fight such a limited war, or use the navy to pursue other objectives (such as regime change or territorial annexation), he still enjoys a good deal of discretion. The president may order naval vessels to convoy U.S. commercial vessels. Or he may decide that offensive attacks on the enemy's navy and privateers would best safeguard U.S. naval commerce.

Even when Congress declares a far more circumscribed war, many decisions remain within the purview of the president. In the so-called Quasi-War (1798–1800), Congress, as a means of protecting U.S. commerce, sanctioned the capture and destruction of only some armed French vessels.[128] Despite the war's seemingly narrow scope, President John Adams was left with much discretion. He might have authorized attacks only on lightly armed French vessels. Or he might have authorized attacks only when U.S. vessels had superior firepower.

Battlefield Command

The Constitution makes the president a general of generals. But his status as first general does not necessarily speak to the delicate matter whether the president may command at the head of an advancing army. May the president assume battlefield command? Or may he command only from afar?

This question may seem trivial. Yet there has long been a sense that magistrates are more dangerous when they assume personal command of an army. Soldiers might become blindly loyal to their leader and be goaded into overthrowing the government. The specter of an Oliver Cromwell was familiar in the eighteenth century. Some thought that Washington might use the army to seize power during the Revolution, a conjecture that made his resignation in 1783 praiseworthy. George III supposedly declared that if Washington resigned his commission and returned to private life, he would be "the greatest man in the world."[129]

A few state constitutions forbade commanders in chief from taking the field unless they first secured the approval of an executive council.[130] Presumably, councils would judge whether the risks of field command were warranted. Other constitutions granted commander-in-chief authority with no constraints on personal command, implying that the commander in chief could command in person.[131] One specifically noted that its governor could lead troops in battles outside state borders,[132] and another brimmed with indications that the commander could lead in person.[133]

Despite fears of a president turned dictator with an army at his back, the Constitution permits the chief executive to take personal command because it never provides otherwise. Presidents need not be armchair commanders, leading the military from afar.[134] Though the New Jersey Plan barred field command,[135] the prohibition never found its way into the Constitution, suggesting that the Framers never incorporated any such restriction. While Anti-Federalists exclaimed that a president might use field command as a means of seizing power,[136] no Federalist ever denied that the president could command in person.

Washington led the militia for a time during the Whiskey Rebellion before retiring to the nation's capital. His presence throughout the campaign was unnecessary because the aged chief had able assistants both in the form of Alexander Hamilton and the state commanders in chief. Nonetheless, had Washington wanted to lead the entire expedition, he certainly could have done so.

Military Duties

The president's powers over the military are accompanied by duties. The commander in chief must wage wars that Congress declares, because congressional declarations of war are not suggestions or requests. Moreover, subject to certain constraints, the president must honor and execute military statutes that Congress enacts in the same way that any admiral or general must obey the laws.

Waging Declared Wars

Some suppose that though Congress can declare war, the commander in chief cannot be ordered to wage hostilities.[137] This muscular understanding of what it means to be a commander in chief lacks a sound historical basis. During the Revolutionary War, no one could have imagined that either the English or the American commanders in chief could decline to wage the war that their superiors had declared. The muscular reading also unduly minimizes the declare-war power. Formal war declarations from the eighteenth century always commanded the military to wage war against the enemy. For example, George III's declaration against Spain in 1762 "will[ed] and require[d] ... generals and commanders of our forces, ... and all other officers and soldiers under them, by sea and land, to do and execute all acts of hostility against the said King of Spain, his vassals and subjects."[138]

The Constitution contains nothing that suggests a departure from the established view that commanders in chief (along with the rest of the military) had to wage a declared war. To the contrary, if a declaration of war becomes law, waging war is obligatory so long as it is constitutional. The Faithful Execution Clause requires the president to take care that a war declaration be faithfully executed.[139]

Early declarations of war, both formal and informal, authorized the president to use the armed forces to carry the declaration into effect.[140] While such declarations could be read as merely granting the president an option to wage war, they are better read as implicitly triggering the duty to faithfully prosecute the war. By creating a state of war and by authorizing the president to use the military, these declarations required (albeit implicitly) the president to wage war. Of the 1812 declaration, Justice Joseph Story noted that because Congress had declared war, the president was "bound to carry it into effect."[141]

At the same time, the president's duty to prosecute wars does not negate his other constitutional authorities. First, he can seek peace. Shortly after the 1812 declaration, James Madison supposedly tried to strike a peace with England.[142] If he had negotiated a peace treaty and the Senate had consented to it, he would have ended the state of war. Second, the president likely can agree to an armistice of the type that brought hostilities to a close in the Spanish-American War and the Korean War. The president presumably has the power to make armistices as part of his grant of generic executive power.[143] So while Congress can force the president to wage war, the president may exploit changes in circumstance and take a different course. The president's ability to end a war or to end active hostilities in some ways mirrors his ability to seek changes to, or repeal, statutes that he must otherwise faithfully execute.

Executing Military Statutes

The president's duty to implement declarations of war is an important example of a generic constitutional duty. If Congress has power over some area of governance, the chief executive must obey and execute any statutes pertaining to that power. The president's role as commander in chief does not change the equation, for this role does not exempt him from his faithful-execution duties.

In the late eighteenth and early nineteenth centuries, Congress enacted dozens of detailed statutes regulating the military. Congress specified the size of the army and navy, the stationing of the army, areas of naval patrol, army training and tactics, ways of firing weapons, wartime targets, and the branches of the armed forces that could participate in wars. These statutes reflected Congress's sweeping power over the military, derived from the constitutional authorities to declare war, raise and fund the armed forces, and make rules for their government and regulation.[144]

Despite the often-intrusive nature of these statutes, no early commander in chief claimed that legislative micromanagement was unconstitutional or that he could ignore such laws. To the contrary, they honored such statutes, never questioning their constitutionality or their duty to implement them. The words of the first secretary of war, Henry Knox, reflect the practices of early commanders in chief. When one governor sought authority for offensive measures against an Indian nation that had declared war, Knox replied that such operations were impermissible until Congress authorized them. Should Congress order something, however, the president would obey: "Whatever they [Congress] direct, will be executed by the Executive."[145]

Congressional Power over the Commander in Chief

This chapter's claim of significant but circumscribed authority for the commander in chief is in striking contrast with the extravagant claims made by modern presidents. Recent commanders in chief have insisted

that the Constitution cedes them considerable autonomy in military operations. Without such autonomy, they claim that they are not truly *commander* in chief. Some advocates of this view argue that if Congress can
direct operations, the nation has not 1 commander, but 535. In short,
modern commanders in chief claim that their office implies an ample
sphere of independence, one inconsistent with sweeping legislative power.

The best textual case for this autonomy arises not from the
Commander in Chief Clause but from the failure to carry over certain
language from the Articles of Confederation to the Constitution. Under
the Articles, Congress not only could govern and regulate the military,
but also had express authority to "direct[] their operations."[146] Though
the Constitution renews the power to govern and regulate the army and
navy, it lacks text indicating that Congress can "direct[] their operations." One possible implication is that because the Constitution does not
renew the grant to direct military operations, Congress no longer has that
power. By implication, the commander in chief has sole power to direct
operations.

Though this argument for the operational autonomy of the commander in chief seems strong at first glance, further probing reveals its
weakness. The power to make rules for the government and the regulation of the armed forces is a sweeping power. The same power, over any
other subject, is understood to convey broad power over that matter. For
instance, Congress's power to make "all needful Rules and Regulations
respecting the Territory or other Property belonging to the United
States"[147] is widely understood to give Congress comprehensive authority
over the nation's territories and property, power of the sort that a state
legislature has over its own territory. Just as there are no subject-matter
limits to Congress's regulatory power over the territory and property of
the United States, so too are there no subject-matter limits to its regulatory power over the military. The omission of a specific clause related to
operations was likely due to its redundancy, for that lesser power was
included in the greater power to govern and regulate the armed forces. In
much the same way, though the Articles specifically granted the power to
impose postage on mail, and although Congress, under the Constitution,
lacks such an express grant,[148] no one doubts that Congress can impose
postage. In fact, the implication that Congress may direct military opera-

tions is far more robust, because while the powers to declare war and to create rules for the government and regulation of the armed forces seem to clearly subsume the lesser included power to direct military operations, one can conceive of a power to create post offices and roads that does not encompass a power to charge postage.

Modern advocates of a sphere of military autonomy for the president seem unaware that the Continental Congress had an express power to direct operations. As noted earlier, they rest their claim on the bare fact that the Constitution makes the president the commander in chief. But the Constitution's text and structure give us many reasons to doubt that the office implies command without restraint. Though Article II never specifically constrains the commander in chief, it should be obvious that he is subject to a host of limitations. For instance, he cannot order the military to withdraw funds from the treasury, because his authority over the public force, considerable as it is, cannot be used to usurp the appropriations power.[149] Nor can he order the navy to divert commerce to particular ports, because doing so would violate the bar on port preferences.[150] Finally, in peacetime, the commander in chief cannot quarter soldiers within a home without the owner's consent; in time of war, involuntary quartering is at the discretion of Congress.[151]

More fundamentally, the claim that the office of commander in chief necessarily implies some military autonomy rests on a fundamental misunderstanding of the office that has no basis in eighteenth-century practice. Before the Constitution, every commander in chief was a subordinate; none were autonomous. The commander in chief of the British army was wholly subservient to the Crown. Moreover, as noted earlier, the title of commander in chief was not confined to the highest-ranked officer. It was associated with *any* military office that controlled a subunit of an army or navy. England had regional commanders in chief for specific areas of the empire, for example, a commander in chief for India;[152] it had colonial commanders in chief, for example, Colonel George Washington, commander in chief of the Virginia militia during the French and Indian War;[153] and finally, it had unit commanders in chief, such as captains and colonels. England had hundreds of commanders in chief, none of which were autonomous, because each had superiors.

This understanding of "commander in chief" as a subordinate office was not a casualty of the Revolution. Many constitutions made their state commanders in chief subject to legislative control.[154] Moreover, apparently no state commander had any exclusive military powers.[155] Yet they were no less commanders in chief.

The same sense of a commander in chief existed in the Continental Congress, for it directed George Washington throughout the war.[156] His commission obliged him to "observe and follow" congressional orders.[157] Moreover, he was not the only army commander in chief, for Congress created regional army commanders in chief[158] subordinate to Washington and Congress. Similarly, there was a commander in chief "of the fleet"[159] under the sole control of Congress.[160] Washington and the other American military men were not any less commanders in chief because they had to follow the commands of others.

The Constitution contains nothing suggesting that it meant to create a novel, autonomous species of commander in chief. It too assumed that commanders in chief would be subordinate officers. Consider the president's status as commander in chief of the militia. Whenever the president commands the state militias, pursuant to a law passed by Congress, he necessarily commands the state commanders in chief.[161] In creating a system in which multiple commanders in chief are subordinate to the president, the Constitution reflects the prevailing sense that the office of commander in chief did not come with any constitutionally protected autonomy. Put another way, state commanders in chief are not effectively divested of their offices every time the federal commander in chief directs them. The same is true when Congress directs the federal commander.

Early federal statutes clearly recognized that commanders in chief could be directed. Militia statutes specifically recognized that state commanders in chief were subordinate to the president.[162] Other federal statutes referred to subcommanders in chief in the army and navy,[163] each subordinate to the president. And as recounted earlier, Congress passed dozens of statutes regulating the military and militias, most of which constrained the commander in chief, thereby demonstrating that both Congress and early presidents understood that Congress could direct the military and its commander. The absence of vetoes suggests that no early president had constitutional objections to statutes that limited when, where, and how the military and militia might be deployed.

Within the executive branch, the subordinate status of commanders in chief was apparent. In 1798, President John Adams made George Washington "Commander in Chief of all the armies" in a bid to revitalize the army.[164] Neither man supposed that the president had thereby conferred upon Washington any autonomy from the constitutional commander in chief. Washington's commission provided that he served at Adams's pleasure and that he was to "Follow such Orders and Directions from time to time, as he shall receive" from Adams and from any president in the future.[165] This was conclusive evidence that both presidents understood that a commander in chief could command and yet still be subordinate.

In short, American usage and practice conformed to British traditions. Americans were quite familiar with the idea that there could be multiple commanders in chief in a single branch of the military. While each commander in chief enjoyed circumscribed military authority, none enjoyed a sphere of exclusive powers that ceded them a measure of military independence.[166] The president is commander in chief of the army, navy, and federalized militia in the same way that continental commanders in chief, including Washington, served under the control of the Continental Congress and in the same way that English commanders in chief served under the Crown. There is little or no founding-era support for the modern proposition that the office of commander in chief grants the president any constitutionally illimitable military autonomy.

Constraints on Congressional Direction of Military Operations

Though the office of commander in chief did not change with the advent of the Constitution, and though the Constitution does not affirmatively grant the president any military autonomy, a mixture of policy, institutional, and constitutional factors practically ensures that the Constitution's commander in chief will not be as subservient to Congress as the Continental Army's commander in chief was to the Continental Congress.

Regardless of what the Constitution authorizes Congress to do, members may see eye to eye with John Locke and conclude that certain decisions are typically best left to the discretion of the commander in chief.[167] Legislators often will recognize that when rules are too detailed, the handling of fluid situations becomes impossible. Sometimes decisions must be left to the discretion of those who have the most knowledge. Relatedly, when Congress enacts detailed rules, it may find it difficult to alter those rules quickly. After all, wars do not pause during congressional recesses. For all these reasons, Congress often is reluctant to micromanage the military's wartime operations.

Even when members wish to micromanage military operations, Congress often finds it difficult or impossible to do so. Many military decisions must be made in real time, in the heat of battle. Decisions like when to advance on a particular battlefield cannot possibly be determined by a distant legislature. Even with modern communications, it is impossible for a ponderous, bicameral legislature to make such decisions. Congress will never be able to dictate that a particular platoon advance or retreat.

Moreover, the Presentment Clause guarantees that the president has ten days to consider any bill passed before either vetoing it or permitting it to become law.[168] Any president who wishes to undermine congressional direction of ongoing military operations may issue contrary orders at any point from the time Congress begins to consider a bill until the time it becomes law. Between the time when members of Congress propose a bill and when it becomes law, almost two weeks might elapse.

Finally, the president's veto makes it tough for Congress to direct particular operations. Should Congress try to order a battlefield retreat, the president surely would veto the measure. In most cases, vetoes (or the threat of them) will preclude military micromanagement that the president opposes.[169]

Besides the Presentment Clause, a number of other provisions limit Congress's ability to direct military operations. The Commander in Chief Clause limits congressional power by implicitly denying Congress the power to create independent admirals and generals. If Congress could make portions of the army and navy independent, the president would not be commander in chief of the entire army and navy. Similarly, Congress cannot create an independent military department and vest it with the authority to decide matters such as a war's objectives and the equipment to be used in the war. Whatever wartime discretion Congress elects not to exercise, it must leave with the commander in chief.

The Constitution's impeachment provisions likewise constrain congressional power over the commander in chief because they implicitly bar Congress from treating the commander in chief as an at-will employee. During the Revolutionary War, dismissal of the army's commander in chief was a distinct possibility as some members of the military and Congress conspired to have George Washington removed after some setbacks.[170] Such removal would have been possible for any reason and could have occurred by a simple majority vote in the unicameral Continental Congress. Indeed, Congress sacked the navy's commander in chief for incompetence.[171] Under the Constitution, however, the only means of ousting the commander in chief is quite daunting. The House must impeach, and two-thirds of the Senate must find the commander in chief guilty of a high crime or misdemeanor.[172]

The president's ability to nominate and appoint also limits congressional power. By using its power to appoint all military officers,[173] the Continental Congress forced Washington to work with generals whom he regarded as deficient and with others who coveted his job.[174] Under the Constitution, the president may nominate all military officers.[175] Moreover, he may remove all military officers.[176] Hence, he can never be forced to work with incompetent, insubordinate, or disloyal subcommanders.

The Opinions Clause[177] suggests something about the scope of presidential power over the military. In particular, Congress likely cannot require the commander in chief to seek the advice and consent of others before making decisions. The clause provides that the president has the right to consult the heads of the executive departments, perhaps implying that he cannot be forced to consult.[178] Just as importantly, Congress arguably lacks constitutional authority to require the president to consult with others before exercising his constitutional powers. Though Washington, as commander in chief of the Continental Army, believed he had to consult with a council pursuant to a Continental Congress resolve,[179] any such requirement would be improper under the Constitution. Congress cannot replace the unitary commander in chief with a plural "Commander Council" that would effectively usurp and exercise the president's residual military authority.

Finally, the president may mitigate what he takes to be a harsh system of military justice. The president may pardon all federal offenses, including military ones.[180] Moreover, he may decline to prosecute military officers, just as he may decline to prosecute in the civilian context. For instance, the president may decide that a military trial would serve no purpose because an injured soldier already had suffered enough.

All in all, the president's other constitutional powers have a significant bearing on his control over the military. The president can delay and veto intrusive congressional micromanagement; can determine, to a large extent, who gets military appointments and who continues to serve as officers; and can mitigate any harsh military punishments that Congress chooses to enact. Collectively, these constraints on congressional power ensure that presidents generally will enjoy wide latitude over the military.

Conclusion

When Hamilton said that the president would be but the "first General and Admiral" of the nation,[181] he did not unduly downplay the power of the commander in chief. To be sure, the commander in chief has the authority common to military commanders, a power to direct that extends to all units of the armed forces. Yet this authority to command was subject to familiar limits. Like other commanders, the president cannot decide that the nation should wage war. Nor can he create and impose military punishments. Moreover, like ordinary generals and admirals, the president has superiors whose directions he must obey. The subordinate status of commanders in chief was well known, because every prior commander in chief, both in England and America, was subject to control; none had any autonomy by virtue of his office.

Furthermore, notwithstanding the president's status as commander in chief, Congress enjoys a sweeping, almost plenary power over the military. Exercising its powers to declare war and to make rules for the government and regulation of the military, Congress may regulate almost all aspects of the military, including operations. Early Congresses directed the military in a host of ways, creating military crimes, specifying training rules, authorizing the use of military force in rather limited ways, and even deciding which enemy assets to target and where the navy ought to patrol.

Yet despite Congress's far-reaching war and military powers, a number of factors limit the extent to which it can micromanage the military. Congress often is unable or unwilling to regulate distant battlefields. Even if Congress tries to micromanage the military, the president has many ways to constrain its meddling. He may delay or veto bills that regulate the military. He may nominate his military subordinates and dismiss them at will. He may mitigate harsh military punishments. Finally, there are constitutional constraints on Congress. It can neither create independent military officers nor require the commander in chief to consult with others as he exercises his residual authority as commander in chief. So while the Commander in Chief Clause makes the president but a "first general and admiral," the rest of the Constitution virtually guarantees that the president will enjoy great latitude over the military.

CHAPTER EIGHT

THE EXECUTIVE POWER "OF APPOINTING, OVERSEEING, AND CONTROLLING THOSE WHO EXECUTE THE LAWS"

What made the executive "the active principle" or "moving force" of all governments? It was not merely the powers to execute the law, steward foreign relations, and defend a nation, but also the authority to direct the officers who help animate those powers. Without officers serving as instruments of the chief executive, grants of executive power would have been largely illusory.

The English Crown was the "fountain" and "parent" of offices, having the power to create offices unilaterally.[1] The Crown appointed to the offices it created and could remove all officers serving at its pleasure. For good reason, King George III noted that ministers were his "tools" and "instruments."[2] Because the Crown could do little without its subordinates, the "chief royal prerogative was 'that the King names, creates, constitutes, and removes all the great Officers of the Government.'"[3]

The U.S. chief executive is not the fountain of offices. Congress creates them and may specify their qualifications, duties, and powers. Moreover, the Constitution requires the president to secure the Senate's consent before appointing high officers. Despite these checks, executive officers serve as the president's tools because the Constitution does not modify this customary and vital attribute of executive power. Executive officers execute the law, manage foreign relations, and guard the nation, all under presidential direction.[4]

Office Creation

In America, the power to create offices gradually came to rest with assemblies. During the colonial era, governors and assemblies both created offices.[5] In the states, the power to create offices likely rested with the assemblies.[6] At the national level, the Continental Congress created all continental offices.

The Constitution suggests that Congress retained its monopoly on office creation. The Appointments Clause speaks of presidential appointment of ambassadors, Supreme Court justices, and "all other Officers . . . which shall be established by Law."[7] Setting aside the president's ability to make treaties (which the Supremacy Clause makes "supreme law"), only Congress can make law, meaning that only it can create offices. The absolute bar on legislators from serving in offices created during their current legislative term points in the same direction.[8] The bar reflects the fear that members might establish offices and seek immediate appointment to them in the hopes of securing lucrative posts.

The Appointment Clause's origins suggest that only Congress may create offices. When considering an earlier provision dealing with appointments, James Madison proposed that the Constitutional Convention "obviate doubts that [the president] might appoint officers without a previous creation of the offices by the Legislature."[9] His successful amendment permitted the president to appoint "to offices," rather than the previous power to appoint "officers."[10] Perhaps believing that Madison's amendment was still unclear, the convention made another change, providing that the president could appoint "to all offices which may hereafter be created by law."[11] A committee later deleted that language, and the delegations approved the amended clause.[12] Toward the end of the convention, one delegate moved "that no officer shall be appd but to offices created by the Constitution or by law." After his motion lost, delegates decisively rejected a similar one.[13] In its waning days, the convention endorsed the Appointments Clause.[14]

Consistent with the view that the Constitution grants Congress the power to create offices, Congress created nearly all of them, including departmental secretaries, the attorney general, district attorneys, collectors, judges, and generals.[15] Overseas postings were the exception. Congress never created such offices. Instead, the president decided on a destination ("France") and grade (for example, "minister plenipotentiary") and forwarded a nomination to the Senate. If the latter consented, the president appointed to the posts he had created.[16]

Three justifications for the unilateral presidential creation of diplomatic posts seem plausible. First, overseas postings, whether treaty negotiators, ambassadors, or consuls, may not be "offices" under the Constitution.[17] But this lumps together dissimilar postings. While one might conclude that treaty negotiators do not hold offices, since their duties are meant to be transient,[18] that logic hardly applies to ambassadors or consuls, both of which are no less permanent than any domestic officer. In practice, early Senates routinely confirmed ambassadors and consuls, suggesting that they were seen as "officers of the United States." These persons also received the commissions due officers,[19] and many—including James Madison—spoke of ambassadors and consuls as occupying offices.[20] The idea that ambassadors and consuls are not officers and do not hold offices seems mistaken.

A second argument rests on the Appointment Clause's text. If one imagines that the qualification "which shall be established by law," applies only to "other officers of the United States" and not to justices and "other public Ministers and Consuls," perhaps the president may create overseas offices and Supreme Court justiceships. This reading is belied by a statute that set the number of justices (six), thereby creating those offices.[21] Needless to say, it would be odd for the Appointments Clause's provision "which shall be established by law" to apply to Supreme Court judges and all other offices, but not to the earlier categories (ambassadors, other public ministers, consuls).

The last justification for the president's creation of diplomatic offices arises from his executive power over foreign affairs. Given the president's generic foreign affairs authority, perhaps legislators concluded that the statutory creation of diplomatic offices might encroach upon the president's authority to recognize foreign nations and governments. While weighty, this concern hardly establishes that the Constitution bars Congress from creating diplomatic offices, for Congress could have created these offices without intruding upon the president's recognition power. Congress could have created generic diplomatic offices, leaving rank and destination to the president's discretion. Alternatively, Congress could have specified diplomatic rank but not destination. It might have created four ministers resident and three ministers plenipotentiary, leaving the president to determine their destinations. Finally, Congress could have specified destination and grade, but still granted the president some flexibility regarding the offices. For instance, it might have passed a statute providing "that the President, *at his discretion*, may send a minister to reside at the Court of St. James." If the president did not wish to send an emissary to Great Britain, the law would not have forced his hand. None of these statutes would have encroached upon the president's recognition authority, for none would have compelled him to do anything.

It seems likely that President Washington's creation of diplomatic offices was a constitutional misstep. If so, it was a misstep that has been replicated hundreds, perhaps thousands of times over the course of two centuries. When it comes to foreign postings, presidents continue to create offices, exercising a power long resting with monarchs.

As one might surmise, the power to create offices encompasses ancillary authorities. Congress may specify an office's authority and duties. The first Congress took this approach with the treasury offices and the attorney general.[22] Alternatively, Congress may cede the president the discretion to determine the contours of an office, as when it permitted Washington to choose which of his executive powers over foreign relations the secretary of foreign affairs would help carry into execution.[23]

Implicit in a finite list of powers and duties is an office's limited scope, meaning that the statutory description of the office is usually exhaustive. Example: The president likely cannot strip away the commerce secretary's statutory authority and grant it to the treasury secretary. If the president could add or reshuffle powers, he would enjoy the power to create offices, rendering the congressional monopoly over office creation illusory.

Second, the power to create offices enables Congress to set maximum tenures. In the wake of the Decision of 1789 (discussed later), Madison noted that Congress could limit tenure by statute.[24] Early Congresses agreed, occasionally establishing maximum terms.[25] They also provided that an officer's tenure automatically ended if the officer was convicted of certain offenses,[26] thus bypassing the impeachment process.

Qualifications and Exclusions for Offices

Though the Constitution fixes qualifications for the president and members of Congress, it does not set qualifications for executive or judicial officers. Hence, the Constitution leaves the vast majority of federal offices open to almost all, since it does not bar foreigners or the immature from serving as generals, secretaries, or judges. As far as the Constitution is concerned, the secretary of defense could be a seventeen-year-old Bengali.

This is not to say that anyone may serve as an officer. Rather than establishing qualifications, the Constitution establishes exclusionary rules. Officers cannot simultaneously serve in Congress. Relatedly, a member of Congress cannot resign and serve in any civil office created during the member's legislative term or whose salary was augmented during that term.[27] Finally, those whom the Senate bars from office by virtue of an impeachment conviction cannot occupy federal office again.[28]

Because the power to create offices implies the ancillary authority to dictate what sorts of people are fit to occupy those offices, Congress may set statutory qualifications. The first Congress provided that attorneys general and district attorneys had to be "meet" persons "learned in the law."[29] Curiously, district judges merely had to reside in their districts.[30] Financial qualifications were perhaps most common. Statutes effectively limited certain offices to those who could post bonds, which were meant to ensure that the officers did not abscond with federal property. The treasurer of the United States had to post a $150,000 bond, with "sufficient sureties," before assuming office.[31] Some collectors and surveyors had to post congressionally required bonds as high as $60,000.[32] Such qualifications extended to offices outside the treasury, such as overseas consuls.[33] Finally, other laws disqualified those who had been convicted of certain offenses.[34]

The statutory imposition of qualifications and exclusions was not entirely unforeseen. Before ratification, James Madison noted that without the bar on religious tests, Congress might impose one: "The constitution of necessary offices being given to the Congress, the proper qualifications seem to be evidently involved."[35] After ratification, a congressman observed that the "law may with propriety say, what shall be the qualification and what the disqualification of the officer."[36] Until James Monroe complained three decades later, no president seems to have claimed that Congress could not impose qualifications on offices.[37]

Congressional power to establish powers, tenure, and qualifications for offices arises from the same clause that permits it to create offices: the Necessary and Proper Clause.[38] Congress may create offices and specify their powers, duties, tenure, and qualifications in order to help implement the federal government's powers.

Nomination

Though Congress may set qualifications, it cannot impose such narrow criteria that it effectively selects individuals. That is because the Constitution expressly grants the president the power to nominate to offices.[39] Congress's implicit power to set qualifications must be limited, lest it be used to usurp the president's explicit nomination authority. Put another way, qualifications that do not leave room for presidential choice are not necessary and proper, because they improperly encroach upon the nomination power. Because the powers to create qualifications and to nominate do not share a neat boundary, discerning when Congress has intruded upon the president's power to nominate sometimes may prove difficult.

Relatedly, Congress likely cannot impose qualifications that have little to do with the office, such constraints not being necessary and proper for someone to implement federal power. It is one thing for Congress to require that army doctors be trained in medicine. It is another for it to mandate that they belong to a particular political party. The former constraint relates to the reason for establishing the office; the latter has nothing to do with medicine.[40]

The first president nominated over 350 persons.[41] When relevant, he took into account expertise, as when he rejected his nephew's bid to be a district attorney.[42] He always considered personal integrity,[43] and his pragmatism led him to favor the nation's "first characters," hoping their luster would rub off on the regime.[44] He considered geographic diversity for major offices and local residence for field posts.[45]

In choosing whom to nominate, he sought the advice of citizens and state officials, sometimes making inquiries about worthy men during his travels. But members of Congress had the most sway. Legislative influence predated the Constitution, as when members of the Continental Congress recommended deputy postmasters to the postmaster general.[46] Members of the new Congress continued the tradition, backing their favorites for field and national posts and denigrating their rivals and enemies. Thomas Jefferson once claimed that Washington passed over those who would generate "any material opposition,"[47] suggesting the weight that the president attached to legislative opinion.

The Senate's Share of Executive Power: Advising and Consenting to Appointments

Some precursors of the president, like the Crown and the colonial governors, could appoint unilaterally and hence lacked a distinct power to nominate.[48] Some colonial governors could nominate judges and executive counselors, but could appoint them only with the consent of their council.[49] In other instances, one chamber of an assembly might nominate, and the appointment would be made by an act of the entire legislature.[50]

The state constitutions contained even greater variation. Often, the assembly or the governor could appoint certain officers unilaterally.[51] Sometimes, the legislature could nominate multiple persons to the same post, and the governor would select from the pool.[52] Other constitutions granted the governor, acting in conjunction with some other entity, the power to appoint, never indicating who could put forward names for consideration.[53] In Massachusetts, the governor could nominate, but could appoint only with a council's advice and consent.[54]

The Constitution adopts the last framework. Several delegates wanted to vest the appointment power exclusively with the president, while others sought to lodge a portion with the Senate.[55] One proposal gave the Senate the power to appoint Supreme Court justices and ambassadors.[56] Additionally, delegates resolved that Congress could appoint the treasurer, as was the custom in many states.[57] A committee later proposed the

Constitution's nomination and appointment scheme, which, though criticized, passed without objection.[58] Still later, the convention eliminated
Congress's power to appoint the treasurer, leaving the office to be filled
under the normal appointment rules.[59]

The Appointments Clause was meant to unite presidential responsibility with the security of a senatorial check.[60] Some Anti-Federalists complained about the Senate's role, claiming a violation of Montesquieu's
separation maxim. Either the president would become the Senate's tool
or he would dominate it. Others claimed that the president should appoint without any check.[61] And still others wished for a distinct executive
council that could check presidential appointments.[62]

Washington understood the importance of making sound appointments, predicting that it would be "one of the most difficult & delicate
parts" of his job.[63] The rejection of Benjamin Fishbourn as a revenue
collector for Georgia proved him prescient. The Senate rejected
Fishbourn in August 1789 because of the opposition of Senator James
Gunn of Georgia.[64] After the rebuff, Washington entered the Senate
chambers, seeking an explanation. Out of respect for the president,
Gunn offered one, but denied that the Senate had any duty to explain.[65]
Washington later submitted a message asking senators to communicate
their objections before rejecting a nominee and to avail themselves of the
information that led to his choice.[66] Thereafter, Washington sought the
advice of senators before making a nomination rather than waiting for
their objections. By the time of the Adams administration, nominations
to local posts likely would fail if they lacked the prior approval of the relevant state delegations.[67] These early practices were the genesis of senatorial courtesy, the practice of members deferring to each other regarding
nominees to local posts.

In the wake of Fishbourn's defeat, the Senate formed a committee to
consult with the president about the proper means of carrying out its advice and consent functions.[68] The president sent a memorandum to the
committee, arguing that written communications were most appropriate
for nominations. If the president attended in person, some senators might
be reluctant to disparage a nominee because doing so might embarrass
the president. Moreover, the president might be argumentative or silent,
either of which would be awkward. Washington concluded that just as

the president need not explain his nominations, so too the Senate need not justify its refusals.[69]

In a second memorandum, penned within days of the first, Washington shifted ground. The Senate was a council to the president, said Washington.[70] Because it was the president's council, he could determine the time, place, and manner of consultation, even obliging the Senate to come to the president.[71] By rule, the Senate adopted his suggestions, providing that nominations might be made in writing or in person. If in person, the president might come to the Senate or might convene it elsewhere. The rules also provided that senators "shall attend" any such meeting and that the president could be present during voice votes.[72]

These early understandings suggest that the president may insist that the Senate vote on his nominees because, as his council, it must act on his nominations in much the same way that heads of departments must advise the president when requested. In other words, the Constitution arguably requires the Senate to consider nominees and treaties, meaning that indefinite delay on such matters is likely unconstitutional. To be sure, the Senate need not drop all business and may seek additional information about candidates and treaties. But it cannot interminably delay the consideration of either. Though the president has no legal means of forcing the Senate to consider treaties and nominations, he repeatedly may convene it and try to persuade senators to vote.[73]

Appointments

After the Senate consents, the president must appoint, for the former's imprimatur does not make an officer of a nominee.[74] The Constitution never specifies when or how an office vests, an uncertainty that became the subject of a now-famous early Supreme Court case. In *Marbury v. Madison* (1803), Chief Justice John Marshall claimed that President John Adams's signature on William Marbury's commission made the latter's appointment complete.[75] But he also equivocated, arguing that other notorious "public act[s]" might make an appointment complete.[76] President Jefferson later excoriated Marshall, insisting that an appointment vested only with the commission's delivery.[77] Others might have supposed that acceptance of the office was necessary to vest it.[78]

The great chief justice was clearly right that neither delivery of the commission nor acceptance of the office was necessary to consummate an appointment. A contemporary dictionary defined "to commission" as "to empower; to appoint,"[79] making clear that at least sometimes the act of commissioning is the act of appointing. Moreover, early practices indicate that neither delivery nor acceptance was necessary to appoint to an office. Instead, appointments might precede or coincide with the signing of commissions. The commissions of the Crown and the Continental Congress support this sequence.[80] President Washington's actions suggested the same understanding. Sometimes Washington spoke of a person being appointed before he received a commission.[81] Some commissions noted that the president "do[es] appoint" a particular person,[82] suggesting that the signing of the commission made the appointment. Further, the president's letters signaled that an appointment could vest irrespective of whether the appointee agreed to serve. In one letter, Washington notified John Rutledge of his "appointment" to the Supreme Court and went on to note that the commission was enclosed.[83] Those refusing to serve were said to have resigned.[84]

Evidence that appointment could precede delivery of the commission also comes from a surprising source. In 1790, Secretary of State Thomas Jefferson wrote a memorandum distinguishing appointing from commissioning. He divided the appointment of foreign ministers into five distinct aspects: destination, diplomatic grade, nomination, appointment, and commission. "[A]ppointment does not comprehend the neighboring acts of nomination, or commission,"[85] he insisted.

Yet just as President Jefferson was wrong to claim that an office can vest only upon delivery, Chief Justice Marshall was mistaken in insisting that an office can never vest upon commission delivery or office acceptance. First, the Constitution hinted that recess appointments were to be made via commission delivery. The Recess Appointments Clause provides that the president "shall have Power to fill up all Vacancies that may happen during the Recess of the Senate, by granting Commissions which shall expire at the End of their next Session."[86] The language could be read to suggest that recess appointments would be made by the act of "granting commissions."[87] If granting commissions meant delivering them, then at least recess appointments would be made by commission delivery. Second, the federal law requiring the secretary of state to affix the seal to commissions provided that the secretary had to "affix the said seal to all civil commissions, to officers of the United States, to be appointed by the President."[88] The text could be read as hinting that even after sealing, the appointment was incomplete—the officers were still "to be appointed." Third, Chief Justice Marshall endorsed the delivery theory for pardons. Writing for the court in 1833, he claimed that a "pardon is a deed, to the validity of which delivery is essential."[89] He never noted the apparent inconsistency with *Marbury* or suggested why pardons might be different from commissions.

What of acceptance being treated as the point at which an office vests? Acceptance had to matter in certain cases. For instance, suppose the president unilaterally appointed a senator to a low office during the Senate's recess. The Constitution forbids members of Congress from simultaneously serving as officers of the United States. If the president could appoint a senator to an office without his or her consent, the president has the power to oust legislators from Congress.[90] The point is that in certain situations, it makes little sense to suppose that the president can involuntarily divest persons of their current stations by appointing them to new offices. If that is so, then acceptance is sometimes necessary for an appointment to vest, whatever the president may desire.

So Marshall was wrong to insist that delivery and acceptance were necessarily irrelevant, and Jefferson was wrong to declare that delivery was all that mattered. The error that afflicted both was in supposing that the Constitution enshrined one particular means of appointing, to the exclusion of other modes. There is no constitutionally prescribed means of vesting offices.

The better view is that because the Constitution does not specify when an appointment must vest, it implicitly cedes discretion to the president. When appointing a secretary, the president can decide that the appointment vests as soon as the Senate consents. Or he may decide the office vests with the delivery of a commission. If he wishes to use a recess appointment, the president might choose to have the appointment vest if, and only if, the appointee accepts the office. In this way, the president can appoint in a number of ways, varying the method based on the context.

Circumventing the President's Appointments Council

The Constitution creates two means of bypassing the Senate's check on presidential appointments. First, the president may appoint to all vacancies that happen during the Senate's recess, the appointment to expire at the end of the Senate's next session.[91] This exception likely was thought necessary because offices might need to be filled when the Senate was between sessions. As Michael Rappaport has argued, the Recess Appointments Clause likely does not permit the president to fill offices that become vacant when the Senate is in session. More precisely, vacancies do not "happen during the [Senate's] Recess" if the office became vacant while the Senate was in session.[92]

Second, Congress may vest the power to appoint inferior officers in the president, department heads, and the courts of law.[93] This authority was perhaps thought necessary as a means of forgoing Senate confirmation for lesser offices. When proposed late in the Constitutional Convention, it initially failed before passing without dissent after an immediate reconsideration.[94] Although the clause is best read as permitting only Congress to vest intrabranch appointment power (that is, only courts may appoint inferior judicial officers and only executives may appoint inferior executives), the Supreme Court has held otherwise.[95] The effects of judicial appointment of inferior executives are blunted by the president's constitutional power (discussed later) to oust all executives, however appointed.

Commissioning

Under the Constitution, the president must commission all officers of the United States.[96] In England and the colonies, the authority to commission was vested in the executive. In the states, commissioning often was a gubernatorial duty,[97] something obligatory even when governors did not appoint the relevant officials. Given that Congress may permit someone other than the president to appoint inferior officers, the

Constitution contemplates that the president may commission those whom he did not appoint.

Besides a means of appointing to office, commissions served other purposes. First, when those issuing the commission also could create offices, a commission helped define an office's contours. The Crown's commissions to colonial governors often covered pages and pages in length, specifying powers, duties, and checks[98] and serving as quasi constitutions for colonies.[99] In independent America, commissions were far less consequential as a means of defining offices because statutes typically played that role. Still, American commissions might contain instructions illuminating an officer's powers and duties and might oblige others to obey the newly commissioned.[100]

Second, the commission was "public evidence" of the appointment,[101] serving as a police officer's badge might today. President Washington's commissions often began with the following: "To all who shall see these presents—Greeting." It then declared that a particular person had been appointed to a particular office. Officers sometimes had to return commissions upon leaving office,[102] lest they be used to bamboozle unsuspecting citizens. Other times, officers returned commissions in order to signify their fidelity to the public good and the rule of law. In a ceremony full of symbolism, veneration, and tears, Washington returned to the Continental Congress his commission as army commander in chief.[103]

Funding Executive Salaries and Expenses

As noted in Chapter 3, the Crown enjoyed a civil list annuity, typically set by Parliament at the outset of a reign, which was a permanent appropriation used to support all civil officers.[104] The civil list was a means of ceding the Crown a measure of independence because Parliament often lacked the leverage that came from an executive demand for periodic appropriations.[105]

Given that the Constitution guarantees salaries for the president and federal judges, the strong implication is that no other officers have any *constitutional* guarantee of receiving their salaries.[106] Chapter 7 discussed why the Constitution bars a statutory "army list." Though Congress may grant a long-term or permanent appropriation to the navy, the Constitution bars army appropriations that last longer than two years.[107]

The Constitution left open the possibility of a permanent civil list set at the outset of a president's administration. Yet early Congresses never gave up their means of influence. Instead, they passed annual appropriations.[108] Moreover, Congress specified salaries for officers, meaning the president could not set salaries himself.[109] Congress also set the fees that officers could retain from funds collected from the public.[110]

The Executive Power of Superintendence

Because Congress creates and funds executive offices, and because one of its chambers checks who may serve in office, legislators exercise considerable sway over executive officers. Yet once officers are in office, the president directs them in their day-to-day functions because the superintendence of executive officers is one of the most vital features of the executive power, and the Constitution never modified or abrogated that feature. These executives help the chief executive prosecute offenders, defend the nation, and treat with foreign nations.

William Blackstone noted that the king was "not only the chief, but properly the sole, magistrate of the nation; all others acting by commission from, and in due subordination to him."[111] Other chief magistrates had the same relationship with their officers. A minister for Louis XVI noted that one must

> distinguish executive power from its immense chain of intermediate agents . . . who, in all governments, definitively exert the executive power, or consummate its last act. It is to these agents that the function of executing the laws exclusively devolves; and, consequently, the executive power, considered as an attribute of sovereign power, consists in a right to give to its agents the order of executing the laws; . . . and the power of rendering them responsible for the execution. Such is the just and precise definition of executive power. It was in this manner that our kings exerted it in France; and in this manner that it has been exerted in England, and in all governments whatever; because it is impossible that it can be otherwise.[112]

In America, chief executives directed those immediately responsible for executing the laws, conducting diplomacy, and stewarding the nation's defense. As we have seen, in the colonies and especially in the states, the executive often lacked the power to create offices or appoint to them. Nonetheless, chief executives directed officers in their law enforcement, defense, and foreign-relations functions.[113] At the national level, the Continental Congress enjoyed the executive power of superintendence. The Articles granted Congress the power "to appoint such . . . civil officers as may be necessary for managing the general affairs of the United States under [congressional] direction."[114]

Delegates to the Constitutional Convention realized that their proposed executive would direct officers. Gouverneur Morris predicted: "There must be certain great officers of State; a minister of finance, of war, of foreign affairs &c. These he presumes will exercise their functions in subordination to the Executive."[115] Charles Pinckney similarly noted that the chief executive "will be empowered, whenever he conceives it necessary, to inspect the Departments of Foreign Affairs, of War, of Treasury," and that "[t]his inspection into the conduct of the Departments will operate as a check upon those Officers, keep them attentive to their duty, and may be the means in time not only of preventing and correcting errors, but of detecting and punishing mal-practices."[116] Late in the convention, Morris and Pinckney proposed that the heads of four departments—war, treasury, foreign affairs, and marine—serve at the president's pleasure and help him "conduct[] the Public affairs."[117] The convention never adopted this plan, perhaps judging that including a list of departments in the Constitution was unnecessary and unwise.

While the convention deliberated, Americans urged that the delegates create an executive power able to direct executives. One told Washington that there ought to be an executive council with power "to superintend the Collection of the federal Revenue—to direct arrangements in the military or naval departments—to appoint and commission proper persons to act under their direction."[118] The delegates failed to create such a council, creating a unitary executive instead.

In the states, the Constitution's creation of a supreme executive was well understood. Sometimes subordinates were left unmentioned, since individuals focused on presidential control. Consider the claim that the president would "superintend[] the execution of the laws of the Union,"[119] a statement implying that the president would direct executives. Others specifically discussed the president's relationship to other executives. Publius wrote that "[t]he administration of government" in "its most usual and perhaps in its most precise signification" lies "within the province of the executive department." Conducting foreign negotiations, preparing budgets, disbursing appropriated funds, and directing wars—these and other matters of a like nature were executive functions:[120] "The persons therefore, to whose immediate management these different matters are committed, ought to be considered as the assistants or deputies of the chief magistrate; and, on this account, they ought to derive their offices from his appointment, at least from his nomination, and ought to be subject to his superintendence."[121]

At the North Carolina ratifying convention, we find confirmation of Hamilton's claim. Some delegates feared that federal tax collectors might harass citizens. One responded that if revenue officers oppressed residents, the people could hold the president responsible: "The President is the superior officer, who is to see the laws put in execution. . . . Were it possible to suppose that the President should give wrong instructions to his deputies, . . . citizens . . . would have redress in the ordinary courts of common law."[122]

Anti-Federalists likewise understood that the president would superintend. *The Federal Farmer* argued that law execution was best entrusted "to the direction and care of one man."[123] A unitary executive was "peculiarly well circumstanced to superintend the execution of laws with discernment and decision, with promptitude and uniformity."[124] Again, declaring that the president would "direct[]" and "superintend" execution indicated that he could command subordinate executives.

After ratification, people spoke of a chief executive's power to command other executives. Justice James Wilson highlighted the advantages of executive unity. When "the executive power of government is placed in the hands of one person, who is to direct all the subordinate officers of that department; is there not reason to expect, in his plans and conduct, promptitude, activity, firmness, consistency, and energy?"[125] Wilson went on to describe an executive that bore a strong resemblance to Washington, the sitting president. In the House, a representative spoke of a secretary as being only "a finger of [the president's] hand" and said that the other secretaries were equally instruments.[126] A federal district judge noted the necessity of subsidiary officers to support the president:

"The business of the executive, is too extensive and various to be performed by one man. Many of its duties must be performed by subordinate Ministers, who are to be considered as assistants to the President."[127] A critic of Washington (and the presidency) said the federal executive had "a power for superintending the execution of the federal laws."[128] Someone more inclined to a robust executive noted that "subordinate executive officers, are the nerves of the public strength, to be united in the office of the chief executive magistrate, and subject to his controul."[129]

From the outset, the first president saw matters the same way. In 1789, when a French diplomat sought personal negotiations, Washington declined.

> [I]n most polished nations, a system [is] established, with regard to the foreign as well as the other great Departments, which, from the utility, the necessity, & the reason of the thing, provides that business should be digested & prepared by the Heads of those Departments. The impossibility that one man should be able to perform all the great business of the State, I take to have been the reason for instituting the great Departments, & appointing officers therein, to assist the Supreme Magistrate in discharging the duties of his trust. And, perhaps I may be allowed to say of myself, that the Supreme Magistrate of no State can have a greater variety of important business to perform in person, than I have at this moment.[130]

Washington understood that across nations, inferior executives, including the most prominent ministers, functioned to assist the chief executive. And he read the Constitution as not altering that familiar system.

Washington controlled the executive branch in a manner impossible today, resolving problems in the bowels of his administration. For instance, he admonished an executive to repair to the capital to carry out his functions, and that if he could not promise "immediate and steady" attendance to duty, he ought to resign.[131] On one occasion, the chief executive granted a leave of absence for a marshal and permitted his deputy to serve in his stead,[132] while at another time Washington insisted that a marshal issue judicial process himself rather than use a deputy.[133] When one officer became ill and could not function, Washington said he would "de[lay] making any new appointment" until necessary to do so, a clear signal that he might fire the officer.[134]

The president's control had dimensions extending well beyond episodes of dereliction. In a bid to avoid offending the French government, he considered creating government-wide rules to govern executives in their interactions with French exiles.[135] As recounted in Chapter 5, when his secretaries were absent from the capital, the president assumed direct control of their departments.[136] Finally, because the president directed the attorney general, district attorneys, marshals, commissioners of various sorts, and territorial governors, his control extended beyond the three great departments of Treasury, War, and State. In almost all these cases, he implicitly relied on constitutional authority to justify his direction, for most statutes said nothing about presidential intervention or control. That is to say, the president understood the Constitution as granting him a general power of superintendence over executive officers.

In a letter to his departmental chiefs, Thomas Jefferson recounted "with exactness" how Washington oversaw his subordinates. When letters came in, they were sent to the appropriate department. Then began a process of almost military precision: "[I]f an answer was requisite, the Secretary of the department communicated the letter & his proposed answer to the President. . . . [I]f a doubt of any importance arose, [the president] reserved it for conference. [B]y this means he was always in accurate possession of all facts & proceedings in every part of the Union, & to whatsoever department they related."[137] Washington, said Jefferson, "formed a central point for the different branches [of the executive]; preserved an unity of object and action among them; exercised that participation in the gestion of affairs which his office made incumbent on him, and met himself the due responsibility for whatever was done."[138] President Washington acted very much like a modern day Office of Management and Budget, ensuring that there was "unity of action & direction in all the [executive] branches of the government." The president's "power of decision," claimed Jefferson, left no scope for effective obstruction, because opponents could not "change the course of the Executive power."[139]

The best chronicler of early administrative practices, Leonard White, said that under prevailing practice and Federalist orthodoxy, Washington was the "undisputed master" of his branch.[140] The president regarded the secretaries as "dependent agencies," so much so that "[a]ll major decisions in matters of administration and many minor ones were made by the

President."[141] Much as George III had done in England, the president treated executive officers as his tools and instruments.

For all these reasons, it is a mistake to imagine that when Congress creates offices, it cedes them a portion of the "executive power."[142] More accurately, Congress creates offices and specifies what authorities and duties may be attached to them. The president fills the offices and, in the case of executive officers, conveys executive authority to them. Consistent with this conclusion, early commissions specified that the president "authorize[d] and empower[ed]" individuals.[143] In sum, while Congress specifies the metes and bounds of an executive office, the president empowers the officer.

Direction, Not Micromanagement

The "undisputed master" did not decide everything within his branch. For instance, he did not regularly second-guess the claims settlement of accounting officers. He once asserted that it was improper to interfere with claims and that he could not possibly attend to all of them.[144] At another time he said intercession was possible "in cases of [official] malpractice."[145] On a third occasion, he asserted that he did not interfere with claims unless they came before him "in the form of an act."[146]

Sometimes, the president was reluctant to intervene in other contexts. After an ousted deputy postmaster asked Washington to reinstate her, the president responded that he "uniformly avoided interfering with any appointments which do not require [his] official agency," and noted that the postmaster general had appointment power.[147] When one speculator complained about the commissioners charged with planning the new capital, Washington claimed that "[i]t was not . . . the intention of the Law" that the president "should enter into the detail" of the commissioners' work.[148] Similarly, when the architect Pierre L'Enfant complained about the same capital commissioners, Washington told him that the commissioners stood "'between you and the President of the United States,' they being the persons from whom alone you are to receive your directions."[149]

Finally, Washington's toleration of one of Thomas Jefferson's subordinates merits attention. Jefferson had hired Philip Freneau to serve as a part-time departmental translator.[150] Freneau also published the *National Gazette*, a daily newspaper relentlessly critical of the administration.[151] According to Jefferson, Washington had so denounced Freneau in 1793 that he took it as a signal to fire Freneau.[152] Jefferson refused to take the hint.[153]

What accounts for Washington's occasional reluctance to intervene? One might suppose that he read statutes that conveyed claim settlement and appointment authority to others as evincing legislative decisions to rest final authority with others, decisions he had to respect. In other words, he might have concluded that when a law authorized a specific officer to make a decision, only that officer could take action, and that the president ought not interfere, much less direct the final decision.

Regarding claim settlement, President Jefferson took this view: "[W]ith the settlement of the accounts at the Treasury I have no right to interfere in the least. [T]he Comptroller is a law officer. [H]e is the sole & supreme judge in all claims for money against the US[] and would no more receive a direction from me as to his rules of evidence than one of the judges of the supreme court."[154] One nineteenth-century attorney general, William Wirt, universalized the argument, claiming that whenever a statute authorized a particular officer to make a decision, the president had no right to interfere or revise the decision. He cited the absurdity of having the president decide all accounting questions as a reason why the president could have no constitutional power to revise the decisions of claims officers.[155]

In their legal arguments, both Jefferson and Wirt were mistaken. The comptroller and his accountants were bound to have latitude in practice. That leeway stemmed from their knowledge of accounts and claims, something the president could acquire only through an inordinate expenditure of time. It did not stem from the Constitution itself and could not stem from statutes. Contrary to Jefferson's claim, the president could revise the decisions of the accounting officers. The Constitution makes the president "the constitutional EXECUTOR of the laws,"[156] and hence, he is the *constitutional* law officer. The comptroller's status as a "law officer"—an officer charged with executing—could not preclude supervision, for the president routinely controlled numerous other law officers.[157] Contrary to Wirt's claim, the Constitution's grant of executive power means that the president has the authority to make any executive decision, even when a statute lodges a particular type of decision with some subordinate officer. That no president can review all claims against the federal government does not establish that the president lacks constitutional authority to review such claims, any more than the president's evident inability to review the millions of military decisions made by military officers signals that he cannot command generals and privates. To paraphrase Washington, the impossibility that one man could transact all executive business himself required the creation of subordinate officers. That very impossibility hardly proves that executive officers—civil, foreign, and military—can be made independent of the Constitution's chief executive.

When we delve into Washington's practice, we see that his occasional reluctance to intervene was grounded in pragmatism, not in law. His reticence with respect to Freneau reflected unique circumstances. Even as he despised Freneau, Washington desperately wanted to retain Jefferson. Washington could not oust Freneau himself, nor order Jefferson to do so, for either order would have hastened Jefferson's exit. The most that could be done was to hint that Jefferson ought to fire Freneau, which is precisely what Washington apparently did. That way, if Jefferson did nothing there would be no open rupture. The same logic explains why the latter ignored the implicit request. Jefferson knew that he could retain Freneau so long as Washington wished to retain him. Jefferson the subordinate had quite a bit of leverage over Washington the superior.

In some instances the president overcame his aversion to intervening. L'Enfant eventually secured presidential intervention, although not the sort he sought; his abrupt dismissal came not from his immediate supervisors, but from an incensed Washington.[158] The notion that the commissioners had exclusive authority over L'Enfant was nowhere to be found. The speculator who complained about the commissioners secured presidential oversight because the chief executive investigated the charges, finding them largely meritless.[159] The president's stated reluctance to interfere with monetary claims did not prevent him from delving into accounting matters and issuing orders.[160] Nor did it stop him from reviewing the claims (and complaints) of one shady bondholder.[161] Washington eventually sided with Hamilton and the comptroller,[162] both of whom asserted that the bondholder should not receive any payments. He reached that conclusion only after receiving opinions from Hamilton and Edmund Randolph about whether the holder had a valid claim against the federal treasury.[163]

Though Washington evidently did not intervene in all cases, his failure did not reflect a belief that he lacked the constitutional power to intervene. Rather his reasons for sometimes wielding a light touch were grounded in efficiency and policy. The president could not decide every executive detail, no matter how insignificant, for he would be overwhelmed with trifles. The light touch also furthered a sound reluctance to routinely second-guess subordinates. Doing so would undercut the subordinate's authority and perhaps sunder the bond with the president. Washington also knew his limits. What he said about commercial treaties—"that [he] was so little acquainted with *commercial affairs*" and "incompetent"[164]—obviously was true of many subjects. Ignorance about accounts, claims, and other matters was a reason to adopt something of a hands-off attitude, for the president could not acquire expertise in every matter that crossed his desk. Finally, the reluctance to intervene reflected the occasional need to appear "as little implicated as possible in the specific approbation of a particular measure proceeding from" an officer.[165] Washington understood that the better process consisted of initial consideration by officers statutorily charged with tasks, followed by his review if necessary. This mirrors the procedure that Washington described in 1789.[166] And it matches Jefferson's account of the president's approach to executive decision making.[167]

For all these reasons, it would be a mistake to suppose that Washington regarded executives as autonomous or that he believed the Constitution did not authorize his direction of them. As we have seen, Washington regularly interceded in matters large and small, directing the treasury secretary, territorial governors, collectors, and attorneys. The statutes creating such offices rarely authorized presidential direction, meaning that his authority usually stemmed from the Constitution's grant of executive power. Such statutes were, in all material respects, similar to the acts creating district commissioners, postmasters, accounting officers, and the comptroller.

Opinions

Some scholars argue that the Opinions Clause—which empowers the president to demand from department heads written opinions related to their official duties[168]—casts doubt on the claim that the president may direct executives.[169] Under this view, the clause was necessary in order to grant the power to demand opinions. Without it, the president would lack any authority to command opinions. If that conclusion is sound, however, it suggests that insofar as the Constitution is concerned, the president may not direct these principal officers; he may only demand their opinions.

The radical idea that the Constitution leaves the president a bystander in law execution and foreign affairs, with power only to demand opinions from departmental heads, lacks a sound foundation in text or history. As a textual matter, it disregards the executive power and other grants to the executive, clauses that indicate presidential control of executive officers. Moreover, it is inconsistent with what was said about presidential authority both before and after the Constitution's ratification, with many noting that the president would direct and superintend executives. Finally, the radical reading is wholly *inconsistent* with early practice, for, as noted earlier, President Washington regularly directed executive officers. He evidently did not regard himself as being limited to asking their written opinions on subjects related to their statutory duties.

Fortunately, there is a more plausible reading of the clause. In *Federalist* 74, Hamilton claimed the Opinions Clause is "a mere redundancy in the plan; as the right for which it provides would result of itself from the office."[170] The right to demand opinions arose from the office because, by virtue of his executive power, the president was the chief executive, empowered to direct executive officers. Hamilton had said as much earlier, calling executives "assistants" subject to the president's "superintendence."[171]

The manner in which President Washington sought and received advice supports Hamilton's claim that the clause was redundant, for the president and his subordinates paid no attention to the clause's seeming limitations. Despite the limitation that opinions had to relate to an officer's "duties," Washington demanded all sorts of advice—policy, statutory, constitutional—from his department heads. For example, he asked Hamilton and Jefferson for their opinions on the constitutionality of the first Bank of the United States; both complied,[172] even though neither had a statutory duty to opine on the constitutionality of legislation. Moreover, though the clause speaks of "written opinions," Washington routinely sought and received oral advice.[173] By the middle of his first term, Washington had instituted cabinet meetings, at which officers would express opinions.[174] These meetings typically ranged beyond the statutory duties of any particular officer, often yielding nothing but oral advice. Needless to say, if the clause was the only constitutional authority that the president had over departmental heads, Washington should not have demanded oral advice or written opinions about matters beyond their statutory duties.

Though the clause was redundant, it was so in important ways. First, the clause served as a visible "substitute[] for a council,"[175] making it clear that the president would not lack for advice. Americans were accustomed to advisory councils. The Crown had its cabinets and councils, and similar bodies advised state governors. In a break with the past, the Constitution lacked a generic council; the Senate's role extended only to appointments and treaties. Though the president undoubtedly would have had the implicit power to demand advice, the clause made the principle explicit in order to stave off criticism.

Second, the word "opinions" suggests that the ultimate decisions were the president's, not the principal officers'. Under the clause, the president may demand opinions related to facts, law, and public policy so that he may make informed decisions about law execution, foreign affairs, and the military.[176] "[T]he President will personally have the credit of good, or the censure of bad measures; since, though he may ask advice, he is to use his own judgment in following or rejecting it,"[177] said James Iredell at the North Carolina Convention.

Third, the clause confirmed that the president was the superior executive officer. Rather than imagining an arm's-length "information exchange," the clause assumes a hierarchy.[178] In his *Lectures on Law*, Justice James Wilson declared that executive power ultimately rested with the president: "In the United States, our first executive magistrate is not obnubilated [i.e., beclouded] behind the mysterious obscurity of counsellors. Power is communicated to him with liberality, though with ascertained limitations. To him the provident or improvident use of it is to be ascribed."[179] The power and the responsibility are his because he is the superior officer. As Akhil Amar observes, "With the Opinion Clause, the Framers rejected a committee-style Executive Branch in favor of a unitary and accountable President, standing under law, yet over Cabinet officers."[180]

Finally, as noted in Chapter 7, the Opinions Clause suggests that Congress cannot obligate the president to seek advice before exercising his constitutional and statutory authority. On certain matters—treaties and appointments—the president must get the advice of senators. On all other matters, the clause gives the president the option of seeking advice ("The President . . . *may* require the Opinion"), implying that the president decides when he should secure advice. Hence, Congress likely cannot require that the president seek advice before deciding matters such as whom to pardon or which bills to veto.

Removal

Even as the president directed the holdover secretaries and their departments the moment he entered office, some in Congress sought to insulate his successors from his control. In the discussions leading to the creation of the Department of Foreign Affairs—the debates preceding the so-called Decision of 1789—some representatives suggested that department heads were supposed to be free agents.[181] A small minority argued that officers could be removed only via impeachment, an absurd claim grounded on the fact that the Constitution mentioned removal only in that context. Another group argued that the Constitution empowered Congress to decide by statute whether the president could remove whom he chose. A third faction claimed that the president could remove officers only with the Senate's concurrence, arguing that because the Senate's approval was necessary to appoint, it also was necessary to remove. James Madison said this argument envisioned a "two-headed monster," with officers striving to satisfy both the president and senators.[182]

Arrayed against these groups was a much larger House faction maintaining that because the president was empowered to execute the law and was made responsible for a faithful execution, the better reading of the Constitution was that it granted the president the power to remove via its grant of executive power.[183] As James Madison put it, "Is the power of displacing, an executive power? I conceive that if any power whatsoever is in its nature executive, it is the power of appointing, overseeing, and controlling those who execute the laws."[184] He further argued that there was a "chain of dependence" in which the lowest, middle, and highest officers "will depend, as they ought, on the President."[185] The Massachusetts representative Fisher Ames echoed what Washington had said in another context: "The constitution places all executive power in the hands of the President, and could he personally execute all the laws, there would be no occasion for establishing auxiliaries." But since personal presidential execution of all the laws was impossible, the president needed "assistants."[186] Ames noted too that the "executive powers are delegated to the President, with a view to have a responsible officer to superintend, control, inspect, and check the officers necessarily employed in administering the laws."[187] Another member observed that officers were "the eyes and arms" of the president, "the instruments of execution."[188]

The Madisonians ultimately prevailed, and the House passed a bill that implicitly recognized a presidential power to remove. Unlike a previous version, the final bill cannot be read as granting the power to remove; instead, it discusses what would happen if the president removed the secretary of foreign affairs, text designed to make clear the authors' view that the president had a constitutional power to remove.[189]

The Senate evenly split on this question. Some agreed that the president had a constitutional power to remove,[190] while others denied any such power.[191] The vice president broke two ties, thereby ushering in a law that implied that the Constitution granted the president a power to remove all executives.[192] Acts creating the Department of Treasury and the Department of War had the same wording, confirming the Decision of 1789.[193]

Later statutes usually lacked text implicitly assuming that the president had a constitutional power to remove. Nonetheless, members understood that the president could remove. In 1800, a senator said the president could remove "every officer of the United States . . . at his pleasure."[194] Moreover, the conventional wisdom regarded the first Congress as endorsing the view that the grant of executive power included the authority to remove executives.[195] Even representatives who previously had believed that executive officers were independent of the president came to regard that view as erroneous.[196] Hamilton, who as Publius seemed to have argued that the Senate's concurrence was necessary to remove,[197] admitted that his earlier reading of the Constitution was mistaken.[198]

Washington agreed with Congress, concluding that he could oust his assistants. His views are evident in the commissions he issued and the removals he made. Although we lack copies of all the commissions that Washington signed, "during pleasure" commissions went to attorneys, a comptroller, a marshal, a collector, an inspector, and commissioners of various sorts. No statute authorized Washington to issue commissions with at-pleasure tenure. Acting on his belief that he could remove, Washington ousted over two dozen officers, including military officers, diplomats, consuls, collectors, and surveyors.[199] Again, no federal act sanctioned the removals. After he left office, Washington wrote that if an agent "is fd. incompetent, remiss in his duty, or pursuing wrong courses," the president must oust the agent lest the president be held responsible for the agent's dereliction.[200]

Reacting to the spoils system, later politicians reopened a question that had seemed settled. In the nineteenth century, men such as Daniel Webster disparaged the Madisonian claim that the executive power enabled the president to remove. By the Civil War, Congress had enacted a number of statutes that required the president to obtain the Senate's consent before removing certain officers. When President Andrew Johnson removed the secretary of war unilaterally, the House impeached him and the Senate came within one vote of convicting him. Removal cases found their way to the Supreme Court. The court eventually embraced the Madisonian view,[201] only to later read the removal power rather narrowly and to sanction statutory limits on its exercise.[202]

Modern Scholarly Attempts to Discern a Disunified Executive

Some scholars maintain that early presidential control of officers was less than complete because the Constitution implicitly recognized that officers and departments might have their own powers and duties and not be subject to presidential direction. Some also contend that Congress created nonexecutive departments outside the president's purview. The claims have textual elements, grounded in the Constitution, and historical elements, based on early statutes and practice.

Powers and Duties of Executive Officers and Departments

One respected scholar, Peter Strauss, argues that the Constitution supposes that departments and officers have their own powers and duties.[203] As evidence, he cites the Necessary and Proper Clause and the Opinions Clause. The former speaks of the "powers" of departments, while the latter refers to the "duties" of principal officers. If departments have their own powers and if principal officers their own duties, the president cannot treat departments and officers as if they were merely his instruments. Rather, the president can intervene only if departments and officers are unfaithfully executing the law. In cases of unfaithful execution, the president, citing the Faithful Execution Clause, may direct and, if need be, remove. But mere disagreement with an officer's lawful exercise of statutory discretion never justifies presidential direction or removal, says Strauss.

Problems bedevil this claim. In the case of executive departments and officers, the Constitution never grants powers and specifies only one duty—the duty to provide opinions to the president. Though Congress can specify the powers that departments and officers may exercise, it cannot strip away the president's executive authority and convey it elsewhere. As George Washington and others noted, when departments and officers exercise power, they implement the president's powers to execute laws, defend the nation, and treat with foreign countries. The departments were "instituted to relieve the President from the details of execution,"[204] as Jefferson put it, not to relieve him of his constitutional powers. Furthermore, early practice refutes the notion that departments and officers have powers and duties that are peculiarly theirs. Usually without any statutory warrant, President Washington directed departments and officers in ways inconsistent with the notion that they had powers and duties outside the reach of the constitutional executor of the laws. If the Constitution contemplated independent power and duties for departments and their officers, the first president and the rest of the executive branch (from secretaries to the lowest officers) failed to decode it properly, for the former "decided the course to be pursued" and the latter followed that course.[205]

Though subordinate executive officers have powers and duties derived from their offices, those powers and duties are no less the president's, whatever a statute might decree. We could say much the same thing about superiors and subordinates in many relationships. A colonel generally must use force to defend the nation. With no contradiction, we can say that the commander in chief has a superior power and the same duty. Similarly, the president's power to execute the law is superior to a law officer's statutory power because the president's authority derives from the Constitution.

The Possibility of Nonexecutive, Administrative Departments

Though the original Constitution mentioned departments in three places, only the Opinions Clause mentions *executive* departments. Two eminent professors, Larry Lessig and Cass Sunstein, suggest that "executive departments" are a subset of a broader class of "departments," a category that includes nonexecutive departments.[206] For instance, under the Appointments Clause, Congress can vest appointment authority in the "Heads of Departments," meaning that Congress can vest such authority in the head of any department, executive or otherwise. In contrast, because the Opinions Clause refers only to executive departments, it does not authorize the president to demand the opinions of the "principal officers" of the nonexecutive departments. The more general point is that the president lacks constitutional authority over these nonexecutive departments precisely because they are not executive, in much the same way he cannot direct the federal courts because they are not executive.

Lessig and Sunstein assert too that the Founders distinguished "administration" and "administrative" from "execution" and "executive." Under this theory, the president had a constitutional right to direct "executive" functions, consisting of those powers and duties described after the Executive Power Clause.[207] Hence, he could direct the execution of laws relating to military and foreign affairs because Article II, sections 2 and 3 supposedly granted him control over such areas.[208] In contrast, "administrative" functions consisted of implementing the laws enacted by Congress to effectuate its Article I powers, such as the taxation and postal powers.[209] Congress, via the Necessary and Proper Clause, could decide what role, if any, the president would play in the "administration" of "administrative" laws.[210] Congress therefore could forbid any presidential role in implementing administrative laws relating to the treasury and the post office.[211]

In his recent book on the first century of administrative law, Jerry Mashaw makes a different point, arguing that the Constitution "left a hole where administration might have been." He perceives an administrative gap because he supposes that the Vesting Clause of Article II is vacuous and that the Constitution is "silent" on most administrative matters.[212] He thus rejects the claim that the president was to have "directive authority over all administrative functions."[213]

The use of "Heads of Departments" in one clause and "principal officers of the executive departments" in another was (and is) inconsequential. Both referred to those who would help the president implement his powers over law execution, defense, and foreign relations.[214] The Opinions Clause mentions "executive" departments because a precursor was amended to eliminate a presidential power to demand opinions of the chief justice of the Supreme Court.

At the founding, there was no distinction between "administrative" and "executive." "Administration" meant "the active or executive part of government," indicating that these terms were synonyms.[215] Unsurprisingly, founding-era references to "administration" mentioned the president's central role in execution;[216] Washington, for example, repeatedly discussed his "administration" of government.[217] Moreover, there is no evidence that anyone divided functions, departments, and laws into two categories—executive and administrative—putting only the former under the president's control. Washington controlled all those charged with executing the laws.[218] In sum, usage in the eighteenth century tracked modern usage, which treats "the administration" and "administration of the laws" as synonyms for "the executive" and its "execution of the laws."

Was Treasury a Nonexecutive Department?

The claim that the Constitution contemplates nonexecutive departments may never have been made had early laws not lent surface plausibility to it. Congress labeled the War Department and the Foreign Affairs Department as "executive," but not Treasury.[219] The missing adjective leads some to suppose that Treasury was not executive. Some scholars add that the comptroller executed his functions without any presidential control.[220]

The adjective's absence was immaterial. Treasury was an executive department under the Articles of Confederation;[221] it was seen as such in the drafting,[222] ratifying,[223] and early congressional debates.[224] Before the creation of the Treasury Department, some in Congress said that its secretary should not report to Congress, on the grounds that doing so would grant undue influence to the executive,[225] a complaint grounded in the secretary's executive status. In addition, Congress recognized that the department's officers were executive. A mere nine days after the Treasury Act's passage, an act granting salaries to "the Executive Officers of Government" included all Treasury officers.[226] After the act's passage, members of Congress continued to perceive the department and its officers as executive.[227]

Washington certainly believed that Treasury was an executive department, for he directed it from the outset.[228] He ordered customs agents to monitor the activities of foreign ships that might violate American neutrality.[229] By calling out the militia to suppress the Whiskey Rebellion, he aided excise men in their tax collection.[230] The chief executive not only removed Treasury officials who neglected their duties,[231] he also reviewed their requests for leave,[232] a level of control inconsistent with the notion that Treasury was the first independent agency.

Hamilton, the first secretary of the Treasury, knew that according to the Constitution, he was the president's aide. In a draft letter to Congress written on Washington's behalf, Hamilton observed that "the Executive Power collects the tax and brings it into the Treasury,"[233] a statement identifying the department's functions as executive. In practice, the secretary acted as a subordinate. For instance, Hamilton sought permission to use Treasury's statutory authority to remit a fine.[234] Moreover, Hamilton's famous opinion on the constitutionality of the Bank of the United States stemmed from Washington's "order."[235] Given the lack of statutory authority for this "order," it fairly proves that Washington and Hamilton believed that Treasury was an executive department.

Those who claim that the comptroller "was not directly within the President's control"[236] cite James Madison. In the first Congress, Madison asserted that the comptroller—who would decide "upon the lawfulness and justice of the claims and accounts subsisting between the United States and particular citizens"—possessed judicial and executive features.[237] Given the office's supposedly blended nature, Madison proposed that the comptroller should hold office for a fixed term "unless sooner removed by the President."[238] This amendment supposedly envisioned the comptroller's independence.

The problems with this claim are legion. As Madison noted, his proposal was meant to make the comptroller highly responsive to Congress.[239] This in no way detracted from presidential authority to remove; in fact, his proposal expressly assumed an unqualified presidential removal power.[240] Moreover, his proposal went nowhere, because he withdrew it after criticism from his allies.[241] Why an amendment withdrawn by its author should be understood as conferring independence on the comptroller is something of a mystery. In any event, neither the Treasury Act nor any other early statute conferred an independence-enhancing tenure upon the comptroller.

In fact, the comptroller was an executive officer and was subject to presidential control. The act supplying salaries for "executive" officials covered the comptroller. Moreover, an early comptroller commission, issued to Oliver Wolcott, noted that the comptroller served at pleasure. Finally, Washington directed his comptroller.[242] There is no sound basis for imagining that the comptroller was, or was meant to be, independent of President Washington.

Conclusion

Congress is a necessary partner when it comes to officers and offices. Under the Constitution, only Congress can create offices, meaning that it may decide the powers associated with them, establish qualifications, and set maximum tenures. Congress also controls the purse strings, enabling it to set salaries and establish budgets for officers and departments. The Senate plays an additional, critical role, for it must consent to appointments.

Once in office, executive officers serve as the president's instruments. Officers are the vital means by which executive will becomes united to action. Without subordinates, the executive power is feckless and cannot possibly serve as the active force, since so few aspects of executive power can be exercised without the aid of others. Because executive officers help exercise presidential powers and because they exist to relieve the chief executive of the burden of executive details, the president may direct their execution of the law and their actions related to foreign relations and defense.

CHAPTER NINE

"NOT A SINGLE PRIVILEGE IS ANNEXED TO HIS CHARACTER"

The breadth of the "executive power" may cause some to wonder whether the Vesting Clause cedes all of the powers enjoyed by the eighteenth-century English Crown. Responding to the claim that the executive power included a power to remove executives, the South Carolina representative William Smith, in 1789, wondered whether the president inherited other Crown powers: "Can the President establish corporations? Can he prevent citizens from going out of the country?"[1] Smith knew that the president could do neither. He reasoned that "[w]hat powers are executive . . . will depend upon the nature of the Government." In a democracy, the removal power could not rest with the executive, insisted Smith.[2]

Though mistaken about removal, Smith's general assertion was on the mark. Like all words and phrases, the meaning of "executive power" may vary across time and across nations. Powers deemed "executive" in one government might not exist in another. Some powers generally considered executive nonetheless might rest with the legislative branch in a particular nation, making it possible that they will lose their executive tinge over time. Other powers generally deemed legislative or judicial may come to be seen as executive powers in a country where the executive en-joys them.

The president's executive power differs in important respects from the powers vested in some of his eighteenth-century counterparts. Some powers enjoyed by the Crown and colonial governors disappeared in America. Other executive powers rest with Congress and are best under-stood as exceptions to the Article II grant of executive power to the presi-dent. Because understanding the original presidency requires some sense of what it cannot do and what privileges it lacks, this chapter considers powers and privileges sometimes deemed executive that nonetheless do not rest with the president because neither the executive power nor any-thing else in Article II conveys them.[3]

Powers Foreign to the Constitution

Some powers occasionally seen as executive in the eighteenth century are alien to the Constitution. The English Crown's ecclesiastical powers are an obvious starting point. Though the Crown led the Anglican Church, could appoint bishops, and sat as a court of last resort in ecclesi-astical disputes,[4] the U.S. president undoubtedly lacks such powers. He has no such powers because the United States can have no established church[5] and because the Constitution bars the taking of religious test oaths,[6] making it impossible for the executive power to have a sectarian valence. Similarly, though the Crown was the fountain of honors and cre-ated nobles, knights, and rights of precedence and privilege among citi-zens,[7] the president is powerless in this realm. The Constitution expressly bars the "United States" from granting "titles of nobility."[8]

Powers Granted to Congress

In 1776 Thomas Jefferson wrote a draft constitution for Virginia. After noting that the "executive powers shall be exercised in manner follow-ing," Article II proposed an "Administrator" who would have "the power formerly held by the king."[9] Yet the draft went on to deny the administra-tor a host of the Crown's executive powers: the powers to declare war and make peace; to raise an army and navy; to issue letters of marque and reprisal; to establish offices, corporations, ports, lighthouses, and markets; to coin money; to lay prolonged embargoes; to regulate weights and measures; and to make denizens of aliens (grant rights short of citizenship).[10]

Though Article II of the U.S. Constitution lacks a similar list of exceptions to the executive power, the president lacks such authorities nonetheless. Section 8 of Article I grants all these powers to Congress, creating a series of implied exceptions to the executive power. As noted in Chapter 7, with respect to war and military matters, Congress may declare war, issue letters of marque and reprisal, and raise, fund, and equip the army and navy; the president clearly lacks such powers. With respect to commercial matters, the Constitution grants Congress the powers to regulate commerce, establish weights and measures, and coin money. These affirmative grants have long been understood to deny the president any such powers. Similarly, the president lacks power to confer commercial privileges upon individuals. Again, the grants to Congress of the commerce, patent, and copyright powers are best read as indirectly denying the president any power to grant monopolies or create corporations with limited liability. Finally, the president cannot make citizens or denizens; at the federal level, Congress has such authority under its naturalization, commerce, and necessary and proper powers.[11] In *Federalist* 69, Hamilton made some of these points, when he distinguished the president from the Crown. "The one can confer no privileges whatever: The other can make denizens of aliens, noblemen of commoners, can erect corporations with all the rights incident to corporate bodies. The one can prescribe no rules concerning the commerce or currency of the nation: The other is in several respects the arbiter of commerce, and in this capacity can establish markets and fairs, can regulate weights and measures, can lay embargoes for a limited time, can coin money, can authorise or prohibit the circulation of foreign coin."[12]

More generally, the president lacks not only the powers granted to Congress, but also any legislative power. The Constitution text never grants him any authority to make rules that alter legal rights and responsibilities. This inability largely mirrored the incapacity of state executives. Governors and executive councils generally did not enjoy lawmaking power. If state executives could make what laws they wished, the veto power that some enjoyed[13] would have served little purpose. After all, if they could make law, they could repeal bothersome statutes, new and old. Similarly, the execution duties of state executives[14] likely presupposed the absence of lawmaking power. Requiring faithfulness to laws enacted by others ensured that lawmaking rested with those who made laws and not with executives.

The Constitution's structure points to the same conclusions. The idea that the president may veto bills and sometimes prevent them from becoming law presupposes that he lacks a generic power to make or unmake law, for if he had the latter power, the veto shrinks into irrelevance. Furthermore, as Justice Hugo Black observed, "[T]he President's power to see that the laws are faithfully executed refutes the idea that he is to be a lawmaker."[15] More accurately, his execution *duty* seems in great tension with the idea that he may make laws.

Stripped as he is of the powers over commerce, monopolies, corporations, and so forth, the president is more purely executive than either the Crown or some state executives (for example, those that could make law in narrow ways such as imposing embargoes).[16] The president may prevent a bill from becoming a law and may pardon certain offenses, but the Constitution never grants him any authority to make, modify, or repeal laws.

Emergency Prerogative

For some, the idea that the U.S. chief executive must have some sort of emergency power is appealing. That attraction rests on the sense that there will be crises during which existing laws are lacking in some way and in which reliance upon Congress will prove imprudent, either because Congress cannot convene or because internal division will leave it paralyzed, unable to rise to the challenge. When the fate of the nation is in the balance or numerous lives at stake, some suppose that the active principle of government must act and remedy the defects of the standing laws. The executive alone has the capacity and energy to ensure that the nation weathers the storm.

Over time, several conceptions of an executive emergency power have surfaced. John Locke claimed that the executive had "prerogative" or a "power to act according to discretion, for the public good, without the prescription of the law, and sometimes even against it."[17] Such a power was necessary because lawmakers were not always in session, were too deliberate to manage crises, and could not foresee the future and enact laws that met every contingency.[18] When Abraham Lincoln asked, "[A]re all the laws, *but one*, to go unexecuted, and the government itself go to pieces, lest that one be violated?"[19] he seemingly endorsed the Lockean view that it was lawful for the executive to violate some laws as a means of preserving the entire system of laws.

Perhaps recognizing the awkwardness of saying that it could be legal to violate the law, Lincoln refined his argument: "[M]easures, otherwise un-constitutional, might become lawful, by becoming indispensable to the preservation of the constitution, through the preservation of the na-tion."[20] One scholar has dubbed this the "Constitution of Necessity," in which an emergency makes actions legal that would be illegal in ordinary times.[21] Under this view, the executive power, the commander-in-chief authority, and the duty to preserve, protect, and defend the Constitution collectively cede the president power to do what is necessary to avert and mitigate severe emergencies.

The conception of prerogative found in William Blackstone's *Commentaries* was narrower than this in some ways and broader in others. Blackstone spoke of the Crown having a "discretionary power of acting for the public good, where the positive laws are silent."[22] Of the presi-dent, Theodore Roosevelt similarly claimed that he could do anything ex-cept things affirmatively prohibited by the Constitution or Congress.[23] Properly speaking, neither Blackstone nor Roosevelt argued for an emer-gency power. Yet both supposed that the executive could do anything left unforbidden, a power exceptionally useful during crises.

Another possibility is hinted at in the work of some scholars. They seem to envision a presidential power to take transitory measures, leaving ultimate decisions for Congress. The case is compelling: the president is the only constitutional officer on duty twenty-four hours a day, seven days a week.[24] As such, he must be able to take temporary steps to prevent and mitigate crises, for if he cannot, no one can. When Congress convenes, it may ratify those measures or allow them to lapse. Some argue that a few of Lincoln's unilateral Civil War measures were constitutional as tempo-rary measures.[25]

Despite the appeal of these conceptions, the Constitution does not grant the president any temporary or permanent emergency power, even during the direst crises. The Founders well understood that leaders occasionally would have to take extreme measures in order to save lives or defeat an invader. But the undeniable need for such measures did not legalize them. More precisely, the founding generation did not, via their constitutions, federal and state, grant their chief executives any sort of generic emergency power, temporary or otherwise.

Consider the plight of the Revolutionary War executives. In the face of a powerful enemy and a populace of mixed loyalties, these administrators needed to secure supplies, apprehend spies, and maintain civil government. Though state constitutions typically made their chief executives commanders in chief and almost always granted them executive power, state governors could not take all measures they deemed necessary during the war. Margaret Burnham MacMillan, the foremost historian on Revolutionary War governors, observed that state constitutions granted executives "limited powers entirely inadequate for dealing with . . . emergencies."[26]

The impotence of state executives can be seen in the recurring need for crisis legislation. Most such laws granted specific authority, such as taking war material or detaining and punishing Tories.[27] Occasionally, a broader delegation was necessary. An extraordinary South Carolina law granted dictatorial powers. While the legislature was in recess, the governor could "do everything necessary for the public good except" executing someone without trial.[28] Whether sweeping or specific, emergency legislation always came with an expiration date. Sometimes the crisis delegation would last while the legislature was recessed.[29] At other times it would last for as little as two weeks.[30]

Sweeping authority often triggered trepidation. Before the Virginia assembly ceded broad powers to Patrick Henry, one legislator supposedly declared that Henry would "feel my dagger in his heart" should he become a dictator.[31] When Thomas Jefferson was governor, a similar measure that sought to establish a dictatorship failed,[32] only to pass in a different form when a new governor took office.[33]

When legislative measures lapsed, the governors understood that they lacked the crisis powers formerly ceded. A Virginia governor lamented his inability to send the militia outside the state. The power was part of a "particular temporary Act which has been several times continued for short periods and is now extinct, as indeed are all Laws giving extraordinary powers to the governor."[34] With a measure of embarrassment, the Pennsylvania Executive Council's president told General Washington that the council could not seize supplies because temporary statutory authority had expired:[35] "It may seem strange . . . that we have not legal power to impress a single horse or wagon, let the emergency be what it will, nor have we any legal power whatever over property in any instance of public distress . . . In this state of imbecility . . . we regret our inability to answer the public expectation with the keenest sensibility."[36] One governor spoke for most when he lamented the lapse of legislation, for it meant he was "left to the Constitution which may do in Peace but is by no means adapted to war."[37]

And yet the constitutions were not wholly bereft of emergency executive authority. Some executives, whether singular or plural, could summon the state legislature, allowing the latter to approve emergency measures that the executive might take or had already taken.[38] The ability to summon suggested that the executives lacked a generic emergency power, for had such a power been readily available there would have been no need to summon the assembly. Moreover, a handful of executives could impose short-term embargoes,[39] meaning that only the legislatures could enact ones of longer duration.

Sometimes the press of necessity was irresistible, leading executives to take unauthorized crisis measures. Such unilateral executive action—often dealing with supplies—was illegal. When Washington pushed George Clinton of New York to secure some flour, the governor illegally seized it.[40] Another time, Clinton cautiously refused to give an order to seize necessary nails but advised officers to seize them nonetheless, claiming that necessity justified their seizure.[41] Essentially, he was advising them to act illegally and bear the responsibility. As he later admitted, "[I]t is not in my Power as Gov'r [to impress] & I ought to be cautious how I walk."[42]

In the wake of illegal crisis measures, governors regularly sought post hoc legislative sanction.[43] After one governor illegally transferred cannons to Washington's army, he obtained legislative sanction.[44] Another legislature "legalize[d] certain acts" of its governor, concluding that they were "evidently productive of general good and warranted by necessity."[45]

The Continental commander in chief was no more powerful than his state counterparts. More than a year after creating the office, Congress conveyed a long list of temporary powers, including the power to raise army units; to set pay for all the new soldiers; to call forth the militias from the several states; to displace and appoint all officers under the rank of brigadier general; to take any private property with reasonable compensation; and, finally, to arrest and confine those opposed to the Revolution as well as those who refused to take continental currency as payment. These powers were to last six months.[46] The unmistakable implication of the temporary crisis resolution was that the commander in chief previously lacked the powers to take property, raise armies, appoint and displace officers, and arrest traitors. Subsequent congressional resolutions renewed some powers, albeit with constraints. For instance, Congress conveyed a takings power.[47] Yet it was granted for only sixty days and was exercisable only within seventy miles of headquarters.[48] The Continental Congress apparently believed that its commander in chief enjoyed emergency powers only when it delegated them.

During the drafting of the Constitution, there seems to have been little discussion of the president acting in emergencies. At first blush, this might seem surprising. But upon a more careful perusal of the Constitution, one can see why the Founders might have supposed that the Constitution vested adequate emergency authority. The Constitution conspicuously provides that Congress may provide for calling forth the militia to suppress insurrections and repel invasions. Moreover, as Hamilton observed in *The Federalist*, the federal government had the powers "to raise armies—to build and equip fleets—to prescribe rules for the government of both—to direct their operations—to provide for their support," each of which helped the federal government handle "national exigencies."[49] In later numbers of *The Federalist*, Hamilton noted that a taxation power was necessary to handle the expenses associated with "exigencies."[50] All these powers belong to Congress, creating the inference that Congress may enact statutes that grant the president the means necessary to help the nation to weather crises.

Of course, the president has powers useful during a crisis. He may pardon, a useful tool for pacifying rebellions.[51] During a Senate recess, he may appoint to offices that became vacant during the recess, something also perhaps necessary during an invasion or rebellion. Moreover, the Constitution grants the president the power to convene one or both congressional chambers on "extraordinary Occasions," language that calls to mind an emergency.[52] But that is about as far as his crisis authorities go. An implication of the power to convene Congress is that if there is an emergency and Congress has not previously delegated sufficient crisis authority, the president may convene Congress and request additional funds, the authority to impress supplies, and other powers. The convening authority would have been unnecessary if the chief executive could take all actions necessary to manage "extraordinary occasions."

Episodes during the Washington administration confirm the absence of a presidential emergency power. When faced with a crisis, Washington took limited measures within his constitutional competence, such as issuing pardons in the aftermath of a rebellion and ordering defensive measures in the face of invasions. Anything beyond those limited measures required legislative sanction, because Washington understood that he lacked a generic emergency power to do whatever was necessary to avert or weather crises.

Recall the Whiskey Rebellion in western Pennsylvania. In the face of this revolt against the excise tax, Washington did not feel at liberty to do whatever was necessary to crush it. He offered inducements, promising pardons to those who would reconcile themselves to the excise law. He did not call out the militia on the basis of his constitutional authority alone. Instead, he satisfied the congressional statute that authorized the president, in limited circumstances, to summon the militia. Before the president could call forth the militia, a judge would have to conclude that the ordinary means of law execution were inadequate.[53] Only after Justice James Wilson made this finding did Washington summon the militia.[54] By following the militia law, the president recognized that the Constitution authorized only Congress to determine when the militia could execute federal law.

Congress must have agreed that the president lacked a generic crisis power, for it would not have granted him the power to summon the militia in limited circumstances if it thought that he already enjoyed a constitutional power to do whatever was necessary during emergencies. Strengthening the inference that only Congress could provide when civilian forces might be summoned, the Militia Act limited which militias the president might summon. The president could deploy a state's militia across state borders only when Congress was not in session. When Congress was in session, a state militia could be used only within its home state, unless Congress enacted a new law.[55]

Similarly, Washington's actions in the face of the Creek and Cherokee invasions reveal his view that he lacked a generic emergency power. After these tribes invaded and attacked frontier towns, declaring war formally and informally, the president authorized defensive measures only. He specifically forbade any offensive measures, such as sending raiding parties into Indian territory, because, he said, only Congress could authorize such measures, as part of its power to declare war.[56] Once again, if he thought he had a generic emergency power, Washington might have done anything necessary to weather these crises, including ordering the destruction of Indian towns.

A third crisis, related to a plague afflicting Philadelphia, is especially interesting. In the summer of 1793, while Congress was in recess, yellow fever wracked the city. It eventually killed thousands. Before the onset of the plague, Congress had provided that it would reconvene in Philadelphia. Needless to say, Washington thought it extremely inadvisable for Congress to meet in the city. Unsure of his constitutional and statutory authority and wary of taking some action that might "make further food for scriblers,"[57] Washington asked his three principal aides (Jefferson, Hamilton, and Randolph), Jonathan Trumbull (Speaker of the House), and James Madison whether he could convene Congress outside Philadelphia by using his authority to convene both chambers "on extraordinary Occasions."[58]

Madison and Jefferson concluded that neither the Constitution nor the statutes permitted the executive to change where Congress met.[59] Hamilton and Randolph hedged, arguing that the power to convene could be used to move Congress, but only when there was an "unforeseen occurrence in the public affairs," such as a war, that made it necessary to convene Congress *early*.[60] Trumbull claimed the president could summon

Congress elsewhere, using his power to convene them on extraordinary occasions.[61]

Missing from these opinions is any whiff of an executive crisis power. Even though the president had sought opinions on his ability to move Congress during an emergency, no one mentioned the possibility of his exercising an executive crisis authority. Had Madison or Jefferson thought the president enjoyed such a power, they would have argued that although the power to summon Congress did not permit convening it outside Philadelphia, the executive power (or some other) was up to the task. Similarly, had Hamilton, Randolph, or Trumbull thought that the president could convene Congress elsewhere pursuant to his executive power, they would have said that the power to summon Congress on extraordinary occasions was supplemented by an executive prerogative, a power capable of handling a plague or any crisis.[62]

Washington decided to do nothing. As the days passed, the fever receded, mooting the legal question.[63] In April 1794, a law conveyed to the president the power to convene Congress in whatever location he chose so long as the reason had to do with the health or safety of members.[64] Legislators likely agreed that the president lacked a crisis power to summon Congress elsewhere, and hence endorsed a statutory fix.

Throughout the crises facing the state and federal governments, no executive ever claimed either a permanent or a temporary emergency power. Though state executives were always on duty and at the helm (no less than the future federal executive) and faced existential threats, none of them thought they had a permanent or temporary power to take or transfer property, to suppress peaceful Tories, or to send the militia outside the state. Washington confronted his own emergencies, first as commander in chief of the Continental Army and later as president. He never imagined that because he served the nation twenty-four hours a day, seven days a week (in both capacities) that he could take whatever emergency measures he deemed necessary. Washington understood that extraordinary times did not grant him extraordinary powers.

If founding-era executives lacked an emergency power, temporary or otherwise, that raises the question of how governments were supposed to weather the inevitable crises that buffet a nation. The primary answer was via legislation. Sometimes the legislature would delegate crisis authority in advance. At other times, the executive would convene the legislature in the teeth of a crisis and seek authority on an as-needed basis.

But there was a more perilous option. Sometimes executives were expected to take bold, illegal measures and seek absolution afterward. In opposing a grant of a removal power in 1789, one representative stated, "It would be better for the President to extend his powers on some extraordinary occasions, even where he is not strictly justified by the Constitution."[65] The representative praised a revolutionary governor's willingness to take unconstitutional measures and the legislature's subsequent approval of them. The pattern of executives exceeding their authority and later seeking indemnification "corresponds with the practice under every limited Government," said the representative.[66]

Much later, Thomas Jefferson endorsed the custom. Speaking of the Louisiana Purchase, he observed that because the treaty with France went "beyond the constitution," he would have to "rely on the nation to sanction an act done for its great good, without its previous authority."[67] Later still, Jefferson expanded on the idea of actions motivated by a "higher obligation":

> A strict observance of the written laws is doubtless one of the high duties of a good citizen, but it is not the highest. The laws of necessity, of self-preservation, of saving our country when in danger, are of higher obligation. To lose our country by a scrupulous adherence to written law, would be to lose the law itself, with life, liberty, property and all those who are enjoying them with us; thus absurdly sacrificing the ends to the means. . . . The officer who is called to act on this superior ground, does indeed risk himself on the justice of the controlling powers of the constitution, and his station makes it his duty to incur that risk. But those controlling powers, and his fellow citizens generally, are bound to judge according to the circumstances under which he acted.[68]

Jefferson understood that even though executives lacked a crisis power, they occasionally should take illegal measures and seek the public's forgiveness.

Some might question whether congressional authority was (or is) sufficient to manage all exigencies. But if we put ourselves in the shoes of the Founders, the appeal of legislative primacy during emergencies seems plain. The nation and states had just weathered a severe crisis under a re-gime of legislative control of crisis powers. If the system had been good enough to secure independence from the British Empire, the Founders likely would have thought it good enough for future crises. Moreover, founding-era constitution makers might have feared provisions that auto-matically made the executive a dictator during emergencies. Justice Robert Jackson speculated that the Founders might not have conveyed a generic emergency power to the federal government out of fear that such a provision "would tend to kindle emergencies."[69] His claim is somewhat misbegotten, because Congress has all the power needed to weather a cri-sis. But if we consider his fear with the executive in mind, the appeal of Jackson's intuition is plain. A presidential emergency power that could suspend constitutional principles (like legislative control of appropria-tions) might kindle the tendency of executives to seize and retain dictato-rial powers, as Julius Caesar and others did in other republics. Far better for such powers to come via temporary statutes so that the executive would appreciate that emergency powers were appropriate only in the direst of situations. Or better for the executive to act illegally, knowing that if the acts were seen as unjustified, he might be sanctioned for them. These were the standard American means of handling emergencies, as opposed to a unilateral and often too hasty reliance on an executive pre-rogative, temporary or otherwise, to suspend all legal constraints.

Suspending Habeas Corpus

Suspensions of the privilege of habeas corpus are a subspecies of emergency power. Because one revered president suspended the privilege, it makes sense to treat this question separately. Are suspensions different from other emergency powers, meaning that the president may suspend the writ? Or should they be left to the legislature, like the vast majority of crisis measures?[70]

In the spring of 1861, early in the Civil War, Abraham Lincoln autho-rized military commanders to suspend the writ of habeas corpus.[71] His suspensions triggered a firestorm, with many denying that the president could take such action. In a July 1861 message to Congress explaining his emergency measures, Lincoln alluded elliptically to the opinion of Chief

Justice Roger Taney, an opinion that insisted that only Congress could suspend the privilege of the writ.[72] Lincoln emphatically disagreed. He noted that the Suspension Clause[73] never specified *who* could suspend the writ. Surely the president could suspend: "it cannot be believed the framers of the instrument intended, that in every case, the danger [of invasion or rebellion] should run its course, until Congress could be called together."[74] He ended with a promise of a lengthy opinion from his attorney general and an acknowledgment that Congress might pass whatever habeas legislation it wished.[75] Two years later, the president more clearly asserted that "the commander-in-chief . . . is the man who holds the power, and bears the responsibility" for suspending habeas corpus.[76]

After initially staying mum about habeas,[77] Congress finally enacted a suspension statute in mid-1863.[78] This statute limited the effectiveness of any suspension and was intentionally ambiguous about whether Congress believed that the president had a constitutional power to suspend.[79] In a subsequent suspension—his broadest yet—the president pointedly relied upon the Constitution *and* the statute.[80]

The Constitution does not authorize the president to suspend. As a matter of text, the Constitution never hints that the president has a constitutional power, much less a constitutional right, to suspend laws. As a matter of structure, the Suspension Clause is found in Article I, section 9, which generally consists of limitations on the legislature. The clause's placement suggests that only Congress can suspend the privilege. Moreover, because suspending the privilege authorizes detention, thereby eliminating a judicial check on the executive, the idea that the Constitution silently empowers the president to eliminate that check seems implausible.

History buttresses these intuitions. After the enactment of the Habeas Corpus Act of 1679, the first English suspension of the writ occurred a decade later. After William III informed the Commons that he wished to indefinitely imprison several persons on suspicion of treason, the Commons resolved to pass a bill authorizing the Crown to suspend. The Lords, however, drafted an address asking the king to suspend the writ unilaterally. The Commons refused to accede to such an address, insisting that suspension could occur only via a statute, an action consistent with the ban on statutory suspensions found in the Declaration of Rights.[81] The Commons prevailed, and Parliament enacted a series of short suspensions of the writ.[82] Ever since, only Parliament has suspended habeas corpus, the Crown having no power to suspend statutes.[83] Blackstone noted that "the happiness of our constitution is, that it is not left to the executive power to determine when the danger of the state is so great as to render [suspension] expedient. For the Parliament only, or legislative power, whenever it sees proper, can authorize the crown, by suspending the habeas corpus act for a short and limited time, to imprison suspected persons."[84]

England bequeathed this tradition to America. Amanda Tyler notes that before the Constitution's creation, five states suspended the writ of habeas corpus and that in each instance, suspension occurred via statute.[85] Some state constitutions, such as that of Massachusetts, contained language strongly suggesting that only the legislature could suspend the writ: "The privilege and benefit of the writ of *habeas corpus* shall be enjoyed in this Commonwealth in the most free, easy, cheap, expeditious and ample manner; and shall not be suspended by the Legislature, except upon the most urgent and pressing occasions, and for a limited time not exceeding twelve months."[86] While Massachusetts did not expressly bar executive suspensions, the text implied that only the legislature could suspend. After all, if the governor had a concurrent power, that power would neither be limited in time nor constrained by the condition that suspensions occur only "upon the most urgent and pressing occasions."

Commentary before and after ratification assumed that Congress had a monopoly on suspension. A proposal floated at the Philadelphia Convention assumed that only the legislature could suspend.[87] In Massachusetts, two judges assumed that only the legislature could suspend the writ, speaking of the clause as limiting Congress.[88] In Virginia, speakers repeatedly noted that Congress could suspend;[89] one remarked that national suspensions would be on the same footing as in England, namely, that the legislature alone could suspend.[90] In Pennsylvania, one delegate noted that the Habeas Clause was "restrictive of the general legislative powers of Congress."[91] The New York ratifying convention proposed limiting the length of a suspension, a curb tied to "passing the act for such suspension."[92] Supporters in that convention, including Alexander Hamilton, John Jay, and Gouverneur Morris, almost certainly believed that only Congress could suspend. If not, their proposal would have left the executive's power to suspend wholly untrammeled.

Outside the conventions, Americans knew that Congress alone could suspend.[93] A Massachusetts editorial noted that Congress could suspend and thereby "empower" the president to imprison people.[94] After ratification, John Marshall, Joseph Story, William Rawle, and St. George Tucker claimed that the power rested with Congress.[95] The first time Congress took up the matter, in the wake of the Aaron Burr conspiracy, legislators did not imagine that the president could suspend the writ himself.[96]

Perhaps recognizing that the case for a generic executive power is extremely weak, some have argued for a temporary suspension power. When the nation's existence hangs in the balance and Congress is out of session, then and only then may the president suspend. Some have suggested that Lincoln convened Congress so that it could judge whether to prolong his temporary suspensions.[97]

While the policy arguments for a temporary executive suspension power are compelling, the Constitution does not grant the president such a power. Nothing in the Constitution suggests a temporary suspension power. Nothing that preceded it hints at such a power. English and American executives invariably relied upon legislative suspensions, never suspending the writ on their own. They perhaps recognized that though they were to be vigilant guardians of their constitutions, they nonetheless lacked an implied power to suspend habeas corpus, even temporarily. Finally, president Lincoln's example in no way supports a temporary power. He championed a robust executive suspension power, not a temporary one exercisable only so long as Congress was adjourned. His delegations of suspension authority lacked expiration dates.

Martial Law

Lincoln's unilateral enforcement of martial law on civilians makes it appropriate for us to consider the original presidency's power in this area too. Just as the president lacks a generic crisis power or a targeted power to suspend habeas corpus, so too he lacks a power to decide that portions of the United States should be governed by the military and subject to military justice.

During the Revolutionary era, American executives recognized that they lacked authority to apply military law. As recounted in Chapter 7, congressional resolves created military courts and crimes for soldiers and sailors. Congressional authorization also was necessary if civilians were to be tried for military crimes in military courts. For instance, in 1777 the Continental Congress authorized military justice in areas around Pennsylvania, New Jersey, and Delaware.[98] Because local executives were too feeble to suppress those who aided the British, Congress granted George Washington the power to seize such inhabitants and try them "by a court-martial."[99] Many civilians were court-martialed, and some were executed.[100] When such laws expired or did not apply, Washington knew the military could not detain or try civilians.[101]

State executives likewise lacked constitutional authority to declare martial law, meaning that statutes were the sole authority to impose martial law on civilians. Margaret Burnham MacMillan recounts that some states passed acts granting their executives the authority to "declare martial law" temporarily.[102] Such statutes implied that the governor otherwise lacked such authority, for it would have been pointless to grant limited, constrained authority had the executive enjoyed a generic ability to declare or recognize martial law.[103] Indeed, chief executives lamented that military courts could not try certain individuals because no statute authorized as much.[104]

Nothing about the Constitution suggests a departure from this understanding of the executive's limited wartime authority. The Commander in Chief Clause surely does not grant the president any more authority than the Continental commander had, for it would have been odd to use a familiar *military* title as a means of conveying far greater power over *civilians*. The Vesting Clause's grant of executive power does not alter the analysis, for state executives likewise lacked constitutional authority to impose military justice on civilians, even though most had grants of executive power. Lastly, we should recall that the president lacks constitutional authority to impose military justice on soldiers and sailors,[105] making it unreasonable to suppose that the Constitution authorizes the president to impose such justice on civilians.

During the Whiskey Rebellion, President Washington ensured that his troops arrested the scofflaws, leaving prosecution, judgment, and execution of sentence to civilians in the executive and the judiciary.[106] He specifically told his officers to turn over rebels to the "civil magistrates" for prosecution and trial, recognizing that congressional authority to use the militia did not sanction the trial of civilians before military courts, and that he lacked constitutional authority to impose military justice.[107] The first president's view of the executive's limited constitutional authority prevailed as late as 1815, when President Madison admonished Andrew Jackson for his imposition of martial law on New Orleans, declaring it inconsistent with the "established law of the land."[108] Madison never hinted that Old Hickory's actions would have been permissible had he first secured the president's previous sanction.

Executive Immunity

Richard Nixon once said that "[w]hen the President does it, that means that it is not illegal,"[109] implying that some acts that would otherwise be illegal were lawful if the president took them. Perhaps he was distorting an eighteenth-century English legal principle. The Crown, it was said, could "do no wrong."[110] Although susceptible to many readings,[111] in practice the principle meant that the Crown could not be prosecuted criminally or sued civilly.[112] This immunity was said to arise from the Crown's status as the font of justice, for no tributary court could direct the source of its authority.[113]

The Crown's immunity had consequences for its authority to act. Monarchs could not take certain actions, precisely because such actions would be immune from judicial scrutiny. A chief justice supposedly advised a king that the latter "could not arrest any man for suspicion of treason, or felony, as any of his subjects might"; and he gave an excellent reason for this rule: "because, says [the justice], if the king did wrong, the party could not have his action."[114] In other words, if the king was immune from judicial process, he could not be allowed to do anything that might injure someone, for the victim would have no redress. Absolute immunity necessitated a reciprocal executive debility.

The handicap was inconsequential because the Crown's ministers stood ready to implement orders. These ministers, who had to countersign and implement the Crown's decisions, were responsible for the advice they gave and actions they took. The same chief justice who advised that a monarch could not arrest anyone also observed that an executive order to take an illegal action did not shield those who did the Crown's bidding:

"If the king command me to [wrongfully] arrest a man, and . . . I do arrest him, he [the arrestee] shall have his action of false imprisonment against me, albeit he was in the king's presence."[115] In sum, because the Crown could do no wrong, it was disabled from taking many actions without the intervention of responsible executives, officers who might be civilly sued, criminally prosecuted, and impeached by Parliament.

Americans did not care for the maxim that the king could no wrong. They knew from experience that he could. During the Constitution's creation, the responsible president was repeatedly contrasted with the irresponsible Crown. John Marshall taunted those praising the British Constitution to vote for it and thereby adopt its principle that the executive could do no wrong.[116]

The president is held accountable in three senses. First, presidential electors (and those who select them) may judge an incumbent's actions, both personal and official, when he seeks reelection. Second, when the president commits high crimes and misdemeanors, the House may impeach him and the Senate remove him. Third, the president may be held civilly and criminally liable for actions taken while president.

The third sense of responsibility was (and is) controversial and contested. Some insisted that presidents were beyond judicial reach. Vice President John Adams and Senator Oliver Ellsworth apparently asserted that the president "was not subject to any process whatever; could have no action Whatever, brought against him; was above the power of all Judges [and] Justices." Both claimed that impeachment was the only means of proceeding against a sitting president.[117] Ellsworth seemed to regard the presidency and its occupant as sacred things, insisting that it was "[s]acrilege to touch an Hair of [the president's] head."[118] Much later, when Aaron Burr subpoenaed presidential letters in order to prove that he had not committed treason, Thomas Jefferson denied that the judiciary could command the president, because otherwise the courts "could bandy him from pillar to post, keep him constantly trudging from north to south & east to west, and withdraw him entirely from his constitutional duties."[119] Jefferson's pragmatic argument implied that the president could not be subject to judicial process at all, except via impeachment.

Others advanced more nuanced arguments, ones that seemed to leave open the question whether the president might be subject to some judicial process. As Publius, Alexander Hamilton seemed to argue that impeachment was the only means of proceeding against a president.[120] Almost fifty years later, Justice Joseph Story claimed that the president could not "be liable to arrest, imprisonment, or detention, while he is in the discharge of the duties of his office; and for this purpose his person must be deemed, in civil cases at least, to possess an official inviolability."[121] Hamilton and Story left open the possibility that the president might have a legal duty to testify and supply evidence, even if the judiciary could not punish him in order to secure his cooperation.

A third group read the Constitution as conveying no immunity. Late in the Philadelphia Convention, after a debate on congressional immunities, James Madison raised "the necessity of considering what privileges ought to be allowed to the Executive," suggesting that he read the largely finalized Constitution as *not* granting any privileges or immunities to the president.[122] In the states, people likewise suggested that the president was subject to the jurisdiction of the courts, no less than any other citizen. James Wilson argued that not a "single privilege is annexed" to the president: "[F]ar from being above the laws, he is amenable to them in his private character as a citizen, and in his public character by impeachment."[123] Later, Wilson boasted that the Constitution created no aristocracy: "Does even the first magistrate of the United States draw to himself a single privilege or security that does not extend to every person throughout the United States? Is there a single distinction attached to him in this system more than there is to the lowest officer in the republic?"[124] The answers were evident. No distinctions, no privileges.

In North Carolina, James Iredell seemed to agree, saying that America did not need an executive council because the president was as accountable as any man.

> No man has an authority to injure another with impunity. No man is better than his fellow-citizens, nor can pretend to any superiority over the meanest man in the country. If the President does a single act by which the people are prejudiced, he is punishable himself, and no other man merely to screen him. If he commits any misdemeanor in office, he is impeachable, removable from office, and incapacitated to hold any office of honor, trust, or profit. If he commits any crime, he is punishable by the laws of his country, and in capital cases may be deprived of his life.[125]

The future Supreme Court justice seemed to suppose that the president might be punished while in office. Another North Carolinian supporter of the Constitution agreed, adding that the president was "amenable for any maladministration in his office," namely, for illegal acts carried out under his orders: "Were it possible to suppose that the President should give wrong instructions to his deputies, . . . citizens . . . would have redress in the ordinary courts of common law."[126] The comment suggested that the president was answerable for his official acts in the ordinary courts, just like any other officer. In Massachusetts, "Cassius" claimed that if a president violated his oath, "he would be immediately arrested . . . and summoned to answer for his conduct before a federal court, where strict justice and equity would undoubtedly preside."[127] Finally a Federalist, writing immediately after the Philadelphia Convention, declared that the president was more accountable than members of Congress: *"His person is not so much protected as that of a member of the House of Representatives; for he may be proceeded against like any other man in the ordinary course of law."*[128]

After ratification, some in the Senate supposed that the president might be "put to jail for debt."[129] William Grayson of Virginia argued that the "President is not above the law" and that it was "an absurdity to admit this idea into our government." Indeed, he foresaw "that the President may be sued." He also pointed out that Christina II (of Sweden) had been accused of murder,[130] suggesting that a future president might commit such a crime. Agreeing with Grayson, William Maclay of Pennsylvania insisted the president "is not above the laws." Maclay asked what was to be done if the president committed multiple murders and the Senate was not in session to remove. When one senator claimed that no European monarch had ever murdered anyone, Maclay drolly observed that the claim was "very true in the retail way, Charles the IX of France excepted, they generally do these things on the great Scale."[131] Maclay clearly did not believe that the Constitution either barred criminal prosecution of the president or exalted him above all judicial process.

William Rawle, in his *A View of the Constitution of the United States* (1829), said that private parties could sue any federal executive. "[T]he president would be liable to the action of a person injured in the same manner that a private individual would be. The law makes no distinction of persons," said Rawle, before admitting that the Constitution made one such distinction, a limited one for members of Congress.[132]

Even an Englishman read the Constitution as conferring no immunity. The president, said the Baptist minister William Winterbotham, is "so settled as to secure VIGOUR and ENERGY with ACTUAL RESPONSIBILITY," because the president, "so far from being above the laws, is amenable to them, in his private character, of a citizen."[133] To say that a sitting president has a private character and that he is amenable to the laws is to suggest that a sitting president might be sued and prosecuted like anyone else.

James Wilson had the better view, namely, that the Constitution enshrines a rule of presidential responsibility, and confers no sort of legal immunity. As a matter of text, the executive power should not be understood to convey such immunity, temporary or permanent, because even if the executive power in England could do no wrong, Americans well understood that the president could. The impeachment provisions assume as much. Moreover, the limited and express congressional immunity from arrest while traveling to or from Congress suggests that the president lacks a far broader immunity, either with respect to his official or personal acts. As noted, James Madison seemed to reach this conclusion during the Philadelphia Convention in the wake of a discussion on legislative privileges, noting that delegates should likewise consider what privileges the president ought to enjoy. That none were added for the president suggests that none were conveyed. Had the Framers wished to grant some form of immunity to the executive, temporary or permanent, official or personal, they would have included an express provision. They had ready examples from Delaware and Virginia; both granted temporary impeachment immunity to their chief executives. Neither could be impeached or convicted while in office.[134] Subsequent constitution makers came to the same conclusion, including immunity provisions for the executive when such provisions were thought necessary.[135]

Constitutional structure points to the same conclusion. Under the Constitution, the president may carry out executive functions unilaterally. Early statutes recognized as much when they vested functions with the president.[136] If the president can execute statutes without the assistance of others, he should be subject to judicial process, lest injury befall Americans without hope of judicial remedy. England could stomach chief executive immunity precisely because kings and queens could not act unilaterally and hence could not harm anyone. By contrast, a rule of legal immunity for the president would mean that so long as he did not enlist the aid of others, he could inflict injury without those injured having a chance of legal redress.

Another structural argument in favor of presidential responsibility relates to the original Constitution's lack of term limits. Immunity while in office seems plausible in the modern age, when the plaintiff or prosecutor must wait no more than ten years to bring suit. Before ratification of the Twenty-Second Amendment, however, the president could serve any number of terms, making it more likely that he might die in office. In that context, immunity in office had vastly different consequences. A dead president could not be criminally prosecuted and punished. Moreover, a president's estate might lack the assets necessary to satisfy a civil judgment. In many cases, the justice delayed as a result of immunity in office would amount to justice denied.

A final structural argument against immunity while in office is that it either leads to injustice or requires an implausibly complex structural inference. A temporary immunity while in office would allow the president to escape liability for all sorts of crimes and torts because the statute of limitations might expire while the alleged criminal or tortfeasor remained in office. Under this system, temporary immunity would approach absolute immunity, making temporary immunity obnoxious. For this reason, proponents of temporary immunity assert that statutes of limitations should be tolled during the president's time in office.[37] This condition makes the idea of temporary immunity more palatable, but only at the cost of rendering the idea of temporary immunity far-fetched. We have to imagine that the Constitution's structure not only silently grants a temporary immunity, but also grants plaintiffs and the government a nontextual tolling of state and federal statutes of limitations. The more intricate an implied structural feature said to be part of the Constitution, the less plausible it is. Needless to say, a rule that would combine temporary immunity and tolling is quite elaborate, so much so that none of those early Americans who favored presidential immunity while in office ever claimed that this immunity was accompanied by a constitutional tolling of all state and federal statutes of limitations.

When we consider the question less abstractly, focusing on the different sorts of amenability (criminal, civil, state, and federal), the plausibility of a constitutional rule of presidential responsibility comes into focus. Consider the most consequential form of amenability, criminal prosecutions. The federal government is unlikely to prosecute the president because the latter controls the instruments of prosecution, at least under the original Constitution. If a federal prosecutor has the temerity to prosecute the president, the president may cut the prosecution short, either by pardoning himself or by ordering a halt to the prosecution. The fact that federal criminal prosecutions of the president are unlikely renders it improbable that the Constitution bars such prosecutions. There is little reason to create implied provisions to handle exceptionally low-probability events.

Of course, there is a chance that a president might welcome an investigation and prosecution as a means of salvaging a tattered reputation. A president who permitted a federal prosecution to proceed would not violate the Constitution, for it does not bar criminal prosecutions of a sitting president.

State criminal prosecutions are troubling because one can imagine an ambitious local prosecutor trying to score political points. But practical factors conspire to make this prospect remote. The Constitution contemplates a capital, where Congress and the executive will reside. Congressional jurisdiction is exclusive over the capital.[138] The president's enforcement jurisdiction within the capital is likewise exclusive. Because presidents spend most of their time in the capital, the chances of them committing crimes within a state are somewhat remote, making it harder for prosecutors to credibly charge them. Again, the remoteness of the seeming menace suggests why constitution makers did not bother enshrining presidential immunity from criminal prosecution.

Private civil suits may seem more problematic because the set of plaintiffs is so large. Yet there is a good deal of common sense and justice in a system in which the president, as a constitutional matter, may be subject to private lawsuits. To see why this is so, we need to recognize that nothing in the Constitution bars the president from suing others. Even if we think that a president should devote all his energies to the nation's business, the president is at liberty to sue tenants, contractors, and those who have injured him. The Constitution should not be read to permit a sitting president to sue any number of Americans but deny them the right to countersue. And if Americans may countersue, there should be no bar to them filing the suit in the first instance.

The notion that a president might be litigious is hardly chimerical, for George Washington was something of a frequent litigant. On a number of occasions while serving as president, citizen Washington threatened suit. His ire was usually directed against debtors, squatters, and trespassers. He told one debtor that he would put his bonds "in suit without delay" if the debtor did not pay him.[139] On another occasion, he gave instructions to his attorney to put another "bond in suit" should a payment demand be refused.[140] When one squatter claimed two hundred acres of land on his property, Washington warned him "in the most pointed manner not to make any settlements thereon." If the squatter encroached on his land, Washington promised that the claimant "must expect to be prosecuted as far as right and justice will admit."[141] After some miscreants chopped down trees and stole "Hoop poles" (farm implements), Washington asked his nephew Bushrod to bring a suit by using George Augustine Washington (another nephew) as the named plaintiff, because Washington was not "willing to have [his] own name called in Court," if it could be avoided.[142] Washington sought the assistance of future chief justice John Marshall to collect a debt and resolve a land dispute. Washington hoped to settle the debt owed him "without a suit," but implied that one might be necessary.[143]

Besides asserting his own rights in state courts, Washington served as an executor of several estates. In 1792, Washington had to answer a complaint in the Virginia High Court of Chancery about a land sale that he had arranged many years earlier for a deceased friend.[144] Washington seemed to be the defendant, because he spoke about being "called upon legally to answer the complaint."[145] What is clear is that Washington expressed exasperation about being continually dragged into courts: "It is really hard that I am so often called before Courts in matters in which I have no interest; but am continually saddled with the expense of defence."[146] If we credit his complaints, the Virginia state courts bandied the first president from "pillar to post."

In 1796, before the same court, Washington was "enjoined" (his word) as an executor of another estate.[147] The decree "[o]rder[ed]" him to deposit the deceased's funds in a bank, presumably to be distributed among the estate's claimants.[148] The decree was something of a relief, since Washington had been party to "many lawsuits and much difficulty."[149] In fact, he was the plaintiff in the case, seeking to bring all claimants before the court. One of his final actions as executor was to publish the court's order in London, where several claimants were thought to reside. The *London Gazette* printed the judicial decree "[o]rder[ing]" "George Washington" to deposit funds with the court.[150] The order drove home the fact that unlike the English, the Americans had a responsible chief executive, one amenable to judicial commands.

While threatening suit, bringing actions, and being summoned by courts, Washington never suggested that he could not be sued. He made no such claims because though the Constitution granted him certain monarchical powers, it did not grant him the full panoply of regal trappings. Washington perhaps understood that although court proceedings would distract him from the nation's business, the Constitution never granted the president immunity from suit.

The judicial proceedings that vexed Washington were of a private nature. None concerned his official acts. But other early presidents were not so lucky. After Thomas Jefferson left office, Edward Livingston sued him. It seems that President Jefferson had ordered governmental officials to remove Livingston's improvements on a batture (a sandbank in the midst of a river) in New Orleans. Because Livingston believed that he owned that portion of the batture, he sued Jefferson in 1810, after Jefferson left office. Jefferson wrote an elaborate, ninety-nine-page defense, never once claiming that because he had ordered the seizure while president, he was entitled to absolute immunity.[151] The fact that Jefferson never mentioned this possibility strongly suggests that he did not believe that presidents had immunity for official acts. Jefferson's implicit understanding of the Constitution is sound, for presidents ought to be held responsible for their official acts, at least as a matter of the Constitution itself.

Executive Privilege

Even if the president is amenable to suits, prosecutions, and judicial process, there is the more limited question whether he enjoys a constitutional privilege to withhold documents and shield conversations from both the courts and Congress—what today is termed "executive privilege." To invoke the privilege, the executive typically orders executive officials to refuse to comply with subpoenas from the courts and Congress. If officials follow the president's commands, he has successfully claimed executive privilege. But if an official chooses to release the information or testify notwithstanding the presidential order, the president can do little to stop it. Invocation of the privilege is successful only if all parties with access to the relevant information agree to keep it under wraps. This privilege might exist because the president has an affirmative constitutional right to refuse information demands. Or it might arise because neither Congress nor the courts have any lawful means, either constitutional or statutory, of obtaining information from the executive. Here the "privilege" flows from the lack of constitutional authority to demand the information.

A range of arguments are said to support the idea of executive privilege. First, perhaps the president's executive power encompasses a right to conceal executive papers and communications. Second, the Constitution might guarantee the president the means necessary to implement his powers and satisfy his duties, including executive privilege. In certain areas, such as military affairs and foreign policy, concealment of information and plans is indispensable.[152] As William Rehnquist put it, the "doctrine itself is an absolutely essential condition for the faithful discharge by the executive of his constitutional duties."[153] A third argument rests on the president's need for candid advice. Without the privilege, the quality of counsel that a president receives will suffer, because officials advising the president will know that a litigant or a prying Congress eventually might divulge their candid and provocative advice to the world.[154]

Though executive privilege would be necessary and proper for carrying into execution the president's powers, the Constitution is better read as never granting any such a privilege. Consider constitutional structure. As discussed in Chapter 8, the chief executive does not have the right to any and all means that might seem to him required for carrying his powers into execution. Only Congress has the necessary and proper authority to help the president implement his powers and duties. By using this authority, Congress can create offices, departments, armies, and a navy; establish their functions and duties; and appropriate funds to cover expenses and salaries. The president can do none of these things on his own. Should Congress decide that there should be no army, that the navy be underfunded, or that there be neither a secretary nor a department of state, it could cripple the president. Compared with executive privilege, officers and departments are infinitely more crucial to the president's ability to wield his constitutional powers effectively. If the Constitution does not grant him a constitutional right to the more significant assistance—secretaries, generals, sailors, and tax collectors—it seems unlikely that it implicitly grants him a less meaningful right of confidentiality. We would have to imagine that though the Constitution grants him no constitutional right to officers, he has an implied right to shield communication with them once offices are created and filled.

Moreover, because executive privilege is conceived of as a right to refuse information demands and not as a right to actually keep matters secret, it is a rather incomplete means of safeguarding information. For instance, if the president had discussions with his cabinet on a controversial topic and one of his cabinet members later chose to share those discussions with the press, Congress, or a court, the current conception of executive privilege does not permit the president to obtain an injunction protecting the confidentiality of those discussions. This powerlessness exists even though the quality of future advice given to the executive undoubtedly would be compromised and though diplomatic or military confidences might be revealed. As executive privilege is currently understood, only a statute could confer a right to keep matters wholly secret, thereby granting the president the right to shut the mouths of garrulous executives.

When we look to text and history, the case for executive privilege becomes no more persuasive. While executive power was understood to encompass authority over law execution, foreign affairs, officers, and war powers, no one, either in England or America, seems to have identified executive privilege as an attribute of the executive power. Though the Crown sometimes withheld documents from Parliament, ministers could be punished for adhering to such decisions, as when Parliament jailed a minister because of his refusal to testify.[155] Such episodes suggest that the Crown lacked a constitutional power to rebuff such demands. Consistent with this conclusion, before the Constitution's ratification, no one argued that the president had executive privilege. Admittedly, Publius and others observed that executives (singular ones especially) were better at keeping secrets than sizable legislatures.[156] But the ability to keep secrets, by itself, did not mean that executives had a *constitutional* right to reject information demands from Congress and the courts.[157] Indeed, comments from the founding suggest that the president did not enjoy the right to rebuff information demands. Recall that James Wilson claimed that not a single privilege was attached to the presidency and that it lacked any shield not available to ordinary citizens.[158] Others said the president was not superior to any citizen,[159] implying that he lacked any privilege shields.

The best case for executive privilege arises from episodes when chambers of Congress sought information during the Washington administration. But even here the evidence is mixed, at best. Three incidents are worth discussing. The first episode concerned an investigation into the massacre of an entire division of the army lead by General Arthur St. Clair.[160] A House committee charged with investigating called upon the secretary of war, Henry Knox, to turn over documents. Knox notified President Washington, who then sought advice. Apparently, the president was worried that "there might be papers of so secret a nature as that they ought not to be given up."[161] Jefferson's cabinet notes suggest agreement on four points:

1. that the house was an inquest, and therefore might institute inquiries.
2. that it might call for papers generally.
3. that the Executive ought to . . . refuse those, the disclosure of which would injure the public. Consequently were to exercise a discretion.
4. that neither the committees nor the House has a right to call on the head of a department, who and whose papers were under the Presidt. alone; but that the committee shd. instruct their chairman to move the house to address the President.[162]

Jefferson indicated that the cabinet ultimately resolved that "there was not a paper which might not be properly produced" and that thus no confrontation would be necessary.[163]

We have good reason to suppose that at least some of the cabinet's discussions were disclosed to members of the House. Two days after the cabinet meeting, the House resolved that the president "be requested to cause the proper officers to lay before this House such papers of a public nature, in the Executive Department, as may be necessary to the investigation of the causes of the failure of the late expedition."[164] Because the House directed a qualified request to the president (only papers of a "public nature" were sought), Abraham Sofaer believes that some aspects of the cabinet meeting were leaked to the House.[165] On one view, the chamber acceded to the cabinet's principles. Yet if all the cabinet's conclusions were accepted, there would have been no need to qualify the House's request. On another view, the House sanctioned presidential discretion to withhold documents precisely because it concluded that it normally had a right to demand and receive all papers. After all, if representatives supposed that the president had constitutional authority to withhold documents, there was no need to make a qualified request; Washington might have refused such papers on his own.

What is clear is that the president never publicly asserted a right to withhold information, and in fact, the president transmitted all relevant documents.[166] Given this fact and the House's qualified request, the episode is at best a weak precedent for executive privilege. The episode equally suggests a congressional view that a chamber could cede discretion to withhold documents.[167] Or perhaps the episode reflected an early penchant for compromise, which, as Louis Fisher points out, has been, and is, the principal means of resolving information disputes between the political branches.[168]

The second incident seems like a better precedent for executive privilege. In January 1794, the Senate considered calling upon the secretary of state to hand over diplomatic letters.[169] The request was likely an attempt to embarrass Gouverneur Morris, the U.S. emissary to France, since his letters were thought to disparage France.[170] There also may have been suspicions (later confirmed) that Morris had tried to smuggle Louis XVI out of the country.[171] The Senate eventually directed its request to the president.[172]

Fearing that disclosure might damage relations with France, the president called his cabinet. Again, members supported the president's right to withhold documents.[173] Perhaps acting on this advice, Washington transmitted redacted correspondence, along with an explanation: "After an examination of [the papers], I directed copies and translations to be made; except in those particulars which, in my judgment, for public considerations, ought not to be communicated."[174] The excisions related to confidential informants and embarrassing commentary about French politicians and society. For example, Morris's comment that "[t]he best picture I can give of the French nation is that of cattle before a thunder storm" was redacted.[175] The Senate never challenged the president's withholding of information.[176]

The Senate's acquiescence might have signaled an understanding that the president could keep certain communications secret.

And yet, other explanations are available. Perhaps the Senate found the furnished materials sufficient for its needs. Just as plausibly, the Senate request may have been made in a context in which requests for information were understood to confer discretion on the president. Sofaer observes that many requests from the chambers contained language similar to the House's authorization of discretionary presidential withholding.[177] Given these prior requests, Washington may have thought that the Senate conferred implicit authority to withhold information. In fact, Attorney General William Bradford argued that every request for information should be construed to permit "those just exceptions which the rights of the Executive and the nature of foreign correspondence require."[178] The president should not assume that "the Senate intended to include any Letters, the disclosure of which might endanger national honor or individual safety."[179] So what may seem a claim of a constitutional privilege may instead have been reliance on an interbranch custom of withholding documents that might harm national interests.

The third incident, involving Washington's request for an appropriation to implement the Jay Treaty, triggered open confrontation. The Jay Treaty was controversial; many insisted that it was one-sided and that Chief Justice John Jay had violated his instructions. Nevertheless, the Senate consented, and the president, amid much pressure to renegotiate the treaty, ratified it.

To judge whether the House should pass a statute necessary to satisfy a treaty obligation, Edward Livingston proposed a resolution requesting Jay's treaty instructions.[180] After receiving advice from some "gentlemen," Livingston amended his motion, excepting "such of said papers as any existing negotiation may render improper to be disclosed."[181] A month-long debate ensued (stretching over three hundred pages in the *Annals of Congress*), culminating in the passage of Livingston's modified request.[182]

Washington turned over nothing, explaining, "I trust that no part of my conduct has ever indicated a disposition to withhold any information which the Constitution has enjoined upon the President, as a duty, to give, or which could be required of him by either House of Congress as a right."[183] Foreign negotiations required caution and secrecy, however. Disclosure, even upon completion of diplomatic talks, "would be extremely impolitic: for this might have a pernicious influence on future negotiations; or produce immediate inconveniences, perhaps danger and mischief, in relation to other powers."[184] Such concerns had led the Framers to vest the treaty power with the president and the Senate only. To accept "a right in the House of Representatives to demand, and to have, as a matter of course, all the papers respecting a negotiation with a foreign Power, would be to establish a dangerous precedent."[185] He added that "[i]t does not occur that the inspection of the papers asked for can be relative to any purpose under the cognizance of the House of Representatives, except that of an impeachment; which the resolution has not expressed."[186] Washington claimed that "a just regard to the Constitution and to the duty of my office . . . forbid a compliance with your request."[187]

Washington's letter may seem like a public assertion of executive privilege notably absent from the other incidents. It was nothing of the sort. He never insisted that he could withhold information whenever he felt it necessary. Rather, his refusal was grounded on the supposed lack of power in the House to demand the papers. Because the House had no role in treaty making, it had no right to the papers. He buttressed this point by noting that he had provided all the relevant papers to the Senate during its consideration of the treaty.[188] In other words, though the disclosure of treaty instructions might lead to "danger and mischief," he had provided precisely this information to the Senate because it had a right to it. Relatedly, he pointedly noted that the House had not indicated any interest in impeachment.[189] The only reason to mention this detail was to signal that he might have complied had the House signaled a possible impeachment.

The House stood its ground. Its first resolution asserted that the House had discretion in implementing the terms of treaties.[190] The second resolution insisted that so long as the information requested related to the "Constitutional functions of the House," no explanation or justification was necessary.[191] Both measures passed by wide margins.[192]

So in the only incident in which Washington publicly explained his information-disclosure policy, he never endorsed anything like executive privilege. After all, he never asserted a right to maintain the secrecy of communications. To the contrary, he implied that he would have complied had the House referred to impeachment. Moreover, the House plainly rejected Washington's refusal, asserting its right to the documents.

All in all, though there was a sense that the president should be able to withhold documents from Congress, there also was a sense that Congress sometimes had a constitutional right to information, particularly if impeachment were in play. The first perception hardly established that the president had a constitutional right to refuse information demands, particularly because many congressional requests expressly permitted the withholding of certain documents. Moreover, the idea of a congressional right to information obviously is in great tension with the notion that the president has executive privilege. Since impeachment is arguably always a possibility, it might seem that a chamber always has a right to access to whatever information it deems necessary to exercise its authorities.

The first executive privilege dispute in the courts occurred during the third presidency. Thomas Jefferson privately suggested that Chief Justice Marshall's first subpoena in the Aaron Burr trial was unconstitutional—recall his comment about being bandied "from pillar to post." Nonetheless, he turned over evidence. As John Yoo notes, the "President publicly accepted the power of the judiciary to summon the executive and his papers."[193] In light of Jefferson's private grouse, this is a fair implication. In turning over evidence demanded by Burr, not once but twice, Jefferson never asserted that although he had a constitutional right to reject subpoenas, he was waiving that right. Jefferson bit his tongue, never publicly proclaiming any privilege. To the world, it must have seemed that he had admitted the power of a court to subpoena him.[194]

Given that the textual and structural arguments strongly cut against the idea of executive privilege and that the early historical case for the privilege is weak, there is little warrant for supposing that the president has a constitutional power to shield conversations and documents from either Congress or the courts. While such an authority would be necessary and proper for the executive, much as officers and funds are, that hardly proves that the president has a constitutional right to rebuff attempts to secure information.

Statutory Powers, Privileges, and Immunities

Though there are some powers and privileges that the Constitution does not confer on the president, in many cases Congress might pass legislation granting the executive additional authorities and immunities.

Using the Necessary and Proper Clause, Congress might enact laws giving the president discretionary powers in the wake of an emergency, as it did when it allowed the president to reconvene Congress elsewhere whenever a plague affected the capital. Or Congress might grant the president the ability to suspend the privilege of habeas corpus. And assuming that nothing in the Bill of Rights bars the use of military courts to try civilians, Congress may authorize such use, as it did during the Revolutionary War.

Similarly, even though the Constitution is best read as conferring neither a litigation immunity nor an informational privilege on the president, Congress can use its necessary-and-proper power to confer either or both upon the executive. Congress could limit the president's susceptibility to judicial process by passing a statute shielding the president, temporarily or otherwise, from prosecutions, suits, and depositions. Or it could provide that the president need not hand over certain sensitive documents to courts and Congress.

An immunity statute would be necessary and proper for carrying into execution the president's constitutional powers in much the same way that the Servicemembers Civil Relief Act, by staying civil proceedings against members of the military, permits them to focus on their duties.[195] If Congress granted civil immunity to the president, it might impose reciprocal constraints on the president's ability to sue others. And Congress could convey some form of temporary criminal immunity to the president.

An executive privilege statute would be useful in much the same way that other evidentiary privileges further important societal interests. If Congress granted executive privilege, it might regulate the assertion of it when the executive branch acts as prosecutor rather than a defendant. After all, when the executive seeks to fine or imprison someone, it seems unfair that the executive might be able to use secrecy to obscure the defendant's possible innocence.[196] Likewise, when the executive acts as a plaintiff in a private civil case, assertions of executive privilege seem rather inequitable. In any event, it is for Congress to weigh these matters and construct the contours of executive immunity and privilege.

Conclusion

The grant of executive power has a somewhat different valence in America than in England and on the Continent. The president has no power to confer privileges such as corporate status, and cannot grant residency status to foreign aliens. The president has no religious authority and cannot regulate foreign commerce.

In other respects, the president faces constraints that were common in England, the colonies, and the states. Like many of his predecessors, he lacks an emergency power, a power to do whatever he deems necessary to avert or manage crises like invasions and rebellions. Instead, he must rely on Congress to delegate emergency authority. Relatedly, the president can neither suspend habeas corpus nor charge civilians in military courts, for such authority has never been part of the executive power in America.

The president also lacks privileges and immunities. So far as the Constitution is concerned, the president can sue and be sued. Indeed, he might even be prosecuted criminally. Moreover, the president lacks a constitutional right to keep secrets from Congress and the courts. Nothing in Article II intimates that the president has a right to every instrument, mechanism, or privilege that he (or we) might deem necessary for the sound functioning of the executive branch.

Yet the Constitution is flexible enough to permit Congress to grant additional powers, privileges, and immunities to the executive. Just as Congress decides whether the president will have the far more significant assistance that comes from officers and departments, it also may determine that the president needs emergency authority, immunity from suit, and evidentiary privileges.

CHAPTER TEN

THE "COMBINED AUTHORITY OF EXECUTION AND LEGISLATION"

The president's relationship to Congress is complex because the Constitution makes it so. On the one hand, the president has a duty to execute the laws of Congress. This responsibility has led some to regard him as something of a constitutionally established servant or page of Congress. A European captured this sense of a dutiful, submissive executive when he said that if we were to personify the legislative and the executive, the latter might say that "[a]ll that this man [the legislative power] has talked of, I will perform."[1]

On the other hand, the president's satisfaction of his duties and the exercise of his powers allow him to shape the laws committed to his execution. He must share information with and recommend measures to Congress. He may convene either or both chambers on extraordinary occasions. He has a qualified veto over legislation, ceding him great sway over the content of new laws. Finally, the constitutional executor may pardon law violations and inevitably wields enforcement discretion.

In sum, the president is simultaneously something of an agent of Congress, a leading influence on its deliberations, and a mitigator of its excesses. Some at the founding thought it made eminent sense for the constitutional executor to shape the laws he was to execute. Others criticized the president's legislative powers; one groused that the president would be a "constituent part of the legislative power" because his veto "in many cases will amount to a compleat negative."[2]

Antecedents

In England, the Crown was conceived of as a "constituent part[]" of Parliament, since the two chambers would enact "advice and consent" resolutions that the Crown could accept or reject.[3] Indeed, English laws expressly provided that the Crown enacted laws with the consent of the chambers. Moreover, within limits established by law, the Crown decided when Parliament would convene, adjourn, and end. Additionally, the Crown not only conducted the elections for the Commons, but also could appoint to the Lords. Finally, the Crown appointed the Speaker of the House of Lords and had a veto on the Speaker of the Commons.[4] In the colonies, governors had similar powers over assemblies.[5]

State executives generally were not seen as elements of the legislatures. Most state executives could summon their legislatures, usually on special occasions,[6] but the implication seems to have been that the legislature generally would act autonomously, since most executives lacked explicit authority to propose legislation.[7] Moreover, most state executives lacked authority to prorogue, adjourn, or dissolve their assemblies.[8] Finally, though some executives had a veto, most did not enjoy such authority.[9] There were some notable exceptions, however, in which the executives had some authority over the legislature. In Massachusetts, the governor wielded a qualified veto,[10] and the New York governor served on the Council of Revision.[11] The first South Carolina Constitution vested "legislative authority" in the president, among others.[12] A few state executives sat ex officio in the legislature.[13]

Convening Congress

Though Congress must assemble annually,[14] it need not meet throughout the year. Because exigencies might flare up during a recess or between sessions, the Constitution authorized the president on "extraordinary Occasions, [to] convene both Houses, or either of them."[15] What constitutes an extraordinary occasion is unclear. Surely war and rebellion would constitute an extraordinary occasion. But what of other calamities?

The question first came up in 1793. As discussed in Chapter 9, a deadly plague of yellow fever struck Philadelphia during the summer. Congress was set to reconvene in Philadelphia, putting members at risk of contracting the disease. The president sought advice about whether he could summon Congress to a safer locale. Alexander Hamilton wrote that the reason must involve a "special object of public business out of the pre-established course,"[16] suggesting that sessions could be called only to consider measures in unusual times. Edmund Randolph cited foreign invasion and claimed that if Congress did not reconvene as required by law, that too would be an extraordinary occasion.[17]

The yellow fever episode was the closest Washington came to convening both chambers. The first presidential summons of Congress as a whole came in 1797, when John Adams called it to discuss France's naval war against the United States.[18] Washington, however, summoned the Senate four times: to consider nominations for federal offices in the new state of Vermont, to take up the Jay Treaty, and to debate nominations for offices throughout the nation.

Three of the special sessions came on the heels of ordinary sessions and lasted but a day.[19] In other words, Washington thrice called the Senate into a short extraordinary session a day or two after its previous session had ended.[20] Two of these stunted special sessions occurred on Inauguration Day, one on his second inauguration and one on his successor's inauguration.[21] On the latter occasion, Washington may have summoned the Senate to allow it to quickly receive and act on John Adams' new nominations.[22] As it turned out, Adams made no nominations that day. One special session, lasting for almost twenty days, focused on the Jay Treaty.[23] Washington used the session to secure Senate action on nominees, too.[24]

Although the president may summon either chamber, it was understood that the power to summon one chamber would primarily, if not exclusively, be used to convene the Senate so that it could act on treaties and nominations.[25] That Washington summoned the Senate to consider nominations on the heels of an ordinary session suggests that the need to act on those nominations might sometimes constitute an "extraordinary occasion."

There is the separate question of where the president may summon the chambers. In the fall of 1793, Madison and Jefferson denied that the president could ever summon Congress to a different place from the one established by law;[26] Edmund Randolph and Hamilton claimed that the president could alter where Congress would meet if he had a reason for summoning Congress early. They concluded that the epidemic, by itself, was no cause for calling Congress early, and hence the summoning power was unavailable.[27] Only the Speaker of the House, Jonathan Trumbull, argued that the president could summon Congress elsewhere under these circumstances.[28] Washington delayed making any decision, and eventually the question became moot as the plague faded.[29]

Though these opinions barely discussed state constitutions,[30] the latter revealed a variety of approaches. Most state frameworks empowered the executive to summon the legislature, without mentioning the power to shift its meeting place. Yet a handful addressed this point. The South Carolina Constitution of 1778 provided that the assembly would meet "at the seat of government unless the casualties of war or contagious disorders should render it unsafe to meet there," in which case the governor (with the consent of his privy council) could establish "a more secure and convenient place of meeting."[31] Similarly, the 1780 Massachusetts Constitution (and the very similar 1784 New Hampshire counterpart) declared that the governor "in case of any infectious distemper prevailing in the place where the [legislature] is next at any time to convene, or any other cause happening, whereby danger may arise to the health or lives of the members from their attendance," may appoint another meeting place within the state.[32] The text specifically authorizing a shift in location suggests that this power existed only when expressly conveyed.[33] That likely was the view of Congress, for in 1794 it authorized the president, under limited circumstances, to alter its meeting place.[34]

Two additional issues merit a few words. First, whether an extraordinary occasion exists is left to the president, who, as the first attorney general put it, "may pronounce definitively and without controul."[35] The fuzziness of "extraordinary occasions" suggests that there can be no judicial review of his decision. Second, legislators cannot "refuse to comply with [his] summons."[36] The power to convene is the power to oblige members of Congress to gather together. Though they can refuse to act on his recommendations, they must convene and hear him out.

Adjourning Congress

The president, unlike some Revolutionary-era state chief executives[37] and the English Crown, cannot prorogue the legislature. In other words, the president cannot terminate a session of a Congress merely because he disapproves of pending bills. Moreover, the president cannot dissolve Congress and call early elections, meaning that he lacks the coercive influence that comes with the power to force early elections on legislators, most of whom wish to remain in office.

Instead, the president has a "mediatorial" power:[38] "[I]n Case of Disagreement between [the two chambers], with Respect to the Time of Adjournment, he may adjourn them to such Time as he shall think proper."[39] In other words, the president can intercede only if there is a disagreement between the chambers. But what sort of disagreement? The phrase "Time of adjournment" is ambiguous because it could refer to when to begin an adjournment (the time *to* adjourn), when to end one (the *length* of an adjournment), or both. At least one Founder supposed that it referred to when to begin an adjournment.[40] No one seems to have endorsed the claim that the president may intercede only when there is a disagreement about when an adjournment should end.

Perhaps the clause is best read as covering both disputes. That is to say, if the chambers cannot agree on when to adjourn for a weeklong recess (for example, on October 1 or October 8), the president may decide when the adjournment will begin and when it will end.[41] Alternatively, if the chambers agree on when to adjourn but cannot agree on the duration of the recess, the president can decide the matter. Both disagreements arguably relate to the "time of adjournment." What does seem clear is that when the power comes into play, the president may decide when the adjournment will end without regard to the chambers' views on that matter.

Presidents might wish to exploit an adjournment disagreement as a means of terminating pending business. For instance, if the Senate wishes to adjourn and the House seeks to remain in session to consider legislation, to hold vexing oversight hearings, or to consider articles of impeachment, the president may force the House to adjourn. Despite the potential utility of forced adjournments, presidents have never used this authority.[42]

Two factors likely explain the nonuse. First, the case in which one chamber proposes one date and the other does no more than suggest another may not be a "disagreement,"[43] because a prolonged impasse might be necessary. For instance, friends with different preferences for lunching spots may not be thought to be in a "disagreement" unless the differences linger for some time or become entrenched. Second, it may be that when the chambers have been at loggerheads about adjournment (either the start day, the length, or both), presidents chose to stay above the fray, concluding that resolving the dispute would only anger members of one or both chambers. Without presidential mediation, the chambers eventually resolved their disagreement.

The State of the Union Clause

The annual State of the Union address is something of a political ritual. After members of Congress, the president's cabinet, the Joint Chiefs of Staff, and Supreme Court justices have taken their seats, the House sergeant at arms shouts of the president's arrival. The president enters and presses the flesh with politicos, some of whom will later savage his speech. In these often-forgettable speeches, the president sells his legislative agenda while television cameras occasionally focus on the soldiers, firefighters, and other heroes sitting in a balcony next to the president's spouse.

The clause that supposedly requires these often silly spectacles is in fact terribly important: "He shall from time to time give to Congress Information of the State of the Union."[44] It is significant because it obliges the president to share information. The first president repeatedly spoke of the duty to share information with Congress.[45] Others recognized this as well. On one occasion, a former representative complained to Washington that President John Adams had made a speech about declaring war against France without supplying the U.S. minister's correspondence that might have been useful in deciding whether to wage war.

The representative insisted, "It is the duty of the President to give information of the State of the Union more especially when the awful event of war is contemplated."[46]

Moreover, the president must share information with Congress from time to time, not merely once a year. Whenever the president shares factual information with Congress—concerning enemies, the economy, or governmental operations—he conveys a state of the union message. Because presidents share information with Congress all the time, presidents issue hundreds (even thousands) of state of the union messages every year.[47] These other messages merely lack the spectacle of the annual address.

Mimicking English practice, Washington and Adams gave speeches at the outset of every regular session of Congress. Because in some years there were two regular sessions, these presidents sometimes gave more than one formal address a year to Congress.[48] Making such speeches at the end of a long intersession made a good deal of sense, for the president clearly would have information about the Union that almost all members of Congress would lack. While members were far away from the capital, the president continued with his tasks, many of which supplied him with critical data.

In a bow to English practices, the chambers formally replied to the president's speeches. These replies tended to praise the president and usually agreed to take up the matters the president recommended. Jeffrey Tulis notes that replies "addressed each point of [the President's] speech and thus constituted a kind of oath on the part of congressmen to do the virtuous deeds" urged by the president.[49] The chambers sent committees to deliver the replies; upon receipt, the president would give a sur-reply.[50] This elaborate system of speeches, addresses, and presidential replies prevailed in the administrations of Washington and Adams.

Thomas Jefferson ended the practice of giving speeches before Congress,[51] believing that it smacked too much of monarchy and that formal replies tended to put the chambers in an awkward position, almost compelling them to agree to the president's agenda without giving them time to judge whether such concurrence was warranted.[52] Woodrow Wilson reinstituted the practice of giving speeches, which became more enduringly reestablished several presidents later.[53]

Although some have suggested that written "state of the union" communications are unconstitutional because such information must be conveyed orally,[54] this is misguided. The Constitution merely requires the president to give information about the state of the union, saying nothing about how that information must be conveyed. Washington's first speech specifically mentioned that he had ordered his subordinates to submit "such papers and estimates as regard *the* affairs particularly recommended to your consideration, and necessary to convey to you that information of *the state* of *the Union*, which it is my duty to afford."[55] In other words, Washington's message not only confirmed that there would be multiple messages in a year, but also mentioned that other state of the union information would be in writing.[56]

The concept of executive information sharing may have been borrowed from the New York Constitution, which in turn reflected the tradition of the English Crown giving a "Speech from the Throne." In New York, the governor had the "duty" to communicate the "condition of the State, so far as may respect his department."[57] The U.S. Constitution does not limit the duty to executive branch matters.

As Vasan Kesavan and Gregory Sidak point out, the State of the Union Clause presupposes that the president has an informational advantage.[58] James Wilson observed that the president "will have before him the fullest information of our situation; he will avail himself not only of records and official communications, foreign and domestic, but he will have also the advice of the executive officers in the different departments of the general government."[59] Other early commentators on the Constitution likewise appreciated the geographic and logistical advantages of Article II. One wrote that "from the nature of the executive office it possesses more immediately the sources, and means of information than the other departments of government."[60]

The Recommendations Clause

The president must not only report facts to Congress, but also propose measures:[61] "He shall ... recommend to their Consideration such Measures as he shall judge necessary and expedient."[62] Why impose a duty to suggest measures? Three reasons come to mind.

First, the president often will have useful advice. "A Landholder" observed that "[i]f lawmakers in every instance, before their final decree, had the opinion of those who are to execute them, it would prevent a thousand absurd ordinances."[63] After ratification, St. George Tucker similarly noted that "any inconveniencies resulting from new laws, or for the want of adequate laws upon any subject, more immediately occur to those who are entrusted with the administration of the government, than to others, less immediately concerned therein."[64]

Second, the Recommendations Clause was necessary to overcome any sense that by proposing measures, the president would be a constitutional trespasser. The clause was originally drafted as a discretionary power, but was later hitched to the State of the Union Clause, a change that made recommendations mandatory. As one delegate said, the change made "it the duty of the President to recommend, & thence prevent umbrage or cavil at his doing it."[65] Even so, some regard executive leadership in the legislative process as a perversion of the Constitution.[66] The Recommendations Clause indicates otherwise; the president does not encroach upon Congress's turf when he clearly states his preferences throughout the legislative process.

Third, the proposing of legislation has its burdens. The ancient Locrians supposedly required those who would propose legislation to come forward with a noose around their neck. If the legislation was deemed bad, the proponent was hanged. If it was deemed good, he was spared.[67] Though the president does not face such penalties, he often will be castigated for his suggestions. The constitutional duty to propose measures can be seen as a modest means of countering the tendencies of timid presidents, who might wish to say nothing about measures that might benefit the nation. As William Rawle put it, this obligation is "not to be dispensed with." The president "would not be guiltless" if he failed to tell Congress what measures he thought were required, particularly in the wake of a crisis.[68]

How detailed must these recommendations be? Not very. President Washington seems to have never proposed actual statutory text; he was content to simply raise issues, leaving the particulars to Congress. "Motives of delicacy" had "uniformly restrained" him "from introducing any topick which relates to Legislative matters, to members of either house of Congress, lest it should be suspected that he wished to influence the question before it."[69] Hence, the duty to propose measures hardly guarantees the executive's robust participation in the legislative process, familiar as that practice is today. The Recommendations Clause merely requires some executive exhortation, leaving the president the option of being more or less active and explicit.

Signing Bills

Most statutes become law when the president signs them. But the Presentment Clause (Article I, section 2, clauses 2 and 3) also provides that if the president fails to sign or veto a bill within ten days of receiving it, the bill automatically becomes a law. The text seems to suggest that while the president cannot sign a bill into law after ten days (because the bill already has become law), he may sign a bill into law before that period has expired, even after Congress has ended its session. That is to say, modern readers understand the text as clearly providing that bills can be signed into law even when Congress is between sessions. Indeed, modern presidents routinely sign bills after a congressional session has ended.

Yet the Founders (and succeeding generations) read the Constitution quite differently. Into the twentieth century, presidents and Congresses hewed to the understanding that the president could sign bills only while Congress was in session.[70] If the president did not sign a bill during the congressional session that generated it, the bill automatically expired at the end of the session. This was not a "pocket veto" (more on this later), but something that we might call an "end of session effacement"—a rule wiping away all bills not perfected into law at the end of the session.

Why did presidents and Congress adhere to this rule when the Constitution never expressly provided as much? They evidently believed that the Constitution adopted the English notion of "session," a word with some baggage. Under English practice, bills had to be perfected into law during the session the legislature enacted them. If bills did not become law within a session, Parliament had to start on them anew. So when a session ended on its own or the Crown prorogued it, any bills not signed into law before the close had to be taken up de novo in the next session.[71] Knowing this, the Crown might prorogue a session as a means of terminating pending legislation that it found troubling, thereby requiring Parliament to start from scratch in the next session.

Americans unconsciously adopted the idea that laws could be made only while the legislature was sitting,[72] likely because there was no perceived need to disinherit it. Under the 1780 Massachusetts Constitution, "any bill or resolve . . . not . . . returned by the governor within five days after it shall have been presented, . . . shall have the force of law."[73] Like the U.S. Constitution, this clause contained nothing signaling that laws could be made only during a session, suggesting that if the governor failed to sign a bill into law within five days of receiving it, it would become law even if the fifth day occurred after a session's expiry. Nonetheless, in 1791 the Supreme Judicial Court advised that its members were "clearly of opinion" that a bill could not become law after the end of a session:[74] "[A] bill or resolve, *after the session is ended*, cannot acquire the force of law."[75] This advisory opinion reflected the Anglo-American view that a bill could not be made law after a session ended, by signature or otherwise. The end of a session terminated all pending business, including bills not signed by the executive.

The end of a session had the same effect under the U.S. Constitution. At the close of his second term, Washington complained that although the "Constitution allows the President ten days to deliberate on *each Bill* that is brought before him," Congress actually allowed him "less than half that time to consider *all* the business of the Session; and in some instances, scarcely an hour to resolve the most important."[76] Washington felt "pressure"[77] because he understood that he had to sign the bills, if at all, before the session ended. In the final two days of its last session, the Fourth Congress presented more than twenty bills.[78] Had the Constitution permitted the signing of bills into law after a session ended, surely Washington would have realized (or someone would have told him) that John Adams might have signed the bills into law. More generally, over his eight years, Washington signed almost one hundred bills into law on the final day of a congressional session. Considered in conjunction with his complaint, this practice fairly indicates that he believed that bills could not become law if they were not perfected during a session.

Subsequent presidents and Congresses embraced the traditional understanding about the perfectibility of bills. At the end of every session, presidents would hunker down in a room attached to the Senate and review enrolled bills as they became available.[79] Often the numbers of bills went into the dozens.[80] To give the president more time to consider whether to sign a bill, sometimes Congress would manipulate clocks.[81] After all, if Congress had set an adjournment for noon on a certain day and the appointed hour had arrived without the president signing all the pending bills, more time would be necessary to ensure that the president had time to consider them. If Congress did not doctor the clock or pass a revised adjournment resolution, much of its legislative efforts might be for naught because the president understandably might refrain from signing bills without first reading them. So great was the strain on the president and Congress that at one point the latter barred the consideration of legislation at the close of sessions.[82]

The few times that a president considered signing a bill after the end of a session, the idea was met with objections. Acting upon the advice of John C. Calhoun and against the advice of others, including John Quincy Adams, President James Monroe decided that a postsession signing could create no law.[83] Monroe's decision may have had an effect on Adams, for when the latter became president, he too went to Congress to sign bills, sometimes signing them until two in the morning.[84] Had President Adams believed that he could sign bills after Congress ended its session, he likely would not have stayed up until two one day and returned the next to read bills and sign those he desired to make law. He likely would have taken ten days to consider the almost fifty bills.

Abraham Lincoln, a constitutional innovator in so many ways, was the first to sign a bill after the termination of a session. His postsession signature of an 1863 bill[85] was criticized by a House committee that complained that the "spirit of the Constitution evidently requires the performance of every act necessary to the enactment and approval of laws to be perfect before the adjournment of Congress."[86] Still, an 1864 statute referred to the disputed legislation as an "Act," perhaps suggesting that Congress as a whole might have regarded the 1863 bill as law.[87] If Congress was confused, it had good company. In 1864, Lincoln objected to a bill given to him minutes before the end of a session as "a matter of too much importance to be swallowed in that way," a complaint that assumed that he only had minutes to consider its terms. Indeed, Lincoln went to Congress to sign bills in the customary office.[88] His presence at the close of the session was wholly unnecessary if he could have signed bills into law after the session ended. Lincoln's adherence to old practices suggested that he perhaps had come to understand that the end of a session terminated the viability of all bills, even those presented to him.

The practice of early presidents certainly conforms to the claim that bills not perfected into law expire at the end of sessions. Yet alternative explanations are available. First, perhaps early presidents wanted to give Congress a chance to override any vetoes. If this was the goal, it is not clear why members could not override the veto when it reassembled in a new session or a new Congress. After all, if legislation does not need to be perfected into law during a single session, nothing prevents the legislature from overriding vetoes in a subsequent session. Moreover, the president might have delayed consideration of bills when override seemed unlikely or impossible. For instance, the president might have deferred reading those bills that had low margins of passage, on the theory that, with respect to such bills, Congress was rather unlikely to override any veto. He then could have read them more deliberately and coolly decided whether to veto them. Had a desire to preserve the override power been a concern, presidents had no need to burn the midnight oil at the end of every session.

Second, it is possible that some presidents believed that they could sign bills into law after a session terminated, but chose not to take the risk that others (such as the courts) would disagree. After all, the penalty for being mistaken was quite high; if these presidents were wrong, the bills they thought had become law with their signature would not be law after all. To avoid this possibility, the more prudent tack was to follow the existing practice. While fear of invalidation by the courts is certainly plausible, the most likely reason is that presidents understood and accepted the traditional understanding of the consequences of session's expiration, namely, that matters that had not yet become law had to be taken up de novo in the next session.

Presidents no longer sit in Congress with their cabinet members at their sides, poring over bills into the wee hours of the morning. Instead, presidents routinely sign bills after Congress has ended its session and members have made their way home. The current system, in which the president may make laws by signing bills after a session ends, is a superior means of lawmaking compared with what preceded it. There is no mad rush to decide whether to sign or veto. Recognizing this, some state constitutions gravitated to the practice, explicitly permitting the postsession signing of bills.[89] Though the parallel change in federal practice bettered the lawmaking process and found sanction from the Supreme Court,[90] if we are to judge this practice by the original Constitution, it is unconstitutional, for it ignores the significance of the end of legislative sessions.

The Qualified Veto

The veto power has a controversial past. The Declaration of Independence's first grievance was that George III had "refused his Assent to Laws, the most wholesome and necessary for the public good."[91] The antipathy toward vetoes was keenly felt in the states. Some Marylanders insisted that "the persons appointed to hold the executive power, [should] have no share or negative in the legislature."[92] One writer claimed that it would be absurd if the "principal Executive power" wielded a veto, because there would be "but little chance for proper freedom, where the making and executing the laws of a State lie in the same hand."[93] Another objected that it was a "solecism" "to invest the different power of legislation and the execution of the laws in the same hands."[94]

Such sentiments predominated in the creation of the state frameworks, only three of which ceded vetoes. While the 1776 South Carolina Constitution granted a veto,[95] the 1778 constitution eliminated it[96] (over President John Rutledge's veto!).[97] New York's governor had a share in the veto. He, along with the chancellor and other judges of the Supreme Court, formed the "Council of Revision." If a council majority objected to a bill, it would not become law unless two-thirds of both chambers overrode the veto.[98] The Massachusetts veto was similar, except that the governor wielded it unilaterally.[99] The state constitution's veto ensured that "a due balance may be preserved in the three capital powers of Government" and that no men would "enact, interpret and execute the laws."[100]

The state experiences led influential delegates at the Philadelphia Convention to favor a veto. Many recognized that in the absence of the veto, assemblies had passed unwise laws and that executives had been subject to legislative caprice and even domination. In contrast, legislatures in states with a veto were seen as more balanced and less prone to enact imprudent laws.

The Virginia Plan provided a veto exercisable through the joint action of the executive and judges.[101] One delegate objected to the connection between the judiciary and the executive, because "the one is the expounder, and the other the Executor of the Laws."[102] Such complaints led to a purely executive veto.[103] Certain delegates wanted an absolute check,[104] on the grounds that such authority was necessary for the executive to defend against legislative encroachments.[105] After lopsided votes against absolute and suspensive vetoes (the latter being a check that would merely delay the enactment of legislation), delegates approved a veto subject to a two-thirds override by each chamber.[106]

Mirroring comments made during the creation of state constitutions, some Anti-Federalists complained that the president's veto generated an unsafe accumulation of authority. One writer, citing Montesquieu, insisted that there could be "NO LIBERTY" when someone could enact tyrannical laws and could ensure their tyrannical execution as well.[107] Another complained that though the president would have the "supreme continental executive power" and be the "supreme conservator of laws," he also enjoyed legislative authority. Notwithstanding his "modest title," the president could "exercise the combined authority of legislation, and execution."[108]

As enacted, the Presentment Clause gives the president three options. First, as discussed earlier, the president can sign a bill, ushering it into law. Second, he can return the bill with his objections to the originating chamber. If two-thirds majorities in both chambers repass the original bill, it becomes law. Third, if the president neither signs the bill nor returns it with objections within ten days after presentment, the bill becomes law. But if the bill cannot be returned to Congress because its adjournment prevents a return, it does not become law. This is the so-called pocket veto scenario.

Despite the clause's seeming simplicity, it has spawned a number of questions. Perhaps the most basic is precisely which measures must be presented to the president. Though the Constitution provides that "Every Order, Resolution, or Vote to which the Concurrence of the Senate and House of Representatives may be necessary . . . shall be presented to the

President of the United States,"[109] Congress has not presented every such matter to the president. Though both chambers must approve constitutional amendments, Congress did not present the first twelve to President Washington. The Supreme Court agreed with Congress, concluding that the amendments were outside the clause's ambit.[110] Similarly, no one imagines that congressional overrides of presidential vetoes must be presented to the president.

Another fundamental question relates to the scope of the veto decision. Some assert that rather than objecting and returning an entire bill to Congress, the president enjoys "line item veto" authority—that is, he may return only the objectionable portions, allowing the rest of the bill to become law.[111] Yet Michael Rappaport has demonstrated that the Constitution never grants the president any such authority.[112] It makes clear that if the president wishes to veto a bill, he must return "it"—the bill—and not just those portions he dislikes. Moreover, the Constitution never imposes upon Congress a single-subject limitation of the type sometimes found in state constitutions. The lack of such a constraint permits Congress to bundle together disparate provisions into a single bill and present the president a motley package. These principles were well understood at the founding. As president, Washington noted that given the "nature of the Constitution, [he had to] approve all the parts of a Bill, or reject it in toto."[113]

Supposing that an unconstrained veto makes the president too powerful, some have claimed that he can veto bills only when his objections are constitutional. Some have gone further, suggesting that only constitutional objections to statutory curbs on presidential power are permissible. Underlying these supposed constraints is the view that the president cannot veto legislation merely because he believes that it is bad policy.

Nothing in the text or early practice supports such constraints. The Constitution does not suggest that the president's objections have to be constitutionally based, much less grounded, in Article II concerns. Though Washington's first veto was grounded in constitutional objections, his second veto listed four policy objections.[114] Moreover, the first veto grounded in a supposed encroachment on presidential power occurred in Andrew Jackson's administration.[115] When modern presidents veto bills based on policy disagreements, they do nothing constitutionally suspect.

Some have objected to veto threats, believing that the president should have a role only after both chambers have passed the same bill. Reflecting the fear of executive influence, there seems to have been a rule that members of Parliament could not mention the Crown's views on legislation, an internal rule reflecting a fear of executive influence.[116] In America, critics such as Daniel Webster castigated Andrew Jackson for suggesting that Congress ought to have sought his advice in framing a bank bill.[117]

The Constitution does not gag the president before presentment. Nothing in the Constitution expressly or implicitly bars the president from commenting on pending legislation. To the contrary, the Recommendations Clause suggests that the president has a duty to comment on legislative matters, a duty that exists even when bills are pending. Moreover, any prohibition on commenting on legislation would have been unprecedented. Even if Parliament had a rule that no member could refer to the monarch's view of legislation, that internal rule hardly prohibited the Crown from expressing its views. Indeed, before ratification of the Constitution, executives armed with a veto often wielded the threat as a means of securing legislation more to their liking. At the Philadelphia Convention, Benjamin Franklin argued against the veto on the grounds that it "was constantly made use of to extort money" from the legislature. In addition, he claimed that governors used veto threats to influence the legislative process: "No good law whatever could be passed without a private bargain with" them.[118]

There are sound reasons for not silencing the president. As noted, the legislature benefits from the executive's information and expertise. Moreover, if he must remain silent until bill enrollment, Congress may squander time crafting and debating bills that will never become law. The Constitution is better read to permit the president to voice his concerns throughout the lawmaking process.

The Pocket Veto

One last veto matter merits attention, namely, the president's much-maligned pocket veto. Ordinarily, if the president does nothing for ten days after presentment (neither signing nor returning the bill), the bill automatically becomes law. That rule, designed to prevent the president

254

from indefinitely delaying a decision on whether to sign a bill, does not apply when "Congress by their Adjournment prevent its [the bill's] Return." Because return is necessary for a successful ordinary veto, the Framers did not want Congress to be able to prevent return and thereby vitiate the president's veto power.

The phrase "pocket veto" comes from critics of President Andrew Jackson who objected that he had vetoed bills by putting them in his pocket at the end of sessions.[119] While many describe the pocket veto as an absolute veto, the commentators greatly exaggerate its effects and importance. Describing the pocket veto as "absolute" implies that Congress is helpless. But this is mistaken. After the president pocket vetoes a bill, Congress may repass the bill well in advance of an adjournment and present it to the president again. If he then issues an ordinary veto, members can attempt to muster the two-thirds majorities necessary to override. Nothing in the Constitution prevents repassage and re-presentment of the exact same bill.

Just as importantly, Congress easily can avoid a pocket veto. To render pocket vetoes impossible, Congress may either remain in session for ten days after presentment of a bill or it may adjourn after presentment, so long as it reassembles by the tenth day after presentment. With adequate planning, the possibility of a pocket veto can be limited to crisis situations in which Congress cannot maneuver to avoid the risk.

A perplexing question is what sorts of adjournments are within the ambit of the pocket veto clause of the Presentment Clause. No one believes that it applies to the routine daily adjournments of Congress, the ones that typically occur in the evening. But which of the other adjournments raise the possibility of a pocket veto? Do the pocket veto provisions apply when Congress has adjourned within a session, at the end of a congressional session, at the end of a particular Congress, or in some combination of these three possibilities?

There are respectable grounds for supposing that the Constitution's pocket veto provision only applies to intrasession adjournments. Recall that the Founders believed that no bill could be made law after the end of a legislative session. All pending bills, even those presented to the executive, that did not become law before a session's termination had to start anew in the next session. Given the prevailing conception of "session," one might suppose that the pocket veto clause refers to intrasession adjournments only because there was no need to adopt the exception to deal with end-of-session issues. If Congress gives a bill to the president and immediately adjourns, the bill cannot become law without repassage and re-presentment. We can draw support for this conclusion from the Massachusetts Supreme Court's 1791 interpretation of its 1780 Constitution. Recall that the constitution provided that a bill would become law after five days unless the governor returned it with objections. There was no express exception for adjournments preventing return. Despite the seemingly absolute nature of the text, the Court concluded that the passage of five days would not make a bill a law when the fifth day fell after the end of a session. That was so because no bill could become law after the end of a session.

We can draw indirect support for the conclusion that the federal pocket veto applies only to intrasession recesses from the provisions of the 1777 New York Constitution. Like the U.S. Constitution, the New York version provided that a bill would become law if the Council of Revision did not return it within ten days of presentment, unless the legislature, by its adjournment, rendered return "impracticable." But the New York Constitution also provided that when return was impracticable for reasons of adjournment, the Council of Revision had to return the bill on the first day of the next meeting of the legislature.[120] Given the end-of-session effacement rule applicable in Anglo-American polities, this latter return requirement would have been pointless after the end of the session. After all, the legislature would have to begin afresh with or without return. If that is so, the only way in which the council could return under this latter provision of the New York Constitution was in the context of a bill presented just before an intrasession recess. In other words, the New York Constitution's return provisions likely were constructed with intrasession adjournments in mind.

If the end-of-session effacement principle applies to the U.S. Constitution even in the absence of any particular clause clearly specifying as much (likely because of the implicit connotation of "session"), then there was no need to include a separate provision dealing with end-of-session adjournments. After the expiration of a session, there was nothing the president could do to revive a bill; neither signing it nor returning it could possibly matter. This in turn suggests that the pocket veto clause was meant to cover intrasession adjournments of Congress. If we understand the pocket veto clause as encompassing only intrasession adjournments—since only those sorts of adjournments "prevent" return of a bill—the first use of the clause occurred in 1867.[121]

Alternatively, one might suppose that the pocket veto exception applies only to end-of-session adjournments, and was added out of an abundance of caution. Despite the concept of session, perhaps the seemingly absolute language of the Presentment Clause—providing that "[i]f any Bill shall not be returned by the President within ten Days . . . the Same shall be a Law"—led some to believe that it was necessary to expressly provide that when Congress prevents the return because both chambers are adjourned, then the automatic law-creating rule does not matter. Because this reading sees the pocket veto exception as applying only at the end of sessions, it would mean that so long as Congress is open for business—so long as the current session has not expired—the president can return his objections, whether or not the originating chamber has adjourned. The theory would be that so long as one chamber still operates during a session, "Congress" is still in place and able to accept objections, with reconsideration to take place after the originating chamber returns from its intrasession adjournment.

Not surprisingly, modern presidents claim that the pocket veto clause applies to both intrasession and end-of-session adjournments. And they seem to believe that if the originating chamber has adjourned but the other remains active, that is an adjournment for purposes of the pocket veto clause. They believe this even though the pocket veto clause speaks of "Congress by their adjournment," language that suggests that both chambers must be adjourned in order to prevent a return.[122]

If we conclude that the pocket veto exception was meant to apply to intrasession recesses only, it is worth asking what, exactly, "prevent[s]" the return of a bill when Congress has adjourned but remains in session. Some imagine that return is prevented merely because when Congress is adjourned, no one is present to accept the president's objections. If an adjourned chamber makes return feasible—say, by designating an agent to accept presidential objections or by creating a return receptacle (like the metal bins for returning library books), then maybe returns are possible (not prevented) even when a chamber has adjourned.[123]

The better reading is that congressional adjournment within a session necessarily prevents return, meaning that the Constitution supposed that the legislature had to be functioning when the executive returned the bill, presumably with an eye to quick reconsideration of the bill. The Constitution's text seems to imagine that by adjourning, Congress automatically prevents return ("unless Congress by their adjournment prevents return"). The 1777 New York Constitution seemed to assume that adjournment necessarily prevented return, because it expressly permitted return when the legislature reconvened.[124] This feature was necessary only if one supposed that return was impossible when the legislature was not sitting. The absence of a similar clause in the U.S. Constitution suggests that Congress necessarily prevents return of a bill when, during a session, it is in recess during the tenth day after presentment.

Furthermore, the Presentment Clause apparently envisions quick consideration of the vetoed bill. After receiving the president's objections, the receiving house "shall enter the Objections at large on their Journal, and proceed to reconsider it." This seems to contemplate reconsideration shortly after receiving the objection. Obviously, prompt reconsideration is impossible if Congress receives the objections just before the start of a three-month recess and does not reconsider the bill until the day after the end of the recess. Again, the text suggests that if both chambers are adjourned on the tenth day after presentment, Congress can do nothing to make return possible.

All in all, the pocket veto likely was meant to apply to intrasession recesses only, since it was impossible for a bill to become law after a session expired. The more important point is that pocket vetoes are not particularly consequential, because Congress can maneuver around them. By delaying its adjournment or by reconvening on the tenth day after presentment, Congress can ensure that presidential return is feasible. If, for some reason, neither expedient is possible, Congress can repass a bill that previously was pocket vetoed and ensure that no new pocket veto is possible.

Interpreting Legislation

As president, Washington generally followed the legislature's intent when executing laws. For instance, though the Northwest Ordinance did not require that all laws passed by the territorial legislature be delivered to Congress, the president concluded that sending them to Congress was "conformable with the intention" of the act, one that enabled Congress to overturn all territorial laws.[125] Whether he felt legally obliged to hand over those territorial laws is unclear.

Better evidence of Washington's devotion to legislative intent can be found in a "novel and very perplexing" legislative episode regarding an act "for the relief and protection of [A]merican seamen."[126] According to Washington, the Committee of Enrollment had omitted "an entire Section of a Bill which had passed both Houses of Congress," a section indicating the manner of authenticating a seaman's proofs of citizenship. The "unaccountable"[127] omission of this section made another part of the act "incapable of being executed."[128]

What was Washington to do? The secretaries of Treasury, War, and State thought that the "object of the Law" could be furthered "by the interposition of the Executive. . . . [in] [t]he form of an act" (an order) that would specify the manner of citizenship verification.[129] The attorney general, along with two attorneys, gave slightly different, more nuanced advice. Rather than treat the whole section as "null & void," the attorney general recommended treating the words "authenticated in the manner hereinafter directed" as superfluous. "[E]very kind of reasonable proof . . . subject to the instructions . . . from the Supreme Executive" would then suffice for authentication.[130]

Washington was "desirous . . . of carrying the *intentions* of the Legislature into effect," but at the same time he was wary of supplying the "defect by the Executive Act."[131] Rather than regarding the section dealing with certificates as inoperable because the law lacked authentication instructions (meaning that no certificates would be issued), Washington fixed the legislative mistake. In particular, he incorporated the gist of the missing section in his instructions to collectors,[132] thereby relying upon the intent of Congress.

Regulating Presidential Power

After the Preamble, the Constitution first establishes a Congress and grants it various powers. Though Article I also empowers the president (by granting veto authority), Article II does most of the work. Some might imagine that this sequence hints at legislative supremacy, under the theory that the Constitution creates the most vital institutions first. Others perhaps derive the notion of legislative supremacy not from the Constitution's ordering but from the idea that since the legislature represents the people, it ought to dominate the president, who is not formally elected by the people. And still others have an intuition that in a democracy, powerful officers must be subject to control, lest they subvert the government. The obvious candidate for controlling the president is Congress.[133]

The textual basis for legislative supremacy is uncertain. The Necessary and Proper Clause is the best candidate for the notion that the Constitution grants Congress a regulatory power over the president. The clause enables Congress to enact all laws "necessary and proper for carrying into execution" the powers of the federal government.[134] One might suppose that a statute that modifies or regulates a presidential power could be considered necessary and proper because it is meant to better implement all federal powers. Should Congress conclude that federal powers, as a whole, are better implemented when the president lacks a pardon power during the last three months of a lame-duck administration, perhaps it may enact laws so limiting the pardon power. In the extreme, Congress might even completely bar the exercise of a presidential power. For instance, maybe Congress could forbid presidential nomination of judges (and allocate that power elsewhere) if it concluded that the judicial power would be better exercised as a result.

Insurmountable difficulties plague the idea that the Necessary and Proper Clause grants Congress sweeping authority to regulate presidential powers. To begin with, there is the textual difficulty of supposing that a clause granting Congress the means of enacting laws meant to help "carry into execution" federal powers could be employed to erect obstacles to the execution of presidential powers. Even if Congress could be said to be carrying into execution some of its legislative powers by limiting the pardoning power, it certainly does not carry into execution the pardon power when it limits exercises of that power. Likewise, a statute that precludes presidential vetoes of appropriation bills hardly carries the veto power into execution.

Moreover, if the Necessary and Proper Clause authorizes the regulation of presidential powers, it likewise sanctions the regulation of *all* federal powers. Under a "regulatory" reading of the Necessary and Proper Clause, Congress could tell courts how to decide pending cases or could subject their decisions to the review of some third party. Likewise, Congress could instruct the electoral colleges not to choose certain candidates as president. It is a mistake to read the clause as authorizing the regulation of all federal powers because Congress would thereby exercise all federal powers. Borrowing from Montesquieu, tyrannical legislation then might be executed and judged tyrannically. The Constitution does not permit such congressional aggrandizement.

Finally, the Constitution's text strongly implies that Congress lacks a generic regulatory power. Certain provisions expressly enable Congress to regulate particular powers granted to other entities. The Constitution grants states the power to regulate federal elections, but also permits Congress to make its own superseding rules.[135] Likewise, the Constitution grants the Supreme Court appellate jurisdiction over certain cases, but allows Congress to make exceptions to that jurisdiction.[136]

In two cases, the Constitution grants Congress a limited power to regulate a presidential power. First, although the president has the power to appoint all officers, by and with the Senate's advice and consent, the Constitution provides that Congress may vest the power to appoint inferior officers with the president, the department heads, and the courts.[137] Second, Article II makes the president the commander in chief of the armed forces and the militia. But Article I grants Congress the authority to make rules for "the Government and Regulation" of the armed forces and the power to "provide for organizing, arming, and disciplining, the Militia."[138]

The presence of specific provisions authorizing congressional regulation of certain presidential powers reinforces the conclusion that Congress lacks generic authority to regulate all constitutionally granted powers. Limitations found in these provisions would be of no consequence if Congress enjoyed a generic power to regulate all federal powers. For instance, if Congress had regulatory authority over presidential powers, it not only could delegate the power to appoint inferior officers to the president, department heads, and the courts of law, but also could assume this power for itself, appointing by statute. Further, Congress could assume or convey to others the far more important power to appoint noninferior officers. The better view is that the Constitution nowhere grants Congress generic authority to regulate or modify presidential powers. Where the Constitution means for Congress to have a power to regulate an authority granted to others, it expressly conveys that authority.

Consistent with these arguments, Gary Lawson and Patricia Granger have argued that the Necessary and Proper Clause does not authorize Congress to reorganize or revamp the Constitution's structural provisions.[139] Any such statute not only would be an improper attempt to restructure powers already granted by the Constitution, but also would be wholly unnecessary. Given that the Constitution already allocates presidential powers, subject to certain checks, it can hardly be necessary for Congress to further regulate these powers, creating still more constraints and curbs.

Even if the Constitution's text does not support a regulatory power, some might imagine that historical practice does. Many celebrated acts of Parliament restrained, modified, and abridged the Crown's powers.[140] Likewise, before 1789, state legislatures enacted laws that regulated constitutionally conveyed executive powers. If these assemblies could regulate executive powers, perhaps Congress might as well.

In this case, neither the English nor state experiences are relevant. In England, no fixed constitutional constraints hemmed in the legislature. Rather, the English Constitution merely reflected existing traditions and laws. Subject to political constraints, Parliament could create new constitutional rights and abolish them at will. In the same way, it could regulate the Crown's powers. When Parliament enacted a statute that modified the Crown's powers, the statute became part of the English Constitution. For these reasons, none of the executive's powers were outside Parliament's reach.[141]

Congress did not inherit or acquire parliamentary supremacy. Under the Constitution, Congress is not supreme, cannot modify the Constitution, and cannot enact whatever laws it wishes. Instead, the Constitution is supreme and unalterable by ordinary legislation. A corollary (and one obvious from a reading of the Constitution) is that Congress is limited to its enumerated powers. Because the Constitution never authorizes Congress to regulate presidential power, Congress lacks such power.

The state experience is irrelevant for a different reason: many state constitutions expressly granted legislatures the power to regulate the executive's powers. For instance, the North Carolina Constitution of 1776 granted the governor specific executive powers but also vested him with "all the other executive powers of government, limited and restrained as by this Constitution is mentioned, and according to the laws of the State."[142] As discussed in Chapter 2, such language invited the state legislature to regulate those non-itemized executive powers—that is, those not specifically enumerated in the Constitution. Other constitutions expressly sanctioned legislative alteration of the executive's power in only limited situations. The Pennsylvania Constitution of 1776, for instance, provided that the executive council could appoint and commission certain officers "except such as are chosen by the general assembly or the people, agreeable to this frame of government, and the laws that may be made hereafter."[143] Hence, that constitution established a default rule of executive appointment subject to laws that might vest appointment authority with the general assembly or the people.[144]

Rather than furthering the notion that Congress may treat constitutional grants of power as default grants, the state constitutions weaken that argument. Notwithstanding express or implied grants of legislative power, each of the state constitutions seemed to assume that the legislature did not have the power to alter the constitution's grants of powers. That implication explains the need for specific authorization to regulate the executive's powers. Moreover, given the variability of the state constitutional provisions, it is hard to suppose that there was some sort of silent consensus that the proposed national legislature had implicit power to regulate the executive. To the contrary, the different approaches suggested a lack of consensus.

In turning from the state constitutions to commentary about them, the same picture emerges. Legislatures that regulated (or sought to regulate) executive powers in unauthorized ways were condemned as violating their constitutions. When the Pennsylvania Assembly intruded upon the executive's powers, others criticized it. The state Executive Council complained that "it was never supposed that any House of Assembly would by special laws ... assume the Executive powers."[145] The Pennsylvania Council of Censors made similar claims about the legislature's usurpation of executive powers.[146] Complaints also were voiced in New York.[147] Because neither the

New York nor the Pennsylvania constitutions authorized the legislature to regulate all the executive's powers, the complaints were appropriate.

Legislative regulation proved so problematic that some complained even when constitutions authorized such regulation. Thomas Jefferson objected that the Virginia legislature had assumed executive and judicial powers and could not be checked, because the legislature had embodied its usurpations in statutes, making it necessary for the other entities to honor the unconstitutional usurpation.[148] As a matter of policy, Jefferson had a point. As a matter of law, he seems mistaken: Virginia's Constitution *authorized* statutory regulation of executive power. This meant that legislative usurpation was constitutional.[149] Still, his complaint suggested a certain unease with legislative regulation of executive power.

Records from the Philadelphia Convention of 1787 suggest that delegates did not believe that they were authorizing generic statutory regulation of the executive. First, apparently no one proposed that the president's powers generally should be subject to congressional regulation.[150] This omission is surprising, given that such provisions were somewhat common in the states. Second, rather than speaking of the possible benefits of legislative regulation of the executive, delegates often worried about encroachment.[151] Had legislative regulation somehow been authorized, there could have been no talk of encroachment. After all, a legislature does not encroach on the executive when it acts pursuant to constitutional authority. Talk of encroachment and usurpation was common in the Pennsylvania State House because delegates understood that Congress could not regulate presidential powers. Third, when delegates added a provision that permitted Congress to regulate a presidential power (appointments), its proponent claimed that the provision was "necessary"—precisely the opposite of what one would expect had there been a general understanding that all presidential powers were subject to regulation.[152]

The ratification debates point to the same conclusion. No one argued that the Constitution permitted Congress to regulate the executive. Indeed, when Anti-Federalists complained that the Constitution created an executive who would be a king, no Federalist ever claimed that Congress could curb some or all of the supposedly monarchical powers. Federalists would have argued as much had the Constitution granted Congress a power to regulate the executive's powers.[153]

During these debates, there was once again talk of legislative encroachment and usurpation. Madison spoke of these problems at great length in several of the *Federalist Papers*.[154] Citing experiences in Virginia and Pennsylvania, Madison claimed that examples of legislative usurpation were plentiful and well known. Had the Constitution authorized legislative regulation, Madison would not have complained about encroachment or usurpation. Madison's claims were predicated on the notion that like the Pennsylvania Assembly, Congress might regulate or encroach upon presidential powers, thereby *transgressing* the Constitution.[155]

After the Constitution's ratification, President George Washington certainly doubted that Congress could regulate his powers. In 1796, when the House sought the treaty instructions that Washington had given to John Jay, the president refused to turn them over, on the grounds that the House had no role in the treaty process and hence had no right to the papers. "[I]t is essential to the due administration of the government that the boundaries fixed by the constitution between the different departments should be preserved," Washington wrote the House.[156] To be sure, the House's request was in the form of a resolution and not a statute.[157] Nonetheless, had the House's request been in the form of a statute, Washington's answer likely would have been the same, because he regarded the House's request as an impermissible encroachment upon treaty making.[158]

A 1792 episode suggests a similar lesson. In March, the president sought Thomas Jefferson's opinion on a House resolution requesting the president to convey the House's congratulations regarding the new French Constitution. Washington "apprehend[e]d[] the legislature wd. be endeavoring to invade the executive."[159] The resolution was a supposed invasion because Washington believed that the Constitution, via the grant of executive power, made the president the sole organ of communication between the United States and other nations, and the sole judge of the content of such communications. One has to suppose that had Congress passed a statute to accomplish the same ends, Washington would have been no less disturbed. He recognized that when Congress usurps or regulates powers granted to others, it transgresses "boundaries fixed by the constitution."[160]

At least some of the president's assistants had the same view. Writing in 1796, the secretary of war, James McHenry, declared that Congress, notwithstanding its ample authority over the military, could not "intrench upon, invalidate or nullify [the] power to pardon offences against the United States."[161]

Evidence from Congress is mixed. During the debates leading to the Decision of 1789, one newspaper reported Elias Boudinot as arguing that Congress alone had "the right of modifying and explaining the powers of the constitution, when there were any doubts respecting the organization of the government."[162] Another paper claimed that Boudinot argued that Congress has a right "to modify principles established by the constitution. . . . A supreme court is established by the constitution; but do gentlemen contend, that we cannot modify that court, direct the manner in which its functions shall be performed, and assign and limit its jurisdiction."[163] A few others made similar claims, all in support of the claim that Congress could grant the president a removal power.[164]

After initially asserting that Congress could convey a removal power, Madison eventually argued that the Constitution itself had granted the president that power. In this context, he denied that Congress could make exceptions to any of the president's powers: "The constitution affirms, that the executive power shall be vested in the President. Are there exceptions to this proposition? Yes there are. The constitution says, that in appointing to office, the Senate shall be associated with the President, unless in the case of inferior officers, when the law shall otherwise direct. Have we a right to extend this exception? I believe not. If the constitution has invested all executive power in the President, I venture to assert that the Legislature has no right to diminish or modify his executive authority."[165] Madison made the exact same argument regarding the legislative and judicial powers, namely, that Congress could create no exceptions to such powers. "[I]t is incontrovertible," Madison wrote, "if neither the legislative nor judicial powers are subjected to qualifications, other than those demanded in the constitution, that the executive powers are equally unabateable as either of the others; and inasmuch as the power of removal is of an executive nature, and not affected by any constitutional exception, *it is beyond the reach of the legislative body*."[166] Madison's speech completely repudiated the idea that executive powers were subject to legislative modification. Though the Constitution contains certain exceptions to executive power, it does not authorize Congress to create further ones. If there was a dominant view in the first Congress on the subject of regulation, Madison likely spoke for that majority.

In sum, we have good reason to reject the notion that Congress can pass statutes that regulate presidential powers. The Constitution nowhere grants Congress the generic power to regulate powers granted by the Constitution. To the contrary, it grants Congress specific powers that permit the regulation of other powers in limited circumstances. Moreover, had the Constitution's makers sought to grant Congress a generic regulatory power, they had ready examples from the state constitutions. The failure to adopt such text, coupled with concerns about legislative usurpation, suggests that people believed that Congress could not regulate the president's powers.

Though Congress can make no law regulating presidential power, it has plenty of leverage. It may disestablish offices and withhold funds, measures that will weaken the presidency because it will lose the instruments often necessary for effectively exercising executive power. These indirect methods can serve to make the president cooperative, without formally usurping, transferring, or regulating the exercise of his powers.

Conclusion

The president's role in the formation, alteration, and execution of legislation gave rise to the complaint that he would wield both legislative and executive power. The complaint was grounded in a sound reading of the Constitution. The latter not only grants the president a host of powers related to convening and adjourning Congress, but also imposes two crucial legislative duties upon him. He must share information with Congress regarding the state of the union and must recommend measures. Though the former provision seems to make him something of a legislative aide, the latter obliges him to influence the legislative agenda by requiring him to opine about the shortcomings of existing law. Finally, the president's veto authority effectively enables him to serve as something of a third legislative chamber, ensuring that the other chambers heed his concerns. All in all, the president serves as a chief legislator because the Constitution permits (and in some cases requires) as much.

CHAPTER ELEVEN

JUDGES AS "SHOOTS FROM THE EXECUTIVE STOCK"

The Constitution says little about the president's connection to the judiciary. Other than his power to nominate and appoint judges and his duty to commission them, nothing else is mentioned. Nonetheless, there is a modern relationship, with established features. The executive branch always executes court judgments, even when it supposes that they are erroneous and even when it is the loser. Federal judges rarely serve simultaneously in the executive branch. Finally, such judges almost never advise the executive on matters of federal law.

Routine executive enforcement of judgments is an inheritance from England. Over centuries, the Crown became further and further removed from the judicial power, gradually losing it altogether and solidifying the distinction between executive and judicial power. But the Crown's officers continued the practice of enforcing judgments, perhaps recognizing that if the Crown could decide who ought to prevail in cases regardless of a court's final judgment, for all practical purposes the Crown would enjoy the judicial power and the two powers would not be meaningfully separated. By vesting the judicial power in distinct courts, the

Constitution implicitly adopted the prevailing system, in which courts decide disputes and the executive enforces their judgments.

The other two modern practices reflect contemporary conceptions of a proper separation of powers, most prominently a sense that the judiciary must be kept as isolated as possible from the executive. Yet the original Constitution never forbade judges from serving in the executive branch or from offering advice to the president. Indeed, some early federal judges served as executive officers, negotiating treaties, among other actions. Many also advised the executive on a host of matters.

So while the original Constitution vested executive and judicial power in different entities and envisioned that the executive would enforce the judgments of the courts, it did not bar overlapping membership in these branches. Nor did it bar the executive from seeking judicial advice, or the judiciary from offering it. In sum, the Constitution did not hermetically seal off these two branches from each other.

A Separate Judicial Power

At one time, judicial and executive powers were not considered distinct; the former was considered a branch of the latter, since both were concerned with executing laws.[1] This practice perhaps reflected the fact that English monarchs sat as judges as late as the fourteenth century.[2] The King's Bench consisted of judges and the monarch,[3] and pleadings described it as "the court of our said lord the king, before the king himself."

Over time, kings stopped serving as judges, leaving the power exclusively to appointed judges.[4] Chief Justice Edward Coke is supposed to have told King James I that he could not "take any cause out of any of his Courts, and give judgment upon it himself."[5] Additionally, though English judges served the Crown as "deputies," they exercised independent judgment, meaning that the Crown could not direct their decisions.[6] As one Englishman put it, judges "are sworn to do justice according to the laws, without any regard to the king's words, letters or commands."[7] English judges were not independent, however, because most had tenure during pleasure. The looming threat of executive removal made some judges rather pliant.

That menace disappeared at the end of the seventeenth century. Parliament guaranteed salaries and granted tenure during good behavior, preventing the Crown from punishing or removing high judges.[8] Because the Crown once distributed justice personally and because it erected courts, all judicial "proceedings [ran] generally in the king's name, they pass[ed] under his seal, and [were] executed by his officers."[9] But all this was a matter of form, not substance. Kings had "delegated their whole judicial power" to judges, who could decide cases without executive direction or fear of reprisal.[10] When a court decided a case, the executive branch had to execute the court's judgment, just as it used to do when the king sat on the bench. As a dictionary put it, judges were "invested with authority to determine any cause,"[11] meaning that they conclusively decided who won and lost. When William Blackstone noted that "judgment on a writ of quo warranto . . . is final and conclusive even against the crown,"[12] he was describing not the unique consequences of that judgment but a general rule. Where courts had jurisdiction, the executive had to enforce their judgments.

Had the Crown a generic power to counter or ignore a judgment, it would have been a backdoor means of resuming the judicial power that monarchs previously had delegated to their judges. By divesting themselves of the judicial power and by signing laws that made judges independent of the executive, English monarchs rendered it "improper" for them to exercise the judicial power themselves.[13] Perhaps the English had come to agree with Montesquieu that when one entity exercises both executive and judicial powers, tyranny might arise.

In the eighteenth century, colonial governors had more judicial authority than their creators. They not only established courts, but also sometimes heard cases, making them "part of the judicial system."[14] For the most part, these governors lacked a criminal jurisdiction,[15] most likely because of the incongruity of deciding cases in which they were parties (as prosecutors). With respect to many civil cases, however, there was no such issue, and governors often served as the last court of appeal. Finally, to maintain sway over judges and to comply with Crown directives, governors tried to grant judges tenure during pleasure.[16] Sometimes they took other measures, such as packing or intimidating courts.[17]

State constitutions tended to establish a somewhat more thorough separation of the judicial and executive powers, at least in the sense of vesting the powers in two distinct entities. Though executives generally lacked judicial power, there were notable exceptions. The New Jersey governor was made chancellor of the Court of Equity and had authority over estates as "surrogate general."[18] In Pennsylvania, the supreme executive council could try impeachments of state officers.[19] Many gubernatorial commanders in chief heard final appeals in courts-martial.[20]

As William Baude has shown, the notion that the executive had to enforce judgments was a bedrock assumption of American jurisprudence.[21] James Wilson noted that "[w]hen the decisions of courts of justice are made, they must, it is true, be executed; but the power of executing them is ministerial," meaning that the executive lacked discretion and had to enforce them.[22] Agreeing with Baude's claim, Philip Hamburger quotes James Iredell as observing that "*if the power of judging rests with the Courts, their decision is final as to the subject matter*" and asking the rhetorical question: "Did ever a Sheriff refuse to hang a Man because he thought he was unjustly convicted of murder?"[23]

Consider also the discussion of judicial power found in *The Essex Result*, a Massachusetts separation-of-powers document discussed in previous chapters: "Every man is to be presumed innocent, until the judicial power hath determined him guilty. When that decision is known, the law annexes the punishment, and the offender is turned over to the executive arm, by whom it is inflicted on him. The judicial power hath also to determine what legal contracts have been broken, and what member hath been injured by a violation of the law, to consider the damages that have been sustained, and to ascertain the recompense. The executive power takes care that this recompense is paid."[24] The *Result* supposed that the executive enforced judgments, regardless of whether the government was prosecutor, defendant, or no party at all.

Notwithstanding the division of executive and judicial power and the duty of the executive to execute judgments, people understood that executive and judicial powers were closely related. As James Madison observed, judges were originally "shoots from the executive stock."[25] Not surprisingly, while many distinguished these powers, some saw judicial power as merely a branch of the executive.[26] Indeed, Thomas Paine went so far as to say that the "judicial power" was "strictly and properly the executive," claiming the former actually ensured that the laws were executed.[27] Paine went too far. The executive often must make parties comply with a judgment, and it often executes the law in contexts in which the courts will rarely if ever intervene. But we might say that the judicial power was more purely "executive" than the executive power. Whereas the former was almost wholly focused on law execution, the latter had several features, some of which were only tangentially related to execution.

The Judicial Power Under the Constitution

The Constitution grants judicial power to the courts, not the president. Given prevailing conceptions at the time of its ratification, the implication was clear. Executive enforcement of judgments was a bedrock (though tacit) feature of the Constitution, in the same way that the Constitution implicitly obliges judges to decide cases consistent with the law. The courts would decide disputes—the winners and losers—and the executive would execute those judgments. As one federal judge put it in his treatise on government, "It is the business of the executive to carry into effect, the decisions of the judiciary."[28]

Despite the hundreds of judicial judgments issued over the eight years of Washington's presidency, no one in the administration seems ever to have claimed that a judgment of a court would not or should not be enforced. These executives likely understood that a judgment supplied the law of the case that the president was to faithfully execute, even if he opposed many or all of the rationales underlying the judgment. The one exception to this rule was express—the pardon power authorized the president to erase or moderate certain judgments favoring the government.

Some scholars deny that the original Constitution incorporates the rule that the executive branch must execute judgments. Michael Stokes Paulsen claims that under the original Constitution, the executive could decide whether to implement judgments.[29] His assertion is partly grounded on Alexander Hamilton's observation that the judiciary had "neither Force nor Will, but merely judgment; and must ultimately depend upon the aid of the executive arm even for the efficacy of its judgments."[30] But saying that the judiciary must rely upon the executive hardly implies that the latter has a constitutional right to ignore judgments. Though the federal government similarly depends upon states to conduct federal elections, no one would say that the states therefore have a constitutional right to refuse to conduct such elections.

Paulsen also grounds his argument on the idea that the branches are coordinate and that no one branch should be supreme in constitutional interpretation.[31] Yet the executive's obligation to enforce judgments does not imply that judicial interpretations of the Constitution are supreme. As discussed below, the president can reject the constitutional interpretations of the courts even as he fulfills his implied constitutional duty. More generally, each branch takes actions that are unreviewable by its counterparts. The finality of judicial judgments no more implies judicial supremacy than the finality of pardons implies executive supremacy.

Members of the Washington administration were well aware of the judiciary's sphere of exclusive authority. In 1795, Attorney General William Bradford denied any authority to interfere in a private dispute over French prizes, saying it would be "improper and unavailing."[32] When the English protested a different suit, he pointed out that just as the Crown could not suppress private suits, the U.S. executive was similarly impotent.[33] To the French minister, Secretary of State Thomas Jefferson explained that once a claim about an improper capture went to a court, "there is no power in this country which could take the vessel out of the custody of that court, till it should decide, itself, whether it had jurisdiction or not."[34] Jefferson spoke a little too loosely. When a private party went to court, the executive could not halt the proceedings, as Jefferson noted. But if the federal government brought suit, the executive certainly could terminate it, as Attorney General Charles Lee observed in 1797.[35]

Washington likewise disclaimed the power to interfere with judicial proceedings. During the Whiskey Rebellion, he commanded a federal district judge to march with the militia. But this was merely an order to be ready to attend to his duties once the militia restored order. Pursuant to Washington's directions, Alexander Hamilton instructed a commander that "the Judge cannot be controuled in his functions."[36] Similarly, when a foreigner sought the distribution of estate assets, Washington noted his incapacity. The foreigner imagined "that the Courts of Justice in this country were under [the President's] control."[37] The president replied that he had "no more right to intermeddle in the Judicial proceedings of the Courts in this Country than you have."[38] Though uttered in the context of state proceedings, the principle applied equally to federal cases.

The Authority of Judicial Opinions

In modern times, judgments sometimes seem less important than the opinions that accompany them. Whereas judgments tersely declare the victor and the relief granted, opinions purport to explain the law, sometimes containing memorable rhetoric. Today, some imagine that the president must treat judicial opinions as if they were authoritative pronouncements about the law that he must obey and execute. Indeed, when people think about constitutional law, the Supreme Court's opinions often come to mind. For some, the opinions of the Supreme Court are part of the Constitution (broadly understood); in many instances, the opinions may seem more important than the text of the Constitution.

Eighteenth-century judicial opinions likely were not regarded as binding on future cases. Instead, there perhaps was a sense that a "decision may bind the unfortunate individual who happens to be the particular subject of it; but it cannot alter the law."[39] Levi Lincoln, Jefferson's attorney general, summed it up best while discussing a case called the *Peggy Schooner:*

> The Supreme Court, who were competent to decide this principle, have determined it in her case [the *Peggy*]. It must, therefore, be considered as binding in this particular instance. Although they have fixed the principle for themselves, and thereby bound others, in reference to the case on which they have adjudicated, it can, I conceive, extend no further. In all other cases in which the Executive or other courts are obliged to act, they must decide for themselves; paying a great deference to the opinions of a court of so high an authority as the supreme one of the United States, but still greater to their own convictions of the meaning of the laws and constitution of the United States, and their oaths to support them.[40]

Again, though courts decided cases once and for all, others could decide the law's meaning in contrary ways, because judicial opinions did not conclusively fix meaning.

Why was there a dichotomy between the treatment accorded to judgments and opinions? To begin with, judicial opinions were oral, not written.[41] When written accounts of opinions were available, they were the product of private reporters who transcribed the oral opinions issued from the bench. These private reports had limited printings and distributions, meaning that they were not widely read.[42] To be sure, there also was no general publication and distribution of statutes; but at least the secretary of state saw to it that the states received copies of laws.[43] There was no similar distribution of federal judicial opinions, making general adherence to their legal reasoning unlikely.

Moreover, in the late eighteenth century, *courts* did not render opinions; individual judges did. For instance, in the Supreme Court's early days, justices issued opinions, with the judgment resulting from the aggregation of individual views. It was not until the early nineteenth century that Chief Justice John Marshall introduced the authoritative "opinion of the Court."[44] In a world where individual judges and justices issued separate opinions, it was often difficult, even impossible, to discern a common thread necessary to derive an authoritative legal pronouncement from a multimember court. Even if the vote to affirm was unanimous, the particular reasons might vary dramatically. One judge might cite jurisdictional reasons for a judgment, another a federal statute, and a third a state constitution. Adherence to the reasoning in an opinion for the court was impossible when there was no "court" opinion.

Even treating the opinion of a single judge as law is fraught with difficulties. Suppose one district judge decided that a military pension statute did not cover members of the militia. Subsequently, in another case, a different district court concluded that the same statute granted benefits to militiamen. And in a third case, a state court trial judge concludes that some members of the militia are covered and some not. If the president had had to regard judicial opinions as binding, he would have found himself in an impossible position, for he could not follow all three opinions in future cases. Supreme Court review might eventually solve the problem of conflicting "authoritative" interpretations. But in the interim (which could last years), the executive would face contradictory "binding" opinions. In a world where judgments matter, there likely was some discomfort with inconsistent judgments across cases. Yet there was no logical problem, because conflicting judgments may be executed without any logical conflict. In a world where judicial opinions are law, however, it would have been impossible for conflicting opinions to simultaneously serve as the law that the president had to execute.

Consider also the traditional structure of litigation and appeal. When litigants prevail and secure the judgment they seek, they have no opportunity to appeal a judicial opinion to a higher court in a bid to overturn aspects of the opinion that the litigants intensely reject. Suppose a merchant makes three arguments in an attempt to recover money from a supplier, and the court rejects two of the arguments but accepts the third and awards judgment to the merchant. She cannot appeal the rejection of her two legal arguments. If judicial opinions create or establish law, however, it makes less sense to deny the merchant the opportunity to appeal those subsidiary decisions, because they may be far more important to her than the individual case that she won. The point is that the U.S. litigation system focuses on who wins and who loses and accords appeal rights to those who face an adverse judgment. In other words, our system is constructed on the view that it is the outcome—the judgment—that really matters, not the opinion or opinions undergirding it.

In sum, because opinions were "underreported, often unwritten, and often seriatim";[45] because they often would yield contradictory indications about what the law meant; and because they were not appealable, we have good reasons for concluding that opinions were not binding statements on the meaning of the law.[46] They were not on par with judgments.

Yet opinions could persuade. When Thomas Jefferson observed, "[W]e take no judge's word for what the law is, further than he is warranted by the authorities he appeals to,"[47] he admitted that opinions could provide a sense of what the law is. Because opinions were reasoned elaborations of what a learned judge took to be the meaning of a law and because they supplied a sense of how courts might resolve future cases, litigants (executive or otherwise) would pay close attention to them. President Washington and his successors may have given weight to judicial opinions out of respect for the learning they represented and out of a pragmatic sense that future courts might adhere to the wisdom found in prior opinions. But any such deference likely arose for practical reasons, not from any constitutional obligation. Though eighteenth-century judges decided cases and controversies by issuing judgments that the executive had to enforce, the judicial power likely did not encompass the formal power to conclusively settle what the law was for the other branches or, for that matter, anyone else.

Judicial Process and the President

Thus far, the relationship between the federal executive and the courts seems rather clear—the president was a litigant in some cases, was the enforcer of all judgments, and would often find wisdom in judicial opinions. Yet there was some early confusion about the president's relationship to the courts. As noted in Chapter 1, the president's link to the judiciary first arose in the context of the bill related to judicial process. The Senate version would have had judges issue writs and process in the president's name. For instance, a judicial summons was to begin with the statement "The President of the United States of America . . . command[s]" the marshal to summon an individual before a court.[48] This mimicked the colonial and British practice,[49] but ran contrary to state practices.[50] After debating whether process should issue in the president's name, the House returned a bill in which process would issue from the "United States."[51] The House's vote likely reflected the sense that because sovereignty did not rest with the president, but with the United States as whole, process should be issued in that name only.[52] While the Senate resisted the change, the House stood firm. Ultimately, Congress's act was silent on the matter, leaving it unresolved.[53]

The Supreme Court stepped into the breach, providing that all of its process would be issued in the "Name of the 'President of the United States.'" The court indicated that its rule would be valid only so long as Congress did not provide another rule by "[l]aw."[54] Why did the court resolve the matter in favor of the president? Perhaps it read the grant of executive power broadly or favored mimicking English customs. Nor should one discount the notion that the justices wished to associate the courts with the nation's most powerful and popular figure. The Supreme Court's standing paled in comparison to that of Washington and his presidency.

Issuing process in the president's name perhaps was a constitutional blunder, not so much because the practice was an "apendage of

Royalty,"[55] but because the president has no constitutional power related to judicial functions. In England, the notion that the Crown commanded people to come to court may have been a vestige of the sense that the king was either personally in court or acted via his judicial deputies.[56] In the United States, there should have been no such notion. The president was not always present in court and was not the font of judicial authority. With respect to writs in particular, he had no authority, except for the duty to see to their execution.

The best case for issuing orders in the president's name is that because he had to enforce judicial orders, it made sense for summons, orders, and so forth to issue in his name. Yet the fact that the executive had to enforce judicial orders against recalcitrant citizens hardly establishes that judicial orders had to issue in his name. Though the president must enforce statutes, no one supposes that Congress ought to preface its laws with words from the president commanding that citizens obey them. Similarly, the courts have judicial power to issue binding orders, and citizens must honor those orders in the same way that they are obliged to follow the laws enacted by legislatures. Furthermore, some judicial orders in the president's name were issued to courts rather than executive officers.[57] In this context, the use of the president's name seems odd, for why would a higher court need to use the president as a means of securing compliance from a lower court? So strong was the sense of presidential power and prestige that some were misled into mimicking practices foreign to the Constitution.

Judges in the Executive Branch

Though the Constitution expressly bars members of Congress from holding executive or judicial offices, it does not explicitly ban people from holding both executive and judicial offices.[58] Dual office holding was common in England and some states, hinting that the failure to expressly ban this practice implied that it might continue. Indeed, Steve Calabresi and Joan Larsen have argued that the absence of an express ban likely reflected a desire to permit judges to serve in the executive branch.[59]

Although some objected to the practice, early chief justices served as executive officers. John Jay served as the first cross-branch officeholder when he simultaneously functioned as chief justice and as a holdover secretary of foreign affairs.[60] Later, the chief justice helped negotiate the Jay Treaty with England. Oliver Ellsworth and John Marshall also had cross-branch appointments, the former serving as chief justice and special envoy to France in 1799, and the latter serving as both secretary of state and chief justice for a very brief period.[61] Finally, Jay served as a commissioner of the public debt[62] and as an inspector of newly minted coins.[63] In these latter cases, statutes directly vested executive functions upon the office of the chief justice, meaning that the president did not nominate or appoint Jay to a new office before the latter assumed the new functions. Nor did the Senate separately consent to his appointment to a reconstituted office.[64]

One early episode might suggest the unconstitutionality of judges serving in the executive branch. After Congress passed a pension act that required "courts" to hear applications for veteran pensions, some judges wrote to the president asserting that they could not adjudicate the claims. Among the reasons they gave were that the duties were not judicial in nature and that the secretary of war could reverse their decisions.[65] The logic of these complaints suggested that judges could perform only judicial functions and could not have their official decisions subject to executive branch review.

Other judges reacted quite differently, however. Some reviewed the applications, acting as nonjudicial commissioners, albeit "in the same court room, or chamber."[66] That is to say, they acted as members of the executive branch, periodically setting aside their status as judges in order to consider pension applications.[67] Others refused to act as executive commissioners, claiming that because Congress had imposed a duty on "courts," it evidently did not wish to impose nonjudicial business upon judges. These latter judges declined to say whether Congress could constitutionally require them to hear claims as "commissioners" rather than as judges.[68] In other words, they sidestepped the question whether judges could serve in the executive branch in a nonjudicial capacity.

Given the conspicuous absence of any express bar on judges serving in the executive branch, the longstanding practices in America and England,

and the examples of John Jay and other chief justices, the better reading of the Constitution is that federal judges could take up executive duties. There was no sound reason for concluding that federal judges could not also serve as executive commissioners under the control of the secretary of war and, by implication, the president.

Indeed the office of "judge" likely encompassed some minimal, vestigial executive functions. Before the Constitution's ratification, state executives sometimes ordered judges, among others, to apprehend alleged lawbreakers.[69] President Washington did the same, generically directing "all officers" to guard against violations of the law and sometimes giving specific orders to judges.[70] While attacking the proposed 1801 disestablishment of certain federal courts, Alexander Hamilton said that judges had two duties—"judicial and ministerial."[71] When acting as a "conservator of the peace, which every judge is ex officio, many things are done not connected with a judicial controversy."[72] Hamilton believed that while judges had both judicial and executive tasks, courts were necessarily confined to the judicial.

In their ministerial, executive capacity, judges were properly subject to presidential control, for ministerial officers are, by their nature, subject to direction.[73] This explains the lack of hue and cry when executives occasionally directed judges, in their capacity as conservators of the peace, to apprehend alleged lawbreakers. Similarly, Chief Justice Jay received "orders" from Washington when he served as secretary of state and as treaty negotiator.[74] The act making the chief justice one of several debt commissioners expressly authorized the president to approve the commissioners' decisions.[75] Though the president could not control how judges decided cases, he could direct them in their executive capacities, because they were exercising his power when acting as executives.[76]

The control mechanisms were obvious when judges occupied a separate, nonjudicial office, for the president could oust the judge from the executive office. For instance, Washington clearly could have removed John Jay as a negotiator had he been dissatisfied with the progress of the treaty talks. When a statute imposed executive duties on judges acting in their judicial capacities, the control mechanisms were less clear. Though these judges were constitutionally obliged to follow the chief executive's instructions relating to executive tasks, they could not be removed from office, because they did not formally occupy a separate executive office. Perhaps the president could have barred particular judges from serving in the executive branch, ex officio, for the president's removal power suggests that Congress cannot force the president to employ officers in whom he lacks confidence.

Judges Advising the President

Another early question was whether the president could seek and receive the opinions of judges on legal matters. A Constitutional Convention proposal that would have permitted the president and Congress to seek the opinions of Supreme Court justices never was put to a vote. A more modest proposal authorizing the president to seek advice from the chief justice met the same fate.[77] Rather than enacting either suggestion, the convention adopted the Opinions Clause, a clause that could be read to suggest that the president could seek opinions only from executives—"he may require the Opinion, in writing, of the principal Officer in each of the *executive* Departments."

Nonetheless, Washington received advice from judges. John Jay advised on matters of law and policy throughout his term as chief justice, although the frequency of his advice decreased after 1790.[78] After the president issued a standing request for advice,[79] justices opined about circuit riding and other matters.[80] As Maeva Marcus and Robert Teir point out, the justices' letters to the president on the Pension Act were, "in the most classic sense, advisory opinions."[81]

All this advice giving was, in the words of Justice James Iredell, "proper."[82] As Stewart Jay points out, the "most natural" reading of the Constitutional Convention's proceedings and its final product is that though the president had no constitutional right to the opinions of judges, the Constitution did not bar either his requests or judicial compliance with them.[83] Indeed, nothing in the Constitution forbids judges, as individuals, from giving legal opinions to friends, family, or politicians.

Despite the seeming constitutionality of extrajudicial advice giving, on one occasion the justices conspicuously declined. In the summer of 1793, at the beginning of the president's second term, the Washington administration sought the Supreme Court's advice on questions related to treaty

interpretation and international law.[84] Though the administration prepared twenty-nine questions, whether it actually sent them to the court is
unclear.[85] What is certain is that the court refused to supply advice, claiming that "[t]he Lines of Separation drawn by the Constitution" between
the branches, "their being in certain Respects checks on each other," and
the role of the Supreme Court as one of "last Resort" constituted "strong
arguments against the Propriety of our extrajudicially" responding to
questions.[86] Justices also cited the president's ability to demand opinions
from department heads as the sanctioned means of receiving advice.

Why did the court decline to give advice? Perhaps justices were concerned that the president would feel obliged to follow their advice, putting him in an awkward position.[87] Maybe the topic was too controversial,
given the intense feelings aroused by the war between England and
France.[88] Conceivably, the best reason had to do with whom the president
asked. By preparing questions to be answered by the court, rather than
by individual justices, the president may have reawakened some concerns
expressed in the wake of the Pension Act, namely, that *courts* could not
give advice. Had the president asked individual justices for their legal
opinions, he might have received answers.[89] This contextual explanation
of the episode makes sense of some of the reasons the justices gave and
also explains their willingness to opine and advise as individuals both before and after the court's 1793 refusal.[90]

William Casto provides a more conspiratorial reason for why the court
declined: Alexander Hamilton may have asked them to demur. Casto
points out that while Hamilton generally fared well in internal deliberations, his influence might have waned had the court opined on the French
treaties. The court might have told Washington that he could privilege
France, an answer inconsistent with the strict neutrality that Hamilton
wished to pursue. Given his success in the cabinet, the better forum for
Hamilton was the cabinet, not the court.[91]

In any event, individual judges routinely gave legal and policy advice to
Washington, notwithstanding the lack of presidential power to demand
opinions from them and the absence of an Article III case or controversy.
The few times that judges shied away from opining are best seen as exercises of discretion. Indeed, justices continued to supply advice to the pres-

ident (and members in Congress) even after the conspicuous failure to do so with respect to the French treaties.[92]

Executive Adjudication of "Private" Disputes

Although the Constitution separates judicial from executive power, on one occasion the executive had to adjudicate a private dispute. In 1793, Washington decided the legality of a wartime capture. The British alleged that a French vessel had improperly captured the *Grange* within the United States, something inconsistent with American neutrality. After reviewing submissions from England and France, the president, concluding that the capture was illegal, ordered restitution. The French privateers complied, perhaps recognizing that the president could settle the dispute.[93]

To resolve future cases, Washington set up a better adjudicative process. The president asked governors to accept applications for relief and to notify the district attorneys of the disputed captures. The attorneys were to give notice to all parties and their nation's consuls and to recommend arbiters to the parties. After arbitration, governors would then carry out the arbitral order. If the parties could not agree on arbiters, however, the U.S. attorney was to take depositions himself and transmit them "for the information and decision of the President."[94] On one occasion, the president faced the embarrassing prospect of rendering a decision based on nothing more than one deposition, the attorney general having found other depositions inadmissible.[95]

Perhaps recognizing that such difficulties might recur, the president sought legislation from Congress, saying that if "the Executive is to be the resort [of aggrieved private parties in capture cases] it is hoped, that he will be authorized by law, to have facts ascertained by the Courts, when, for his own information, he shall request it."[96] In other words, even if the courts would not decide capture cases, the president wanted Congress to require the courts to find facts and thereby aid the president. After all, the courts were in the business of finding facts and were likely adept at doing so.

Parallel with these efforts, Washington sought judicial intervention. District attorneys were instructed to bring suit to have the courts adjudicate the private suits. The administration concluded too that the victims of the capture might bring cases claiming that their vessel had been taken within U.S. waters.[97] The executive favored judicial resolution because executive decisions might anger the losers and their governments. Far better to have a federal judge decide the controversy.

After three district courts concluded that the federal courts lacked jurisdiction over such cases, the Supreme Court came to the rescue, concluding that the federal courts could hear such cases.[98] The executive was thus relieved of the burden of deciding whether wartime captures were legal.

Executive adjudication of private disputes was rather unusual. Indeed, it is hard to imagine another area in which the president would feel obliged to adjudicate such disputes. Nonetheless, such adjudication was in keeping with the notion that the president and courts executed the laws, usually in different ways.

Conclusion

After the break with England, some English conceptions of the judiciary lingered in America. There remained the sense that the judiciary executed the law.[99] There also was the sense that judges decided cases once and for all by issuing final judgments, and that the executive was obliged to enforce those judgments. Finally, there was the understanding that judges simultaneously might serve as executive officers or as informal advisers to a chief executive.

But there also was a departure from a particular English conception. Americans generally had no sense that the chief executive served as the wellspring of judicial power. The absence of this notion meant that Americans were more likely to regard the executive and judicial powers as somewhat distinct. Relatedly, because some Americans regarded the intermixture of the executive and judicial branches as improper, some saw voluntary advice giving and dual office holding as practices to be discouraged or stamped out. Yet the Constitution did not affirmatively forbid either, so President Washington and Congress were left free to draw upon the wisdom of federal judges in various nonjudicial contexts. The president repeatedly sought legal advice from federal judges, and Congress occasionally imposed nonjudicial (executive) tasks upon them.

CHAPTER TWELVE

"WHATEVER REQUISITION THE PRESIDENT SHALL MAKE" AND THE FEDERAL DUTIES OF STATE EXECUTIVES

The states play a crucial role in the selection of high federal officials, for they conduct federal legislative elections and decide how to appoint presidential electors. Once in federal office, members of the political branches may implement their powers without further state assistance. Congress may create the instruments (departments and offices) and supply the funds, allowing the president to execute federal law throughout the nation. In modern times, a significant state role in implementing federal law seems largely unnecessary because of the massive federal bureaucracy and Congress's willingness to make it more massive still.

Things stood rather differently in the Constitution's early years. Because the federal apparatus was much smaller, the assistance of state executives was acutely necessary. Believing that he could insist upon the aid of governors, President Washington repeatedly directed them to arrest lawbreakers and to help implement the foreign policy of the United States. Governors almost always complied. Their routine obedience reflected the understanding that when state executives executed federal law, the Constitution obliged them to take orders from the chief executive.

Despite the Constitution's subordination of state executives to the chief executive on matters of federal law, relying upon state officers somewhat hinders the president. Though he may remove federal executives, he cannot oust state officials who prove uncooperative, incompetent, or venal. The president likely can do no more than bar their future assistance in federal matters. From the president's vantage, his limited leverage over state officers makes dependence on them less attractive and makes it preferable to rely wholly on federal officers.

A Tradition of Commandeering Executives

Under the Articles of Confederation, the Continental Congress could "appoint . . . committees and civil officers as may be necessary for managing the general affairs of the United States under [congressional] direction," perhaps suggesting that only officers so appointed would manage the nation's "general affairs."[1] The Articles also expressly empowered Congress to demand troops and funds from the states, provisions possibly hinting that it could not otherwise commandeer state aid.[2]

Congress never read national power so narrowly, at least when it came to state executives. Rather than appointing a sizable and expensive cadre of federal officials and dispersing them throughout the nation, the Continental Congress treated state executives "as their local agents."[3] That is to say, Congress regularly directed state executives, both before and after the 1781 ratification of the Articles of Confederation. Margaret Burnham MacMillan observes that at the direction of Congress, governors assumed "innumerable minor and major administrative actions," including administering oaths, erecting forts, and supervising and removing federal officers.[4] According to MacMillan, "Many a governor gave fully as much time and energy to work for Congress as he did to his [state] constitutional duties."[5]

Though some state executives took offense at the manner in which Congress occasionally expressed itself,[6] they did not seem to believe that they were free to reject congressional requisitions of their attention and services. Judging by their actions, they perhaps felt obliged to lend a hand to the Confederation in those areas where the continental government was supreme.

A Commandeering Constitution

Though delegates to the Constitutional Convention envisioned a more robust, energetic national executive than the one that preceded it, some hoped that state executives might be called upon to execute federal law, as they had in the past. Connecticut delegates considered proposing that "the laws of the United States ought, as far as may be consistent with the common interests of the Union, to be carried into execution by the judiciary and executive officers of the respective states, wherein the execution thereof is required."[7] Though delegates never took up this proposal, the Constitution rather clearly authorized the federal government to conscript state executives in some situations. Congress may decide when the commander in chief will have the assistance of state militias to execute the laws, suppress insurrections, and repel invasions.[8] After summoning a state militia, the federal commander in chief may direct all its members, including the governor, the state-appointed militia officers, and other state executives.

While the express power to conscript the militia for federal purposes may seem somewhat narrow, some at the founding assumed that state executives would serve national purposes even in the absence of any federal statute requiring as much. For instance, Alexander Hamilton claimed that the state "Magistracy, being equally the Ministers of the law of the land, from whatever source it might emanate, would doubtless be as ready to guard the national as the local regulations from the inroads of private licentiousness."[9] He later elaborated: "[T]he laws of the confederacy . . . will become the SUPREME LAW of the land; to the observance of which, all officers legislative, executive and judicial in each State, will be bound by the sanctity of an oath. Thus the Legislatures, Courts, and Magistrates of the respective members will be incorporated into the operations of the national government, as far as its just and constitutional authority extends; and will be rendered auxiliary to the enforcement of its laws."[10]

Opponents of ratification conceded that the new government might conscript state executives. Patrick Henry and other opponents initially assumed that there would be two different tax collectors, one federal and one state.[11] The Constitution's supporters responded that state collectors might collect state and federal taxes. One noted, "We have state taxes, county taxes, and corporation taxes. How do these operate together? It is true, that in some places they are collected by the same man; and probably also the federal and state taxes will be."[12] Another observed, "The laws can, in general, be executed by the officers of the states. State courts and state officers will, for the most part, probably answer the purpose of Congress as well as any other."[13] Yielding the point, Henry complained that such a system would favor federal coffers.[14]

The common view that state executives would enforce federal law reflected the sense that the Constitution did not implicitly bar the commandeering of state executives. That conclusion stemmed also from a belief that state executives had a duty to enforce the laws of the land, whatever their source.[15] Moreover, though the Articles' system of commandeering state legislatures to supply soldiers and funds was widely seen as a failure, since legislatures often failed to fully satisfy those requisitions, reliance on the services of state executives had been successful enough. Given their history of cooperation with the Continental Congress and its commander in chief of the Continental Army, people reasonably read the Constitution as continuing the system in place under the Articles, a system in which state executives acted as auxiliaries in the enforcement of federal law.[16]

Left uncertain was under what circumstances the state executives would enforce federal law. As noted, some assumed that state executives were obliged to execute federal law without any prior congressional authorization or command. By virtue of being magistrates, state officers had to execute federal law because it was the supreme law of the land and was no less state law than statutes passed by the state assemblies. As Governor Thomas Mifflin of Pennsylvania put it during the Whiskey Rebellion, "That the laws of the Union are the laws of the State, is a Constitutional axiom that will never be controverted."[17] Others assumed that Congress would have to statutorily authorize the use of state officers to enforce federal laws. That seemed to mirror the practice under the Articles, in which resolves of the Continental Congress expressly directed state executives to assist the national government in various ways.

For a host of reasons, the better reading is that Congress must decide when, if ever, state executives may execute federal laws. First, it does not follow that because federal law is also state law (by virtue of the Supremacy Clause) that all state executives must execute all federal laws. No one supposes that all federal executives must execute all federal laws.

As discussed in Chapter 8, Congress determines what resources (departments, officers, funds) are available to the president to execute the laws,
meaning that Congress determines which federal laws each subordinate
federal executive will execute. Nothing would be amiss should Congress
limit the secretary of commerce to the execution of the federal commercial laws and bar her execution of the laws related to naturalization or
patents. Second and relatedly, the same system ought to apply to the use
of state executive resources, for it makes little sense to give Congress a
monopoly on federal resources but grant the president unfettered access
to state resources via the power to unilaterally commandeer the state executives. Third, from a textual perspective, an executive power to commandeer state resources is contrary to the implications of Article I, clause
15. Recall that clause 15 declares that *Congress* (and not the president) may
determine when the militias may be called forth to execute federal law.
But if the president may demand the assistance of state executives (including their militias) whenever he feels the need, section 15 serves no
purpose. Independent of Congress, the president could call forth the
state militias via his power to commandeer state executives.

Commandeering the State Militias and Their Commanders in Chief

In his first term, Washington relied upon a statutory delegation to summon the militia of two states to defend the frontiers of the United States
against Indian invasions.[18] Though governors sent their militias, they did
not attend, probably because Washington had not sought their personal
services.

That changed in the president's second term. Responding to
Washington's call to suppress the Whiskey Rebellion in western
Pennsylvania, three governors marched with their militias. The president
made Virginia governor Henry Lee commander in chief of the expedition, but only when Washington was not in the field. He made the
Pennsylvanian Thomas Mifflin next in command, followed by Governor
Richard Howell of New Jersey. Washington's directions were quite detailed, laying out rules for handling the rebels and aiding the federal
judge accompanying the expedition.[19]

Governors understood that when called into federal service, they were subordinate to the federal commander in chief. For instance, Governor Mifflin publicly averred that due to a "just sense of [his] federal obligations . . . whatever requisition the President of the United States shall make, or whatever duty he shall impose in pursuance of his constitutional and legal powers, . . . will, on my part, be promptly undertaken and faithfully discharged."[20]

Less Extraordinary Law Execution

It may seem that Washington took the view that he could commandeer state resources, including the militias, only pursuant to a federal statute. Had he not relied upon federal statutes in summoning the militias to suppress the Whiskey Rebellion and to defend the frontiers? Yet at other times Washington acted as if he could command the assistance of state executives even when no federal statute compelled such aid. Before summoning the militia to suppress the Whiskey Rebellion, Washington demanded the assistance of the governors to execute the federal excise laws. After charging "*all* Courts, Magistrates, and officers" to enforce those laws, Washington sent a copy of his proclamation to governors in states facing significant resistance to the law. He noted that he had "an entire confidence, that the weight and influence of the [state] Executive . . . will be chearfully exerted . . . to promote on every occasion, a due obedience to the . . . laws of the Union."[21] It was a polite order to use state resources to help enforce the excise laws, but an order nonetheless.

The president demanded assistance too in enforcing American neutrality during the war between Republican France and Europe. Administration officials issued directives to state governors related to the arming of vessels in U.S. ports, the resolution of prize disputes, and the participation of Americans in the war.[22] Interestingly, the administration instructed governors to use their militias when ordinary law enforcement means might prove inadequate.[23] Even if the president could not direct the militias himself, because federal statutory preconditions had not yet been met, his administration apparently believed that he could direct governors to use all the means at their disposal to execute federal law. In a sense, the president circumvented the limits Congress had imposed on summoning the state militias.[24]

The administration seemed to regard state executives as tools to be wielded in the furtherance of federal law. Secretary of State Thomas Jefferson repeatedly spoke of "instructions" to governors to help enforce American neutrality.[25] His successor, Edmund Randolph, similarly referred to the "rules . . . prescribed" to the governors and their "duties" toward these rules.[26] Secretary of War Henry Knox told governors that the president "confides the charge" of intervening whenever the warring nations committed hostilities within their states.[27] In another letter, Knox declared that the president desired that governors halt the arming, equipping, and commissioning of privateers, with "further directions" to come.[28] Finally, Washington himself voiced his frustration when his "orders" to a governor went unheeded.[29]

Governors felt obliged to obey the president. Said Pennsylvania's Mifflin to his legislature: "[I] have uniformly considered a prompt cooperation in all the constitutional measures of the general government, as an important duty."[30] Mifflin's attitude was shared "by nearly all the state executives,"[31] including Henry Lee of Virginia, who spoke of following the path that the president's "instructions enjoin."[32] Though Isaac Shelby of Kentucky doubted the legality of suppressing a private expedition against Spain, he said it was his "duty to perform whatever may be constitutionally required of me . . . by the President."[33]

While Washington never commanded governors to assist in the enforcement of *every* federal law, he likely supposed that the occasional conscription of state executive power was necessary and proper. Like the Continental Congress before him, Washington lacked a large and dispersed federal apparatus. Every federal district had a marshal and might have a few other officers, such as collectors and port wardens. Such minimal manpower was inadequate when faced with certain kinds of misconduct, whether it involved frontiersmen spoiling for a fight with Indians or heavily armed vessels violating America's neutrality.

War Powers

Chapter 7 recounts how certain Indian tribes declared war against the United States. Rather than taking whatever military measures they deemed appropriate—a tack authorized by the Constitution[34]—governors often sought presidential direction. Washington ordered them to engage in defensive operations only. His administration sent letters to neighboring governors making clear that they too were constrained. To Congress, Washington observed that "offensive measures [were] prohibited," leaving that matter for Congress under its declare-war power.[35]

When governors ignored these directives, Washington rebuked them. After the administration ordered Governor Edward Telfair of Georgia to avoid offensive operations, he nonetheless sought authority to invade Indian territory, perhaps believing that the best defense was a punitive offense. He specifically requested that his proposal be "laid before the President."[36] Secretary of War Knox penned a caustic reply: "The President . . . deems the intended expedition against the Creeks as unauthorized by law . . . and as contrary to the instructions heretofore given; and he has directed me to express to your Excellency his expectations that it will not be undertaken."[37] In another letter, Knox admonished the governor to attend to his "duty" and prevent Georgians from sabotaging a peace treaty.[38] As discussed later, these instructions fell on deaf ears.

The next Georgia governor, George Matthews, was more tractable. In 1794, the administration ordered Matthews to "follow[] [a] . . . line of conduct, without delay," relating to squatters on Indian land.[39] Later, the president directed the removal of a "post" erected on disputed territory. Writing for the president, Hamilton said that even "if it was doubtful" whether the post was in Indian territory, it "must be immediately removed."[40] These two letters are full of language indicating the great trust the administration had confided in Matthews and the expectation that he would oblige the president. The reliance was not misplaced, for Matthews was obedient,[41] even asking for "instructions" about what to do with prisoners taken from the illegal settlements.[42]

State governors likely sought direction out of a sense that the federal executive was constitutionally obliged to defend the nation and statutorily authorized to come to the aid of the states. But governors also perhaps perceived that the president was, in some general sense, their constitutional superior on matters of defense. This was obviously true when he used his statutory authority to call forth the militias; after all, a governor might be called to serve as the commander in chief's subordinate. But that subordination was perhaps only slightly less palpable when the president was in the midst of deciding how best to respond to a state request for federal military assistance.

Legal and Practical Limits on Presidential Commandeering of State Executives

Though gubernatorial assistance to the president was the rule and not the exception, sometimes such aid was ineffectual or limited. Moreover, disputes occasionally arose about the legality of presidential directives. As discussed below, one governor, Georgia's Edward Telfair, defied the president, likely because Telfair supposed that the administration was mistaken about federal law.

Occasionally, the problem was poor implementation of Washington's orders. Exercising his executive power over foreign affairs, the president in 1793 barred the warring European nations from arming ships in the United States. To enforce the order, the administration instructed governors to prevent ships from arming in their states' ports. If a foreign government nonetheless augmented a ship's armament, governors were to halt its departure. After the president issued these orders, the French government purchased the *Little Sarah* from a privateer and, while the ship was docked in Philadelphia, added to it ten iron cannons and six swivel cannons.[43] The newly christened *Petite Democrat* then departed Philadelphia, angering Washington. Thomas Jefferson recorded the president's displeasure: "[W]hen the orders were given to the governors to stop vessels arming &c. in our ports even by military force, he took for granted the Govrs. wd use such diligence as to detect those projects in embryo and stop them when no force was requisite or a very small party of militia would suffice."[44] Governor Thomas Mifflin of Pennsylvania compounded his initial error of allowing the ship to increase its armament by failing to halt its departure.[45]

Sometimes state law constrained a governor's ability to comply. In 1794, the Pennsylvania assembly ordered Governor Mifflin to settle Presque Isle, territory also claimed by the Iroquois. In a letter to Mifflin, Washington said that it was "adviseable to suspend for the present" further development of the isle. The president worried that settlement would endanger relations with the Iroquois, perhaps leading to a "rupture."[46]

Already fighting the Wabash Indians, the administration sought to avoid further hostilities. Mifflin suspended the law's execution, but noted that he eventually would resume executing it.[47]

Washington trod lightly here because it seemed clear that he had no authority to order the settlement's suspension. Neither federal nor state law authorized the president or the governor to terminate the isle's development. Nor did Washington have generic authority to order whatever measures he deemed necessary to avoid giving offense to other nations. While the need to avoid another war was critical, Washington did not suppose that he could order Mifflin to halt the isle's development, and so recommended only a temporary delay.[48] Many letters between Mifflin and the administration discussed suspension. The governor complained that since he was acting at the president's behest, the latter ought to share the responsibility.[49]

This episode reveals one limit on the president's ability to order state governors, for the former had no right to compel a governor to suspend the execution of a state law merely because it conflicted with the federal executive's perception of the nation's interests. Because the state law did not conflict with any federal law, the president could not insist that Mifflin permanently suspend the act.[50] The state legislature later passed a law authorizing the prolonged suspension of the original act.[51]

In other instances, disagreements arose about the meaning and scope of federal law. Although Kentucky governor Isaac Shelby initially agreed to suppress a private military expedition against Spanish territory, misgivings cropped up in his mind. He expressed "great doubts" about whether the mere intention to conduct an expedition against another nation was illegal and whether it was proper to "restrain or punish" anyone in advance of any ongoing expedition.[52] The secretary of state took Shelby's letter as an act of defiance, castigating him for equivocating.[53] The president thereafter publicly proclaimed that any military expedition from Kentucky would be illegal.[54] Afterward, Congress passed the Neutrality Act, which penalized neutrality violations.[55] Shelby felt vindicated, claiming that the expeditions had become illegal only after passage of the new act.[56]

One governor defied Washington's instructions. As noted earlier, Washington told Edward Telfair of Georgia to avoid offensive expeditions into Creek territory. Flouting that directive, the governor approved an unsuccessful June invasion. The administration later reiterated its opposition to offensive measures, noting that only Congress could declare war. The command (and the legal claim) fell on deaf ears, for in September the Georgia militia destroyed a town consisting of friendly Creeks.[57] Perhaps the governor believed that the Creeks had to be punished and that he had a lawful right to protect his state.[58] Given that some Creek tribes had declared war,[59] Georgia arguably had a legal right to wage war, for the Constitution provides that states may engage in war when "actually invaded" or in imminent danger of such an invasion.[60]

As these early episodes perhaps suggest, Washington had limited tools of influence at his disposal. He could not remove wayward governors. Nor could he ordinarily prosecute disobedient state executives.[61] The idea of using military force against recalcitrant state executives would have been fantastical. After all, Washington relied upon state governors for help precisely because he otherwise lacked the means to exert great force within their states.[62]

Unhelpful and Unwanted State Execution of Federal Law

Missing from the early years was any instance in which a governor agreed to help implement federal law but refused to follow the president's instructions. Whenever governors assisted the president, they did so on his terms, never contending that they could execute federal statutes as they understood them. Though a state supreme court would later claim that the U.S. Supreme Court could not review a state court's interpretation of federal law,[63] no governor during the first administration made an analogous claim vis-à-vis the supreme federal executive. Had governors claimed a right to execute federal law without regard to the president's directions, their aid would have been far less welcome. Federal officers might have enforced federal laws in one way and state officers in another.

One means of ameliorating this potential disharmony is executive branch review of particular state enforcement decisions. For instance, if a state executive adopted an overly aggressive reading of a federal criminal statute and began prosecuting someone (assuming that Congress had authorized state prosecutions of federal offenses), the victim could appeal to the president for relief. As Chapter 5 observed, the president not only may pardon, but also may order officials to enter a nolle prosequi on behalf of the federal government, indicating that the executive does not wish to prosecute the person before the court. The court must dismiss the prosecution, since even when state executives play an auxiliary prosecutorial role, the president ultimately represents the United States in court. Alternatively, if state executives adopt a lax construction of federal law—say, by concluding that an excise tax does not apply to a particular good—federal officials can ignore the state's interpretation and execute the law under the administration's reading of it.

If the differences of opinion are more pervasive, the president may take more drastic measures. Though the president cannot remove state officers from state office, he may forbid state officers, including governors, from shouldering federal tasks. In other words, the chief executive may decline or reject the assistance of state executives. He may reject such assistance because he is not constitutionally required to accept the aid of those who would undermine the exercise of his constitutional powers. State executives cannot force the president to accept their assistance any more than federal executives can compel the president to accept theirs.

Conclusion

That state executives might be significant, or in some cases the primary, enforcers of federal law may seem somewhat odd today because we live in an age where federal officialdom is so vast. The further notion that the president could direct governors in their execution of federal law may compound the oddity, for governors seem to embody state autonomy and sovereignty.

But in an era of relatively robust state governments and a weak federal government, federal reliance upon state executives made eminent sense. Governors had access to a large roster of state officials and generally could more easily call upon the militia when the president believed that significant uses of force were necessary.

State executives, however, were not wholly reliable tools of the president. While governors generally acted as subordinates, recognizing the supremacy of federal law and the chief executive, they occasionally exhibited an independent streak. When they did so, the president had no easy means of forcing them to obey his directions. And he often had no way of circumventing them.

Given the drawbacks of excessive reliance upon state executives to enforce federal law, it was predictable that, over time, Congress and the president might choose to rely more heavily on federal officials.[64] Congress made it possible by providing the funding and offices, and presidents had many reasons to support such moves. Nonetheless, should modern presidents wish to rely upon state executives to help execute federal law, they can cite the assistance and deference that early state governors usually accorded the first president.

CHAPTER THIRTEEN

THE PRESIDENT AS "GLORIOUS PROTECTOR" OF THE CONSTITUTION

When considering the means and mechanisms of defending the Constitution, the courts immediately come to mind, particularly the U.S. Supreme Court. Knowing of the public's propensity to so regard the courts, some justices claim that they are the Constitution's guardians, with a unique power to divine and settle its meaning.[1]

The Constitution's text never makes the Supreme Court (or the judiciary more generally) its ultimate arbiter and defender. It does little more than oblige federal judges to take an oath to "support" it, the same obligation imposed on all legislators and officers, federal and state.[2] In truth, the Constitution singles out the president, rather than the courts, requiring him to "solemnly swear (or affirm) that [he] will faithfully execute the Office of President of the United States, and will to the best of [his] Ability, preserve, protect and defend the Constitution of the United States."[3]

This oath has three implications. The president cannot violate the Constitution, for doing so would hardly preserve, protect, or defend it. The president must defend the Constitution against violators and aggressors, foreign and domestic. Concretely, he must deploy the resources at his disposal—his office and officers, his veto and voice—to protect the Constitution. Finally, the president must preserve the Constitution, suggesting he must resist attempts to alter it by improper means. In sum, the Constitution makes the president its protector, meaning he must safeguard its features—individual liberties, federalism, and the separation of powers.

The Origins of the Presidential Oath

At their coronations, eighteenth-century English monarchs vowed to "governe the people . . . according to the statutes in Parlyament agreed on, and the laws and customs of the same."[4] This oath reinforced Parliament's supremacy, for it rejected the idea that the monarch could suspend statutes. Of course, other eighteenth-century officials took vows, too. Colonial governors swore fidelity to their commissions and instructions, allegiance to the Crown, and devotion to Parliament's colonial acts.[5] Most state constitutions had generic oaths, applicable to all officers, including the governor.[6] Some states required all officers to promise to never violate the state constitution;[7] others required a defense of the constitution;[8] and still others required a defense of the state's territory.[9] Only Georgia required its chief magistrates to take a unique vow. Its gubernatorial oath required diligent execution of the office, defense of the state and constitution, protection of liberties, execution of the laws, and vacation of the office upon the term's expiration.[10]

At the Constitutional Convention, the idea of a constitutional oath first came up when some sought to secure the support and loyalty of state officials to the proposed new order.[11] Only in late July did a delegation successfully move that national officers take the same oath.[12] In August, a committee suggested that the president take an oath to "faithfully execute the office of President."[13] Later that month, James Madison and George Mason moved that the oath also require the president "to the best of [his] judgment and power preserve protect and defend the Constitution of the" United States.[14] Though James Wilson said the generic oath sufficed, the amendment passed handily, suggesting that many favored a more specific and comprehensive oath.[15]

299

Constitutional Meaning

The president's obligations to the Constitution ("preserve, protect and defend") raise the question of whose sense of the Constitution must the president defend. As discussed in Chapter 11, the best answer is that the chief executive must defend the Constitution as he understands it, for the Constitution neither mandates the generic subordination of the president to another branch nor anoints one as the final arbiter of its meaning. Each branch, in the course of exercising its powers and meeting its duties, must interpret the Constitution for itself. Legislators must decide whether the Constitution authorizes them to vote for bills. Judges must interpret the Constitution as they decide cases regarding governmental actions.

The president likewise must judge the Constitution's meaning. He must decide whether bills and proposed treaties are constitutional. He must determine the scope of his own powers, for example, whether he can terminate treaties or oust officers. And he must gauge the import of his oath to ensure that he stays faithful to it. If the president conducted no independent inquiry and blindly relied upon the opinions of Congress or the courts, he might violate his oath to defend the Constitution, for he would not know whether others had misread the Constitution. Minimally, the president must judge for himself whether the Constitution obliges him to accept the legal conclusions of others.

Early presidents certainly acted as if their constitutional oath required them to reach independent constitutional conclusions. Washington acted on his own constitutional understandings, as when he vetoed an apportionment bill as unconstitutional.[16] Though his cabinet's division on the bill's constitutionality perhaps suggested the reasonableness of Congress's implicit constitutional judgment,[17] Washington elected not to defer to the legislature. The first president also refused to satisfy the request of the House of Representatives for the Jay Treaty negotiation instructions, believing that because the Constitution forbade the House's participation in treaty making, it also barred him from lending any credence to the House's view that it could refuse to fund a treaty.[18]

Successors continued the tradition of independence in constitutional interpretation. In 1804, President Thomas Jefferson wrote: "[N]othing in the Constitution has given [the judges] a right to decide for the Executive, more than to the Executive to decide for them. Both magistracies are equally independent in the sphere of action assigned to them."[19] Andrew Jackson was equally emphatic: "The Congress, the Executive, and the Court must each for itself be guided by its own opinion of the Constitution. . . . The opinion of the judges has no more authority over Congress than the opinion of Congress has over the judges, and on that point the President is independent of both. The authority of the Supreme Court must not, therefore, be permitted to control the Congress or the Executive . . . but to have only such influence as the force of their reasoning may deserve."[20] In sum, while the president certainly could learn from the other branches (as they could from him), he was not obliged to accept their constitutional judgments.

A Bar on Executive Violations

The duty to preserve, protect, and defend the Constitution forbids presidential violations of the Constitution. When Washington declared that his nomination of a sitting senator to the Supreme Court was improper on the grounds that a legislator could not serve in an office created during the legislator's term,[21] the president observed that it was his "duty . . . to declare, that . . . the nomination [was] null by the Constitution."[22] The first president deserves praise for the admission of constitutional error.[23]

Most agree that at some level the Constitution exhorts the president to avoid violating the Constitution himself. Yet at least one chief executive claimed that his oath compelled him to take measures that would ordinarily be constitutional violations. Abraham Lincoln defended his suspension of habeas corpus, asking: "Are all the laws, but one [the constitutional privilege of habeas corpus], to go unexecuted, and the government itself go to pieces, lest that one be violated? Even in such a case, would not the official oath be broken, if the government should be overthrown."[24] Lincoln argued that his oath required him to take measures necessary to save the government and nation, for should either fall, the Constitution would be at an end and the Presidential Oath would be broken. Just as a doctor might have to sacrifice a limb or two to save a patient, so too must the president sometimes sacrifice a few constitutional principles in order to save the Constitution.[25]

Lincoln was mistaken, at least according to the original Constitution. As discussed in Chapter 9, he seemed to suppose that the oath granted crisis powers. Yet oaths do not typically cede powers. No one would imagine that a firefighter or an accountant would acquire vast and murky constitutional powers merely if each likewise took an oath to "preserve, protect, and defend" the Constitution.[26] Rather than surreptitiously ceding powers, oaths require the avower to satisfy the obligations imposed by using resources derived elsewhere. When the 1778 South Carolina Constitution required state officers to use all their "power, [to] support, maintain, and defend the said State,"[27] it did not thereby cede tremendous constitutional powers to each and every state official. It merely obliged each to defend his state using all the lawful means at his disposal, means that stemmed from other sources, constitutional and statutory. The oath did not itself generate and convey resources as a means of ensuring its satisfaction.

Likewise, the Presidential Oath requires the chief executive to preserve, protect, and defend the Constitution, using the constitutional and statutory resources at his disposal. It is not a constitutional license to do whatever the president deems necessary, because the oath nowhere conveys to the president the power to take whatever measures he deems necessary to satisfy it.

President Lincoln also was wrong to argue that parts of the Constitution may be sacrificed in order to save the nation, for the Constitution makes itself paramount. Here it is worth noting that some state constitutions expressly required defense of the state. As noted, the 1778 South Carolina Constitution commanded the governor, among many others, "to . . . support, maintain, and defend the said State against the said King George the Third."[28] Similarly, the Massachusetts Constitution obliged all officers to swear that they would "defend the [state] against traitorous conspiracies and all hostile attempts whatsoever."[29] Such constitutions could be read as making the state's physical defense the topmost obligation, even if a successful defense required the sacrifice of some or all of the state constitution's other provisions. Alternatively, perhaps such constitutions placed the state's continued existence on a par with the constitution's other provisions, meaning that officers faced a difficult choice if the continued existence of the state government required the sacrificing of certain constitutional principles.

In contrast, the oath contains little suggesting that the president may violate the Constitution in order to save the nation. By requiring the president to "preserve, protect, and defend the Constitution" and by not imposing an equal or superior obligation to defend the nation at all costs, the Constitution affirmatively bars presidents from choosing to violate the Constitution in order to save the nation. As a legal matter, the president may not raid the treasury, create a national religion, or abridge the freedom of speech, even if he is certain that doing so will avert the dissolution of the nation. This is not to say that presidents lack a duty to defend the country. It is to say that while presidents must defend the nation, the Constitution never grants them the authority to violate its provisions. Contrary to Lincoln's claim, the Constitution does not authorize the president to sacrifice whatever he deems expendable in order to save the nation.

Admittedly, many would praise a president (or anyone else) who violated the Constitution in a bid to eliminate some moral evil or to save the nation. Constitutional fidelity is not the only value. Yet we should not allow good intentions or exigent circumstances to cloud our judgment to such an extent that we regard a constitutional transgression as something other than a violation merely because we favor the ends it furthers. Better to excuse a president's constitutional violations than to whitewash them in a bid to make them more acceptable, for the latter approach, by making the Constitution's rules more uncertain, increases the likelihood of future breaches.

Defending the Constitution from Violations by Others

Avoiding constitutional violations is not enough, by itself, to satisfy the Presidential Oath. The president must protect and defend the Constitution, meaning that he cannot remain indifferent to the transgressions of others. Assaults on the Constitution (and the government it creates) can come from many quarters, among them his aides, Congress, and the states. We certainly expect presidents to thwart their subordinates' breaches. Because executive officers are under his sway, a resolute president should have a comparatively easy time ensuring that his branch does little or no constitutional harm.[30]

As discussed below, averting and frustrating the constitutional violations of those outside the executive branch may prove more difficult. Opposing the usurpations of entities outside the executive branch often is troublesome because they are unlikely to quietly accept presidential criticisms or passively stand by while the president attempts to thwart their actions. When the president criticizes or blocks constitutional violations by Congress or the states, the censure is often swift and severe.

The Duty to Veto

Some saw the veto as the principal check on unconstitutional bills,[31] likely because presentment was a chokepoint for all federal legislation, whereas judicial review was not. Recent presidents have largely cast aside the shield, preferring to sign unconstitutional provisions into law and simultaneously issue statements that decry those provisions.[32] Executive branch lawyers argue that if the president vetoed all bills with unconstitutional segments, many necessary provisions would never become law.

This "sign and denounce" practice conflicts with the Presidential Oath.[33] When Congress presents a bill containing one or more unconstitutional provisions, the president has a choice. He may veto the bill or allow it to become law. If he elects the latter path, the president helps usher in an unconstitutional law and conspicuously fails to defend the Constitution. It is akin to a soldier who, though sworn to defend the country, nonetheless allows the enemy to pass unmolested. To stay true to his oath, the president must veto bills when he believes that one or more of their provisions are unconstitutional.[34] He can no more sign and denounce then he can "recommend and denounce," that is, recommend legislation while denouncing elements of it as unconstitutional.[35]

Early presidents understood this principle. A letter from Washington on the Bank of United States bill is illuminating. To Alexander Hamilton, the president noted that some had denied the constitutionality of the proposed bank.[36] He noted that it "therefore becomes . . . my duty to examine the ground on [which] the objection is built."[37] Such an examination would have been somewhat pointless, however, had Washington not also supposed that he had a duty to veto the bill if he found it unconstitutional. Jefferson shared this understanding, calling the veto "the shield provided by the constitution to protect against the invasions of the legislature 1. [of] the rights of the Executive 2. of the Judiciary 3. of the states & state legislatures."[38]

All the opinions Washington received—from Jefferson, Alexander Hamilton, and Edmund Randolph—considered only the bank's constitutionality.[39] None addressed the possibility that the president might, as a matter of constitutional discretion, sign a bill containing unconstitutional provisions. The absence of any such discussion suggests that these advisers thought the president had no choice but to veto if he found the bank unconstitutional.

Successors likewise felt obliged to veto bills containing unconstitutional provisions. Even though he favored a public works bill, James Madison asserted that he had "no option" but to veto it.[40] "I am constrained by the insuperable difficulty I feel in reconciling the bill with the Constitution of the United States to return it with that objection," he wrote.[41] In another message, Madison averred that he "could not have otherwise discharged [his] duty" except by vetoing a bill that he thought violated the Establishment Clause.[42] In James Monroe's veto message of a road bill, he wrote: "[I]t is with deep regret, approving as I do the policy, that I am compelled to object to its passage and to return the bill to the House of Representatives, in which it originated, under a conviction that Congress do not possess the power under the constitution to pass such a law."[43] In his famous veto of the bill extending the charter of the Second Bank of United States, Andrew Jackson said he was obliged to veto bills that he deemed unconstitutional.[44]

Arguments in defense of sign and denounce do not withstand scrutiny. Though some argue that the president should not be forced to block statutory provisions that he desires or that the nation desperately needs, this argument conflates constitutionality with expediency. While defending the Constitution, the president often will have to sacrifice his other goals. If no such sacrifices were ever necessary, because necessity or felt need eliminated the possibility of constitutional violation, the oath would be largely irrelevant.

Moreover, a president's willingness to veto bills on grounds of constitutional principle would not necessarily mean that needful provisions would never become law. In the short run, Congress might respond by eliminating the problematic provisions; after all, Congress might prefer a bill shorn of the troublesome provisions to the status quo. In the long run, a new equilibrium might arise, one in which members would recognize that including sections that the president regarded as unconstitutional would trigger a veto. This recognition might lead to the legislative removal of many such provisions out of sense that including them would be somewhat futile.

A very different claim—that because unconstitutional provisions are void there can be no constitutional harm in allowing them to become "law"—is too clever by half. If anyone could propose or endorse unconstitutional measures on the grounds that the measures were irrelevant because they could never have any force, then legislators could vote for wholly unconstitutional bills, judges could join opinions with erroneous constitutional reasoning, and presidents could propose unconstitutional measures. Moreover, this defense of the modern sign-and-denounce practice fails to recognize that once a bill becomes law, the supposedly null provision might yet be enforced by the courts or by a future president. An unconstitutional bill made into putative law is akin to a loaded gun, ready to be misused by someone with a different sense of the Constitution. For example, a president who signs into law a bill that denies due process of law with the intent to ignore it must be aware that successors may faithfully execute the denial.

It is easy to see why some would tolerate sign and denounce. Many have grown accustomed to the idea that the courts play the primary, even the exclusive, role in defending the Constitution. Given the sense that constitutional defense is the judiciary's peculiar job, some might imagine that it is presumptuous for the president to thwart bills that he believes are unconstitutional. Moreover, there are other values besides constitutional fidelity, and it may seem unwise, even foolish to sacrifice those values at the altar of constitutional principle. Still, this understandable attitude about the costs of principled action does not validate the idea that the Constitution is indifferent to, or actually sanctions, decisions to allow unconstitutional bills to become law.

The Duty to Disregard

Sometimes a bill with unconstitutional features overcomes the Constitution's many procedural hurdles and (seemingly) becomes law. A previous president might have had his veto overridden, been a poor defender, or had a different sense of the Constitution. Must a later president faithfully execute putative laws that he believes are unconstitutional? Recent chief executives have claimed the power to disregard such "laws."[45]

Critics assert that the Constitution's text bars presidents from disregarding statutes, even when they believe them to be unconstitutional. If a president could ignore statutes, whatever his reasons, he would not be faithfully executing the law.[46] Moreover, one scholar has claimed that President James Buchanan was the first to disregard a statute on the grounds of its unconstitutionality, some seventy years after ratification.[47] That his predecessors never disregarded laws supposedly suggests that they did not believe they could do so.[48] In sum, the alleged power to disregard unconstitutional statutes strikes critics as a power incompatible with the Constitution.

Critics are right to say that the president lacks the power to ignore unconstitutional laws. Saying that the president has a *power* to disregard statutes suggests that the Constitution grants him discretion, allowing him to enforce laws that he regards as unconstitutional. The idea that the Constitution grants the president a nonenforcement power exercisable at his whim is surely incorrect.[49]

Rather than granting a *discretionary* power to disregard statutes, the Constitution *requires* the president to disregard unconstitutional statutes. To begin with, the Constitution does not authorize the president to enforce unconstitutional laws. At the founding, unconstitutional laws generally were regarded as null and void. Two circumstances led to this conclusion. First, colonials claimed that Parliament had little or no jurisdiction over the colonies and that any acts regulating the colonies were void. Thomas Jefferson argued that because "the British Parliament has no right to exercise authority over" America, colonials could "declare [Parliament's] acts void."[50] Patrick Henry likewise insisted that Virginians could ignore Parliament's unconstitutional laws.[51] Second, a concern for individual rights led Americans to deny that unconstitutional state statutes were law. When state legislatures adopted laws that abridged the rights guaranteed by state constitutions or the natural rights of Englishmen, courts regarded the laws as void. The North Carolina Supreme Court noted that an unconstitutional act must stand "as abrogated and without any effect."[52] In Connecticut, another court concluded that an unconstitutional state law "could not legally operate."[53] And in Virginia, judges and counsel observed that unconstitutional laws were nullities.[54]

Those helping decide the Constitution's shape and fate repeatedly noted that unconstitutional laws were void. Future justice Oliver Ellsworth "contended that there was no lawyer, no civilian who would not say that ex post facto laws were void of themselves."[55] Discussing the Supremacy Clause, the North Carolina governor said that laws repugnant to the Constitution "will be nugatory and void."[56] Patrick Henry agreed that federal "laws in opposition to the Constitution would be void."[57]

Besides averring that an unconstitutional law would not be law at all, participants occasionally referred to the president's defense of the Constitution. In the Pennsylvania ratification convention, James Wilson observed that the president "could shield himself, and refuse to carry into effect an act that violates the Constitution."[58] In *Federalist* 44, James Madison noted that the "success" of a congressional usurpation would "depend on the executive and judiciary departments, which are to expound and give effect to the legislative acts."[59] Madison thereby implied that the other departments could refuse to enforce unconstitutional acts; otherwise, the success of the attempted usurpation would be guaranteed from the moment the supposedly unconstitutional bills became law.[60]

Early presidents held the view that unconstitutional legislative actions were no laws at all and that no one owed any duty to them. Though Washington and Adams never faced the question whether to enforce laws they regarded as unconstitutional,[61] some of their statements suggested that only constitutional laws were binding.[62] Jefferson was the first to claim that constitutional duty barred him from enforcing an unconstitutional statute. Upon taking office, Jefferson faced choices relating to the Sedition Act, an act regulating criticism of federal personnel. First, he decided to pardon those convicted of violating the act. Second, he chose to halt pending Sedition Act prosecutions. By its terms, the act expired on

March 3, 1801,[63] the day before Jefferson took office. Yet the act expressly provided that its expiration would "not prevent or defeat a prosecution and punishment of any offence against the law, during the time it shall be in force."[64] In other words, the act's expiration neither terminated ongoing prosecutions nor barred new prosecutions founded on deeds committed before the act's expiration.

Jefferson ordered his district attorneys to discontinue all ongoing Sedition Act prosecutions, to take care that the Sedition Act was not faithfully executed.[65] The president explained: "[W]henever in the line of my functions I should be met by the Sedition law, I should treat it as a nullity."[66] In letters, Jefferson insisted that the Constitution compelled this stance.[67]

> I discharged every person under punishment or prosecution under the Sedition law, because I considered, & now consider, that law to be nullity, as absolute and as palpable as if Congress had ordered us to fall down and worship a golden image; and that it was as much my duty to arrest its execution in every stage, as it would have been to have rescued from the fiery furnace those who should have been cast into it for refusing to worship their image. It was accordingly done in every instance, without asking what the offenders had done, or against whom they had offended, but whether the pains they were suffering were inflicted under the pretended sedition law.[68]

Jefferson also suggested that he had terminated Sedition Act prosecutions because of the "obligations of an oath to protect the Constitution, violated by an unauthorized act of Congress."[69] The third president evidently believed that his oath prohibited him from enforcing a statute that he regarded as unconstitutional. And he was right because under the original Constitution, an unconstitutional law is no law at all.

The Duty to Pardon

The case for a duty to pardon parallels the duty to veto unconstitutional bills and disregard unconstitutional "laws." Because the president may pardon for any reason, the president clearly may pardon offenses based on constitutional scruples. He may pardon when he believes that the underlying statute attempts to regulate conduct that Congress cannot reach, that the penalties Congress attached to the offense are unconstitutional, or that the procedures for securing the punishment were constitutionally improper. Given his duty to preserve, protect, and defend the Constitution, the president is obliged to wield his pardon pen to forgive convictions and sentences that he regards as unconstitutional. Thomas Jefferson pardoned all those convicted under the Sedition Act for these reasons.

The Duty to Protest

From Washington's time, presidents have issued constitutional warnings and lodged constitutional protests against the measures and opinions of others. These warnings and protests were grounded on the notion that presidents had to speak out against mistaken constitutional claims, lest faulty reasoning take root and spread.

Early in his first term, Washington considered protesting a House resolution as an invasion of his foreign affairs authority, but Jefferson dissuaded him on the grounds that any encroachment was minimal.[70] A constitutional protest had to wait until 1796, when, as discussed earlier, Washington rebuffed the House's supposed encroachment on the treaty power. While deciding whether to appropriate funds to implement the Jay Treaty, the House sought Washington's treaty instructions to John Jay. After citing his duty to "preserve, protect and defend the Constitution," Washington made the following claim: "[A] just regard to the Constitution and to the duty of my office, under all the circumstances of this case, forbids a compliance with your request."[71] The president believed that the House had to implement the treaty, for it had no authority to obstruct its implementation. To supply the Jay instructions to the House, when the latter had no treaty authority, struck him as a dangerous acquiescence in a power grab. Given his oath to protect the Constitution, he felt he had to refuse.

As discussed in Chapters 7 and 12, when it seemed that governors might attack Indian tribes who had declared war, Washington admonished them not to engage in offensive measures. His letters to governors were meant to preserve what he believed was a congressional monopoly on authorizing offensive actions, an exclusivity thought to stem from the Declare War Clause.[72] Though Washington may have been mistaken on the constitutional merits, he properly defended the Constitution as he understood it.

Much later, Andrew Jackson protested the Senate's censure of his removal of a treasury secretary. Repeatedly citing his oath, Jackson claimed that he had no choice but to defend the Constitution, the censure being "not only unauthorized by the Constitution, but in many respects repugnant to its provisions and subversive of the rights secured by it to other coordinate departments." He then expounded on his constitutional role in this regard: "I deem it an imperative duty to maintain the supremacy of that sacred instrument and the immunities of the department intrusted to my care by all means consistent with my own lawful powers, with the rights of others, and with the genius of our civil institutions."[73] Later, Old Hickory rejected the nullification doctrine and threatened to use violence against states that transgressed the Constitution. In a proclamation to South Carolinians, Jackson declared that the doctrine—the idea that states could use force to thwart the enforcement of laws they deemed unconstitutional—was "contradicted expressly by the letter of the Constitution, unauthorized by its spirit, inconsistent with every principle on which it was founded, and destructive of the great object for which it was formed."[74] Jackson ended by warning that he would use force if necessary. Congress subsequently passed the "Force Bill," giving Jackson the full means of enforcing the laws.[75]

Abraham Lincoln took vigorous measures leading up to, and during, the Civil War in a bid to counteract those who had resisted the federal government's lawful authority. Defending his measures, he referred to the Presidential Oath, noting that while those who were poised to secede had taken no oath to destroy the national government, he had taken an oath to preserve, protect, and defend it.[76] Lincoln knew that he had to resist the unconstitutional measures emanating from the states. His mistake was in supposing that in the course of resisting those unconstitutional actions, he might violate the Constitution as a means of better preserving it.

Finally, presidents should protest the less formal pronouncements of other institutions, including the courts. As noted in Chapter 11, the president must enforce judicial judgments, no matter the reasoning that underlies them. But the president should not remain mute in the face of faulty constitutional reasoning found in judicial opinions. Given the prominent role that courts play in shaping constitutional thought and discourse, the president must be willing to engage with their reasoning and criticize errors.[77] The Constitution's grant of limited judicial independence in the form of good-behavior tenure and salary protections does not shield judges from vigorous, hard-hitting criticism.

The Constitutional Preserver

An obscure aspect of the Presidential Oath arguably has interesting ramifications for constitutional interpretation. Some scholars endorse the proposition that the Constitution's meaning properly evolves over time in response to shifting practices, new judicial decisions, and changing morality.[78] Yet the text of the Presidential Oath poses a problem for those favoring a living Constitution.

By requiring the president to "preserve" the Constitution, the oath seems to contemplate a constitution that does not radically change with the times even as politics, the composition of the bench, and public morality do. In the same way that a developer does not "preserve" pristine land by engaging in open-pit mining, the president likewise does not "preserve" the Constitution by reading it as if it evolved with the changing times and by remaining passive while others are actively rewriting it. Though the president must honor Article V amendments because the Constitution contemplates such alterations, he must not ratify other supposed "amendments" that lie outside the proper modes of constitutional change.

Early chief executives acted as if they were obliged to preserve the original Constitution and not participate in its informal amendment. They never considered the possibility that they (or others) could recast a potential constitutional violation as participation in the Constitution's legitimate evolution. For early presidents, the duty to "preserve" the Constitution encompassed a duty not to participate in its informal amendment via creative constitutional interpretation.

Consider again Washington's refusal to hand over to the House documents relating to the Jay Treaty. After explaining that the Constitution granted the House no role in treaty making, he claimed that he could not take any action that hinted that the House had any discretion in treaty implementation, lest a bad "precedent" be established. It was "essential to the due administration of the Government that the boundaries fixed by the Constitution between the different departments should be preserved," a statement suggesting that he saw his task as safeguarding the original sense of the Constitution.[79] Had he thought that the Constitution's meaning could evolve over time, he ought to have decided whether the House should have discretion to refuse to implement a treaty. This possibility never seemed to occur to him.

Obviously, the notion that the president must act to preserve the Constitution is in tension with the modern claim that the Constitution's meaning properly changes over time. But perhaps it poses no irreconcilable inconsistency. If the meaning of the provisions outside Article II can evolve over time, as many insist they have, the duty to preserve the Constitution also might evolve in a way that facilitates a more mutable Constitution. In particular, the duty to preserve, protect, and defend might be understood to permit (or require) the president to recognize and defend entrenched governmental practices and modern constitutional morality as constitutive of the Constitution.

Yet if one embraces a living Constitution, the idea of permanent and meaningful legal constraints on presidential power seems chimerical. In a world where the Constitution properly evolves outside the provisions of Article V, a president who seemingly violates the Constitution always can claim that he is participating in the welcome and inevitable evolution of Article II and the rest of the Constitution. Modern presidents who grab and exercise powers that were once outside the executive's domain can be seen as simultaneously changing and implementing a living Article II.

Implementing the President's Duty

A number of practical questions arise from the Presidential Oath. First, how can the president best satisfy his duty in a world of limited resources? Second, what should the president do to ensure that he receives diverse constitutional opinions and that his ultimate conclusions have lasting influence? Third, what mechanisms serve to check a president's mistaken or overzealous defense of the Constitution?

Limited Resources

Some might suppose that the president's duty to defend the Constitution must supersede all else. There perhaps is no more significant obligation, suggesting that the president must continually consider the actions of all federal and state officials, judge whether they are constitutional, and, when necessary, implement a strategy of opposition and obstruction. He must scrutinize every bill, statute, and governmental action, lest he inadvertently compound someone else's constitutional violations. He can never excuse his shortcomings by citing distractions, such as politics or foreign-policy disputes.

This conception of constitutional duty is unrealistic. If the president had infinite resources, satisfaction of his oath might require his unremitting attention. In the real world, the president has limited resources and must make choices. Should he spend more time considering the constitutionality of a law supposedly violating the Bill of Attainder Clause or a bill that may go beyond Congress's enumerated powers? And how much time and effort should be expended on a convict's plausible claim that he was convicted pursuant to unconstitutional procedures? Answers to such questions cannot be found in the Presidential Oath.

Moreover, the president has competing obligations, precluding an obsession with constitutional questions to the exclusion of all else. The president must expend time and resources to execute constitutional laws, which, of course, will take a good deal of time and resources. He also must faithfully execute the presidential office.[80] Presumably, this duty requires him to use his resources in a manner that best serves the nation. Satisfaction of this aspect of the oath requires him to defend the nation from attack and to appoint hundreds of officers, which in turn entails a consideration of the fitness of even more candidates. And he must perform other tasks, like supplying information on the nation to Congress, recommending legislative measures, receiving foreign ambassadors, and issuing commissions.[81] Because each task requires resources, each will detract from his ability to defend the Constitution.

However the president allocates resources, errors are inevitable. Making choices about which constitutional questions to examine closely will lead to uneven treatment and yield mistakes. The president likely will reach constitutional conclusions that he would have rejected had he allocated resources differently. Similarly, allocating resources toward things besides the Constitution's defense means that sometimes the president will enforce statutes that he might have regarded as unconstitutional had more time been spent on the matter.

A different resource problem arises with respect to the execution of statutes after the president has concluded that they are constitutional: what to do if the courts consistently disagree with the president's conclusions. Consider the case in which the president's decision not to enforce an unconstitutional statute is readily subject to judicial review. If the president's nonenforcement is repeatedly and successfully challenged in court, the president will, at some point, justifiably conclude that continuing to disregard the relevant provisions is a waste of money. Given limited resources, it would be far better to spend time and money in an attempt to fulfill other aspects of his presidential duties. It is silly to imagine that the president must stubbornly refuse to enforce a statute that the courts eventually will compel him to enforce, and it wastes resources that could help satisfy other aspects of his duty.

Consider the mirror situation in which the president concludes that a statute is constitutional but the judiciary consistently rules that it is unconstitutional. In this case, there may be some who suppose that under the Faithful Execution Clause, the president must enforce the statute because, in his mind at least, it is constitutional. Yet stubbornly enforcing the statute in the face of implacable judicial opposition is again a waste of funds. Imagining that the president repeatedly must try to enforce a law that the courts will not permit him to execute unduly minimizes the complicated duties imposed by the Faithful Execution and Presidential Oath Clauses and the rest of Article II. Out of a misguided sense of constitutional duty, the president need not, in the manner of Sisyphus, undertake tasks with little or no chance of success.

The necessary implication of limited resources is that the president will not be able to mount a perfect defense of the Constitution. Ensuring that no one ever violates the Constitution, at the expense of all else, may sound appealing to the constitutional scholar. But the Constitution does not give the president the means of blocking or halting all constitutional violations. It gives him some means (the veto, the pardon, and the implied ability to disregard unconstitutional laws), but it does not cede him the right to commandeer all the resources he deems necessary for a successful defense. His ability to defend against constitutional violations will largely depend on the resources Congress supplies him, an awkward situation given that Congress is one of the entities that the president must check.

Given that defending the Constitution will often prove difficult, it is worth noting that the Presidential Oath does not require a perfect defense. The oath merely requires the president to preserve, protect, and defend the Constitution to the "best of [his] ability," a phrasing that implicitly acknowledges that there likely will be failures arising from resource constraints and personal shortcomings. The Constitution does not suppose that its most prominent guardian will be flawless in its defense.

Advice and Justification

The executive should take measures designed to ensure that the public will view his defenses of the Constitution in much the same way that it generally regards exercises of judicial review. The public has a favorable view of judicial review in part because the courts consider opposing viewpoints on the constitutionality of legislation and because the courts publicly justify their decisions.

One means of ensuring a clash of views is to eliminate the Office of Legal Counsel's quasi monopoly on difficult legal questions.[82] Rather than receiving a single opinion from that office, modern presidents ought to emulate early presidents, who received multiple opinions on legal matters, including questions of constitutional law. Demanding constitutional opinions from numerous department heads makes it much more likely that the president will receive conflicting constitutional advice in much the same way that early chief executives received a variety of legal advice. Another way of generating debate is to invite public comment. Mimicking the manner in which agencies invite remarks on regulations, the executive branch might solicit comments on the constitutionality of bills, statutes, and actions. Sifting through conflicting advice may generate sounder constitutional conclusions.

Another means of securing the public's confidence involves public explanations of constitutional decisions. Though the president is under no obligation to explain his reasoning (at least outside the context of veto messages), publicly revealing the bases of constitutional decisions will tend to increase public confidence in them. Chief executives should justify their constitutional judgments as a means of partly dispelling the notion that their constitutional conclusions are insincere and merely serve to further personal or partisan ends. Moreover, presidents will better influence future actors (executives, legislators, judges, the public) when they supply a public explanation. Written opinions provide something that future presidents, Congresses, and courts can consult in reaching their own conclusions. In contrast, unexplained actions are likely to receive less respectful consideration in the future, precisely because the basis for the actions will be opaque. Finally, the discipline resulting from a public justification may strengthen the president's ultimate constitutional conclusions. A written justification often brings to the surface areas of uncertainty and weakness, leading the writer to explore the issue further and either strengthen or abandon her conclusion. Modern presidents engage in some public constitutional reasoning in various documents; they should do more of it.

Checking the Constitutional Guardian

While the president may seem something of a juggernaut, he is checkable in numerous ways. To begin with, the public may sanction presidents who adopt incorrect or unpopular constitutional readings. Incumbent presidents can lose reelection bids based on the unpopularity of their constitutional interpretations—arguably, John Adams' reelection chances were harmed by his energetic enforcement of the Sedition Act.[83] Indeed, Thomas Jefferson noted the possibility of throwing out constitutional rascals.[84] Moreover, the unpopularity of a president's constitutional vision will inflict collateral damage on the president's policy agenda. Hence, even if a president cannot or will not run for another term, the public's perception of his constitutional reasoning will affect his power and influence.

Congress can check the president as well. Committee hearings and investigations, along with informal meetings, serve as forums for congressional displeasure. In the extreme, the chambers of Congress can invoke their impeachment powers. If sufficiently moved or outraged, the House can impeach and the Senate may convict the president and executive officers for their constitutional failings.

The federal judiciary stands as the most efficient check on the executive. A plaintiff with standing may sue to have the president terminate his obstructionist measures. For instance, if the president denies a subsidy on the grounds that a statutory subsidy is unconstitutional, those with standing may challenge the denial. If such plaintiffs succeed, the courts will issue judgments ordering relief. Moreover, those victimized by perceived presidential overreach may bring suit and argue that presidents have misread the Constitution. The entrenched and constitutionally sound practice of routine executive enforcement of judgments will tend to give the courts the final word in many constitutional disputes.

Finally, state officials can protest and obstruct presidential actions that they believe violate the Constitution. Emulating the New England governors who refused to obey an executive order to summon their state militias during the War of 1812,[85] modern state executives might resist the federal executive and try to thwart its alleged usurpations. Likewise, state legislatures might protest against federal executive actions, just as they protested against federal statutes in the past.[86] No less than their federal counterparts, state courts may issue judgments that frustrate presidential measures based on what the courts believe to be flawed presidential readings of the Constitution.

Conclusion

Before assuming office, the president must vow to "preserve, protect, and defend the Constitution." Because nothing obliges him to adopt the constitutional conclusions of others, he must judge for himself what the Constitution permits and forbids. Otherwise, he runs the risk that he will have failed to satisfy his duty to protect the Constitution because of his blind adherence to the potentially mistaken readings of others.

Relying on his own sense of the Constitution, the president should strive to ensure that neither he nor his administration violates its provisions. But he must keep a watchful eye on Congress, the courts, and the states too. Sometimes the president must act to obstruct unconstitutional measures, as when Congress attempts to enact unconstitutional bills into law. Here the president must veto. When confronted with an unconstitutional law already on the books, he must decline to enforce these putative laws on the grounds that they are nullities. In other instances, the president will lack the ability to obstruct and can do no more than protest.

Because the Constitution does not grant the president all the resources that might be useful for defending it and because of human imperfection, the president's defense will sometimes fall short. Though the Constitution makes the president its "glorious protector,"[87] it cannot make him an infallible one.

CONCLUSION

Executive power seems elusive because although many recognize that executives are men and women of action, the appropriate realm of action is unclear. Does the Constitution itself empower the chief executive to execute the law, or may Congress decide what role, if any, he will have in law execution? Can the commander in chief launch a preemptive war, must he await the enemy's first strike, or must he seek a declaration of war from Congress? Is the president, who is obliged to "preserve, protect, and defend" the Constitution, authorized to take whatever measures are necessary to save the nation, such as suspending habeas corpus and impressing soldiers and supplies, or must he look to Congress for such authority? Perhaps the most important question of all: does the original Constitution even address these and related questions, or are those who seek answers in the original Constitution looking in the wrong place?

Those fearful of executive authority, of the possibility of vigorous and quick presidential action, have tended to claim that his realm of action extends only to those specific grants of authority found in Article II, sections 2 and 3. This reading of the Constitution suggests that it imposes a duty (faithful law execution) with no corresponding grant of power that makes fulfillment of the obligation possible. It imagines also that the president has little or no foreign affairs authority, except for receiving ambassadors and making treaties. Finally, it supposes that the president has no authority over civilian executives, except for the ability to demand written opinions from department heads on matters within their statutory purview. The unrecognizable office that would conform to such constraints bears little resemblance to the one in existence in 1789 and since.

Those who celebrate executive decisiveness, secrecy, and energy go to the other extreme. They read the Vesting Clause's executive power as a grant of all authority necessary to save the nation and its Constitution. Under this reading, the executive can do whatever he believes is necessary in a crisis and, going further, may be able to do anything that the Constitution does not affirmatively forbid. The Vesting Clause is read as sort of a constitutional wild card to be played as a means of dissolving all legal constraints. While a handful of presidents (both heroes and villains) have sometimes championed such readings, these imaginative readings also bear little semblance to the 1789 office.

The Vesting Clause's grant of executive power was neither a wholly superfluous reference to other grants in Article II nor a grant of all power that some president at some time might find necessary and proper. Rather, executive power at the end of the eighteenth century had four components: law execution; control of foreign affairs; command of the military; and the creation, appointment, and direction of officers involved in implementing all three features.

Nations could (and did) constrain these powers in various ways. Though the English Crown had the executive power, Parliament had checked it repeatedly over the course of centuries. While the Crown could start wars, it would typically seek the prior approval of Parliament because only the latter could provide the necessary funds for military operations. Furthermore, Parliament enacted laws limiting the authority of the Crown to wage war to protect foreign possessions. Likewise, despite the Crown's command of the military, only Parliament could create punishments for soldiers and sailors. Colonial America saw a similar pattern. The Crown limited the authority of governors, sometimes barring their exercise of some executive power and at other times requiring the consent of an executive council. The state constitutions went further in constraining the executive. Some transferred executive powers to the legislatures. Others vested executive powers in a council rather than a single executive. And many authorized their legislatures to statutorily regulate the exercise of executive authority.

The Constitution's presidency reflected a partial counterrevolution in separation-of-powers thought. Numerous delegates in Philadelphia regarded the state executives as ciphers, incapable of defending themselves or serving as a bulwark against vortex-like assemblies. They realized that most states lacked a true separation of powers and strove to ensure that the federal executive and Constitution would be different. Moreover, if we believe early critics and skeptics of the Constitution, many delegates were beguiled by the sanguine prospect of a Washington presidency. When considering a singular executive, they may have envisioned in their mind's eye the circumspect, wise, and virtuous Washington and allowed this image to affect their judgment. Can anyone doubt that had there been a constitutional convention after Richard Nixon's resignation that his example would have led to the creation of a feeble executive? Sometimes timing is everything.

Because the president could pardon crimes, veto bills, appoint officers, control the military, and because he would be selected by an electoral college that could reelect him over and over again, many considered Article II's unitary executive an elective monarch, one more powerful than many of the crowned kings of Europe. Observers foreign and domestic, both friends and foes of the Constitution, noted the unmistakable resemblance. The president would be a republican, elective monarch, a king in all but name.

At the same time, the most dreaded executive powers were the ones most checked. Congress's power to declare war meant that the president could not wage war without Congress's prior approval. Congress's authority to provide rules for the government and regulation of the army, navy, and militias would check the commander in chief's control of the military. The president's federative role in foreign affairs was further limited by the many grants of foreign affairs authority to Congress (for example, commerce and letters of marque and reprisal) and by the requirement that significant international commitments (treaties) had to receive the approval of a supermajority of senators. The executive's tendency to use offices as prizes with which to reward allies and friends was tempered by the requirement that he garner the Senate's advice and consent. Finally, Congress not only controlled the purse strings for the executive branch, but also created the executive offices and departments that would serve the chief executive. Without the aid of Congress, there could be no departments, secretaries, generals, or admirals. The legislature would decide whether the chief executive would be the sole federal executive.

Those favoring either a consistently weak or a uniformly strong executive may scoff at the portrait painted here. After all, the book's sketch of the president suggests that the Philadelphia delegates were inconsistent, never quite settling on a theme or a direction for the executive. But collective lawmaking bodies, composed of individuals with diverse preferences, predictably will generate outcomes that cannot be traced to a grand theory. Sometimes, a feature of the presidency conduces toward a strong executive because a coalition formed that favored that particular feature. At other times, a coalition coalesced around another preference, resulting in a weak executive on a particular dimension. Article II emerged from these multiple, unstable coalitions. Very few of the presidency's features were obvious and uncontroversial, either at the Constitutional Convention's outset or at the end. Anyone reading the records of the convention, with its numerous twists and turns, cannot but realize that delegates were hardly fixated on one conception of the executive.

Some two hundred years removed from the creation of the presidency, the constitutional drift is apparent. In some respects, the presidency is imperiled and fettered, at least if we use the original understanding of the Constitution as a baseline. We no longer have a chief executive who superintends all law execution. Instead, Congress has created numerous executive fiefdoms called "independent" agencies, and the Supreme Court has sanctioned their constitutionality. As a result, officers somewhat or largely unaccountable to the chief executive execute vast swaths of federal law. Moreover, the executive's constitutional council often proves obstructionist, for the Senate allows senators to indefinitely delay the consideration of nominees, making a farce of the Senate's advice-and-consent role.

In other respects, the presidency has become far more powerful. Presidents and their advisers regularly claim the right to take the nation to war, something unheard of during the nation's first 150 years. Some presidents have exercised a sweeping emergency power, a power to do whatever is necessary to save the nation. This is in contrast with state governors who believed that they could not impress nails and other supplies during the Revolutionary War, and with President George Washington, who seemed to recognize that even in the face of a deadly plague, he was powerless to convene Congress elsewhere. Finally, consider something as minor as recess appointments. In supposing that they can appoint to offices that become vacant while the Senate is in session, presidents have managed to make a mountainous exception out of what was quite likely a constitutional molehill.

No one can predict the presidency's future direction, except to say that there will be further drift, sometimes making the presidency more regal and other times less so. Likewise, there will continue to be impassioned debate about what type of president the Constitution created, what type of presidency we have today, and what type of executive we ought to have. And as long as there is a unitary executive vested with considerable authority, there will be cries of monarchy and comparisons to George III aplenty.

NOTES

Introduction

1. *See, e.g.*, Curtis A. Bradley & Martin S. Flaherty, *Executive Power Essentialism and Foreign Affairs*, 102 Mich. L. Rev. 545 (2004); Lawrence Lessig & Cass R. Sunstein, *The President and the Administration*, 94 Colum. L. Rev. 1 (1994).

2. Michael D. Ramsey, *Presidential Originalism?*, 88 B.U. L. Rev. 353, 356–57 & n.17 (2008).

3. Arthur M. Schlesinger, Jr., The Imperial Presidency (1973); *see also* Peter Shane, Madison's Nightmare: How Executive Power Threatens American Democracy (2009); Charlie Savage, Takeover: The Return of the Imperial Presidency and the Subversion of American Democracy (2008).

4. The Declaration of Independence (U.S. 1776).

5. *See, e.g.*, The Fettered Presidency: Legal Constraints on the Executive Branch (L. Gordon Crovitz & Jeremy A. Rabkin eds., 1989); *see also* Terry Eastland, Energy in the Executive: The Case for the Strong Presidency 3 (1992) (discussing the claim of a "'fettered' executive").

6. Tim Harper, *Cheney Argues for Nixon-Era Powers*, Toronto Star, Dec. 21, 2005, at A1 ("'Watergate and a lot of things around Watergate and Vietnam, both during the '70s served, I think, to erode the authority . . . the president needs to be effective, especially in the national security area,' Cheney told reporters."); *see also* Bob Woodward, *Cheney Upholds Power of the Presidency*, Wash. Post, Jan. 20, 2005, at A7 ("Vice President Cheney

said in an interview that the proper power of the presidency has finally been restored after being diminished in the wake of the Vietnam War and Watergate.").

7. *See, e.g.,* Martin S. Flaherty, *The Most Dangerous Branch,* 105 Yale L.J. 1725, 1795–98 (1996); Lessig & Sunstein, *supra* note 1, at 32–38, 72; Bradley & Flaherty, *supra* note 1, at 664–79.

8. William H. Harbaugh, The Constitution of the Theodore Roosevelt Presidency and the Progressive Era, *in* The Constitution and the American Presidency 63, 67 (Martin L. Fausold & Alan Shank eds., 1991).

9. Paolo E. Coletta, The Presidency of William Howard Taft 12 (1973).

10. *See generally* Christopher S. Yoo, Stephen G. Calabresi & Laurence D. Nee, *The Unitary Executive During the Third Half-Century: 1889–1945,* 80 Notre Dame L. Rev. 1, 40–47 (2004). While Taft denied there was an "undefined residuum" of presidential power, his theory recognized that the president had implicit powers arising from explicit constitutional and statutory grants. And he recognized that the Vesting Clause of Article II vested power with the president.

11. Youngstown Sheet & Tube Co. v. Sawyer, 343 U.S. 579, 634–35 (1952) (Jackson, J., concurring).

12. Antonin Scalia, *Originalism: The Lesser Evil,* 57 U. Cin. L. Rev. 849, 852 (1989).

13. *See* Letter XI from John Adams to John Taylor, of Caroline, Virginia, In Reply to His Strictures On Some Parts of the Defence of the American Constitutions, in 6 The Works of John Adams 469, 470 (Charles Francis Adams ed., 1851) (recounting and translating comments made in 1788 by William V, prince of Orange).

14. 347 U.S. 483 (1954).

Chapter 1. "A King, Under the Title of President"

1. The Declaration of Independence (U.S. 1776).

2. Thomas Paine, Common Sense (1776), *in* 1 The Writings of Thomas Paine 99 (Moncure Daniel Conway ed., 1894).

3. *See* Brian Palmer, *King Me: Why Do So Many European Countries Still Have Monarchs* (Apr. 30, 2013), *available at* http://www.slate.com/articles/news_and_politics/explainer/2013/04/dutch_coronation_why_does_the_netherlands_still_have_a_monarch.html (describing the low-key style of "bicycle monarchs" in Scandinavia and the Low Countries) (accessed Aug. 19, 2013).

4. *See* Bernard Michael Ortwein II, *The Swedish Legal System: An Introduction,* 13 Ind. Int'l & Comp. L. Rev. 405, 408 (2003).

5. Const. of Malaysia pt. IV, ch. 1, art. 32 (1957).

6. Const. of France, tit. III, ch. II, § I(X) (1791), *in* Benjamin Flower, The French Constitution; With Remarks on Some of Its Principal Articles 44 (1792).

7. Const. of France, tit. III, ch. II, § I(II) (1791), *in id.* at 42.

8. *See, e.g.,* 1 William Blackstone, Commentaries on the Laws of England 235, 239 (University of Chicago 1979) (1765).

9. *See* "monarch, n.1," Oxford English Dictionary, http://www.oed.com/view/Entry/121083 (accessed Aug. 19, 2013).

10. *See* J. L. De Lolme, The Constitution of England 278, 361 (William S. Hein & Co. 1999) (1784) (mentioning that the nobles of Poland, Sweden, and Denmark had diminished their monarchs greatly).

11. *See* Vernon Bogdanor, The Monarchy and the Constitution 5 (1995).

12. Const. of France, tit. III, ch. III, § I(II)–(III) (1791), *in* Flower, *supra* note 6, at 57–58.

13. *See, e.g.,* A Letter to Edmund Burke 13 (1780) (noting that the Crown goes to Parliament before declaring war, out of fear that it might have to retract its declaration should Parliament not grant supplies); *see also* Richard Jebb, A Reply to a Pamphlet, Entitled Arguments for and against an Union 24 (1798) (while the Crown had the power to declare war in theory, Parliament had practical authority); 3 Cobbett's Annual Register 1380–81 (1803) (Charles James Fox claiming that while the Crown has the power to declare war in theory, it first seeks supplies from Parliament).

14. *See* Act of Settlement, 1700, 12 & 13 W. & M. 3, c. 2, § 3 (Eng.).

15. *See* Jeffrey Stephen, Scottish Presbyterians and the Act of Union 1707, at 25 (2007).

16. *See* James Bryce, The Holy Roman Empire 233–43 (1904) (describing the electoral system).

17. Robert Bideleux & Ian Jeffries, A History of Eastern Europe: Crisis and Change ch. 14 (2d ed. 2007) (recounting numerous elections of Polish kings, including one involving 40,000 nobles).

18. *See* Owen Chadwick, The Popes and European Revolution 257–63 (2003).

19. *See* Bogdanor, *supra* note 11, at 5.

20. Baron de Montesquieu, The Spirit of Laws 84 (Batoche Books 2001) (1748).

21. *See* Marisa Linton, *Robespierre's Political Principles, in* Robespierre 45 (Colin Haydon & William Doyle eds., 1999) (quoting Robespierre).

22. J.A., *On the Words Republic and Commonwealth, in* 1 The Monthly Magazine and British Register for 1796, at 179, 181 (1796); *see also* Louise B. Dunbar, A Study in "Monarchical" Tendencies in the United States from 1776–1801, at 83 (1922) (observing that Alexander Hamilton had "emphasized the fact that 'republic' had been 'used in various senses' and 'applied to aristocracies and monarchies'").

23. *See* Benjamin H. Irwin, Clothed in the Robes of Sovereignty: The Continental Congress and the People out of Doors 184–85 (2011).

24. The next several paragraphs draw from Louise Dunbar's extensive study of monarchical sentiment in the Revolutionary and founding eras. *See* Dunbar, *supra* note 22.

25. Robert Haggard, *The Nicola Affair*, 146 Proc. Am. Phil. Soc'y 139, 157 (2002).

26. Dunbar, *supra* note 22, at 46–47.

27. *See generally*, Richard Krauel, *Prince Henry of Prussia and the Regency of the United States, 1786*, 17 Am. Hist. Rev. 44 (1911).

28. *See* Letter from Agent to Lord Dorchester, *in* Report on Canadian Archives 1890, at 97 (Douglas Brymner ed., 1891).

29. *Id.* at 98–99.

30. Letter from George Washington to John Jay (Aug. 15, 1786), *in* 4 The Papers of George Washington: Confederation Series 212, 213 (W. W. Abbott ed., 1995).

31. Letter from George Washington to James Madison (Mar. 31, 1787), *in* 5 The Papers of George Washington: Confederation Series 114, 115 (W. W. Abbott ed., 1997).

32. 1 The Records of the Federal Convention of 1787, at 88 (Max Farrand rev. ed., 1966) [hereinafter Records of the Federal Convention].

33. *Id.* at 425.

34. *Id.* at 66.

35. *Id.*, vol. 2, at 101.

36. *Id.*, vol. 1, at 83; *see also id.*, vol. 2, at 101 (Hugh Williamson claiming that "we should at some time or other have a King").

37. *Id.*, vol. 1, at 71.

38. *Id.* at 86–87.

39. *Id.*, vol. 2, at 36. James McClurg, of Virginia, continued that he was also not "so wedded to Republican Govt. as not to be sensible of the tyrannies that had been & may be exercised under that form."

40. *See* Letter from Nicholas Gilman to Joseph Gilman (July 31, 1787), *in id.*, vol. 3, at 66.

41. *See* Letter from Luther Martin to Daniel Carroll (May 20, 1788), *in id.* at 321. For a survey of the views of particular delegates, *see* Dunbar, *supra* note 22, at 88–92.

42. 1 Records of the Federal Convention, *supra* note 32, at 64–65, 101, 119, 152.

43. *See, e.g., id.*, vol. 2, at 35–36.

44. *Id.*, vol. 1, at 300.

45. *Id.* at 290.

46. *Id.*

47. *Id.* at 300; *see also* Letter from John Adams to Benjamin Lincoln (June 19, 1789), *in* 16 Documentary History of the First Federal Congress, Correspondence: First Session, June–August 1789, at 811, 812 (Charlene Bangs Bickford et al. eds., 2004) (claiming that Massachusetts governor John Hancock was a "limited Monarch" because the Constitution of Massachusetts established a "limited Monarchy") [hereinafter 16 Documentary History of the First Federal Congress]. In truth, the New York and Massachusetts governors might be said to resemble monarchs. The rest were, as James Madison put it, ciphers. *See* 2 Records of the Federal Convention, *supra* note 32, at 35.

48. *See* Frank Prochaska, The Eagle and The Crown: Americans and the British Monarchy 15 (2008). Prochaska notes that "[t]he distinction between absolute monarchy and limited monarchy was often lost on American politicians, particularly anti-Federalists with a political axe to grind."

49. *See* Letter from Alexander Martin to Governor Caswell (Aug. 20, 1787), *in* 3 Records of the Federal Convention, *supra* note 32, at 72, 73; *id.*, vol. 2, at 333 n.12; *see also* John K. Alexander, The Selling of the Constitutional Convention: A History of News Coverage

129 (1990) (quoting the Fairfield Gazette); 1 John R. Vile, The Constitutional Convention of 1787: A Comprehensive Encyclopedia of America's Founding 490 (2005).

50. Dunbar, *supra* note 22, at 82.

51. Extract from the Pennsylvania Journal (Aug. 22, 1787), *in* 3 Records of the Federal Convention, *supra* note 32, at 73–74.

52. *Id.*, vol. 2, at 278.

53. Letter from Thomas Jefferson to James Madison (Mar. 15, 1789), *in* 14 The Papers of Thomas Jefferson 659, 661 (Julian P. Boyd ed., 1958).

54. 2 Records of the Federal Convention, *supra* note 32, at 104; *see also id.*, vol. 1, at 432 (similar comments of Alexander Hamilton).

55. Letter from James Madison to Thomas Jefferson (Oct. 24, 1787), *in* 10 The Papers of James Madison: Congressional Series 205, 208 (Robert A. Rutland et al. eds., 1977).

56. Letter from Pierce Butler to Weedon Butler (May 5, 1788), *in* 3 Records of the Federal Convention, *supra* note 32, at 301, 302.

57. Thomas Paine to the Citizens of the United States (1803), *in* 3 The Writings of Thomas Paine 385, 388 (Moncure Daniel Conway ed., 1895).

58. *Genuine Information*, *in* 3 Records of the Federal Convention, *supra* note 32, at 172, 181, 216.

59. 3 The Debates in the Several State Conventions on the Adoption of the Federal Constitution 485 (Jonathan Elliot ed., 2d ed. 1836) [hereinafter Debates in the Several State Conventions].

60. Cato, Essay IV (Nov. 8, 1787), *in* 14 The Documentary History of the Ratification of the Constitution 7, 10 (John P. Kaminski & Gaspare J. Saladino eds., 1983).

61. 3 Debates in the Several State Conventions, *supra* note 59, at 58.

62. Philadelphiensis, No. XII (Apr. 9, 1788), *in* 17 The Documentary History of the Ratification of the Constitution 60, 62 (John P. Kaminski & Gaspare J. Saladino eds., 1995).

63. An Old Whig V (Nov. 1, 1787), *in* 13 The Documentary History of the Ratification of the Constitution 538, 541 (John P. Kaminski & Gaspare J. Saladino eds., 1981); *see also Rhode Island is Right!*, Mass. Gazette (Dec. 7, 1787), *in* The Antifederalist Papers 39 (Morton Borden ed., 1965) ("the new constitution, which the Convention has proposed to us, is an elective monarchy, which is proverbially the worst government.").

64. Letter from Thomas Jefferson to John Adams (Nov. 13, 1787), *in* 12 The Papers of Thomas Jefferson 349, 351 (Julian P. Boyd ed., 1955); *see also* Letter from Thomas Jefferson to Edward Carrington (May 27, 1788), *in* 13 The Papers of Thomas Jefferson 208, 208 (Julian P. Boyd ed., 1955) (observing that because the president could be reelected, the drawbacks of elective monarchy were inevitable, and if term limits could not be imposed, better to adopt a hereditary monarchy).

65. *See, e.g.*, Charles Pinckney in the United States Senate (Mar. 28, 1800), *in* 3 Records of the Federal Convention, *supra* note 32, at 385, 390.

66. Dunbar, *supra* note 22, at 100.

67. A Bystander, *Account of the Late Revolution in Sweden* (Nov. 14, 1787), *in* 2 The American Museum or Repository 432, 433 (1787).

68. *See* Letter XI from John Adams to John Taylor (1814), *in* 6 The Works of John Adams 469, 470 (Charles Francis Adams ed., 1851) (recounting and translating comments made in 1788 by William V, prince of Orange). *See also* Letter from John Adams to William Tudor (June 28, 1789), *in* 16 Documentary History of the First Federal Congress, *supra* note 47, at 870, 871 (quoting the prince of Orange making this claim in French).

69. Letter from John Adams to William Tudor (June 28, 1789), *in* 16 Documentary History of the First Federal Congress, *supra* note 47, at 870, 871.

70. Max Farrand, *Compromises of the Constitution*, 9 Am. Hist. Rev. 479, 486 (1904).

71. 3 Debates in the Several State Conventions, *supra* note 59, at 222; *see also* An American Citizen II (Sept. 28, 1787), *in* 13 The Documentary History of the Ratification of the Constitution, *supra* note 63, at 264 ("[O]ur president bears *no resemblance to a King*").

72. *See* 3 Debates in the Several State Conventions, *supra* note 58, at 485–86.

73. 3 Literary Diary of Ezra Stiles 293, *as reprinted in* 3 Records of the Federal Convention, *supra* note 32, at 168, 169 (recounting Abraham Baldwin's characterization of the delegates) (emphasis added).

74. Prochaska, *supra* note 48, at 14.

75. *See* The Federalist No. 69, at 348–54 (Alexander Hamilton) (Garry Wills ed., 1982).

76. Notes for Speech (July 12, 1788), *in* 5 The Papers of Alexander Hamilton 149, 150 (Harold C. Syrett ed., 1962).

77. 3 Records of the Federal Convention, *supra* note 32, at 85.

78. Dunbar, *supra* note 22, at 72 (quoting Letter from Nathan Dane to Henry Knox, *as quoted in* Eben Stone, *Parsons and the Constitutional Convention of 1788*, 35 The Essex Institute Historical Collections 81, 89 (1899)).

79. Theobald McKenna, Political Essays Relative to the Affairs of Ireland 195 (1794).

80. Protest Against Paine's "Rights of Man" 30 & n.*, *in* Thomas Paine, Rights of Man (1791).

81. Stephen Jones, The History of Poland, From its Origin as a Nation to the Commencement of the Year 1795, at 393 (1795).

82. 2 Joseph Priestley, Lectures on History, and General Policy 66 (1803); *see also General View of Politics No. 7*, The Tomahawk! or, Censor General, No. IX, Nov. 6, 1795, at 35 (claiming that America had a "mixed Monarchy, with an elective king").

83. 2 William Godwin, Enquiry Concerning Political Justice, and Its Influence on Morals and Happiness 79 (1798).

84. *Id.* at 80.

85. *See* Review of History of the Reign of George III, *in* 20 The Critical Review; or, Annals of Literature 419, 421 (1797).

86. Robert Thomas, The Cause of Truth 315 (1797).

87. Letter from John Jay to Giuseppe Chiappe (Dec. 1, 1789), *available at* http://www.fold3.com/image/1/6594073/, http://www.fold3.com/image/1/6594081/.

88. Letter from Robert R. Livingston to George Washington (May 2, 1789), *in* 2 The Papers of George Washington: Presidential Series 192, 193–94 (Dorothy Twohig ed., 1987).

89. Letter from John Adams to Roger Sherman (July 1789), *in* 6 The Works of John Adams, *supra* note 68, at 429, 430.

90. *Id.*

91. *See* Letter XI from John Adams to John Taylor (1814), *in id.* at 469, 470.

92. Robert Simons, *For the City Gazette*, City Gazette and Daily Advertiser, Mar. 21, 1794, at 2.

93. Benjamin Franklin Bache, Remarks Occasioned by the Late Conduct of Mr. Washington as President of the United States 37–38 (1796) (emphasis omitted).

94. Letter from Samuel Chase to Richard Henry Lee (July 2, 1789), *in* 16 Documentary History of the First Federal Congress, *supra* note 47, at 916, 917.

95. Dunbar, *supra* note 22, at 100.

96. Letter from John Adams to Benjamin Rush (June 9, 1789), *in* 16 Documentary History of the First Federal Congress, *supra* note 47, at 727.

97. *See* Noah Webster, Revolution in France (1794), *in* A Collection of Papers on Political, Literary, and Moral Subjects 22 (1843); *see also id.* at 41 (arguing that "[w]hen all this is done, [the French people] must learn that the *executive* power must be vested in a *single hand*, call him monarch, doge, president, governor, or what they please; and to secure *liberty*, the executive must have force and energy").

98. Prochaska, *supra* note 48, at 19–21.

99. *See* 9 Documentary History of the First Federal Congress: The Diary of William Maclay and Other Notes on Senate Debates 342 (Kenneth R. Bowling & Helen E. Veit eds., 1988) [hereinafter 9 Documentary History of the First Federal Congress].

100. *See* William Roscoe Thayer, George Washington 178–79 (1922).

101. Prochaska, *supra* note 48, at 20 (noting that "Jefferson, who recoiled from such royal usages, thought Washington's address to Congress in 1790 too kingly").

102. 9 Documentary History of the First Federal Congress, *supra* note 99, at 16 (emphasis omitted).

103. Prochaska, *supra* note 48, at 17.

104. 9 Documentary History of the First Federal Congress, *supra* note 99, at 22.

105. Julius Goebel, Jr., History of the Supreme Court of the United States: Antecedents and Beginnings to 1801, at 538–39 (Paul A. Freund ed., 1971).

106. *Id.* at 540.

107. Letter from Thomas Jefferson to James Sullivan (Feb. 9, 1797), *in* 29 The Papers of Thomas Jefferson 289, 289 (Barbara B. Oberg ed., 2002).

108. *Id.*

109. 9 Documentary History of the First Federal Congress, *supra* note 99, at 28.

110. Samuel Johnson, A Dictionary of the English Language (10th ed. 1792) (emphasis added) (entry for "monarch"); *see also* Thomas Sheridan, A General Dictionary of the English Language (1780) (entry for "monarch") (same).

111. Johnson may have had *Antony and Cleopatra* in mind, in which Cleopatra calls herself the "President of my kingdom." *See* William Shakespeare, Antony and Cleopatra, act 3, sc. 7.

112. J. G. A. Pocock, *Monarchy in the Name of Britain: The Case of George III*, in Monarchisms in the Age of Enlightenment: Liberty, Patriotism, and the Common Good 285, 300 (Hans Blom et al. eds., 2007).

113. Jeffrey H. Morrison, The Political Philosophy of George Washington 83 (2009).

Chapter 2. "English Whigs, Cordial in Their . . . Jealousies of Their Executive Magistrate"

1. 1 William Blackstone, Commentaries on the Laws of England 258–59 (University of Chicago 1979) (1765).

2. 4 William Blackstone, Commentaries on the Laws of England 127 (University of Chicago 1979) (1769).

3. 2 William Blackstone, Commentaries on the Laws of England 2 (University of Chicago 1979) (1766); *see also* 1 Blackstone, *supra* note 1, at 259.

4. J. L. De Lolme, The Constitution of England 50 (William S. Hein & Co. 1999) (1784).

5. 1 Blackstone, *supra* note 1, at 245.

6. *Id.* at 249.

7. *Id.* at 250–51.

8. *Id.* at 249.

9. *See generally* Saikrishna Bangalore Prakash, *Exhuming the Seemingly Moribund Declaration of War*, 77 Geo. Wash. L. Rev. 89, 107–20 (2008) (discussing the traditional functions of formal declarations of war).

10. 1 Blackstone, *supra* note 1, at 254.

11. 1661, 13 Car. 2, c. 6, § 1 (Eng.).

12. For a discussion of the Crown's limited authority to enforce its military rules in peacetime England, *see* Saikrishna Bangalore Prakash, *The Separation and Overlap of War and Military Powers*, 87 Tex. L. Rev. 299, 328–29 (2008).

13. 1 Blackstone, *supra* note 1, at 261.

14. *See* Saikrishna Bangalore Prakash, *Fragmented Features of the Constitution's Unitary Executive*, 45 Willamette L. Rev. 701, 702–3 (2009).

15. *See* Saikrishna Prakash, *Removal and Tenure in Office*, 92 Va. L. Rev. 1779, 1817–22 (2006) (citing G.E. Aylmer, The King's Servants: The Civil Service of Charles I, at 69, 106–10 (rev. ed. 1974)).

16. Claude Halstead Van Tyne, The Causes of the War of Independence 242 (1922).

17. D. A. Winstanley, Lord Chatham and the Whig Opposition 3 (1912).

18. Jeremy Black, George III: America's Last King 13 (2006); Christopher Hibbert, George III: A Personal History 244 (1998)

19. 1 Blackstone, *supra* note 1, at 243.

20. A. Mervyn Davies, The Influence of George III on the Development of the Constitution 21 (1921).

21. *Id.* at 19.

22. *See* John Brewer, Party Ideology and Popular Politics at the Accession of George III 116 (1976).

23. For a general discussion of the civil list, *see* E. A. Reitan, *The Civil List in Eighteenth Century British Politics: Parliamentary Supremacy Versus the Independence of the Crown*, 9 Hist. J. 318 (1966).

24. *Id.* at 318 (citing 1 William Blackstone, Commentaries on the Laws of England 335 (7th ed., London 1775)).

25. *Id.* at 332.

26. 1 Blackstone, *supra* note 1, at 150.

27. *Id.*

28. *Id.* at 145–46, 179–82.

29. *Id.* at 388–89.

30. *See, e.g.,* Cyril Ransome, An Advanced History of England from the Earliest Times to the Present Day 829 (2d ed. 1896).

31. 1 Blackstone, *supra* note 1, at 263–68.

32. *Id.* at 263, 460–65.

33. *Id.* at 269.

34. *Id.* at 270.

35. *Id.* at 257–58.

36. *Id.* at 138.

37. *Id.* at 258.

38. *Id.* at 398–99.

39. *Id.* at 106.

40. *See* Rosara Joseph, The War Prerogative: History, Reform, and Constitutional Design 97–99 (2013).

41. *See* Evarts Boutell Greene, The Provincial Governor in the English Colonies of North America 91–165 (1898).

42. *See id.* at 72–90.

43. *See, e.g., id.* at 166–76.

44. *See* Margaret Burnham MacMillan, The War Governors in the American Revolution 30–37 (1943); *see also* Willi Paul Adams, The First American Constitutions 27–48 (Rita Kimber & Robert Kimber trans., 1980).

45. *See* MacMillan, *supra* note 44, at 32–37; *see also* Adams, *supra* note 44, at 42, 45.

46. *See* Adams, *supra* note 44, at 266–71. Not all states created constitutions. Neither Rhode Island nor Connecticut adopted a constitution in the period before the U.S. Constitution. And not all entities that created constitutions were recognized as states within the Confederation. Though Vermont had a constitution and government, the Continental Congress refused to recognize it as a state. Federal recognition came after the

Constitution's ratification in 1791. Even though Vermont was not a state, this book discusses the Vermont Constitutions of 1777 and 1786.

47. Gordon S. Wood, The Creation of the American Republic 1776–1787, at 135–41 (1998).

48. *Id.* at 135.

49. Greene, *supra* note 41, at 194–95.

50. Wood, *supra* note 47, at 136.

51. *See* Del. Const. art. 7 (1776) (stating that the chief magistrate may "exercise all the other executive powers of government . . . according to the laws of the State"); Ga. Const. art. XIX (1777) (same); Md. Const. art. XXXIII (1776) (same); N.C. Const. art. XIX (1776) (same); Va. Const. (1776) (same).

52. Charles C. Thach, Jr., The Creation of the Presidency 1775–1789: A Study in Constitutional History 29 (1922).

53. Massachusetts, New York, and South Carolina were the only states that vested the executive with a veto. New York's governor held the veto power along with the chancellor and other judges on the Supreme Court as a "council of revision." If a majority of that council objected to a bill, it would not become law unless approved by two-thirds of both chambers. N.Y. Const. art. III (1777). The Massachusetts veto adopted as part of the Constitution of 1780 was similar to New York's, except that the governor had unilateral veto authority. Mass. Const. pt. 2, ch. I, § 1, art. II (1780). The South Carolina Constitution of 1776 granted a veto. S.C. Const. art. VII (1776). But the constitution of 1778, which was adopted over the veto of President John Rutledge, eliminated it. *See* Marc W. Kruman, Between Authority and Liberty: State Constitution Making in Revolutionary America 124 (1997).

54. Kruman, *supra* note 53, at 126 (quoting An Address of the Convention . . . to Their Constituents, *in* The Popular Sources of Political Authority: Documents on the Massachusetts Constitution of 1780, at 437 (Oscar Handlin & Mary Handlin eds., 1966)).

55. *See* Del. Const. art. 7 (1776); Ga. Const. art. II (1777); Md. Const. art. XXV (1776); N.C. Const. art. XV (1776); N.J. Const. art. VII (1776); S.C. Const. art. III (1778); Va. Const. (1776).

56. *See* MacMillan, *supra* note 44, at 57. Only Delaware, New York, and South Carolina had terms of office longer than one year (three, three, and two years, respectively). *See* Del. Const. art. 7 (1776); N.Y. Const. art. XVIII (1777); S.C. Const. art. III (1778).

57. Only Massachusetts, New Jersey, New Hampshire, and New York imposed no term limits. *See* Mass. Const. pt. 2, ch. II, § 1, arts. II–III (1780); N.H. Const. pt. II (1784); N.J. Const. art. VII (1776); N.Y. Const. art. XVIII (1776). Other states forbade consecutive terms or required rotation. *See* Del. Const. art. 7 (1776) (president may serve a three-year term and then must wait three years to serve again); Ga. Const. art. XXIII (1777) (governor chosen annually and cannot serve more than one year in a three-year span); Md. Const. art. XXXI (1776) (governor chosen annually but cannot serve more than three successive terms and is ineligible for four years after leaving office); N.C. Const. art. XV

(1776) (governor chosen annually and can serve only three out of six years); Pa. Const. § 19 (1776) (any person serving on the executive council for three consecutive years cannot serve again in the next four); S.C. Const. art. VI (1778) (governor can serve one two-year term every six years); Va. Const. (1776) (governor shall be chosen annually, cannot serve more than three successive terms, and is ineligible for four years).

58. *See* MacMillan, *supra* note 44, at 60. In Georgia, New Jersey, North Carolina, South Carolina, and Virginia, the legislature could appoint to almost all important offices. *See* Kruman, *supra* note 53, at 119–23. The constitutions of Delaware, Maryland, Massachusetts, New Hampshire, and Pennsylvania, however, divided the appointment power between the executive and the legislature. *Id.*

59. *See, e.g.,* Md. Const. art. XXXIII (1776) (providing that the governor can summon the militia with the council's consent); N.Y. Const. art. III (1777) (creating a revisionary council to exercise veto power).

60. *See* Pa. Const. § 3 (1776); Vt. Const. ch. II, § 3 (1777).

61. Thach, *supra* note 52, at 37.

62. *See id.* at 53–54.

63. Mass. Const. pt. 2, ch. I, § 1, art. II; ch. II, § 1, arts. vii–ix (1780).

64. *See* Thach, *supra* note 52, at 44–47.

65. *See* Notes on the State of Virginia (1784), *in* 4 The Works of Thomas Jefferson 20 (Paul Leicester Ford ed., 1904).

66. A Report of the Committee of the Council of Censors, *in* Early American Imprints, 1st Ser. No. 18693, at 3 (1784). For instance, the assembly had improperly ordered the council to prosecute the state's claims against the attainted traitor Joseph Galloway. *Id.* at 15. In this case, the Executive Council also was at fault, for in conferring with the Assembly it had "yielded the executive power to the legislature." Journal of the Council of Censors, *in* Early American Imprints, 1st Ser. No. 18093, at 165 (1784).

67. 2 The Records of the Federal Convention of 1787, at 35 (Max Farrand rev. ed., 1966) [hereinafter Records of the Federal Convention]; *see also* Letter from James Madison to Caleb Wallace (Aug. 23, 1785), *in* 8 The Papers of James Madison 350, 352 (Robert A. Rutland & William M. E. Rachal eds., 1973) (observing that the Virginia executive was the "worst part of a ba[d] Constitution" because it was dependent upon the legislature). Charles Pinckney and Edmund Randolph voiced similar complaints. 4 The Debates in the Several State Conventions on the Adoption of the Federal Constitution 324–25 (Jonathan Elliot ed., 2d ed. 1836); 1 Records of the Federal Convention, *supra*, at 176.

68. Notes on the State of Virginia (1784), *in* 4 The Works of Thomas Jefferson, *supra* note 65, at 17. Indeed, Jefferson's draft of the Virginia Constitution of 1776 reflected such inexperience, with his "Administrator" expressly denied a long list of executive powers. *See* Third Draft of the Virginia Constitution, art. II (1776), *reprinted in* 1 The Papers of Thomas Jefferson 356, 359–60 (Julian P. Boyd ed., 1950).

69. Thomas Jefferson, Autobiography (1821), *in* 1 The Works of Thomas Jefferson 121 (Paul Leicester Ford ed., 1904).

NOTES TO PAGES 34-35

70. James Wilson, Lectures on Law (1790), *in* 1 Collected Works of James Wilson 699 (Kermit L. Hall & Mark David Hall eds., 2007).

71. *See* Jennings B. Sanders, Evolution of Executive Departments of the Continental Congress 1774-1789, at 4, 6 (1935).

72. *Id.* at 4.

73. *Id.*

74. Letter from Alexander Hamilton to James Duane (Sept. 3, 1780), *in* 2 The Papers of Alexander Hamilton 400, 404 (Harold C. Syrett ed., 1961).

75. *Id.*

76. *Id.*

77. *Id.*

78. Letter from George Washington to James Duane (Dec. 20, 1780), *quoted in* Thach, *supra* note 52, at 64.

79. Sanders, *supra* note 71, at 3 (noting that members understood that committees were unwieldy bodies that could not execute with efficiency and dispatch).

80. 19 Journals of the Continental Congress 1774-1789, at 43-44 (Gaillard Hunt ed., 1912). Though the resolution did not state that the Department of Foreign Affairs was an executive department, subsequent proceedings make this clear. *See* 24 Journals of the Continental Congress 1774-1789, at 335 (Gaillard Hunt ed., 1922) (stating that the committee would not consider the secretary of foreign affairs' rank "relative[] to [the] other heads of the Executive Departments," because another committee was considering the same issue); 19 Journals of the Continental Congress 1774-1789, *supra*, at 169 (stating that reporting civil list expenses was unnecessary because Congress was reorganizing "the four great executive Civil Departments").

81. 19 Journals of the Continental Congress 1774-1789, *supra* note 80, at 125-27. Later resolutions continued to refer to these departments as "executive departments." *See* 23 Journals of the Continental Congress 1774-1789, at 722 (Gaillard Hunt ed., 1914); 28 Journals of the Continental Congress 1774-1789, at 213 (John C. Fitzpatrick ed., 1933). The officers within these departments were seen as "executives." *See* Letter from James Duane to George Washington (Jan. 29, 1781), *in* 16 Letters of the Delegates to Congress 633 (Paul H. Smith et al., eds., 1989).

82. Thach, *supra* note 52, at 70.

83. Letter from Thomas Jefferson to Edward Carrington (Aug. 4, 1787), *in* 5 The Works of Thomas Jefferson 319 (Paul Leicester Ford ed., 1904).

84. Henry Barrett Learned, The President's Cabinet 51-52 (1912).

85. *Id.* at 51 (quoting Letter from a person in Philadelphia, *in* 1 George Bancroft, History of the Formation of the Constitution of the United States 298, 299 (1882)).

86. Letter from Alexander Hamilton to George Washington (July 3, 1787), *in* 3 Records of the Federal Convention, *supra* note 67, at 53.

Chapter 3. Constituting "His Highness" the President

1. Letter from James Warren to John Adams (Jan. 28, 1785), *in* 16 The Papers of John Adams 498, 499 (Gregg L. Lint et al. eds., 2012).

2. Jay Caesar Guggenheimer, *The Development of the Executive Departments, 1775–1789, in* Essays in the Constitutional History of the United States in the Formative Period, 1775–1789, at 116, 162–63 (J. Franklin Jameson ed., 1889).

3. Letter from Gouverneur Morris to General Greene (Dec. 24, 1781), *in* 1 The Life of Gouverneur Morris 238, 239 (Jared Sparks ed., 1832).

4. 1 The Records of the Federal Convention of 1787, at 21, 244, 292 (Max Farrand rev. ed., 1966) [hereinafter Records of the Federal Convention]; *id.*, vol. 3, at 606.

5. Pa. Const. §§ 3, 19–20 (1776).

6. Va. Const. (1776).

7. 1 Records of the Federal Convention, *supra* note 4, at 292; *id.*, vol. 3, at 606.

8. *Id.*, vol. 1, at 65.

9. *Id.*

10. *Id.*

11. *Id.*

12. *Id.*

13. *Id.* at 66.

14. *Id.*

15. *Id.* at 88–89.

16. *Id.* at 96. Wilson's claim was particularly odd, given that Pennsylvania had a plural executive council. Its president was, at best, first among equals.

17. *Id.*

18. *Id.* at 97.

19. *Id.* at 244.

20. *Id.* at 111–12; *id.*, vol. 2, at 100–101.

21. *Id.*, vol. 2, at 29.

22. 2 The Debates in the Several State Conventions on the Adoption of the Federal Constitution 480 (Jonathan Elliot ed., 2d ed. 1836) [hereinafter Debates in the Several State Conventions].

23. The Federalist No. 70, at 360 (Alexander Hamilton) (Garry Wills ed., 1982).

24. *Id.* at 356.

25. *See, e.g.,* A Landholder, No. VI (Dec. 10, 1787), *in* 3 The Documentary History of the Ratification of the Constitution 487, 489 (Merrill Jensen ed., 1978) (stating that "Secrecy, vigor, dispatch, and responsibility require that the supreme executive should be one person").

26. The Federal Farmer No. 14 (Jan. 17, 1788), *in* 20 The Documentary History of the Ratification of the Constitution 1035, 1038 (John P. Kaminski et al. eds., 2004).

27. *Id.*

28. 9 The Documentary History of the Ratification of the Constitution 1097–98 (John P. Kaminski et al. eds., 1990).

29. *See* Henry Barrett Learned, The President's Cabinet 9–36 (1912).

30. *See* Evarts Boutell Greene, The Provincial Governor in the English Colonies of North America 72–90 (1898).

31. *Id.* at 81, 137, 145.

32. *Id.* at 86.

33. Va. Const. (1776).

34. *See* Del. Const. arts. 7, 9, 10 (1776). When constitutions required only the "advice" of a council, it was unclear whether the chief executive merely had to consult with the council or whether its approval was necessary.

35. Ga. Const. art. VIII (1777); Vt. Const. ch. II, § XVI (1786); Joseph E. Kallenbach, The American Chief Executive: The Presidency and the Governorship 23 (1966). *See also* Margaret Burnham MacMillan, The War Governors in the American Revolution 62 (1943) (noting that New Jersey and New Hampshire had executive councils that served as upper legislative chambers).

36. Mass. Const. pt. 2, ch. I, § 2, art. VIII (1780); N.J. Const. art. XII (1776); Kallenbach, *supra* note 35, at 24–25.

37. 1 Records of the Federal Convention, *supra* note 4, at 97.

38. *Id.*, vol. 2, at 328–29.

39. *Id.* at 335–37.

40. *Id.* at 367.

41. *Id.*

42. *Id.* at 599.

43. *Id.* at 541.

44. *Id.* at 542.

45. *Id.*

46. *Id.*

47. *Id.*

48. *Id.*

49. *Id.*

50. Extract from a Letter (Nov. 14, 1787), *in* 8 The Documentary History of the Ratification of the Constitution 156, 157 (John P. Kaminski & Gaspare J. Saladino eds., 1988) (saying that Senate would advise on all important executive matters).

51. George Mason's Objections to the Constitution of Government, *in id.* at 43, 44.

52. *Id.* at 44.

53. Marcus II (Feb. 27, 1788), *in* 16 The Documentary History of the Ratification of the Constitution 242, 243 (John P. Kaminski & Gaspare J. Saladino eds., 1986).

54. 4 Debates in the Several State Conventions, *supra* note 22, at 109.

55. *Id.* at 109–10.

56. The Federalist No. 70, *supra* note 23, at 358 (Alexander Hamilton).

57. *Id.* at 358–59.

58. *Id.* at 359.

59. *Id.* at 361.

60. Samuel Johnson, A Dictionary of the English Language (10th ed. 1792) (entry for "monarch").

61. *Id.* (entry for "president") (numbers and usage examples omitted).

62. U.S. Const. art. I, § 3.

63. *See* Jennings B. Sanders, The Presidency of the Continental Congress, 1774–89: A Study in American Institutional History 33–41 (1930).

64. Articles of Confederation of 1781, art. IX.

65. Del. Const. art. 7 (1776).

66. S.C. Const. art. XXX (1776). The 1778 Constitution changed the title to "governor." S.C. Const. art. III (1778).

67. N.H. Const. pt. II (1784). A draft constitution put to a vote in 1781 called for a "governor," but it was defeated, in part, because the executive was too strong. The next constitution put to the people called for a "president" and weakened the executive considerably. *See* Lynn W. Turner, The Ninth State: New Hampshire's Formative Years 26–29 (1983).

68. One state had a governor and a president of an executive council. *See* Ga. Const. arts. II, XXV (1777).

69. Pa. Const. § 20 (1776) (granting executive authority to the council but making the president commander in chief).

70. *See* Kallenbach, *supra* note 35, at 16.

71. Thomas Jefferson, Third Draft of the Virginia Constitution, art. II (1776), *in* 1 The Papers of Thomas Jefferson 356, 359 (Julian P. Boyd ed., 1950).

72. *See* Albany Plan of Union, *in* The Political Thought of Benjamin Franklin 83, 84 (Ralph Ketcham ed., 2003).

73. Letter from Henry Knox to George Washington (Jan. 14, 1787), *in* 4 The Papers of George Washington: Confederation Series 518, 522 (W. W. Abbot ed., 1995).

74. 1 Records of the Federal Convention, *supra* note 4, at 292.

75. *Id.*, vol. 3, at 599.

76. *Id.*, vol. 2, at 171. The committee initially mooted the creation of a "Governor of the united People & States of America," *id.*, vol. 2, at 145, before settling on "President." *Id.* at 171. Members of the committee presumably borrowed either from Charles Pinckney's plan or from the Pennsylvania Constitution. *See* Kallenbach, *supra* note 35, at 40 n.18.

77. 2 Records of the Federal Convention, *supra* note 4, at 171.

78. *See id.* at 597. The Committee of Detail's report included the title, *id.* at 185, and the convention never altered this resolution before sending it to the Committee of Style. *Id.* at 497 (making clear that "Excellency" was part of the Constitution as late as September 4, 1787).

79. A similar question apparently arose in the Continental Congress, namely, whether its president should be known as "Excellency or Honor." *See* Sanders, *supra* note 63, at 11 n.1.

80. Ga. Const. art. II (1777).

81. Mass. Const. pt. 2, ch. II, § 1, art. I (1780).

82. 21 Journals of the Continental Congress 1774–1789, at 1143–44 (Gaillard Hunt ed., 1912) (commander in chief and president referring to each other as "excellency").

83. 1 Annals of Congress 36 (1789) (emphasis omitted).

84. 9 Documentary History of the First Federal Congress: The Diary of William Maclay and Other Notes on Senate Debates 31 (Kenneth R. Bowling & Helen E. Veit eds., 1988) [hereinafter 9 Documentary History of the First Federal Congress].

85. *See* James H. Hutson, *John Adams' Title Campaign*, 41 New Eng. Q. 30, 34 (1968). In private, Adams argued that "excellency" was beneath the office's dignity, since it was a "provincial or diplomatic title of the lowest order." *Id.*

86. 9 Documentary History of the First Federal Congress, *supra* note 84, at 31.

87. 1 Annals of Congress 35–36 (1789).

88. *Id.*

89. Stuart Leibiger, Founding Friendship: George Washington, James Madison, and the Creation of the American Republic 119 (1999). The Muhlenberg family (originally of Pennsylvania) has passed down a claim that Washington wished to be called "His Mightiness." There are reasons to doubt this. *See id.* at 119; *see also* Stanley Elkins & Eric McKitrick, The Age of Federalism 763–64 n.25 (1993).

90. Leibiger, *supra* note 89, at 119.

91. *Id.*

92. Letter from Comte de Moustier to Comte de Montmorin (June 9, 1789), *in* 16 Documentary History of the First Federal Congress, Correspondence: First Session, June–August 1789, at 729, 734 (Charlene Bangs Bickford et al. eds., 2004) [hereinafter 16 Documentary History of the First Federal Congress].

93. *Id.* (emphasis omitted).

94. Articles of Confederation of 1781, art. VI.

95. *See, e.g.,* 11 Journals of the Continental Congress 1774–1789, at 700 (Worthington Chauncey Ford ed., 1908).

96. Letter from Henry Beekman Livingston to George Washington (June 12, 1789), *in* 2 The Papers of George Washington: Presidential Series 477, 478 (Dorothy Twohig ed., 1987).

97. Letter from James Walton to George Washington (Mar. 29, 1790), *in* 5 The Papers of George Washington: Presidential Series 291, 292 (Dorothy Twohig et al. eds., 1996).

98. *See* Letter from Samuel Carleton to George Washington (Feb. 12, 1790), *in id.* at 133, 133; Letter from Nathaniel Pendleton to George Washington (July 23, 1789), *in* 3 The Papers of George Washington: Presidential Series 292, 292–94 (Dorothy Twohig ed., 1989).

99. *See* Maud C. Cooke, Social Life 451 (1896); Madeleine Vinton Dahlgren, Etiquette of Social Life in Washington 5, 7 (1873). A later author argued that it was "less correct" and "less American" to use "His Excellency." *See* Leigh H. Irvine, Irvine's Dictionary of Titles 40 (1912).

100. Letter from Comte de Moustier to Comte de Montmorin (June 9, 1789), *in* 16 Documentary History of the First Federal Congress, *supra* note 92, at 729, 734.

101. 2 John R. Vile, The Constitutional Convention of 1787: A Comprehensive Encyclopedia of America's Founding 616 (2005) [hereinafter The Constitutional Convention of 1787].

102. *See* 9 Documentary History of the First Federal Congress, *supra* note 84, at 29, 37, 112. The title was slightly less flowery than the "Right Honorable" favored by John Adams. *See id.* at 66.

103. *See, e.g.,* Letters to President Obama: Americans Share Their Hopes and Dreams with the First African-American President 24, 39, 150, 244 (Hanes Walton et al. eds., 2009).

104. Bill of Rights (1689) 1 W. & M. 2, c. 2 (Eng).

105. Minority of Heir to the Crown Act, 1766, 5 Geo. 3, c. 27 (Eng).

106. Act of Settlement, 1700, 12 & 13 W. & M. 3, c. 2 (Eng).

107. *See* Va. Const. (1776) (containing no restraints); N.Y. Const. art. XVII (1777) (governor must be "a wise and descreet freeholder").

108. Md. Const. art. XXX (1776). North Carolina required £1,000, five years residence, and an age of thirty years. N.C. Const. art. XV (1776).

109. *See* N.H. Const. pt. II (1784).

110. S.C. Const. arts. III, V. (1778). Using the same categories, Massachusetts had more-forgiving tests. Its governors had to be Christians, resident for seven years, and own more modest amounts of property (£1,000). Mass. Const. pt. 2, ch. II, § 1, art. II (1780).

111. Del. Const. art. 12 (1776). North Carolina decreed that "no person who shall deny the being of God, or the truth of the Protestant religion, or the divine authority of either the Old or New Testaments, or who shall hold religious principles incompatible with the freedom and safety of the State" could hold office. N.C. Const. art. XXXII (1776). New Jersey limited officers to peaceful members of "any Protestant sect." N.J. Const. art. XIX (1776). The Maryland Constitution merely required belief in "the Christian religion." Md. Const. art. LV (1776).

112. U.S. Const. art. II, § 1.

113. Richard Krauel, *Prince Henry of Prussia and the Regency of the United States, 1786,* 17 Am. Hist. Rev. 44, 46–48 (1911). The prince supposedly demurred, wondering whether America would give up its republican ways and speculating that if a king were needed, France might better supply one. *Id.* at 49.

114. Letter from Alexander Martin to Governor Caswell (Aug. 20, 1787), *in* 3 Records of the Federal Convention, *supra* note 4, at 72, 73; *see also* John K. Alexander, The Selling of the Constitutional Convention: A History of News Coverage 129 (1990) (citing the Fairfield Gazette); 1 The Constitutional Convention of 1787, *supra* note 101, at 490.

115. Letter from John Jay to George Washington (July 25, 1787), *in* 5 The Papers of George Washington: Confederation Series 271, 271–72 (W. W. Abbot ed., 1997).

116. *See* Letter from George Washington to John Jay (Sept. 2, 1787), *in id.* at 307.

117. 2 Records of the Federal Convention, *supra* note 4, at 494.

118. Act of Mar. 26, 1790, 1 Stat. 104. The statute seemed to adopt the jus sanguinis view that "natural born citizens" included not only those born in the United States but also those born to United States citizens abroad.

119. *See* 2 Records of the Federal Convention, *supra* note 4, at 367, 498.

120. Justice Joseph Story said no. *See* James C. Ho, *Presidential Eligibility, in* The Heritage Guide to the Constitution 189, 190 (Edwin Meese III et al. eds., 2005).

121. The Federalist No. 64, *supra* note 23, at 326 (John Jay).

122. *See* Michael Nelson, *Constitutional Qualifications for President,* 17 Pres. Stud. Q. 383, 389–90 (1987).

123. 2 Records of the Federal Convention, *supra* note 4, at 249.

124. *See* Letter XVI of Agrippa (Feb. 5, 1788), *in* 5 The Documentary History of the Ratification of the Constitution 863, 868 (John P. Kaminski et al. eds., 1998).

125. 2 Records of the Federal Convention, *supra* note 4, at 341–42.

126. Sanders, *supra* note 63, at 43 n.51. Peyton Randolph remained the Speaker of the Virginia House of Burgesses; John Jay continued as chief justice of the New York Supreme Court; and Thomas McKean persisted as the chief justice of the Pennsylvania Supreme Court. *See id.* at 11–12, 19–22.

127. Shlomo Slonim, *The Electoral College at Philadelphia: The Evolution of an Ad Hoc Congress for the Selection of a President,* 73 J. Am. Hist. 35, 35 (1986).

128. *See* 2 Records of the Federal Convention, *supra* note 4, at 110 (discussing numerous ideas).

129. *Id.*, vol. 3, at 166.

130. 1 William Blackstone, Commentaries on the Laws of England 185–86 (Univ. of Chicago 1979) (1765).

131. For a discussion of these machinations, see chapter 3 of Julia Swift Orvis, A Brief History of Poland (1916).

132. *See* Del. Const. art. 7 (1776); Ga. Const. art. II (1777); Md. Const. art. XXV (1776); N.C. Const. art. XV (1776); N.J. Const. art. VII (1776); S.C. Const. art. III (1778); Va. Const. (1776). Only the Massachusetts, New Hampshire, New York, and Vermont constitutions provided for popular election. *See* Mass. Const. pt. 2, ch. II, § 1, art. III (1780); N.H. Const. pt. II (1784); N.Y. Const. art. XVII (1777); Vt. Const. ch. II, § XVII (1777). The royal charters of Rhode Island and Connecticut likewise authorized a popular vote. Kallenbach, *supra* note 35, at 17. Most of these states threw the executive's election to the legislature if no candidate received a popular majority. The Pennsylvania Constitution employed a mixed selection. Each county's voters elected one member of the Executive Council, and the General Assembly and the council selected the president from these councilors. Pa. Const. § 19 (1776).

133. 1 Records of the Federal Convention, *supra* note 4, at 68.

134. *Id.*

135. *Id.*

136. *Id.* at 80.

137. *Id.* at 81.

138. *Id.* at 174.

139. *Id.*, vol. 2, at 32.

140. *Id.* at 57–58, 99–101.

141. *Id.* at 105.

142. *Id.* at 114–15.

143. *Id.* at 108–9.

144. *Id.* at 116.

145. *Id.* at 404.

146. *Id.* at 401–3.

147. *Id.* at 497–98.

148. *Id.* at 527.

149. The Federal Farmer No. 14 (Jan. 17, 1788), *in* 20 The Documentary History of the Ratification of the Constitution, *supra* note 26, at 1035, 1037.

150. The Federalist No. 68, *supra* note 23, at 344–45 (Alexander Hamilton).

151. *Id.* at 345.

152. *Id.* at 344. Hamilton may have understated the opposition. Some Anti-Federalists complained that the convention had proposed an elective monarchy, with its attendant ills. *See* Chapter 1 and text accompanying notes 62–63.

153. The Federalist No. 68, *supra* note 23, at 346 (Alexander Hamilton).

154. 4 Debates in the Several State Conventions, *supra* note 22, at 122; *id.* at 58 (the president is chosen by "the people."); *id.* at 74 (the president is "to be chosen by electors appointed by the people."); *id.*, vol. 2, at 154 ("The president is chosen by the electors, who are appointed by the people.").

155. *Id.*, vol. 4, at 105 (stating that legislatures might direct the appointment of electors however they wished). *See also* Extract from a Letter (Nov. 28, 1787), *in* 8 The Documentary History of the Ratification of the Constitution, *supra* note 50, at 177, 178 ("The President is elected by persons nominated by the legislature of each state.").

156. 4 Debates in the Several State Conventions, *supra* note 22, at 105 (State legislators could not appoint, "because, as they were to direct the manner of appointing, a law would look very awkward, which should say, 'They gave the power of such appointments to themselves.'").

157. *Id.* (Some "were of opinion that the people at large were to choose them, and others thought the state legislatures were to appoint them.").

158. U.S. Const. art. II, § 1.

159. *See* Donald R. Deskins, Jr., et al., Presidential Elections 1789–2008, at 3 (2010). One state, Massachusetts, seemed to abuse its power, altering the mode of selecting electors for every election from 1796 to 1828. *See* 2 H. V. Ames, The Proposed Amendments to the Constitution of the United States 85 n.2 (1897).

160. Deskins, *supra* note 159, at 3.

161. *See* 1 Letters of Mrs. Adams, The Wife of John Adams lviii (Charles F. Adams ed., 1840) (referring to John Adams barely getting a majority in the "electoral colleges"); Robert Walsh, *An Argument on the Right of the Constituent to Instruct His Representative in Congress*, 4 Am. Rev. Hist. & Pol. 137, 165 (1812) (discussing "electoral colleges" and "colleges of presidential electors"); "Preamble and Resolutions asserting the right of the state Legislatures to instruct their Senators in the Congress of the United States" of the Virginia Legislature (Feb. 20, 1812), *in* Supplement Containing the Acts of the General Assembly of Virginia, of a Public and Generally Interesting Nature, Passed Since the Session of Assembly Which Commenced in the Year One Thousand Eight Hundred and Seven 158, 163 (1812) (discussing whether "colleges of presidential electors" can receive instructions); 3 The Weekly Register 63 (H. Niles ed., 1813) (discussing the number of votes in the "several electoral colleges" for president).

162. *See* Letter from Alexander Hamilton to James Wilson (Jan. 25, 1789), *in* 5 The Papers of Alexander Hamilton 247, 248–49 (Harold C. Syrett ed., 1962).

163. *See* Yanek Mieczkowski, The Routledge Historical Atlas of Presidential Elections 18–19 (2001).

164. Kallenbach, *supra* note 35, at 78.

165. *See* Bruce Ackerman, The Failure of the Founding Fathers 89–91 (2005).

166. *See* David P. Currie, The Constitution in Congress: The Jeffersonians, 1801–1829, at 39–65 (2001).

167. *See, e.g.,* Richard Cust, Charles I: A Political Life 453–65 (2005).

168. Const. of France tit. III, ch. II, § I(V)–(VII) (1791), *in* Benjamin Flower, The French Constitution; With Remarks on Some of Its Principal Articles 14, 38–39 (1792).

169. Greene, *supra* note 30, at 49.

170. *Id.* at 86.

171. *See* Del. Const. art. 7 (1776) (three years); N.Y. Const. art. XVIII (1777) (same); S.C. Const. art. III (1778) (two years).

172. *See* Del. Const. art. 7 (1776) (the president could serve a three-year term and then had to wait three years to serve again); Ga. Const. art. XXIII (1777) (the governor to be chosen annually and could not serve more than one year in a three-year span); Md. Const. art. XXXI (1776) (the governor to be chosen annually but could not remain in office more than three consecutive years and was not reeligible until having been out of office for four years); N.C. Const. art. XV (1776) (the governor could serve only three years in six successive years); Pa. Const. § 19 (1776) (any person serving as a counselor for three consecutive years could not serve again in the next four); S.C. Const. art. VI (1778) (the governor could serve one two-year term every four years); Va. Const. (1776) (the governor to be chosen annually but could not remain in office longer than three years successively and would not be reeligible until four years after he left office). Only Massachusetts, New Jersey, New Hampshire, and New York imposed no term limits. *See* Mass. Const. pt. 2, ch. II, § 1, arts. II–III (1780); N.H. Const. pt. II (1784); N.J. Const. art. VII (1776); N.Y. Const. art. XVIII (1777).

173. The Federalist No. 53, *supra* note 23, at 270 (James Madison).

174. Founding the American Presidency 98 (Richard J. Ellis ed., 1999).

175. *Id.*

176. *Id.*

177. *Id.*

178. 1 Records of the Federal Convention, *supra* note 4, at 85; *id.*, vol. 2 at 33–36.

179. *Id.*, vol. 2, at 36.

180. *Id.*

181. *Id.*, vol. 1, at 64; *id.*, vol. 2, at 51, 116.

182. *Id.*, vol. 1, at 21.

183. *Id.*, vol. 2, at 33.

184. *Id.* at 111–12.

185. *Id.* at 525.

186. Letter from Thomas Jefferson to James Madison (Dec. 20, 1787), *in* 12 The Papers of Thomas Jefferson 438, 440 (Julian P. Boyd ed., 1955); *see also* 3 Debates in the Several State Conventions, *supra* note 22, at 483–84 (George Mason complaining that president would serve for life).

187. Cato, Essay IV (Nov. 8, 1787), *in* 14 The Documentary History of the Ratification of the Constitution 7, 8 (John P. Kaminski & Gaspare J. Saladino eds., 1983).

188. *Id.* at 9.

189. *See generally* The Federalist No. 72, *supra* note 23, at 366–70 (Alexander Hamilton).

190. *See* Michael J. Korzi, Presidential Term Limits in American History: Power, Principles, and Politics 32 (2011).

191. U.S. Const. amend. XXII.

192. *See* 1 Blackstone, *supra* note 130, at 271–96.

193. *Id.* at 297.

194. Christopher Hibbert, George III: A Personal History 78 (1998).

195. *Id.* at 210.

196. Greene, *supra* note 30, at 175.

197. *Id.* at 174.

198. *Id.* at 175.

199. Pa. Const. § 36 (1776); Vt. Const. ch. II, § XXII (1786).

200. N.C. Const. art. XXI (1776) (The governor and officers "shall have adequate salaries, during their continuance in office.").

201. Del. Const. art. 7 (1776) ("An adequate but moderate salary shall be settled on him."); N.H. Const. pt. II (1784) ("The president and council shall be compensated for their services from time to time by such grants as the General Court shall think reasonable."); Va. Const. (1776) ("An adequate, but moderate salary shall be settled on him.").

202. *Compare* S.C. Const. art. XXXIV (1776) ("That the following yearly salaries be allowed to the public officers ... The president and commander-in-chief nine thousand pounds."), *with* S.C. Const. art. XXXVII (1778) ("That adequate yearly salaries be allowed to the public officers of this State, and be fixed by law.").

203. *See* Mass. Const. pt. 2, ch. II, § 1, art. XIII (1780).

204. *Id.*

205. 1 Records of the Federal Convention, *supra* note 4, at 21, 244.

206. *Id.* at 81–85.

207. *Id.*, vol. 2, at 61.

208. First Inaugural Address (Apr. 30, 1789), *in* 2 The Papers of George Washington: Presidential Series, *supra* note 96, at 173, 176.

209. Act of Sept. 24, 1789, 1 Stat. 72.

210. 1 Annals of Congress 659 (1789).

211. David P. Currie, The Constitution in Congress: The Federalist Period 1789–1801, at 33 (1997).

212. Va. Const. (1776) ("An adequate, but moderate salary shall be settled on him.").

213. Richard J. Ellis, The Development of the American Presidency 253 (2012).

214. 1 Annals of Congress 659–62 (1789).

215. Act of Sept. 24, 1789, 1 Stat. 72.

216. Act of July 1, 1790, 1 Stat. 128.

217. James F. Vivian, The President's Salary: A Study in Constitutional Declension, 1781–1990, at 9 (1993).

218. Act of Sept. 11, 1789, 1 Stat. 67.

219. 2 Records of the Federal Convention, *supra* note 4, at 497–98.

220. *Id.* at 498.

221. *Id.* at 537.

222. *Id.* at 536–37.

223. *Id.* at 537.

224. The vice president would seem to have no meaningful role on whether to consent to a treaty, since he may vote only when the Senate is "equally divided." If the Senate were so arrayed with respect to a treaty, the vice president's vote would not secure the two-thirds support necessary for approval.

225. U.S. Const. amend. XII.

226. Sanders, *supra* note 63, at 33–34.

227. Letter from John Adams to Benjamin Lincoln (May 26, 1789), *quoted in* Linda D. Guerrero, John Adams' Vice Presidency, 1789–1797, at 185 (1982).

228. Letter from John Adams to John Hurd (Apr. 5, 1790), *quoted in id.*

229. Letter from John Adams to Abigail Adams (Dec. 19, 1793), *in* 1 The Works of John Adams 459, 460 (Charles Francis Adams ed., 1856).

230. 9 Documentary History of the First Federal Congress, *supra* note 84, at 30.

231. Guerrero, *supra* note 227, at 134.

232. *Id.* at 128.

233. Jack D. Warren, *John Adams, in* Vice Presidents: A Biographical Dictionary 11–12 (L. Edward Purcell ed., 2010).

234. Standing Rules of the Senate, Rule XIX (2010). The rules on debate say nothing about vice presidential participation, leading some to conclude that the vice president cannot participate. *See, e.g.*, 1 Robert Byrd, The Senate, 1789–1989, at 442 (1989).

235. 1 Records of the Federal Convention, *supra* note 4, at 292.

236. *Id.*, vol. 2, at 186.

237. *Id.* at 427.

238. *Id.* at 499.

239. N.Y. Const. art. XX (1777).

240. 2 Records of the Federal Convention, *supra* note 4, at 535.

241. *Id.*, vol. 1, at 102–3 & n.14.

242. *Id.* at 110–11.

243. *Id.*, vol. 2, at 186.

244. *Id.* at 427.

245. While suffering from a fever, Jefferson indicated to Washington that nothing but "absolute inability" would prevent him from meeting the next morning. Letter from Thomas Jefferson to George Washington (July 11, 1793), *in* 26 The Papers of Thomas Jefferson 482, 482 (John Catanzariti ed., 1995). Jefferson's letter suggests that acute sickness could constitute "inability," in a colloquial sense at least.

246. Letter from George Washington to the Secretaries (Apr. 4, 1791), *in* 20 The Papers of Thomas Jefferson 141, 142 (Julian P. Boyd ed., 1992).

247. Letter from Thomas Jefferson to the President (Apr. 17, 1791), *in id.* at 144, 144–46.

248. *See* William R. Casto, Foreign Affairs and the Constitution in the Age of the Fighting Sail 105–6 (2006).

249. Shirley Anne Warshaw, Powersharing: White House-Cabinet Relations in the Modern Presidency 16 (1996).

250. U.S. Const. amend. XXV.

Chapter 4. The Executive Power as the "Active Principle in All Governments"

1. In making these points, I borrow from my work with Michael Ramsey. *See* Saikrishna B. Prakash & Michael D. Ramsey, *The Executive Power over Foreign Affairs*, 111 Yale L.J. 231 (2001).

2. John Locke, Two Treatises of Government and A Letter Concerning Toleration 164–65 (Yale University Press 2003) (1689).

3. Baron de Montesquieu, The Spirit of Laws 173 (Batoche Books 2001) (1748).

4. John Adams, Defence of the Constitutions of the Government of the United States, *in* 4 The Works of John Adams 271, 579 (Charles Francis Adams ed., 1851).

5. An Address of the Convention for Forming a Constitution of Government for the State of New Hampshire, 1781, *in* Manual of the Constitution of the State of New Hampshire 93, 98 (James Fairbanks Colby ed., 1912).

6. 1 Jacques Necker, An Essay on the True Principles of Executive Power in Great States 1 (1792) [hereinafter True Principles of Executive Power]; *see also* 2 Speeches of M. de Mirabeau the Elder Pronounced in the National Assembly of France 145 (James White trans., 1792) (describing executive power as the "faculty of acting").

7. Samuel Johnson, A Dictionary of the English Language (10th ed. 1792) (entry for "executive").

8. M. J. C. Vile, Constitutionalism and the Separation of Powers 67 (2d ed. 1998).

9. Michael D. Ramsey, *The Textual Basis of the President's Foreign Affairs Power*, 30 Harv. J.L. & Pub. Pol'y 141, 142–43 (2006).

10. A New General English Dictionary (William Pardon ed., 1771) (entry for "England").

11. Thomas Jefferson, Third Draft of the Virginia Constitution, art. II (1776), *in* 1 The Papers of Thomas Jefferson 356, 359 (Julian P. Boyd ed., 1950).

12. *Id.* at 360.

13. *Id.*

14. Theophilus Parsons, The Essex Result (1778), *in* 1 American Political Writing During the Founding Era, 1760–1805, at 481, 494 (Charles S. Hyneman & Donald S. Lutz eds., 1983).

15. Remarks on an Act Granting to Congress Certain Imposts and Duties (Feb. 15, 1787), *in* 4 The Papers of Alexander Hamilton 71, 75 (Harold C. Syrett ed., 1962).

16. The Federalist No. 72, at 366 (Alexander Hamilton) (Garry Wills ed., 1982).

17. John Adams, Thoughts on Government (1776), *in* 1 American Political Writing During the Founding Era 1760–1805, *supra* note 14, at 402–9.

18. Letter from Edward Rutledge to John Jay (Nov. 24, 1776), *in* 5 Letters of Delegates to Congress, 1774–1789, at 538 (Paul H. Smith ed., 1979).

19. *E.g.*, Remarks on an Act Granting to Congress Certain Imposts and Duties (Feb. 15, 1787), *in* 4 The Papers of Alexander Hamilton, *supra* note 15, at 75 (claiming that Congress had "executive power"); Theophilus Parsons, The Essex Result (1778), *in* 1 American Political Writing During the Founding Era 1760–1805, *supra* note 14, at 494 (same).

20. Evarts Boutell Greene, The Provincial Governor in the English Colonies of North America 108–9 (1898).

21. Gordon S. Wood, *Foreword: State Constitution-Making in the American Revolution*, 24 Rutgers L.J. 911, 914–17 (1993).

22. *See* Chapter 1, text accompanying notes 12–15.

23. Locke, *supra* note 2, at 105, 137.

24. 1 True Principles of Executive Power, *supra* note 6, at 4.

25. 1 The Records of the Federal Convention of 1787, at 65 (Max Farrand rev. ed., 1966) [hereinafter Records of the Federal Convention].

26. The Federalist No. 70, *supra* note 16, at 355 (Alexander Hamilton).

27. *E.g.*, 1 Records of the Federal Convention, *supra* note 25, at 71; *id.*, vol. 2, at 100–101.

28. The Presidential Protest (May 7, 1834), *in* 4 The Works of Daniel Webster 103, 134 (1851).

29. Chapter 2, text accompanying notes 44–69.

30. Saikrishna Prakash, *New Light on the Decision of 1789*, 91 Cornell L. Rev. 1021, 1041 (2006).

31. The Appointing and Removing Power (Feb. 16, 1835), *in* 4 The Works of Daniel Webster, *supra* note 28, at 179, 186.

32. *Id.*

33. Youngstown Sheet & Tube Co. v. Sawyer, 343 U.S. 579, 587 (1952) (treating the Vesting Clause as a reference to other powers explicitly given to the executive in Article II instead of as an independent source of executive authority); *id.* at 640–41, 641 n.9 (Jackson, J., concurring) (claiming that there would have been no need for the "Opinion Clause" and other specified powers if the Vesting Clause actually conveyed power).

34. Bruce Ledewitz, *The Uncertain Power of the President To Execute the Laws*, 46 Tenn. L. Rev. 757, 797 (1979) (noting the Executive Power Clause is a "probably empty grant" of power); Lawrence Lessig & Cass R. Sunstein, *The President and the Administration*, 94 Colum. L. Rev. 1, 47–50 (1994) (arguing that the Vesting Clause conveys little more than the enumerated executive powers); Morton Rosenberg, *Presidential Control of Agency Rulemaking*, 23 Ariz. L. Rev. 1199, 1209 (1981) (arguing that the Executive Power Clause "locates the situs of power but not its content").

35. The Appointing and Removing Power (Feb. 16, 1835), *in* 4 The Works of Daniel Webster, *supra* note 28, at 179, 187.

36. *Id.* at 186, 188 (recognizing that authority granted after the Vesting Clause was executive authority).

37. *See* Steven G. Calabresi & Saikrishna B. Prakash, *The President's Power to Execute the Laws*, 104 Yale L.J. 541, 576–79 (1994); Steven G. Calabresi & Kevin H. Rhodes, *The Structural Constitution: Unitary Executive, Plural Judiciary*, 105 Harv. L. Rev. 1153, 1196 n.216 (1992).

38. *See* U.S. Const. art. II, § 2, cl. 1 ("[H]e shall have Power to grant Reprieves and Pardons for offenses against the United States, except in Cases of Impeachment.").

39. *See* U.S. Const. art. II, § 2, cl. 2.

40. *See* Saikrishna Bangalore Prakash, *Exhuming the Seemingly Moribund Declaration of War*, 77 Geo. Wash. L. Rev. 89, 107–20 (2008).

41. Pacificus No. 1 (June 29, 1793), *in* 15 The Papers of Alexander Hamilton 33, 39 (Harold C. Syrett ed., 1969). After the convention's close, Hamilton presented Madison with a more complete plan, one that he wished he had proposed. Article I, section 2 of the plan granted the president the "Executive power, with the qualifications hereinafter specified." 3 Records of the Federal Convention, *supra* note 25, at 619.

42. Pacificus No. 1 (June 29, 1793), *in* 15 The Papers of Alexander Hamilton, *supra* note 41, at 33, 39.

43. The Federalist No. 41, *supra* note 16, at 210 (James Madison).

44. A case can be made that the introductory executive provisions of the Massachusetts and New Hampshire Constitutions did nothing more than establish a title and number. Massachusetts provided that "[t]here shall be a supreme executive magistrate, who shall be styled 'The governor . . . .' and whose title shall be 'His Excellency.'" Mass. Const. pt. 2, ch. II, § 1, art. I (1780); *see also* N.H. Const. pt. II (1784). But even here, describing the governor as a "supreme executive magistrate" likely implied that the governor had powers normally enjoyed by such a magistrate and limited by the subsequent constraints.

45. *See* Steven G. Calabresi, *The Vesting Clauses as Power Grants*, 88 Nw. U. L. Rev. 1377, 1381 (1994) ("This plain meaning understanding is confirmed by the use of the verb 'vest' in two other constitutional provisions where 'vest' is clearly used to refer to the *placing of power and authority in the hands of a named actor.*").

46. *See generally* U.S. Const. art. II, §§ 2–3.

47. *See* U.S. Const. art. I, § 7, cl. 2 (identifying the president as a person by using "he" and "his").

48. The Federalist No. 41, *supra* note 16, at 210 (James Madison).

49. As noted in Chapter 2, neither Rhode Island nor Connecticut adopted constitutions before 1787. *See* Chapter 2, note 45. Moreover, as noted in this chapter, neither Massachusetts nor New Hampshire had grants of "executive power" or their equivalent. *See supra* note 44 and accompanying text. Hence the discussion that follows omits consideration of them.

50. Pa. Const. § 3 (1776); N.J. Const. art. VIII (1776); Vt. Const. ch. II, § 3 (1777); Vt. Const. ch. II, § III (1786).

51. N.Y. Const. art. XVII (1777).

52. Va. Const. (1776); Ga. Const. art. XIX (1777).

53. Del. Const. art. 7 (1776); Md. Const. art. XXXIII (1776); N.C. Const. art. XIX (1776).

54. S.C. Const. art. XXX (1776); S.C. Const. art. XI (1778).

55. Ga. Const. art. XIX (1777).

56. S.C. Const. arts. XXX, XXVI (1776).

57. *Id.* art. XXVI.

58. *Id.* art. VIII.

59. The 1778 South Carolina Constitution had the same provisions. *See* S.C. Const. arts. XI, XVII, XXXIII (1778).

60. Va. Const. (1776).

61. *Id.*

62. *Id.*

63. *Id.* Other constitutions granted generic executive power but barred prorogations and adjournments. *See, e.g.,* Del. Const. art. 10 (1776); Md. Const. art. XXIX (1776).

64. *See* N.C. Const. art. XIX (1776); S.C. Const. art. XXX (1776).

65. Md. Const. art. XXXIII (1776).

66. *Id.*

67. *Id.*

68. *Id.* art. XLVIII.

69. *Id.* art. XXXIII. One might suppose that the phrase referred solely to the powers to pardon, embargo, and appoint. But that is unlikely. There was no reason to use that phrase to encompass the pardon and embargo powers, since those two powers closely followed on the heels of the generic grant. Moreover, the phrase could not have referred to the appointment powers, because those were checked by participation of the executive council and hence were *not* exercisable by the governor alone.

70. Del. Const. art. 7 (1776).

71. *Id.* arts. 9, 10, 21.

72. N.J. Const. art. VIII (1776).

73. N.Y. Const. art. XVII (1777).

74. *Id.* art. XVIII.

75. *See, e.g.,* N.J. Const. (1776); Md. Const. (1776); Del. Const. (1776); S.C. Const. (1776); S.C. Const. (1778).

76. Some constitutions imposed a duty of faithful execution. *E.g.,* N.Y. Const. art. XIX (1777); Pa. Const. § 20 (1776). But as noted in Chapter 5, such faithful-execution duties did not grant power to the executive. Rather, such clauses presupposed the existence of a power *granted elsewhere* to execute the law.

77. Montesquieu, *supra* note 3, at 173–74.

78. N.C. Const. Declaration of Rights, art. IV (1776).

79. Md. Const. Declaration of Rights, art. IV (1776).

80. Va. Const. Declaration of Rights, § 5 (1776).

81. S.C. Const. art. VII (1776).

82. S.C. Const. art. II (1778).

83. N.Y. Const. art. II (1777). The Pennsylvania, New Hampshire, North Carolina, and Vermont Constitutions had the same structure—a generic legislative grant followed by some particularized powers.

84. *Id.* arts. V, XII, XVI.

85. Margaret Burnham MacMillan, The War Governors in the American Revolution 63 (1943).

86. Charles C. Thach, Jr., The Creation of the Presidency, 1775–1789: A Study in Constitutional History 118 (1922).

87. *See* MacMillan, *supra* note 85, at 226.

88. *See id.* at 178 n.54; *see also* 1 Annals of Congress 530 (1789) (noting controversy within the states).

89. Curtis A. Bradley & Martin S. Flaherty, *Executive Power Essentialism and Foreign Affairs,* 102 Mich. L. Rev. 545, 579–80 (2004).

90. 1 Records of the Federal Convention, *supra* note 25, at 21.

91. *Id.* at 292.

92. *Id.*, vol. 3, at 599. The New Jersey Plan did not propose anything resembling the Constitution's vesting clause. *Id.*, vol. 1, at 244.

93. *Id.*, vol 2, at 132.

94. *Id.* at 129, 134 n.3.

95. Thach, *supra* note 86, at 111.

96. 2 Records of the Federal Convention, *supra* note 25, at 185.

97. Thach, *supra* note 86, at 115–16.

98. Pa. Const. § 3 (1776).

99. S.C. Const. art. XI (1778).

100. 2 Records of the Federal Convention, *supra* note 25, at 401.

101. *Id.* at 565, 590.

102. Thach, *supra* note 86, at 139.

103. *E.g*, N.C. Const. art. I (1776) (conveying "legislative authority" without qualifications to the Senate and the Commons).

104. *See* text accompanying notes 30–32.

105. Letter from James Madison to Thomas Jefferson (Sept. 6, 1787), *in* 12 The Papers of Thomas Jefferson 102, 102 (Julian P. Boyd ed., 1955).

106. Thach, *supra* note 86, at 138.

Chapter 5. "The Constitutional Executor of the Laws"

1. M. J. C. Vile, Constitutionalism and the Separation of Powers 45 (2d ed. 1998).

2. Samuel Johnson, A Dictionary of the English Language (10th ed. 1792) (entry for "executive").

3. Alexander Hamilton 33, 43 (Harold C. Syrett ed., 1969).

4. Noah Webster, Rudiments of English Grammar 64 (1790); *see also* Nathaniel Chipman, Sketches of the Principles of Government 119 (1793) ("It is the business of the executive to carry into effect . . . the constitutional laws.").

5. John Locke, Two Treatises of Government and A Letter Concerning Toleration 164 (Yale University Press 2003) (1689).

6. Baron de Montesquieu, The Spirit of the Laws 173 (Batoche Books 2001) (1748).

7. 1 William Blackstone, Commentaries on the Laws of England 257, 259 (University of Chicago 1979) (1765).

8. 1 Jacques Necker, An Essay on the True Principles of Executive Power in Great States 4 (1792); *see also* Philip Withers, History of the Royal Malady 81–82 (1789) ("Executive Power is that energy by which the Legal Resolutions of the People are carried into Effect."); J. L. De Lolme, The Constitution of England 159 (William S. Hein & Co. 1999) (1771) (describing how the executive power ensured "that [the laws] may have weight, and continue in force"); Joseph Priestley, Lectures on History and General Policy 284 (1788) (noting that executive power was "a power of enforcing the sanctions of the laws"); John Young, Essays on the Following Interesting Subjects 41 (1794) (stating that the king has executive power and that "it belongs to him to put [the laws] in execution").

9. Thomas Jefferson, A Summary View of the Rights of British America, *in* Tracts of the American Revolution 1763–1776, at 256, 274 (Merrill Jensen ed., 1967).

10. Joseph Galloway, A Candid Examination of the Mutual Claims of Great Britain and the Colonies, *in id.* at 350, 356.

11. *Id.* at 374–75. The Crown executed the laws in the colonies via its governors. *See* Evarts Boutell Greene, The Provincial Governor in the English Colonies of North America 65, 139 (1898) (describing the "governor" as "the centre of the local administration, the chief executive," and stating that it was his duty "to see that the laws were duly enforced"); *see also* Marcus Wilson Jernegan, The American Colonies 1492–1750, at 276 (1929) (The governor's "general duty was to enforce the laws.").

12. *E.g., "The Interest of America"* (1776), *in* Colonies to Nation 1763–1789, at 315, 318 (Jack P. Greene ed., 1967) (decrying the mixing of legislative and executive power and noting that "where the making and executing the laws . . . lie in the same hand" there "can be but little chance for proper freedom"); *Four Letters on Interesting Subjects* (1776), *in id.* at 311, 313–14 (declaring that while government is generally divided into three parts, there were really only two powers in any government, "the power to make laws, and the power to execute them; for the judicial power is only a branch of the executive").

13. Theophilus Parsons, The Essex Result (1778), *in* 1 American Political Writing During the Founding Era 1760–1805, at 480, 494 (Charles S. Hyneman & Donald S. Lutz eds., 1983).

14. *Id.* at 500.

15. *Id.*

16. An Address of the Convention for Forming a Constitution of Government for the State of New Hampshire, 1781, *in* Manual of the Constitution of the State of New Hampshire 93, 98 (James Fairbanks Colby ed., 1912).

17. Noah Webster, Sketches of American Policy 7 (1785).

18. *See* Vt. Const. ch. II, § XI (1786); Vt. Const. ch. II, § 18 (1777); N.Y. Const. art. XIX (1777); Pa. Const. § 20 (1776).

19. *See* Ga. Const. art. XXIV (1777) (the governor must take an oath that "the laws and ordinances of the State be duly observed, and that law and justice in mercy be executed in all judgments").

20. *See* Margaret Burnham MacMillan, The War Governors in the American Revolution 65–66 (1943).

21. *See id.* at 61–64.

22. *Id.* at 72 (observing that revolutionary assemblies in large part left "the routine execution of its acts in the hands of the governor or president"); Willi Paul Adams, The First American Constitutions 272 (Rita Kimber & Robert Kimber trans., 1980) (observing that "[n]one of the constitutions attempted to limit the powers of the executive solely to carrying out the laws passed by the legislature"); 3 The Debates in the Several State Conventions on the Adoption of the Federal Constitution 201 (Jonathan Elliot ed., 2d ed. 1836) [hereinafter Debates in the Several State Conventions] (Virginia Governor Edmund Randolph noting that every state executive executed the laws).

23. *See* MacMillan, *supra* note 20, at 115–18.

24. Letter from Thomas Jefferson to Edward Carrington (Aug. 4, 1787), *in* 11 The Papers of Thomas Jefferson 678, 679 (Julian P. Boyd ed., 1955).

25. John Adams, A Defence of the Constitutions of Government of the United States of America, *in* 4 The Works of John Adams 271, 581 (Charles Francis Adams ed., 1851).

26. 1 The Records of the Federal Convention of 1787, at 21 (Max Farrand rev. ed., 1966) [hereinafter Records of the Federal Convention].

27. *Id.* at 244.

28. *Id.*, vol. 3, at 606.

29. *Id.*, vol. 1, at 292.

30. *Id.*, vol. 2, at 132.

31. *Id.* at 132, 185.

32. *Id.*, vol. 1, at 66.

33. *Id.* at 67.

34. *See, e.g., id.* at 65.

35. *Id.*, vol. 2, at 34. Gouverneur Morris later made the same point. If the executive were selected by Congress, Congress would "perpetuate & support their usurpations by the influence of tax-gatherers & other officers, by fleets armies &c." *Id.* at 403–4. In other words, if Congress selected the executive, Congress could use the executive's law enforcement machinery as a means of oppression.

36. *Id.*, vol. 1, at 110.

37. 2 Debates in the Several State Conventions, *supra* note 22, at 461.

38. A Jersyman: To the Citizens of New Jersey (Nov. 6, 1987), *in* 3 The Documentary History of the Ratification of the Constitution 149 (Merrill Jensen ed., 1978).

39. 4 Debates in the Several State Conventions, *supra* note 22, at 58.

40. Republicus (Mar. 1, 1788), *in* 8 The Documentary History of the Ratification of the Constitution 446, 448 (John P. Kaminski & Gaspare J. Saladino eds., 1988).

41. *Id.* at 449.

42. The Federal Farmer, No. 14 (Jan. 17, 1788), *in* 20 The Documentary History of the Ratification of the Constitution 1035, 1042 (John P. Kaminski et al. eds., 2004); *see also* Citizen of New Haven (Jan. 7, 1788), *in* 15 The Documentary History of the Ratification of the Constitution 280, 282 (John P. Kaminski & Gaspare J. Saladino eds., 1984) (remarking, "The united wisdom and various interests of a nation should be combined in framing the laws. But the execution of them should not be in the whole legislature.").

43. 2 Debates in the Several State Conventions, *supra* note 22, at 128.

44. A Federal Republican, A Review of the Constitution (Nov. 28, 1787), *in* 14 The Documentary History of the Ratification of the Constitution 255, 273 (John P. Kaminski & Gaspare J. Saladino eds., 1983).

45. 4 Debates in the Several State Conventions, *supra* note 22, at 329.

46. Noah Webster, A Citizen of America, *in* Friends of the Constitution: Writings of the "Other" Federalists 1787–1788, at 373, 380 (Colleen A. Sheehan & Gary L. McDowell eds., 1998).

47. *Id.; see also id.* at 405 (observing that the supreme executive was "invested with power to enforce the laws of the union").

48. The Federal Farmer No. 14 (Jan. 17, 1788), *in* 20 The Documentary History of the Ratification of the Constitution, *supra* note 42, at 1035, 1039. Others who had previously advocated term limits had a change of heart. North Carolina delegates to the Philadelphia Convention had sought to limit the president to a single term. 4 Debates in the Several State Conventions, *supra* note 22, at 103. Returning the president "into the common mass of the people" would ensure that "they would feel the tone they had given to the administration of the laws [which] was the best security the public had for their good behavior." *Id.* After considering opposing arguments, however, one delegate endorsed the lack of term limits. *Id.* at 104 (comments of William Davie).

49. Essays by a Farmer (Mar. 25, 1788), *in* 5 The Complete Anti-Federalist 40, 42 (Herbert J. Storing ed., 1981).

50. Essays by a Farmer (Feb. 29, 1788), *in id.* at 16, 21.

51. 3 Debates in the Several State Conventions, *supra* note 22, at 201.

52. Proclamation of Neutrality (Apr. 22, 1793), *in* 32 The Writings of George Washington 430 (John C. Fitzpatrick ed., 1939).

53. Pacificus No. 1 (June 29, 1973), *in* 15 The Papers of Alexander Hamilton, *supra* note 3, at 33, 43.

54. *Id.* at 40.

55. *Id.* at 41.

56. Helvidius No. I (Aug. 24, 1793), *in* 15 The Papers of James Madison: Congressional Series 66, 69 (Thomas A. Mason et al. eds., 1985).

57. James Wilson, Lectures on Law (1790), *in* 2 Collected Works of James Wilson 747, 878 (Kermit L. Hall & Mark David Hall eds., 2007); 10 Annals of Congress 613 (1800) (John Marshall noting, "[The president] is charged to execute the laws. A treaty is declared to be a law. He must then execute a treaty."); James Kent, 1 Commentaries on American Law 253 (1826) ("The object of this [executive] department is the execution of the law."); Thomas Paine, Dissertation on First Principles of Government (1795), *in* 3 The Writings of Thomas Paine 256, 276 (Moncure Daniel Conway ed., 1895) ("All the parts in the governments of the United States of America that are called THE EXECUTIVE, are no other than authorities to superintend the execution of the laws.").

58. *See* Lawrence Lessig & Cass R. Sunstein, *The President and the Administration*, 94 Colum. L. Rev. 1, 2 (1994).

59. Saikrishna Prakash, *The Chief Prosecutor*, 73 Geo. Wash. L. Rev. 521, 533–35 (2005) [hereinafter The Chief Prosecutor] (summarizing these claims).

60. Lessig & Sunstein, *supra* note 58, at 16.

61. *Id.* at 16–17.

62. For a general discussion of the rebellion, *see* William Hogeland, The Whiskey Rebellion: George Washington, Alexander Hamilton, and the Frontier Rebels Who Challenged America's Newfound Sovereignty (2006).

63. Letter from George Washington to Alexander Hamilton (Oct. 1, 1792), *in* 32 The Writings of George Washington, *supra* note 52, at 173, 174 (noting direction to attorney general); *see also* Letter from George Washington to Edmund Randolph (Oct. 1, 1792), *in id.* at 171 (expressing his "desire" that Randolph attend the proceedings).

64. Fourth Annual Address to Congress (Nov. 6, 1792), *in id.* at 205, 209.

65. Letter from George Washington to William Rawle (Mar. 13, 1793), *in id.* at 386.

66. Proclamation (Mar. 19, 1791), *in* 31 The Writings of George Washington 250 (John C. Fitzpatrick ed., 1939).

67. Fifth Annual Address to Congress (Dec. 3, 1793), *in* 33 The Writings of George Washington 163, 167 (John C. Fitzpatrick ed., 1940).

68. Proclamation of Neutrality (Apr. 22, 1793), *in* 32 The Writings of George Washington, *supra* note 52, at 430–31.

69. Proclamation (Dec. 12, 1792), *in id.* at 260–61.

70. *See* Letter from George Washington to Edmund Randolph (Mar. 27, 1793), *in id.* at 404 (agreeing that a district attorney should be ordered to represent William Bingham). Bingham had been sued for his actions as representative of the United States in Martinique. Bingham v. Cabbot, 3 U.S. (3 Dall.) 19, 20 (1795).

71. *See* Letter from George Washington to Edmund Randolph (Oct. 1, 1792), *in* 32 The Writings of Washington, *supra* note 52, at 171, 172; United States v. Lawrence, 3 U.S. (3 Dall.) 42, 48–49 (1795) (Attorney General William Bradford noting the president's motives for intervening).

72. Susan Low Bloch, *The Early Role of the Attorney General in Our Constitutional Scheme: In the Beginning There Was Pragmatism*, 1989 Duke L.J. 561, 602–6 (1989); Maeva Marcus & Robert Teir, Hayburn's Case: *A Misinterpretation of Precedent*, 1988 Wis. L. Rev. 527, 534–39.

73. Marcus & Teir, *supra* note 72, at 537.

74. Extract of a Letter from Richard Harrison to Timothy Pickering (Oct. 3, 1795), *in* 1 American State Papers: Foreign Relations 626, 627 (Walter Lowrie & Matthew St. Clair Clarke eds., 1833).

75. The Chief Prosecutor, *supra* note 59, at 558–60.

76. *Id.* at 560–61.

77. *Id.* at 561–62.

78. 10 Annals of Congress 184 (1800).

79. *Id.* at 615 (1800).

80. U.S. Const. art. I, § 8, cl. 15.

81. *Id.* art. II, § 2, cl. 1 (declaring that the president is commander in chief of the militias of the several states when called into national service).

82. 2 Records of the Federal Convention, *supra* note 26, at 69.

83. *Id.*, vol. 1, at 245 (providing that the executive could call forth the "power of the Confederated States" to enforce federal acts and treaties).

84. Philadelphiensis IX (Feb. 6, 1788), *in* 16 The Documentary History of the Ratification of the Constitution 57, 58 (John P. Kaminski & Gaspare J. Saladino eds., 1986).

85. *See* 3 Debates in the Several State Conventions, *supra* note 22, at 436. Interestingly, some supporters of the Constitution thought the militia insufficient for law execution and that more "regular forces" (i.e., the army) would be necessary. *See id.*, vol. 4, at 260–61 (comments of Charles Pinckney).

86. *See* Robert W. Coakley, The Role of Federal Military Forces in Domestic Disorders 1789–1878, at 25 (1988).

87. Act of May 2, 1792, 1 Stat. 264.

88. *Id.* § 2.

89. *See* Coakley, *supra* note 86, at 26.

90. Act of June 5, 1794, §§ 7–8, 1 Stat. 381, 384.

91. Coakley, *supra* note 86, at 37, 43.

92. *Id.* at 50–53.

93. *Id.* at 54–55, 60, 63 (Washington issuing various instructions to the militias).

94. Letter from George Washington to Charles Mynn Thruston (Aug. 10, 1794), *in* 33 The Writings of George Washington, *supra* note 67, at 464, 465; *see also* Letter from George Washington to Daniel Morgan (Oct. 8, 1794), *in id.* at 522, 523 (worrying that if the rebels were not subdued, all governments in the United States might fall).

95. Letter from George Washington to Alexander Hamilton (Sept. 7, 1792), *in* 32 The Writings of George Washington, *supra* note 52, at 143, 144.

96. U.S. Const. art. II, § 3.

97. *E.g.*, Peter M. Shane, *Independent Policymaking and Presidential Power: A Constitutional Analysis*, 57 Geo. Wash. L. Rev. 596, 613 (1989).

98. F. W. Maitland, The Constitutional History of England 302–3 (1908).

99. Carolyn A. Edie, *Tactics and Strategies: Parliament's Attack Upon the Royal Dispensing Power 1597–1689*, 29 Am. J. Legal Hist. 197, 199 (1985).

100. *See* Bill of Rights, 1689, 1 W. & M., c. 2 (Eng.).

101. The Frame of the Government of Pennsylvania, art. VIII (1682), *in* William Penn and the Founding of Pennsylvania: A Documentary History 123, 124 (Jean R. Soderlund ed., 1983) ("[T]he Governour and Provincial Council shall take care, that all laws, statutes, and ordinances, which shall at any time be made within the said Province, be duly and diligently executed.").

102. *See* 1 Debates in the Several State Conventions, *supra* note 22, at 334 (Rhode Island's ratification convention expressing its sentiments along with ratification); *id.*, vol. 4, at 243 (North Carolina's Declaration of Rights expressing the same sentiment); *id.*, vol. 3, at 658 (Virginia's proposed amendments to the Constitution expressing the same sentiment).

103. Vt. Const., ch. I, cl. XVII (1786); *id.* ch. II, § XI.

104. *See* N.C. Const. Declaration of Rights, art. V (1776); Md. Const. Declaration of Rights, art. VII (1776); Mass. Const. pt. I, art. XX (1780).

105. 1 Records of the Federal Convention, *supra* note 26, at 103–4.

106. Remarks on Mr. Monroe's "View of the Conduct of the Executive of the United States," *in* 13 The Writings of George Washington 452, 455–56 (Worthington Chauncey

Ford ed., 1892); *see also id.* at 470 (mocking the idea that the president may declare a "treaty null and void").

107. Act of Mar. 27, 1794, §§ 1, 9, 1 Stat. 350, 351.

108. Letter from George Washington to the Senate and House of Representatives (Mar. 15, 1796), *in* 34 The Writings of George Washington 499, 500 (John C. Fitzpatrick ed., 1940).

109. Act of Apr. 20, 1796, 1 Stat. 453.

110. Letter from William Symmes to Peter Osgood (Nov. 15, 1787), *in* 4 The Complete Anti-Federalist, *supra* note 49, at 54, 60.

111. Bruce Ledewitz, *The Uncertain Power of the President to Execute the Laws*, 46 Tenn. L. Rev. 757, 797 (1979); *see also* Thomas O. McGarity, *Presidential Control of Regulatory Agency Decisionmaking*, 36 Am. U. L. Rev. 443, 465–66 (1987).

112. 1 Op. Att'y Gen. 624, 625 (1823).

113. *See supra* text accompanying note 101.

114. Pa. Const. § 20 (1776).

115. N.Y. Const. art. XIX (1777). Vermont too borrowed from the Pennsylvania Constitution, and because it too had a plural executive, it placed the faithful-execution responsibility on its governor and council. *See* Vt. Const. ch. II, § XI (1786); Vt. Const. ch. II, § 18 (1777).

116. N.Y. Const. art. XVII (1777); Pa. Const. § 3 (1776).

117. MacMillan, *supra* note 20, at 65–66.

118. 3 Pennsylvania Archives: Papers of the Governors 804, 808, 816 (George Edward Reed ed., fourth ser. 1900).

119. *Id.* at 841.

120. 2 Records of the Federal Convention, *supra* note 26, at 132 (vesting the president with the power "to carry into Execution the national Laws").

121. *Id.* at 185.

122. *E.g., id.* at 538 (James Wilson noting that "[g]ood laws are of no effect without a good Executive").

123. The Federalist No. 77, at 391 (Alexander Hamilton) (Garry Wills ed., 1982). Hamilton's observation, when read in conjunction with the comments of the Pennsylvania and New York executives, suggests that the clause's duty was often overshadowed by the power that the duty presupposed.

124. *See e.g.,* Letter from William Symmes to Peter Osgood (Nov. 15, 1787), *in* 4 The Complete Anti-Federalist, *supra* note 49, at 54, 60 (saying that Constitution granted the power to faithfully execute to one person).

125. Proclamation (Sept. 15, 1792), *in* 32 The Writings of George Washington, *supra* note 52, at 150, 151.

126. Proclamation (Sept. 25, 1794), *in* 33 The Writings of George Washington, *supra* note 67, at 507, 508 (quoting U.S. Const. art II, § 3).

127. *Id.*

128. Proclamation (Mar. 24, 1794), *in id.*, at 304, 305.

129. Pacificus No. 1 (June 29, 1793), *in* 15 The Papers of Alexander Hamilton, *supra* note 3, at 39.

130. *See, e.g.*, Letter from George Washington to Edmund Randolph (Mar. 11, 1793), *in* 32 The Writings of George Washington, *supra* note 52, at 382.

131. Proclamation (Aug. 26, 1790), *in* 31 The Writings of George Washington, *supra* note 66, at 99.

132. Letter from George Washington to James McHenry (July 13, 1796), *in* 35 The Writings of George Washington 136, 138 (John C. Fitzpatrick ed., 1940) (emphasis omitted).

133. Leonard D. White, The Federalists: A Study in Administrative History 27 (1948).

134. Letter from George Washington to Henry Knox (Oct. 15, 1793), *in* 33 The Writings of George Washington, *supra* note 67, at 130 ("The heads of Departments being absent the disputes arising between the agents of the Powers at war, and other matters, are transmitted immediately to me.").

135. 1 Journal of the Executive Proceedings of the Senate of the United States of America 25 (1789).

136. Address of the House of Representatives to George Washington (Nov. 28, 1794), *in* 1 A Compilation of the Messages and Papers of the Presidents: 1789–1897, at 162, 163 (James D. Richardson ed., 1897) [hereinafter 1 Messages and Papers of the President].

137. *See* Saikrishna Prakash, *The Essential Meaning of Executive Power*, 2003 U. Ill. L. Rev. 701, 801–2 (2003) (discussing these arguments in further detail).

138. 1 Blackstone, *supra* note 7, at *258–59.

139. *Id.* at 259; *see also* 4 William Blackstone, Commentaries on the Laws of England 2 (University of Chicago 1979) (1769) (The king "is supposed by the law to be the person injured by every infraction of the public rights belonging to that community, and is therefore in all cases the proper prosecutor for every public offence."); *id.* at 177 (asserting that by virtue of his "executory power of the law," the king may prosecute those public wrongs that violate the laws of nature, that result in a breach of peace, and that threaten to subvert civil society).

140. *Id.*, vol. 1, at 259.

141. 4 Debates in the Several State Conventions, *supra* note 22, at 111; *see also* 2 Records of the Federal Convention, *supra* note 26, at 426 (James Wilson pointing out that preconviction pardons might be used "to obtain the testimony of accomplices").

142. The Federalist No. 74, *supra* note 123, at 378 (Alexander Hamilton); *see also* 4 Debates in the Several State Conventions, *supra* note 22, at 112 (James Iredell voicing the same idea).

143. United States v. Wilson, 32 U.S. (7 Pet.) 150, 160 (1833).

144. W.H. Humbert, The Pardoning Power of the President 9 (1941).

145. *See* K. J. Kesselring, Mercy and Authority in the Tudor State 83–89, 131–33 (2003).

146. *Id.* at 128–31.

147. *Id.* at 16, 58, 60, 64.

148. *Id.* at 58.

149. *Id.* at 61.

150. *See* Christen Jensen, The Pardoning Power in the American States 3–8 (1922); *see also* Greene, *supra* note 11, at 124–26.

151. 4 Blackstone, *supra* note 139, at 390.

152. N.Y. Const. art. XVIII (1777); Del. Const. art. 7 (1776); Md. Const. art. XXXIII (1776); N.C. Const. art. XIX (1776).

153. N.H. Const. pt. II, cl. 39 (1784); Mass. Const. pt. II, ch. 2, § 1 art. VIII (1780); N.J. Const. art. IX (1776); Va. Const. cl. 29 (1776).

154. Pa. Const. § 20 (1776); Vt. Const. ch. II, § XI (1786) (including the governor on the executive council).

155. S.C. Const. art. XI (1778); S.C. Const. art. XXX (1776).

156. Edward McCrady, The History of South Carolina in the Revolution 1775–1780, at 215 (1901).

157. David Lee Russell, The American Revolution in the Southern Colonies 309 (2000).

158. *See, e.g.,* Mass. Const. pt. II, ch. 2, § 1, art. VIII (1780); N.C. Const. art. XIX (1776).

159. Del. Const. art. 7 (1776); N.C. Const. art. XIX (1776); Va. Const. cl. 29 (1776).

160. Mass. Const. pt. II, ch. 2, § 1, art. VIII (1780); *see also* N.H. Const. pt. II, cl. 39 (1784).

161. N.Y. Const. art. XVIII (1777); Vt. Const. ch. II, § XI (1786); Vt. Const. ch. II, § 18 (1777); Pa. Const. § 20 (1776).

162. Ga. Const. art. XIX (1777).

163. MacMillan, *supra* note 20, at 178.

164. Russell, *supra* note 157, at 309.

165. Charles D. Rodenbough, Governor Alexander Martin: Biography of a North Carolina Revolutionary War Statesman 124 (2004).

166. MacMillan, *supra* note 20, at 178 n.53.

167. *E.g,* 8 Journals of the Continental Congress 1774–1789, at 550 (Worthington Chauncey Ford ed., 1907); 9 Journals of the Continental Congress 1774–1789, at 1067 (Worthington Chauncey Ford ed., 1907).

168. 2 Journals of the Continental Congress 1774–1789, at 122 (Worthington Chauncey Ford ed., 1905); 3 Journals of the Continental Congress 1774–1789, at 383 (Worthington Chaucney Ford ed., 1905).

169. George Washington, General Orders (Feb. 6, 1783), *in* 26 The Writings of George Washington 102, 103 (John C. Fitzpatrick ed., 1938); *see also* George Washington, General Orders (July 4, 1779), *in* 15 The Writings of George Washington 364 (John C. Fitzpatrick ed., 1936) (granting a general pardon to soldiers under a sentence of death).

170. Bruce Chadwick, George Washington's War: The Forging of a Revolutionary Leader and the American Presidency 425–26 (2004).

171. *Id.* at 161–62.

172. 1 Records of the Federal Convention, *supra* note 26, at 21.

173. *Id.* at 292.

174. *Id.*, vol. 2, at 419.

175. *Id.*

176. *Id.* at 419–20.

177. *Id.* at 426, 626–27.

178. *Id.* at 626–27. Others believed that the legislature should have no pardon authority, likely because they wished for the power to rest with the president. *Id.*

179. 10 The Documentary History of the Ratification of the Constitution 1378–79 (John P. Kaminski & Gaspare J. Saladino eds., 1993) (George Mason complaining about treason, pardoning before conviction, and the president screening himself); 6 The Documentary History of the Ratification of the Constitution 1362 (John P. Kaminski & Gaspare J. Saladino eds., 2000) (delegate claiming the pardon will be used by the president to screen himself).

180. *See e.g.*, 4 Debates in the Several State Conventions, *supra* note 22, at 112–14 (comments of James Iredell).

181. *See e.g.*, The Federalist No. 74, *supra* note 123, at 377 (Alexander Hamilton); 4 Debates in the Several State Conventions, *supra* note 22, at 111 (comments of James Iredell).

182. U.S. Const. art. II, § 2, cl. 1.

183. 4 Blackstone, *supra* note 139, at 387.

184. Ex Parte Garland, 71 U.S. 333, 380 (1867); 2 William Blackstone, Commentaries on the Laws of England 254 (University of Chicago 1979) (1766).

185. *See e.g.*, James Pfiffner, *Pardon Power*, *in* The Heritage Guide to the Constitution 203, 203 (Edwin Meese III et al. eds., 2005). The Pardon Attorney's webpage claims that "[u]nder the Constitution, the President's clemency power extends only to federal criminal offenses." *See* U.S. Dep't of Justice, Office of Pardon Attorney, http://www.justice.gov/pardon (last accessed Sept. 8, 2013).

186. A Dictionary of the English Language, *supra* note 2 (entry for "offence") (listing both "crime" and "transgression" as definitions).

187. *Cf.* Ex Parte Grossman, 267 U.S. 87, 117–18 (1925) (denying that other uses of "offenses" in the Constitution limit the meaning of "offenses" in the pardon clause).

188. *See* The Laura, 114 U.S. 411, 413–14 (1885) ("It may be conceded that . . . the President, under the general, unqualified grant of power to pardon offences against the United States, may remit fines, penalties, and forfeitures of *every description arising under the laws of Congress.*") (emphasis added).

189. *See* Maitland, *supra* note 98, at 302–5 (distinguishing pardons, suspensions, and dispensations); Francis Stoughton Sullivan, Lectures on the Constitution and Laws of England 186 (1776) (distinguishing dispensations and pardons).

190. *See* William F. Duker, *The President's Power to Pardon: A Constitutional History*, 18 Wm. & Mary L. Rev. 475, 513–18 (1977) (describing a controversy over pardons during Reconstruction).

191. *See* 20 Op. Att'y Gen. 330–32 (1892).

192. *See* Cynthia Herrup, *Negotiating Grace, in* Politics, Religion and Popularity in Early Stuart Britain 124, 126 (Thomas Cogswell et al. eds., 2002) ("Monarchs issued general pardons when, where and as they chose.").

193. *E.g,* Thomas Gage, Proclamation of Amnesty in Boston to All but Samuel Adams and John Hancock (June 12, 1775), *in* The Boisterous Sea of Liberty: A Documentary History of America From Discovery Through the Civil War 175, 175–76 (David Brion Davis & Steven Mintz eds., 1998) (offering pardons to Americans who reconciled to the king).

194. Kesselring, *supra* note 145, at 60, 64–65, 67.

195. John P. Kaminski, George Clinton, Yeoman Politician of the New Republic 64 (1993).

196. *See* George Washington, General Orders (Feb. 6, 1783), *in* 26 The Writings of George Washington, *supra* note 169, at 102, 103.

197. *See* The Federalist No. 74, *supra* note 123, at 378 (Alexander Hamilton); 4 Debates in the Several State Conventions, *supra* note 22, at 112 (comments of James Iredell).

198. Proclamation (July 10, 1795), *in* 34 The Writings of George Washington, *supra* note 108, at 232, 233.

199. Proclamation (May 21, 1800), *in* 1 Messages and Papers of the Presidents, *supra* note 136, at 293–94.

200. Proclamation (Feb. 6, 1815), *in* 2 A Compilation of the Messages and Papers of the Presidents: 1789–1897, at 543, 544 (James D. Richardson ed., 1897).

201. Habeas Corpus Act, 1679, 31 Car. 2, c. 2, § 12 (Eng.).

202. Act of Settlement, 1701, 12 & 13 W. & M. 3, c. 2 (Eng.).

203. *See* Duker, *supra* note 190, at 487–97.

204. Act of Settlement, 1701, 12 & 13 W. & M. 3, c. 2 (Eng.).

205. Duker, *supra* note 190, at 496 n.109.

206. *See generally* Brian C. Kalt, Note, *Pardon Me? The Constitutional Case Against Presidential Self-Pardons,* 106 Yale L.J. 779 (1996).

207. 6 The Documentary History of the Ratification of the Constitution, *supra* note 179, at 1361–62.

208. *See Governor Stevens' Famous Pardon of Himself, in* 25 Wash. Hist. Q. 229, 230 (1934) (reprieve issued on July 10, 1856).

209. Act of Mar. 2, 1853, §2, 10 Stat. 172, 173.

Chapter 6. The "Transaction of Business with Foreign Nations is Executive Altogether"

1. *See, e.g.,* Va. Const. (1776) (providing that the governor, with the advice of a council, would "exercise the executive powers of government").

2. Many of the arguments in this chapter were first developed in two articles written with Michael Ramsey. *See generally* Saikrishna B. Prakash & Michael D. Ramsey, *The*

Executive Power over Foreign Affairs, 111 Yale L.J. 231 (2001) [hereinafter Executive Power over Foreign Affairs]; Saikrishna Prakash and Michael Ramsey, *Foreign Affairs and the Jeffersonian Executive: A Defense*, 89 Minn. L. Rev. 1591 (2005). The chapter also draws from Abraham D. Sofaer, War, Foreign Affairs, and Constitutional Powers: The Origins (1976) and Michael D. Ramsey, The Constitution's Text in Foreign Affairs (2007).

3. U.S. Const. art. II, § 1.

4. Executive Power over Foreign Affairs, *supra* note 2, at 282.

5. *Id.* at 254–55.

6. *See, e.g.,* James Wilson, Lectures on Law (1790), *in* 2 Collected Works of James Wilson 878 (Kermit L. Hall & Mark David Hall eds., 2007) (discussing the traditional understanding of executive power and claiming that "[t]he person at the head of the executive department had authority, not to make, or alter, or dispense with the laws, but to execute").

7. W. B. Gwyn, The Meaning of the Separation of Powers 5 (1965); *see also* Francis D. Wormuth, The Origins of Modern Constitutionalism 61–62 (1949) (making the same observation).

8. *See generally* Saikrishna B. Prakash, *The Essential Meaning of Executive Power*, 2003 U. Ill. L. Rev. 701 (2003).

9. *See* M. J. C. Vile, Constitutionalism and the Separation of Powers 66 (2d ed. 1998). Vile notes that the Reverend George Lawson had previously observed that the executive power had external and internal components. *Id.* at 62 (citing George Lawson, An Examination of the Political Part of Mr. Hobbs his Leviathan 8 (1657)). Harvey Mansfield traces the foreign affairs component of executive power even earlier, to the sixteenth-century writings of Niccolò Machiavelli. Harvey C. Mansfield, Jr., Taming The Prince: The Ambivalence of Modern Executive Power 135–36 (1989).

10. John Locke, Two Treatises of Government and A Letter Concerning Toleration 165 (Yale University Press, 2003) (1689).

11. *Id.*

12. *Id.*

13. *See id.* at 137 (noting that "executive power" determines "how far injuries from without [society] are to be vindicated"); *see also id.* at 156–57 (referring to executive power as the authority to prevent or redress foreign injuries and to secure society from invasion).

14. Baron de Montesquieu, The Spirit of Laws 173 (Batoche Books 2001) (1748).

15. *Id.*

16. According to William Gwyn, Montesquieu thought that responsibility for foreign relations was executive in nature because it involved the execution of the law of nations. Gwyn, *supra* note 7, at 101 n.3.

17. Vile, *supra* note 9, at 111–12.

18. 1 William Blackstone, Commentaries on the Laws of England 242 (University of Chicago 1979) (1765); *id.* at 233 (claiming that the executive's prerogatives are necessary to "maintain the executive power in due independence and vigour").

19. *Id.* at 245.

20. *Id.*

21. *Id.* at 249.

22. *Id.*

23. *Id.* at 245.

24. 2 Thomas Rutherforth, Institutes of Natural Law 54–55 (1756).

25. J. L. de Lolme, The Constitution of England 50 (William S. Hein & Co. 1999) (1784); *see also* John Craig, 1 Elements of Political Science 245 (1814) (noting that executive power conducts "the foreign policy of the state"); Thomas Mortimer, The Elements of Commerce, Politics and Finances 274 (1772) (the "executive part of [the] government" is entrusted to the king, "especially with regard to foreign affairs"); British and Foreign History for the year 1796 *in* New Annual Register for the Year 1796, at 3, 288 (1797) ("The executive power" divides into two "branches, that which superintends the administration of justice within the state, and that which maintains the external relations with foreign powers.").

26. 17 The Parliamentary Register 301–5 (1802).

27. *See* 2 Speeches of M. de Mirabeau The Elder, Pronounced in the National Assembly of France 111, 119 (James White trans., 1792).

28. Charles Alexandre de Calonne, Considerations on the Present and Future State of France 220 (1791); *see also* 2 Speeches of M. de Mirabeau, *supra* note 27, at 219 (calling such a system "strange").

29. Theophilus Parsons, The Essex Result (1778), *in* 1 American Political Writing During the Founding Era 1760–1805, at 480, 494 (Charles Hyneman & Donald S. Lutz eds., 1983).

30. John Adams, Defence of the Constitutions of Government of the United States of America, *in* 5 The Works of John Adams 3, 69 (Charles Francis Adams ed., 1851).

31. Remarks on an Act Granting to Congress Certain Imposts and Duties (Feb. 15 1787), *in* 4 The Papers of Alexander Hamilton 71, 75 (Harold C. Syrett ed., 1962).

32. Evarts Boutell Greene, The Provincial Governor in the English Colonies of North America 109 (1898).

33. *Id.* at 106–7.

34. Ramsey, *supra* note 2, at 129; Margaret Burnham MacMillan, The War Governors in the American Revolution 272 (1943).

35. Congress—Proceedings as to Protection due French Consuls (Aug. 2, 1779), *in* 3 The Revolutionary Diplomatic Correspondence of the United States 272, 273 (Francis Wharton ed., 1889).

36. Letter from Josiah Bartlett to Meschech Weare (July 20, 1778), *in* 10 Letters of Delegates to Congress 317, 318–19 (Paul H. Smith ed., 1983).

37. Thomas Jefferson, Third Draft of the Virginia Constitution, art. II, *in* 1 The Papers of Thomas Jefferson 356, 359 (Julian P. Boyd ed., 1950).

38. *Id.* at 360.

39. S.C. Const. art. XXVI (1776).

40. The 1778 Constitution contained almost identical constraints. *See* S.C. Const. art. XXXIII (1778) (providing "[t]hat the governor and commander-in-chief shall have no power to commence war, or conclude peace, or enter into any final treaty without the consent of the senate and house of representatives").

41. *See, e.g.,* Jack Rakove, The Beginnings of National Politics: An Interpretive History of the Continental Congress 383 (1979); Martin S. Flaherty, *History Right? Historical Scholarship, Original Understanding, and Treaties as "Supreme Law of the Land,"* 99 Colum. L. Rev. 2095, 2106 (1999); Martin S. Flaherty, *The Most Dangerous Branch,* 105 Yale L.J. 1725, 1764–65 (1996).

42. The Essex Result, *supra* note 29, at 494.

43. Letter from James Madison to Caleb Wallace (Aug. 23, 1785), *in* 8 The Papers of James Madison: Congressional Series 350, 352 (Robert A. Rutland & William M. E. Rachel eds., 1973).

44. Letter from John Jay to Giuseppe Chiappe (Dec. 1, 1789), *available at* http://www.fold3.com/image/1/6594073/, http://www.fold3.com/image/1/6594081/ (last visited Sept. 9, 2013); Letter from Thomas Jefferson to Edmond Charles Genet (Dec. 9, 1793), *in* 27 The Papers of Thomas Jefferson 500 (John C. Catanzariti ed., 1997) (same); 9 The Documentary History of the Ratification of the Constitution 986 (John P. Kaminski & Gaspare J. Saladino eds., 1990) (comments of Edmund Randolph); 2 The Documentary History of the Ratification of the Constitution 474 (Merrill Jensen ed., 1976) (comments of James Wilson); 6 The Documentary History of the Ratification of the Constitution 1325 (John P. Kaminski & Gaspare J. Saladino eds., 2000) (comments of Theophilus Parsons); Comments of Lorde Hawke, *quoted in* Letter from Thomas Jefferson to George Hammond (May 29, 1792), *in* 23 The Papers of Thomas Jefferson 551, 558 (Charles T. Cullen ed. 1990). For a discussion of Congress's executive role, *see* Executive Power over Foreign Affairs, *supra* note 2, at 275–76.

45. 19 Journals of Continental Congress 1774–1789, at 43–44 (Gaillard Hunt ed., 1912).

46. Elmer Plischke, U.S. Department of State: A Reference History 11 (1999); *see also* Jay Caesar Guggenheimer, The Development of the Executive Departments, 1775–1789 (1889), *in* Essays in the Constitutional History of the United States in the Formative Period 1775–1789, at 116, 163 (J. Franklin Jameson ed., 1889) (describing the secretary as being treated as a "congressional clerk"). *But see* Henry Barrett Learned, The President's Cabinet 58 (Yale Univ. Press 1912) (claiming that Secretary John Jay was the "chief executive of the Confederation").

47. Letter from John Jay to Thomas Jefferson (Dec. 14, 1786), *in* 10 The Papers of Thomas Jefferson 596, 598 (Julian P. Boyd ed., 1954).

48. Letter from John Jay to George Washington (Jan. 7, 1787), *in* 4 The Papers of George Washington: Confederation Series 502 (W. W. Abbot, ed., 1995). *See also* Letter from John Jay to Thomas Jefferson (Aug. 18, 1786), *in* 10 The Papers of Thomas Jefferson, *supra* note 47, at 271 (criticizing "unseasonable Delays and successive Obstacles in obtaining the Decision and Sentiments of Congress").

49. Letter from George Washington to Henry Knox (Feb. 3, 1787), *in* 5 The Papers of George Washington: Confederation Series 7, 9 (W. W. Abbot, ed., 1997) (claiming that government was slow, could not keep secrets, and had improperly combined legislative, executive, and judicial powers); Letter from Thomas Jefferson to Edward Carrington (Aug. 4, 1787), *in* 11 The Papers of Thomas Jefferson 678, 679 (Julian P. Boyd ed., 1955) (noting that Congress was enmeshed in executive details).

50. 1 The Records of the Federal Convention of 1787, at 21 (Max Farrand rev. ed., 1966) [hereinafter Records of the Federal Convention]. By way of contrast, the new Congress was to enjoy "the Legislative Rights vested in Congress by the Confederation." *Id.*

51. *Id.* at 292.

52. *Id.*, vol. 3, at 606.

53. *Id.*, vol. 1, at 65.

54. *Id.* at 65–66.

55. *Id.* at 70.

56. *Id.* at 63.

57. *Id.*, vol. 2, at 177, 182.

58. *Id.* at 183.

59. *Id.* at 185.

60. *Id.* at 343. The secretary, along with others, was to advise the president with written opinions. *Id.*

61. *Id.* at 297.

62. *Id.* at 318.

63. 4 The Debates in the Several State Conventions on the Adoption of the Federal Constitution 127 (Jonathan Elliot ed., 2d ed. 1836) [hereinafter Debates in the Several State Conventions].

64. *Id.* at 127–28. *See also id.* at 113 (Iredell assuming that the president could send spies to other nations).

65. The Federalist No. 84, at 442 (Alexander Hamilton) (Garry Wills ed., 1982).

66. A Native of Virginia, Observations upon the Proposed Plan of Federal Government, *in* 9 The Documentary History of the Ratification of the Constitution, *supra* note 44, at 655, 681–82.

67. 2 The Documentary History of the Ratification of the Constitution, *supra* note 44, at 466; *see also* 4 Debates in the Several State Conventions, *supra* note 63, at 116–17 (complaining about the Senate's executive role in treaties); *id.* at 125 (protesting that the Senate tries impeachments of the executive even though it has extensive executive powers).

68. The Address and Reasons of Dissent of the Minority of the Convention of the State of Pennsylvania to their Constituents, *in* 2 The Documentary History of the Ratification of the Constitution, *supra* note 44, at 618, 634.

69. Letter from Richard Henry Lee to Edmund Randolph (Oct. 16, 1787), *in* 8 The Documentary History of the Ratification of the Constitution 61 (John P. Kaminski & Gaspare J. Saladino eds., 1988).

70. Cassius I, *in* 9 The Documentary History of the Ratification of the Constitution, *supra* note 44, at 641, 644.

71. 4 Debates in the Several State Conventions, *supra* note 63, at 269. Given the implication of the South Carolina Constitutions of 1776 and 1778 that executives typically enjoyed the power to make treaties, *supra* notes 39–40, the delegate's comments should hardly be surprising.

72. 4 Debates in the Several State Conventions, *supra* note 63, at 28.

73. In The Federalist No. 69, Hamilton suggested that in the absence of a national government, the treaty power might rest solely with the state executives. The Federalist No. 69, *supra* note 65, at 352 (Alexander Hamilton). This comment was premised on the notion that stewardship of foreign affairs was an executive concern. But Hamilton later denied that treaty making was executive. The Federalist No. 75, *supra* note 65, at 380 (Alexander Hamilton). His latter claim should be understood as a feeble attempt to lessen the sting of the charge that the Senate ought to have no role in treaty making.

74. Letter from George Washington to Sidi Mohammed (Dec. 1, 1789), *in* 4 The Papers of George Washington: Presidential Series 354 (Dorothy Twohig ed., 1993). Washington said much the same to Louis XVI, explaining that because of changes in the system of government, he had the honor of corresponding with the French king. Letter from George Washington to Louis XVI (Oct. 9, 1789), *in id.* at 152.

75. Letter II from John Adams to Roger Sherman (July 1789) *in* 6 The Works of John Adams 429, 430 (Charles Francis Adams ed., 1851).

76. Letter from John Jay to Giuseppe Chiappe (Dec. 1, 1789) *available at* http://www.fold3.com/image/1/6594073/, http://www.fold3.com/image/1/6594081/ (last visited Sept. 9, 2013). In another letter, Jay noted that Washington had the "supreme executive Authority." Letter from John Jay to Francisco Chiappe (Dec. 1, 1789) *available at* http://www.fold3.com/image/6594057/, http://www.fold3.com/image/6594065/.

77. Letter from Thomas Jefferson to George Washington (Apr. 24, 1790), *in* 5 The Papers of George Washington: Presidential Series 342, 343 (Dorothy Twohig et al. eds., 1996).

78. 6 The Diaries of George Washington 68 (Donald Jackson & Dorothy Twohig eds., 1979). Madison would later contradict this claim in his Helvidius letters, arguing that the Executive Power Clause did not grant any foreign affairs powers. But Helvidius was unconvincing. *See infra* notes 116–24.

79. Columbus No. III (Dec. 1793), *in* 1 Writings of John Quincy Adams 160, 170–71 (Worthington Chauncey Ford ed., 1913).

80. 10 Annals of Congress 613–14 (1800).

81. Pacificus No. 1 (June 29, 1793), *in* 15 The Papers of Alexander Hamilton 33, 38 (Harold C. Syrett ed., 1969).

82. *Id.* at 39.

83. Act of July 27, 1789, 1 Stat. 28, 28–29 (1789).

84. *Id.* § 2. Representative Hartley perhaps expressed the dominant view of the department and the secretary when he observed that the "business of the secretary of foreign

affairs is of an executive nature, and must consequently be attached to the executive department." *See* 11 Documentary History of the First Federal Congress 1789–91: Debates in the House of Representatives, First Session 905 (Charlene Bangs Bickford et al. eds., 1992). For a discussion of Congress's decision to admit that the president enjoyed a removal power, *see* Saikrishna Prakash, *New Light on the Decision of 1789*, 91 Cornell L. Rev. 1021 (2006) (discussing removal power over department officials, including the secretary of foreign affairs).

85. Act of July 27, 1789 § 1, 1 Stat. 28–29 (1789).

86. *See* Ramsey, *supra* note 2, at 76.

87. 10 Annals of Congress 613 (1800).

88. *See supra* text accompanying note 74.

89. 5 Annals of Congress 32 (1796).

90. Letter from Thomas Jefferson to Edmond-Charles Genêt (Nov. 22, 1793), *in* 27 The Papers of Thomas Jefferson, *supra* note 44, at 414.

91. Memoranda of Consultations with the President (Mar. 12, 1792), *in* 23 The Papers of Thomas Jefferson, *supra* note 44, at 261.

92. Executive Power over Foreign Affairs *supra* note 2, at 318–19.

93. Ramsey, *supra* note 2, at 77.

94. Executive Power over Foreign Affairs, *supra* note 2, at 298–300.

95. Act of July 27, 1789 § 1, 1 Stat. 28–29 (1789).

96. *See* Letter from Thomas Jefferson to Thomas Pinckney (June 11, 1792), *in* 24 The Papers of Thomas Jefferson 59, 60 (John T. Catanzariti ed., 1990) (describing Pinckney's duties as emissary to Britain and noting that other foreign officers had "instructions" to share information); *see also* Executive Power over Foreign Affairs, *supra* note 2, at 309.

97. Executive Power over Foreign Affairs, *supra* note 2, at 309 (describing removal of Gouverneur Morris and James Monroe). Monroe wrote perhaps the first administration tell-all, defending his conduct as emissary to France. *See* James Monroe, A View of the Conduct of the Executive in the Foreign Affairs of the United States (1797). Although quite critical of the Jay Treaty and the administration's treatment of France, he never intimated that the president lacked authority to direct U.S. diplomats.

98. Executive Power over Foreign Affairs, *supra* note 2, at 299, 305–7.

99. *Id.* at 312.

100. *Id.* at 313.

101. *See, e.g., id.* at 321.

102. Letter from Thomas Jefferson to Edmond Charles Genet (Dec. 9, 1793), *in* 27 The Papers of Thomas Jefferson, *supra* note 44, at 500, 501.

103. Executive Power over Foreign Affairs, *supra* note 2, at 339–40.

104. *Id.* at 324–26. *See generally* Treaty of Alliance (Feb. 6, 1778), 8 Stat. 6 (1778).

105. *See* Executive Power over Foreign Affairs, *supra* note 2, at 328–40 (discussing in more depth the events leading up to, and dissent over, the Neutrality Proclamation).

106. J. H. W. Vezijl, 10 International Law in Historical Perspective 51–58 (1979); *see also* William R. Casto, Foreign Affairs and the Constitution in the Age of the Fighting Sail 93 (2006).

107. Ramsey, *supra* note 2, at 79–80.

108. Casto, *supra* note 106, at 50; Letter from Thomas Jefferson to Jean Baptiste Tenant (May 15, 1793), *in* 26 The Papers of Thomas Jefferson 42, 43–44 (John T. Catanzariti ed., 1995).

109. Casto, *supra* note 106, at 50–52. The president's policy caused Genêt, the French emissary, to sputter that it was "incontestible" that the Treaty of Commerce permitted France to arm in U.S. ports. *Id.* at 57.

110. Letter from Thomas Jefferson to James Madison (July 7, 1793), *in* 26 The Papers of Thomas Jefferson, *supra* note 108, at 443, 444.

111. Letter from Thomas Jefferson to James Madison (June 29, 1793), *in id.* at 401, 403 (declaring that the United States at peace was not "illegal" but was "improper"); Letter from Thomas Jefferson to James Madison (June 23, 1793), *in id.* at 346.

112. *See* Letter from Thomas Jefferson to James Madison (Mar. 24, 1793), *in* 25 The Papers of Thomas Jefferson 442, 442 (John T. Catanzariti ed., 1992).

113. George Washington to the Senate (Jan. 4, 1792), *in* 23 The Papers of Thomas Jefferson, *supra* note 44, at 18.

114. Letter from Thomas Jefferson to Gouverneur Morris (Aug. 16, 1793), *in* 26 The Papers of Thomas Jefferson, *supra* note 108, at 697, 704.

115. David N. Mayer, The Constitutional Thought of Thomas Jefferson 230–31 (1994).

116. Helvidius No. 2, *in* 15 The Papers of James Madison: Congressional Series 80, 81–82 (Thomas A. Mason et al. eds., 1985).

117. Helvidius No. 1, *in id.* at 66, 69, 72.

118. *Id.* at 72.

119. Sofaer, *supra* note 2, at 114–15.

120. Executive Power Over Foreign Affairs, *supra* note 2, at 335–39 (concluding that "Madison's views, at least to the extent that he rejected the executive power theory, are essentially incoherent").

121. Act of July 27, 1789, § 1, 1 Stat. 28–29 (1789).

122. *See supra* text accompanying note 78.

123. Casto, *supra* note 106, at 79.

124. Detached Memoranda (Jan. 1820), *in* 1 The Papers of James Madison: Retirement Series 600, 620 (David B. Mattern et al. eds., 2009).

125. *See, e.g.*, Anthony J. Bellia, Jr. & Bradford R. Clark, *The Federal Common Law of Nations*, 109 Colum. L. Rev 1, 49–52 (2009).

126. *Id.* at 52.

127. Gerhard Casper, Separating Power 53–55 (1997).

128. U.S. Const. art. I, § 9, cl. 7 ("No Money shall be drawn from the Treasury, but in Consequence of Appropriations made by Law.").

129. *See* Md. Const. art. XXXIII (1776) (the governor may impose thirty-day embargoes during recess of the general assembly in order to prevent the departure of ships and the export of commodities); S.C. Const. art. XXXV (1778) (the governor may impose thirty-day embargoes during recess of the legislature); Del. Const. art. 7 (1776) (the president, with the consent of the council, may impose thirty-day embargoes during recess of the legislature); N.C. Const. art. XIX (1776) (same authority for governor); Pa. Const. § 20 (1776) (the executive council may impose thirty-day embargoes during recess of House).

130. Executive Power over Foreign Affairs, *supra* note 2, at 349.

131. Act of June 4, 1794, 1 Stat. 372 (1794).

132. *See, e.g.*, Va. Const. (1776) (declaring that the three powers must be kept separate and distinct).

133. *See, e.g.*, The Federalist No. 47, *supra* note 65, at 243–46 (James Madison) (noting such objections).

134. For a discussion of the original understanding of how treaty interpretation powers were distributed, see John Yoo, *Politics as Law?: The Anti-Ballistic Missile Treaty, the Separation of Powers, and Treaty Interpretation,* 89 Cal. L. Rev. 851 (2001).

135. The Federalist No. 49, *supra* note 65, at 255 (James Madison).

136. Letter from Thomas Jefferson to Gouverneur Morris (Aug. 16, 1793), *in* 26 The Papers of Thomas Jefferson, *supra* note 108, at 697, 711.

137. Letter from Thomas Jefferson to Edmond-Charles Genet (Nov. 22, 1793), *in* 27 The Papers of Thomas Jefferson, *supra* note 44, at 414 (stating that the Constitution "has ascribed to [the president] alone the admission or interdiction of foreign agents").

138. *See* George Washington to the United States Senate and House of Representatives (Jan. 20, 1794), *in* 15 The Papers of George Washington: Presidential Series 97 (Christine S. Patrick ed., 2009).

139. Letter from Thomas Jefferson to James Madison (Aug. 3, 1793), *in* 26 The Papers of Thomas Jefferson, *supra* note 108, at 606 (noting the unanimous decision to demand Genêt's recall).

140. *See* Columbus No. III (Dec. 1793), *in* 1 Writings of John Quincy Adams, *supra* note 79, at 170–71.

141. *See* Saikrishna Bangalore Prakash, *Exhuming the Seemingly Moribund Declaration of War,* 77 Geo. Wash. L. Rev. 89, 103–4 & n.56 (2008); 15 Annals of Congress 153 (1806) (John Quincy Adams claiming that some dismissals involving "national difference" are "virtual declaration[s] of war").

142. *See, e.g.*, Treaty of Amity, Commerce and Navigation, Between His Britannic Majesty and the United States of America, by their President, with the Advice and Consent of their Senate, U.S.-G.B., Nov. 19, 1794, 8 Stat. 116, 128–29, art. 26 (1794) (providing that "[i]f at any time a rupture should take place (which God forbid) between his Majesty and the United States . . . such rupture shall not be deemed to exist . . . until the respective ambassadors or ministers, if such there shall be, shall be recalled, or sent home on account of such differences").

143. 15 Annals of Congress 156 (1806) Adams's position in 1806 differed from his writings as Columbus. In 1793, Adams said that the president had an absolute right to dismiss foreign emissaries, but that he might be impeached if dismissal led to a war. *See* Columbus No. III (Dec. 1793), *in* 1 Writings of John Quincy Adams, *supra* note 79, at 174–75 (the president may exercise his powers in a way that produces a war). The writings can be reconciled if one supposes that while the president cannot take acts that are implicit or virtual declarations of war, he may take acts that so anger another nation that it elects to wage war against the United States. In other words, the president may not declare war, either formally or informally, but may take acts that, in the end, trigger a war. For a greater discussion of the war power, see Chapter 7.

144. Helvidius No. 5 *in* 15 The Papers of James Madison: Congressional Series, *supra* note 116, at 113, 115–16.

145. *See* Letter from James Madison to Edmund Pendleton (Jan. 2, 1791), *in* 13 The Papers of James Madison: Congressional Series 342, 343–44 (Charles F. Hobson & Robert A. Rutland eds., 1981).

146. Act of July 7, 1798, 1 Stat. 578.

147. *See* Letter from Oliver Ellsworth et al. to John Marshall (Oct. 4, 1800), *in* 2 American State Papers: Foreign Relations 342 (Walter Lowrie & Matthew St. Clair Clarke eds., 1832) (the statute declaring treaties void derived validity "from an exercise of the constitutional prerogative of declaring war").

148. *See generally*, Thomas Jefferson, Opinion on French Treaties (Apr. 28, 1793), *in* 25 The Papers of Thomas Jefferson, *supra* note 112, at 608–18; Stanley Elkins & Eric McKitrick, The Age of Federalism 339–40 (1993). In a later episode, some disagreed with the notion that the president could withdraw from treaties. In the wake of Andrew Jackson's military adventures in Florida, one minority committee report claimed that even when another nation violates a treaty, the treaty would remain part of the supreme law of the land that the president was sworn to enforce unless it was "revoked or annulled by Congress." Report of the Minority (Jan. 12, 1819), *in* 1 American State Papers: Military Affairs 736, 742 (Walter Lowrie and Matthew St. Clair Clarke eds., 1832).

149. *See* Pacificus No. 3 (July 6, 1793), *in* 15 The Papers of Alexander Hamilton, *supra* note 81, at 65, 67 (quoting Vattel).

150. The discussion that follows applies only to self-executing treaties (those that purport to create domestic law). I do not believe that the president must adhere to non-self-executing treaties, for in my view they do not create any domestic law. For a discussion of the distinction between self-executing and non-self-executing treaties, *see* Ramsey, *supra* note 2, at 168–71.

151. For a general discussion of why the president cannot violate a treaty, *see id.* at 160–73.

152. Letter from George Washington to the Senate (Aug. 11, 1790), *in* 6 The Papers of George Washington: Presidential Series 237, 238 (Mark A. Mastromarino ed., 1996).

153. Letter from Alexander Hamilton to George Washington (May 20, 1796) *in* 20 The Papers of Alexander Hamilton 190, 193 (Harold C. Syrett ed., 1974).

154. 10 Annals of Congress 613 (1800) (comments of John Marshall during congressional debate) ("[The president] is charged to execute the laws. A treaty is declared to be a law. He must then execute a treaty.").

155. *See* Pacificus No. 1 (June 29, 1793), *in* 15 The Papers of Alexander Hamilton, *supra* note 81, at 33, 41 (noting that it was the "right and duty of the Executive to judge of, or to interpret, those articles of our treaties which give to France particular privileges, in order to the enforcement of those privileges"); Helvidius No. 3 (Sept. 7, 1793), *in* 15 The Papers of James Madison: Congressional Series, *supra* note 116, at 95, 99 (noting that the executive had no more right "to suspend the operation of a treaty in force as a law, than to suspend the operation of any other law").

156. *Cf.* Ralston Hayden, The Senate and Treaties: 1789–1817, at 30 (1920) (stating that Washington thought he had to enforce a treaty or renegotiate it).

157. 10 Annals of Congress 614 (1800).

158. *Id.* at 614–15 (1800).

159. Curtis A. Bradley and Martin S. Flaherty, *Executive Power Essentialism and Foreign Affairs*, 102 Mich. L. Rev. 545, 552, 636 (2004).

160. U.S. Const. art. II, § 3 (listing duties to take care that laws are faithfully executed, to provide information about the state of the union, to receive ambassadors, and to recommend legislation).

161. *Cf.* The Federalist No. 69, *supra* note 65, at 352 (Alexander Hamilton) (referring to the clause as a matter of dignity rather than an authority).

162. 1 Coleman Phillipson, The International Law and Custom of Ancient Greece and Rome 311 (1911).

163. Emmerich de Vattel, The Law of Nations 682–83 (Béla Kapossy & Richard Whatmore ed., 2008) (1758).

164. Benjamin H. Irvin, Clothed in Robes of Sovereignty: The Continental Congress and the People Out of Doors 178 (2011).

165. *See* 11 Journals of Continental Congress 1774–1789, at 698–99 (Worthington Chauncey Ford ed., 1908).

166. *See, e.g., id.* at 752; 22 Journals of Continental Congress 1774–1789, at 246–87 (Gaillard Hunt ed., 1914); 28 Journals of Continental Congress 1774–1789, at 466–67 (John C. Fitzpatrick ed., 1933).

167. Irvin, *supra* note 164, at 183–84.

168. *See id.* at 174, 175, 183–84, 208–9, 266.

169. *See id.* at 174–76.

170. Pacificus wrote about two powers that he claimed could be implied from the duty to receive ambassadors. First was the decision whether to recognize a new government in another nation. By declining to recognize the new government's ambassador, the executive would be deciding not to recognize the new government. Second, if the executive declined to recognize a new government's ambassador, the executive was deciding that any treaties

with that nation were suspended. *See* Pacificus No. 1 (June 29, 1793), *in* 15 The Papers of Alexander Hamilton, *supra* note 81, at 33, 41. Madison denied that the duty to receive ambassadors included even this limited train of power, citing Publius as an authority. *See* Helvidius No. 3 (Sept. 7, 1793), *in* 15 The Papers of James Madison: Congressional Series, *supra* note 116, at 95, 97. Helvidius and Publius have the better argument on how best to read the Reception Clause. On the question whether the Vesting Clause grants generic executive power, something that Publius never squarely addressed, Pacificus deserves the palm.

171. Greene, *supra* note 32, at 106–10.

172. The Federalist No. 69, *supra* note 65, at 352 (Alexander Hamilton).

173. 1 Records of the Federal Convention, *supra* note 50, at 292.

174. *Id.* at 425–26.

175. *Id.*, vol. 2, at 183.

176. *Id.* at 297. While true enough, the claim was beside the point. One could agree with the claim and still argue that for the purposes of treaties, the Senate should serve as a plural executive.

177. *Id.* at 392.

178. *Id.* at 498.

179. *Id.* at 538.

180. *Id.* at 547–50.

181. *See supra* text accompanying note 67.

182. *See* George Mason's Objections to the Constitution, *in* 8 The Documentary History of the Ratification of the Constitution, *supra* note 69, at 40, 43–44.

183. 9 Documentary History of the First Federal Congress: The Diary of William Maclay and Other Notes on Senate Debates 130 (Kenneth R. Bowling & Helen E. Veit eds., 1988) (emphasis omitted).

184. 6 Memoirs of John Quincy Adams 427 (Charles F. Adams ed., 1875) (Adams recounting story told by William H. Crawford).

185. Hayden, *supra* note 156, at 23–24 n.4.

186. 1 Journal of the Executive Proceedings of the Senate of the United States of America 61–62 (1790) [hereinafter Journal of Executive Proceedings].

187. Hayden, *supra* note 156, at 83–86.

188. *Id.* at 85.

189. *Id.* at 35.

190. 1 Journal of Executive Proceedings, *supra* note 186, at 230–31 (1797).

191. Hayden, *supra* note 156, at 58–69.

192. 1 Journal of Executive Proceedings, *supra* note 186, at 9 (1789).

193. *See id.* at 58 (1790) (Washington noting that proposed treaty was subject to ratification by the president).

194. Hayden, *supra* note 156, at 46–48 (declining the Senate's invitation to expend funds without an appropriation as a means of implementing a treaty).

195. Message of the President (Mar. 30, 1796), *in* 35 The Writings of George Washington 2–5 (John C. Fitzpatrick ed., 1940) (stating that treaties were obligatory on Congress and that the latter always had implemented them).

196. 5 Annals of Congress 771 (1796).

197. *Id.*

198. 1 Journal of Executive Proceedings, *supra* note 186, at 66–68 (1791).

199. *Id.* at 77 (1791).

200. *Id.* at 66 (1791).

201. *Id.* at 77 (1791).

202. Michael D. Ramsey, *Executive Agreements and the (Non)Treaty Power*, 77 N.C. L. Rev. 133, 199 (1998).

203. *Id.* at 162–64.

204. Executive Power over Foreign Affairs, *supra* note 2, at 264.

Chapter 7. "First General and Admiral of the Confederacy"

1. This chapter draws on several works of mine. *See Exhuming the Seemingly Moribund Declaration of War*, 77 Geo. Wash. L. Rev. 89 (2008); *The Separation and Overlap of War and Military Powers*, 87 Tex. L. Rev. 299 (2008) [hereinafter Separation and Overlap of War and Military Powers]; *Unleashing the Dogs of War: What the Constitution Means by "Declare War,"* 93 Cornell L. Rev. 45 (2007) [hereinafter Unleashing the Dogs of War]; *A Two-Front War*, 93 Cornell L. Rev. 197 (2007) [hereinafter A Two-Front War].

2. John Locke, Two Treatises of Government and A Letter Concerning Toleration 168 (Yale University Press 2003) (1689).

3. Baron de Montesquieu, The Spirit of the Laws 173 (Batoche Books 2001) (1748).

4. 2 Thomas Rutherforth, Institutes of Natural Law 54 (1756).

5. The Federalist No. 74, at 377 (Alexander Hamilton) (Garry Wills ed., 1982); *see also* 4 The Debates in the Several State Conventions on the Adoption of the Federal Constitution 107 (Jonathan Elliot ed., 2d ed. 1836) [hereinafter Debates in the Several State Conventions] (claiming that "[i]n almost every country, the executive has the command of the military forces").

6. Charles Alexandre de Calonne, Considerations on the Present and Future State of France 218 (1791).

7. 2 The Records of the Federal Convention of 1787, at 52 (Max Farrand rev. ed., 1966) [hereinafter Records of the Federal Convention]; *see also id.*, vol. 1, at 181 (comments of Edmund Randolph) (noting that executive would be "commander of the militia").

8. *See* Louis Fisher, Presidential War Power 3–12 (1995); John Hart Ely, War and Responsibility: Constitutional Lessons of Vietnam and Its Aftermath 3–5 (1993); Michael J. Glennon, Constitutional Diplomacy 80–84 (1990); Harold Hongju Koh, The National Security Constitution: Sharing Power after the Iran-Contra Affair 78–84 (1990); William Michael Treanor, *Fame, the Founding, and the Power to Declare War*, 82 Cornell L. Rev. 695, 756 (1997).

9. *See* Michael D. Ramsey, *Textualism and War Powers*, 69 U. Chi. L. Rev. 1543, 1549–52 (2002) (noting that congressionalists who believe that Congress has a monopoly on the decision whether to wage war have relied upon practices and statements from the Founders rather than text). Though I differ with Professor Ramsey on several significant matters, his work in this area has influenced me greatly.

10. *See* John Yoo, The Powers of War and Peace 7–9, 105, 152 (2005); John C. Yoo, *The Continuation of Politics by Other Means: The Original Understanding of War Powers*, 84 Calif. L. Rev. 167, 174 (1996) [hereinafter The Continuation of Politics by Other Means]; Henry P. Monaghan, *Presidential War-Making*, 50 B.U. L. Rev. (Special Issue) 19, 32 (1970).

11. *See, e.g.*, Phillip Bobbitt, *War Powers: An Essay on John Hart Ely's* War and Responsibility: Constitutional Lessons of Vietnam and Its Aftermath, 92 Mich. L. Rev. 1364, 1384 (1994) (noting that the Korean War and the French naval war "were conducted without benefit of a declaration of war"); J. Gregory Sidak, *To Declare War*, 41 Duke L.J. 27, 40 (1991) (citing the Korean and Vietnam Wars as undeclared wars).

12. *See* The Federalist No. 25, *supra* note 5, at 123 (Alexander Hamilton) ("[T]he ceremony of a formal denunciation of war has of late fallen into disuse.").

13. *See* Michael D. Ramsey, The Constitution's Text in Foreign Affairs 227 (2007).

14. *See* The Continuation of Politics by Other Means, *supra* note 10, at 246–47 (describing the Declaration of Independence as a declaration of war).

15. *See, e.g.*, The Annual Register, or a View of the History, Politics, and Literature, for the Year 1779, at 411 (1780) (describing the announcement of a treaty of alliance as a "true declaration of war").

16. Unleashing the Dogs of War, *supra* note 1, at 73.

17. 6 The Parliamentary Debates from the Year 1803 to the Present Time lxxiii (William Cobbett et al. eds., 1812).

18. 1 Jacques M. Necker, An Essay on the True Principles of the Executive Power in Great States 273 (1792).

19. *See, e.g.*, Letter from King George III to Frederick North (July 18, 1778), *in* 2 The Correspondence of King George the Third with Lord North from 1768 to 1783, at 205 (W. Bodham Donne ed., 1867) (claiming that France, by engaging the British navy, had "cast off the mask and declared war"); J. F. Maurice, Hostilities Without Declaration of War 44 (1883) (quoting Alexander I of Russia's claim that "Napoleon, by a sudden attack on our troops at Kowno, has declared war"). English courts shared the same understanding of "declare war" whether voiced in Parliament or by monarchs. *See* Ramsey, *supra* note 9, at 1585 ("Where is the difference, whether war is proclaimed by a Herald . . . or whether war is announced by royal ships, and whole fleets, at the mouths of cannon?" (quoting The Maria Magdalena (1779) 165 Eng. Rep. 57 (Adm.) 58)).

20. Letter from John Adams to Samuel Adams (Feb. 14, 1779), in 3 The Revolutionary Diplomatic Correspondence of the United States 47, 48 (Francis Wharton ed., 1889) (noting that war between Britain and France was "sufficiently declared by actual hostilities in most parts of the world").

21. See 10 The Parliament History of England 825, 831 (William Cobbett ed., 1812) (observing in 1738 that "of late most wars have been declared from the mouths of cannons, before any formal declaration").

22. Unleashing the Dogs of War, *supra* note 1, at 66, 110; A Two-Front War, *supra* note 1, at 210.

23. A Two-Front War, *supra* note 1, at 208–10.

24. Unleashing the Dogs of War, *supra* note 1, at 95–96; A Two-Front War, *supra* note 1, at 209–10.

25. *See* Lucius Crassus, The Examination No. 1 (Dec. 17, 1801), *in* 25 The Papers of Alexander Hamilton 444, 455–56 (Harold C. Syrett ed., 1977).

26. Letter from George Washington to William Moultrie (Aug. 28, 1793), *in* 13 The Papers of George Washington: Presidential Series 570 (Christine S. Patrick ed., 2007) ("The Constitution vests the power of declaring War with Congress, therefore no offensive expedition of importance can be undertaken until after they shall have deliberated upon the subject, and authorised such a measure."); Letter from Henry Knox to George Washington (Oct. 9, 1792), *in* 11 The Papers of George Washington: Presidential Series 212 (Christine S. Patrick ed., 2002) (Henry Knox noting to Washington that the cabinet, including Hamilton, agreed that even though Cherokee tribes had declared war, a governor ought to be told that no offensive measures could be undertaken).

27. Unleashing the Dogs of War, *supra* note 1, at 101–3 (recounting that both Adams and Hamilton believed that France had waged war against the United States and concluding that any measures beyond repelling attacks required congressional sanction under the declare-war power).

28. *See* Act of May 28, 1798, 1 Stat. 561; Act of June 13, 1798, 1 Stat. 565; Act of Jan. 30, 1799, 1 Stat. 613.

29. Unleashing the Dogs of War, *supra* note 1, at 103–5.

30. *Id.* at 105.

31. Act of June 18, 1812, 2 Stat. 755.

32. *See* 2 Records of the Federal Convention, *supra* note 7, at 318–19.

33. The Pennsylvania Convention (Dec. 11, 1987), *in* 2 The Documentary History of the Ratification of the Constitution 550, 583 (Merrill Jensen ed., 1976); *see also* Rufus King & Nathaniel Gorham, Response to Elbridge Gerry's Objections (Oct. 31, 1787), *in* 4 The Documentary History of the Ratification of the Constitution 186, 190 (John P. Kaminski & Gaspare J. Saladino eds., 1997) (applauding the Constitution's requirement that chambers must act with the president to declare war because "as war is not to be desired and always a great calamity, by increasing the Checks, the measure will be difficult").

34. Letter from George Washington to William Moultrie (Aug. 28, 1793), *in* 13 The Papers of George Washington: Presidential Series, *supra* note 26, at 570.

35. *See, e.g.,* 3 Joseph Story, Commentaries on the Constitution of the United States 60–62 (1833) (equating declaring war with the decision to wage it, noting that the Founders chose to restrain the power to make war by vesting it with Congress, and that Congress

may exercise the power by authorizing hostilities); William Rawle, A View of the Constitution of the United States of America 110 (2d. ed. 1829) ("The power of *declaring war* . . . forms the next branch of powers exclusively confided to [C]ongress."); James Kent, Dissertations: Being the Preliminary Part of a Course of Law Lectures 66 (1795) ("[W]ar can only be commenced by an act or resolution of [C]ongress."); 1 Blackstone's Commentaries: With Notes of Reference, to the Constitution and Laws, of the Federal Government of the United States; and of the Commonwealth of Virginia app. at 270 (St. George Tucker ed., 1803) (explaining that the power to make war rests with the people's representatives and that the president is limited to a veto).

36. *See, e.g.*, Letter from James Madison to Thomas Jefferson (Apr. 2, 1798), *in* 17 The Papers of James Madison: Congressional Series 104 (David B. Mattern et al., 1991) (asserting that because history had revealed executive branches to be the "most interested in war," the Constitution, "with studied care, vested the question of war" in Congress); Letter from Henry Knox to William Blount (Oct. 9, 1792), *quoted in* Letter from Henry Knox to George Washington, *in* 11 The Papers of George Washington: Presidential Series, *supra* note 26, at 212, 213 n.3 (instructing a military commander to "confine all [his] operations to defensive measures" until after "[t]he Congress[,] which possess the powers of declaring War," had assembled); Letter from Henry Knox to Henry Lee (Oct. 9, 1792), *quoted in id.* (explaining that only members of Congress "are invested with the powers of War").

37. Early Congresses never passed resolutions explicitly stating that the president could not declare war. Yet their statutes implied as much. When presidents sought congressional direction on whether to fight a war, *see, e.g.*, Message from James Madison to Congress (June 1, 1812), *in* 4 The Papers of James Madison: Presidential Series 432, 432–38 (J. C. A. Stagg et al. eds., 1999), Congress passed declarations of war rather than resolving that presidents could declare war on their own. *See, e.g.*, Act of June 18, 1812, 2 Stat. 755 (declaring war between the United States and Great Britain).

38. Letter from Thomas Jefferson to James Madison (Sept. 6, 1789), *in* 15 The Papers of Thomas Jefferson 392, 397 (Julian P. Boyd ed., 1958).

39. For an account of the numerous functions served by declarations, *see* Exhuming the Seemingly Moribund Declaration of War, *supra* note 1, 107–20.

40. *See* Rosara Joseph, The War Prerogative: History, Reform, and Constitutional Design 96–99 (2013).

41. Separation and Overlap of War and Military Powers, *supra* note 1, at 316–17.

42. 1 William Blackstone, Commentaries on the Laws of England 250 (University of Chicago 1979) (1765) (noting that the power to issue letters of marque and reprisal "is nearly related to, and plainly derived from, that other of making war").

43. Separation and Overlap of War and Military Powers, *supra* note 1, at 317–18.

44. 1 Blackstone, *supra* note 42, at 254.

45. Bill of Rights, 1689, 1 W. & M., c. 2 (Eng.).

46. Americans recognized that Parliament determined whether there would be an army within Britain. *See* Marcus IV, *in* 16 The Documentary History of the Ratification of

the Constitution 379, 384 (John P. Kaminski & Gaspare J. Saladino eds., 1986) ("[I]t is . . . in the power of Parliament to authorise the keeping up of any number of troops for any indefinite time.").

47. *See, e.g.*, John Childs, *The Restoration Army 1660–1702*, *in* The Oxford Illustrated History of the British Army 48, 55 (David Chandler ed., 1994) ("[Charles II] had very little money and the English constitution insisted that the Crown could only raise additional revenue through parliament.").

48. The Federal Farmer No. 18 (Jan. 25, 1788), *in* 20 The Documentary History of the Ratification of the Constitution 1070, 1073–74 (John P. Kaminski et al. eds., 2004) (claiming that power properly rests with the people's representatives in Great Britain).

49. U.S. Const. art. I, § 8, cl. 1, 12–13 ("The Congress shall have the Power . . . To raise and support Armies . . . [and] To provide and maintain a Navy.").

50. Act of Apr. 30, 1790, 1 Stat. 119.

51. Act of Mar. 27, 1794, § 1, 1 Stat. 350, 350.

52. *Id.* §§ 2–8, 1 Stat. 350, 350–51.

53. Act of June 30, 1798, § 5, 1 Stat. 575, 576.

54. U.S. Const. art. I, § 8, cl. 12.

55. Act of Apr. 30, 1790, § 1, 1 Stat. 119, 119.

56. Act of Mar. 27, 1794, § 9, 1 Stat. 350, 351.

57. U.S. Const. art. I, § 8, cl. 12 (granting Congress the power "[t]o raise and support Armies," but also providing that "no Appropriation of Money to that Use shall be for a longer Term than two Years.").

58. *Id.* § 9, cl. 7 ("No Money shall be drawn from the Treasury, but in Consequence of Appropriations made by Law.").

59. *See infra* Chapter 8.

60. The Federalist No. 24, *supra* note 5, at 116 (Alexander Hamilton). In Federalist No. 26, Hamilton noted that state constitutions had the same schema. *See id.* No. 26, at 127 (Alexander Hamilton) ("The power of raising armies at all under [state] constitutions, can by no construction be deemed to reside any where else, than in the legislatures themselves.").

61. *See* 10 The Documentary History of the Ratification of the Constitution 1371, 1379 (John P. Kaminski & Gaspare J. Saladino eds., 1993) (claiming "that the army and navy were to be raised by Congress, and not the President"); 4 Debates in the Several State Conventions, *supra* note 5, at 107–8 (claiming that Congress, not the president, could raise armies).

62. *See* Letter from George Washington to the United States Senate and House of Representatives (Aug. 10, 1789), *in* 3 The Papers of George Washington: Presidential Series 413 (Dorothy Twohig ed., 1989) (asking Congress to authorize the army's continued existence).

63. *See* Letter from George Washington to Alexander Spotswood (Mar. 15, 1794), *in* 15 The Papers of George Washington: Presidential Series 388 (Christine S. Patrick ed., 2009) (assuming that Congress would decide whether there would be a navy).

64. *E.g.*, Act of June 30, 1798, § 3, 1 Stat. 575, 576.

65. *E.g.*, Act of May 28, 1798, § 3, 1 Stat. 558, 558.

66. This power partly arose from statute and partly from custom, making it unclear the extent to which the Crown had constitutional power to call out the militia.

67. *See* Joyce Lee Malcolm, *Charles II and the Reconstruction of Royal Power*, 35 Hist. J. 307, 323, n.67 (1992) (discussing the limitations on the king's power over the militia as evidenced by the militia acts passed by Parliament in 1661, 1662, and 1663).

68. *See* 1661, 13 Car. 2, c. 6, § 4 (Eng.) (a statute suggesting that only standing law could allow the militia to be sent overseas); *see also* 1662, 14 Car. 2, c. 3, § 7 (Eng.) (codifying a maximum five-shilling fine or twenty-day imprisonment for a soldier for each instance of not performing his duties).

69. *See* 1663, 15 Car. 2, c. 4, § 7 (Eng.) (specifying munitions that "Musquetiers" and horsemen must bring to "every Muster, Training and Exercise").

70. U.S. Const. art. II, § 2, cl. 1 ("The President shall be Commander in Chief of the Army and Navy of the United States, and of the Militia of the several States, when called into the actual Service of the United States.").

71. Proclamation (Aug. 7, 1794), *in* 16 The Papers of George Washington: Presidential Series 531, 533–34 (David R. Hoth & Carol S. Ebel eds., 2011) (Washington noting his compliance with existing law in calling forth the militia).

72. U.S. Const. art. I, § 9, cl. 7.

73. *See* Childs, *supra* note 47, at 54 (stating that because the army was not recognized within the law of Britain, the Articles of War could not be enforced against soldiers before British courts).

74. *See id.* (noting that while purely military offenses were adjudged before courts-martial, stoppage of pay, suspension, or dismissal were the only options for punishment).

75. *Id.*

76. *See id.* at 56 (referring to the awkwardness that resulted during James II's reign when it was difficult to punish the considerable number of soldiers who deserted after 1685).

77. *See* Markus Eder, Crime and Punishment in the Royal Navy of the Seven Years' War, 1755–1763, at 41–42 (2004) (explaining that passage of the Laws and Ordinances Martial Code was the first of several early attempts to enforce discipline in the Royal Navy).

78. *See* 1688, 1 W. & M., c. 5 (Eng.).

79. *Id.*

80. *See* Mark A. Thomson, A Constitutional History of England, 1642 to 1801, at 293 (1938) ("[T]he Act was in some respects vague. It made no mention of the King's power, if any, to issue articles of war, although it was necessary that he should do so if discipline was to be maintained.").

81. *See id.* at 295–96 (describing how, over time, Parliament granted the Crown greater powers over military discipline and the authorization to apply the articles of war).

82. *See* Childs, *supra* note 47, at 54 (explaining that because the Mutiny Act gave legal recognition to the army and its courts-martial, the lapse of the act meant the army was

no longer recognized under the law, thus limiting the army's punishments to stoppage of pay, suspension, or dismissal); Thomson, *supra* note 80, at 294 ("During the interval [when the Mutiny Act lapsed] the Army was kept under tolerable discipline, but how it was done is a mystery."). In the American colonies, governors could execute the "law martial" only in times of war and even then only with the consent of their executive councils. Evarts Boutell Greene, The Provincial Governor in the English Colonies of North America 99 (1898).

83. 3 Journals of the Continental Congress 1774–1789, at 378–87 (Worthington Chauncey Ford ed., 1905) (creating rules for the navy); 2 Journals of the Continental Congress 1774–1789, at 111–22 (Worthington Chauncey Ford ed., 1905) (creating articles of war for the army).

84. 3 Journals of the Continental Congress, *supra* note 83, at 381–82; 2 Journals of the Continental Congress, *supra* note 83, at 113, 116.

85. Articles of Confederation of 1781, art. IX, § 4, para. 4.

86. *See* Act of Sept. 29, 1789, § 4, 1 Stat. 95, 96 (providing that the articles of war created by the Continental Congress would continue to apply to the army under the new Constitution). Because the navy was created later, its articles were delayed. Act of July 1, 1797, § 8, 1 Stat. 523, 525 (providing that sailors and marines shall be governed by rules established in 1775 by the Continental Congress).

87. As Publius, Hamilton could be read to suggest that he believed that the Crown also was a commander in chief. The Federalist No. 69, *supra* note 5, at 349–50 (Alexander Hamilton).

88. *See* Francis D. Wormuth & Edwin B. Firmage, To Chain the Dog of War: The War Power of Congress in History and Law 105 (1989) (explaining that Charles I introduced the term "commander in chief" into English law with the appointment of the Earl of Arundel in 1639).

89. The commission of one early army commander in chief noted that all officers and soldiers were to obey the commander's orders. *See* Commission of George Monck as Captain-General (Aug. 3, 1660), *in* Daniel MacKinnon, 2 Origins and Services of the Coldstream Guards 239, 246 (1833).

90. A Military Dictionary, Explaining and Describing the Technical Terms, Phrases, Works, and Machines Used in the Science of War (G. Robinson et al., 1778) [hereinafter A Military Dictionary] (entry for "General of an Army").

91. *Id.* (entry for "Captain").

92. *Id.* (entry for "Colonel").

93. Although the office is most associated with the British army, the Royal Navy also had commanders in chief. *See* 19 Geo. 3, c. 6 (1789) (Eng.) (authorizing court martial of Augustus Keppel, Commander in Chief of a fleet).

94. A Military Dictionary, *supra* note 90 (entry for "General of an Army").

95. *See* Vt. Const. ch. II, § 18 (1777) (stating that the "Governor shall be commander-in-chief of the forces of the State"); Ga. Const. art. XXXIII (1777) (stating that the governor

"shall be captain-general, and commander-in-chief over all the militia"); N.Y. Const. art. XVIII (1777) (stating that the governor shall be commander in chief of all the militia); N.J. Const. art. VIII (1776) (same); N.C. Const. art. XVIII (1776) (same); Del. Const. art. 9 (1776) (stating that the president may act as "commander-in-chief" of the militia); Pa. Const. § 20 (1776) (stating the state president shall be commander in chief of the "forces of the state"); S.C. Const. art. III (1776) (describing the state president also as the commander in chief).

96. Mass. Const. pt. II, ch. 2, § 1, art. VII (1780). Whether the omission of the army was an oversight is unclear. The New Hampshire Constitution contained a virtually identical provision. N.H. Const. pt. II, cl. 38 (1784).

97. Mass. Const. pt. II, ch. 2, § 1, art. VII (1780).

98. *Id.*

99. 2 Journals of the Continental Congress, *supra* note 83, at 96.

100. 6 Journals of the Continental Congress 1774–1789, at 1045 (Worthington Chauncey Ford ed., 1906).

101. A Military Dictionary, *supra* note 90 (entry for "General of an Army").

102. Mass. Const. pt. II, ch. 2, § 1, art. VII (1780).

103. 2 Records of the Federal Convention, *supra* note 7, at 318.

104. *Id.*

105. *See* Letter from Thomas Jefferson to George Washington (Mar. 27, 1791), *in* 19 The Papers of Thomas Jefferson 625 (Julian P. Boyd ed., 1958); Letter from George Washington to Thomas Jefferson (Apr. 1, 1791), *in* 8 The Papers of George Washington: Presidential Series 35 (Mark A. Mastromarino ed., 1999). Authority from the federal government might have been unnecessary, since states had retained constitutional authority to repel invasions. U.S. Const. art. I, § 10, cl. 3 (implying that states may "engage in War" when "actually invaded").

106. *See* Unleashing the Dogs of War, *supra* note 1, at 100–101 (discussing letters from two governors requesting the authority to conduct offensive operations).

107. *See* A Two-Front War, *supra* note 1, at 213–14.

108. *See generally* Unleashing the Dogs of War, *supra* note 1, at 101–5.

109. *See* Solicitor, U.S. Dep't of State, Right to Protect Citizens in Foreign Countries by Landing Forces 34 (2d. rev. ed. 1929) (listing several incidents of "[s]imple protection of American citizens located in disturbed areas").

110. *See* Unleashing the Dogs of War, *supra* note 1, at 117 (giving examples of other military actions that were not meant to signal a decision to wage war).

111. For a discussion of the difficult dividing line between permissible uses of force and informal declarations of war, *see id.* at 116–19.

112. Generals have sometimes failed to observe implied limits on their authority. *See, e.g.,* D. A. Jeremy Telman, *A Truism that Isn't True? The Tenth Amendment and Executive War Power,* 51 Cath. U. L. Rev. 135, 162–63 (2001) (discussing General Andrew Jackson's unauthorized attack on Seminole Indians and Spanish forts in Florida, and noting that James Monroe admitted that neither he nor Jackson had legal authority to order such attacks).

113. *See* Stephen C. Neff, War and the Law of Nations: A General History 18 (2005).

114. Emer de Vattel, The Law of Nations 228 (Béla Kapossy & Richard Whatmore eds., 2008) (1758).

115. Abraham D. Sofaer, War, Foreign Affairs, and Constitutional Powers: The Origins 156 (1976).

116. Fifth Annual Message (Dec. 3, 1805), *in* 1 A Compilation of the Messages and Papers of the Presidents: 1789–1897, at 370, 372 (James D. Richardson ed., 1896) [hereinafter 1 Messages and Papers of the Presidents].

117. Letter from Thomas Jefferson to Robert Smith (Sept. 3, 1807), *in* 10 The Works of Thomas Jefferson 490, 491 (Paul Leicester Ford ed., 1905).

118. In 1789, Congress made piracy a crime. Act of Apr. 30, 1790, §§ 8–12, 1 Stat. 112, 113–15. Not until 1819 did Congress expressly authorize the president to use the navy to combat pirates. Act of Mar. 3, 1819, 3 Stat. 510. A statute enacted in 1798 might have extended to pirates. Act of May 28, 1798, 1 Stat. 561 (authorizing the use of the navy to seize vessels "committing depradations" against U.S. vessels).

119. President Jefferson's dealings with the so-called Barbary Pirates are not to the contrary. Jefferson apparently did not believe he had the constitutional authority to order offensive measures against Tripolitan vessels. *See* First Annual Message (Dec. 8, 1801), *in* 1 Messages and Papers of the Presidents, *supra* note 116, at 314 (noting that the president could not order offensive measures against Tripoli). His belief likely stemmed from the view that these so-called pirates were really not pirates at all. Jefferson believed that the Tripolitan ships attacking U.S. merchant vessels were authorized agents of the Tripoli government, which had declared war. *Id.* at 326. Hence, Jefferson regarded the Tripolitan corsairs as either privateers or elements of the Tripolitan navy. Because they were not true pirates, Jefferson understood that he lacked the constitutional authority to authorize offensive action against them.

120. *See* A Military Dictionary, *supra* note 90 (entry for "General of an Army") (noting that he who "commands in chief" may issue orders); *see also* Mass. Const. pt. II, ch. 2, § 1, art. VII (1780) (providing that the Massachusetts commander in chief may instruct the navy and the militia).

121. *Cf.* Mass. Const. pt. II, ch. 2, § 1, art. VII (1780) (expressly providing that the commander in chief may train the navy and the militia).

122. *See, e.g.*, George Washington, General Orders (July 6, 1777), *in* 10 The Papers of George Washington: Revolutionary War Series 205, 205–6 (Robert F. Haggard & Mark A. Mastromarino eds., 2002) (expressing concern with the lack of discipline and ordering soldiers to attend a parade and an exercise).

123. *See supra* note 82 and accompanying text.

124. For a discussion of the president's power to remove executive officers, military and civil, *see* Saikrishna Prakash, *Removal and Tenure in Office*, 92 Va. L. Rev. 1779 (2006).

125. *See infra* Chapter 8.

126. *See* Act of June 18, 1812, 2 Stat. 755 (general authorization to use the armed forces to wage war against the United Kingdom).

127. *See* Act of Mar. 3, 1815, 3 Stat. 230 (authorizing the use of the navy against Algerian cruisers for the protection of U.S. commerce); Act of Feb. 6, 1802, 2 Stat. 129 (authorizing the use of the navy against Tripolitan cruisers for the protection of U.S. commerce).

128. Act of July 9, 1798, § 1, 1 Stat. 578, 578 (authorizing capture in U.S. waters and on the high seas, but omitting authority to capture in French waters).

129. Gordon S. Wood, The Radicalism of the American Revolution 206 (1991).

130. Vt. Const. ch. II, art. XI (1786); Pa. Const. § 20 (1776); Md. Const. art. XXXIII (1776).

131. *See, e.g.,* N.C. Const. art. XVIII (1776) (making the governor commander in chief without any constraint on personal command).

132. N.Y. Const. art. XX (1777).

133. Mass. Const. pt. II, ch. 2, § 1, art. VII (1780).

134. 3 Debates in the Several State Conventions, *supra* note 5, at 96–97 (noting that the president might command in person).

135. 1 Records of the Federal Convention, *supra* note 7, at 244.

136. Luther Martin, Genuine Information IX (Jan. 29, 1788), *in* 15 The Documentary History of the Ratification of the Constitution, 494, 495 (John P. Kaminski & Gaspare J. Saladino eds., 1984). *Cf.* An Old Whig, No. V (Nov. 1, 1787), *in* 13 The Documentary History of the Ratification of the Constitution 538, 542 (John P. Kaminski & Gaspare J. Saladino eds., 1981) (worrying that army might be loyal to a beloved commander in chief who wished to cling to power).

137. *See* The Continuation of Politics by Other Means, *supra* note 10, at 304.

138. King of Great Britain's Declaration of War Against the King of Spain, *in* 3 Naval and Military Memoirs of Great Britain from 1727 to 1783, at 340, 341–42 (R. Beatson ed., 1804). The Spanish formal declaration more tersely noted that "proper orders should be sent to all parts of [Spanish] dominions . . . for acting offensively against the enemy." *Id.* at 342–43.

139. U.S. Const. art. II, § 3, cl. 4 ("[H]e shall take Care that the Laws be faithfully executed.").

140. *See, e.g.,* Act of Feb. 6, 1802, § 2, 2 Stat. 129, 130 (recognizing that a state of war existed and authorizing the use of the navy against Tripoli for the protection of commerce); Act of June 18, 1812, 2 Stat. 755 (declaring that war exists and authorizing the president to use the armed forces to wage war).

141. Brown v. United States, 12 U.S. (8 Cranch) 110, 153 (1814) (Story, J., dissenting). Some of the later formal declarations were more direct, requiring the president to wage war against the enemy. *See, e.g.,* Act of Apr. 25, 1898, 30 Stat. 364 ("direct[ing]" the president to wage war against Spain).

142. *See* Mark Zuehlke, For Honour's Sake: The War of 1812 and the Brokering of an Uneasy Peace 84–86 (2006); Frank Arthur Updyke, The Diplomacy of the War of 1812, at 136–37 (1915).

143. *See generally* Ramsey, *supra* note 13, at 174–93 (describing why the president may make international agreements that do not constitute treaties).

144. Separation and Overlap of War and Military Powers, *supra* note 1, at 330–50.

145. *See* Letter from Henry Knox to William Blount (Dec. 29, 1794), *in* 1 American State Papers: Indian Affairs 634, 635 (Walter Lowrie & Matthew St. Clair Clarke eds., 1832).

146. Articles of Confederation of 1781, art. IX, § 4, para. 4.

147. U.S. Const. art. IV, § 3, cl. 2.

148. *Compare id., with* U.S. Const. art. I, § 8, cl. 7.

149. Separation and Overlap of War and Military Powers, *supra* note 1, at 323.

150. U.S. Const. art. I, § 9, cl. 6.

151. *Id.* amend. III.

152. *See* T.A. Heathcote, *The Army of British India, in* The Oxford Illustrated History of the British Army, *supra* note 47, at 376, 378 (discussing the commanders in chief of India, Bengal, and Madras).

153. Commission (Aug. 14, 1755), *in* 2 The Papers of George Washington: Colonial Series 3, 3–4 (W. W. Abbot ed., 1983) (appointing Washington as "Colonel of the Virga Regimt & Commander in Chief of all the Forces now rais'd & to be rais'd for the Defense of this H: Majesty's Colony").

154. *See* David J. Barron & Martin S. Lederman, *The Commander in Chief at the Lowest Ebb—Framing the Problem, Doctrine, and Original Understanding*, 121 Harv. L. Rev. 689, 780–85 (2008) [hereinafter Commander in Chief at the Lowest Ebb] (discussing how state commanders in chief had to exercise their functions subject to legislative direction).

155. *Id.* at 782.

156. *See* Sofaer, *supra* note 115, at 21 (noting the Continental Congress's instruction of Washington).

157. 2 Journals of the Continental Congress, *supra* note 83, at 96 (providing that Washington was "to regulate [his] conduct in every respect by the rules and discipline of war, (as herewith given you[]) and punctually to observe and follow such orders and directions . . . as you shall receive from this, or a future Congress of these United Colonies.").

158. *See* 7 Journals of the Continental Congress 1774–1789, at 218, 252 (Worthington Chauncey Ford ed., 1907) (directing the regional commanders in chief). Letters referred to these regional commanders in chief as well. *See, e.g.,* Letter from the Board of War to the Executive Committee (Feb. 7, 1777), *in* 6 Letters of Delegates to Congress, 1774–1789, at 229 (Paul H. Smith ed., 1980) (describing General Philip Schuyler as commander in chief of the Northern Department).

159. *See* 3 Journals of the Continental Congress, *supra* note 83, at 443 (naming Ezek Hopkins as commander in chief of the fleet).

160. *See, e.g.,* Gardner Weld Allen, 1 A Naval History of the American Revolution 90–92, 112–15 (1913) (noting the Continental Congress's instruction of the naval commander in chief and that he was censured for failing to follow its orders).

161. *See supra* note 95 and accompanying text.

162. *See* Act of May 8, 1792, §§ 4, 6, 10, 1 Stat. 271, 272–74 (mentioning state commanders in chief).

163. *See* Act of Mar. 2, 1799, §§ 6, 11, 1 Stat. 709, 715–17 (discussing prize money to go to naval commanders in chief and rules or regulations made by "any commander in chief"); Act of Mar. 3, 1797, § 4, 1 Stat. 507, 508 (providing that a brigadier general, "while commander in chief," is entitled to double rations).

164. *See* Commission of George Washington as Lieutenant General and Commander in Chief (July 4, 1798), *quoted in* Letter from George Washington to John Adams (July 13, 1798), *in* 2 The Papers of George Washington: Retirement Series 402 n.1 (W. W. Abbot ed., 1998).

165. *Id.*

166. This modest but still significant conception of the commander-in-chief authority continued into modern times. Until October 2002, the United States followed the British practice of having regional commanders in chief. *See* Rowan Scarborough, Rumsfeld's War: The Untold Story of America's Anti-Terrorist Commander 134 (2004) (noting that defense secretary Donald Rumsfeld banned the use of "commander in chief" to describe regional commanders, asserting that the Constitution provided that there could be only one commander in chief). Notwithstanding their titles, no one could have thought that these regional commanders had any autonomy vis-à-vis the Constitution's commander in chief.

167. Locke, *supra* note 2, at 171.

168. U.S. Const. art. I, § 7, cl. 2.

169. *See* U.S. Const. art. I, § 7, cl. 2. One of President Washington's two vetoes related to a military bill meant to discharge some troops. He objected on policy grounds, and the troops remained in service. Veto Message (Feb. 28, 1797), *in* 1 Messages and Papers of the Presidents, *supra* note 116, at 203, 203–4.

170. Some members sought to replace Washington with General Horatio Gates. *See* Edward G. Lengel, General George Washington: A Military Life 276–78 (2005).

171. Allen, *supra* note 160, at 188.

172. U.S. Const. art. I, § 2, cl. 5; *id.* § 3, cl. 6; *id.* art. II, § 4.

173. *See* Articles of Confederation of 1781, art. IX, § 4, para. 4 (Congress had the power to appoint "all officers of the land forces, in the service of the United States, excepting regimental officers," and "all the officers of the naval forces").

174. *See* Bruce Chadwick, General Washington's War: The Forging of a Revolutionary Leader and the American Presidency 258–61, 285, 376–77 (2004) (discussing numerous controversies associated with the congressional power to appoint generals and Washington's frustration with seeing more qualified officers passed over in favor of incompetents).

175. In truth, the Constitution creates a default rule of presidential nomination and appointment. But Congress may vest the appointment of inferior officers, including military officers, in the department heads, the courts of law, or the president. The Constitution specifically provides: "[The president] shall nominate, and by and with the Advice and Consent of the Senate, shall appoint Ambassadors, other public Ministers and Consuls, Judges of the supreme Court, and all other Officers of the United States . . . but the

Congress may by Law vest the Appointment of such inferior Officers, as they think proper, in the President alone, in the Courts of Law, or in the Heads of Departments." U.S. Const. art. II, § 2, cl. 2.

176. *See supra* notes 124–25 and accompanying text.

177. U.S. Const. art. II, § 2, cl. 1 (providing that the president may "require the Opinion, in writing, of the principal Officer in each of the executive Departments, upon any subject relating to the Duties of their respective Offices").

178. *Cf.* 4 Debates in the Several State Conventions, *supra* note 5, at 110 (James Iredell observing that the president may ask for advice but must take responsibility for any decision made).

179. He believed as much because a resolve of Congress seemed to require such consultation. 2 Journals of the Continental Congress, *supra* note 83, at 101 (authorizing Washington to use his discretion and directing him to consult with a "council of war"). Congress eventually said that it never meant to require Washington to consult with a council of war. 7 Journals of the Continental Congress, *supra* note 158, at 196–97. For a discussion of this ambiguity, *see* Commander in Chief at the Lowest Ebb, *supra* note 154, at 778–80.

180. U.S. Const. art. II, § 2, cl. 1 ("[The president] shall have Power to grant Reprieves and Pardons for Offences against the United States, except in Cases of Impeachment.").

181. The Federalist No. 69, *supra* note 5, at 350 (Alexander Hamilton).

Chapter 8. The Executive Power "of Appointing, Overseeing, and Controlling Those Who Execute the Laws"

1. 1 William Blackstone, Commentaries on the Laws of England 261 (University of Chicago 1979) (1765).

2. John Brewer, Party Ideology and Popular Politics at the Accession of George III, at 116 (1976).

3. *Id.* (quoting Ministerial Usurpation Displayed, and the Prerogatives of the Crown, with the Rights of Parliament and of the Privy Council, considered in an appeal to the people 20 (1760)).

4. This chapter draws extensively from Steven G. Calabresi & Saikrishna B. Prakash, *The President's Power To Execute the Laws*, 104 Yale L.J. 541 (1994); Saikrishna Prakash, *The Essential Meaning of Executive Power*, 2003 U. Ill. L. Rev. 701; Saikrishna Bangalore Prakash, *Hail to the Chief Administrator: The Framers and the President's Administrative Powers*, 102 Yale L.J. 991 (1993); Saikrishna Prakash, *Removal and Tenure in Office*, 92 Va. L. Rev. 1779 (2006); Saikrishna Prakash, *Fragmented Features of the Constitution's Unitary Executive*, 45 Willamette L. Rev. 701 (2009); Saikrishna Prakash, *New Light on the Decision of 1789*, 91 Cornell L. Rev. 1021 (2006).

5. Evarts Boutell Greene, The Provincial Governor in the English Colonies of North America 110, 138–39 (1898).

6. Some early state constitutions assumed that only the legislature could create offices. *See* Pa. Const. art. IX, § 24 (1790) (limiting the legislature's ability to create certain offices); Ky. Const. art. XII, § 26 (1792) (same). These constitutions hint that the power to create offices was assumed to be a legislative power.

7. U.S. Const. art. II, § 2, cl. 2 ("[The President] shall nominate, and by and with the Advice and Consent of the Senate, shall appoint Ambassadors, other public Ministers and Consuls, Judges of the supreme Court, and all other Officers of the United States, whose Appointments are not herein otherwise provided for, and which shall be established by Law: but the Congress may by Law vest the Appointment of such inferior Officers, as they think proper, in the President alone, in the Courts of Law, or in the Heads of Departments."). Despite the text, the clause actually means to refer to "offices" created by law, for if laws could establish actual "officers," a separate appointment would be unnecessary.

8. U.S. Const. art. I, § 6, cl. 2.

9. 2 The Records of the Federal Convention of 1787, at 405 (Max Farrand rev. ed., 1966) [hereinafter Records of the Federal Convention].

10. *Id.*

11. *Id.*

12. *Id.* at 497–99.

13. *Id.* at 550, 553.

14. *Id.* at 628.

15. *See generally* Act of Sept. 24, 1789, 1 Stat. 73 (creating federal judgeships, district attorneys, and the attorney general); Act of Sept. 2, 1789, § 1, 1 Stat. 65, 65 (declaring "[t]hat there shall be a Department of Treasury, in which shall be the following officers, namely: a Secretary of the Treasury, to be deemed head of the department; a Comptroller, an Auditor, a Treasurer"); Act of March 3, 1791, § 5, 1 Stat. 222, 222–23 (delegating to the president power to create generals, quartermaster, and chaplain). There were some who believed that the president could create offices. The Senate could check the president by refusing to approve nominees, leaving the offices empty. And the House could check by refusing to grant salaries. *See* 9 The Documentary History of the First Federal Congress: The Diary of William Maclay and Other Notes on Senate Debates 109–10 (Kenneth R. Bowling & Helen E. Veit eds., 1988).

16. *See* Saikrishna B. Prakash & Michael D. Ramsey, *The Executive Power over Foreign Affairs*, 111 Yale L.J. 231, 309–10 (2001).

17. 1 Annals of Congress 721 (1789) (member claiming that Congress did not need to create offices for negotiators because the positions were too ephemeral); Letter from James Madison to James Monroe (May 6, 1822), *in* 9 The Writings of James Madison 89, 91–93 & n.1 (Gaillard Hunt ed., 1910) (claiming that the "places" of ministers or consuls are created by the law of nations). For a longer but no less persuasive defense of the latter claim, see 7 Op. Att'y Gen. 189 (1855).

18. In fact, treaty negotiators underwent the normal process, suggesting that the president and the Senate regarded them as officers. *See, e.g.*, 1 Journal of the Executive

Proceedings of the Senate of the United States of America 150, 152 (1794) (the president nominating, and the Senate consenting to the appointment of, John Jay as treaty envoy to Great Britain).

19. *See* Letter from Thomas Jefferson to William Short (Apr. 30, 1790), *in* 16 The Papers of Thomas Jefferson 395, 395–96 (Julian P. Boyd ed., 1961) (as the Constitution required, the president signed a commission for Short as chargé d'affaires).

20. *See e.g.,* The Federalist No. 42, at 212 (James Madison) (Garry Wills ed., 1982) ("[T]he mission of American Consuls ... may *perhaps* be covered under the authority given by the 9th article of the Confederation, to appoint all such civil officers as may be necessary for managing the general affairs of the United States.").

21. *See* Act of Sept. 24, 1789, § 1, 1 Stat. 73, 73.

22. *See id.* at § 35, 1 Stat. 92–93 (creating the attorney general and specifying duties); Act of Sept. 2, 1789, 1 Stat. 65 (creating the treasury secretary and specifying duties).

23. *See* Act of July 27, 1789, § 1, 1 Stat. 28, 28–29.

24. *See* Letter from James Madison to Edmund Pendleton (June 21, 1789), *in* 12 The Papers of James Madison: Congressional Series 251, 252 (Charles F. Hobson & Robert A. Rutland eds., 1979) (Congress may limit the "duration of the appointments" to office.). In *The Federalist Papers*, Madison seemed to confirm that view. The Federalist No. 39, *supra* note 20, at 191 (James Madison) ("The tenure of the ministerial offices [i.e., executive offices] generally will be a subject of legal regulation."). Some thirty years later, Madison claimed otherwise. *See* Letter from James Madison to James Monroe (Dec. 28, 1820), *in* 9 The Writings of James Madison, *supra* note 17, at 41, 43 (claiming that a law limiting tenure to four years was unconstitutional).

25. *See, e.g.,* Act of Feb. 27, 1801, § 11, 2 Stat. 103, 107 (five-year terms for justices of the peace); Act of Apr. 30, 1790, § 1, 1 Stat. 119, 119 (three-year terms for commissioned army officers); Act of Sept. 24, 1789, § 27, 1 Stat. 73, 87 (four-year terms for marshals).

26. *See* Removal and Tenure in Office, *supra* note 4, at 1804–6.

27. U.S. Const. art. I, § 6, cl. 2 ("No Senator or Representative shall, during the Time for which he was elected, be appointed to any civil Office under the Authority of the United States, which shall have been created, or the Emoluments whereof shall have been increased during such time; and no Person holding any Office under the United States, shall be a Member of either House during his Continuance in Office.").

28. U.S. Const. art. I, § 3, cl. 6.

29. Act of Sept. 24, 1789, § 35, 1 Stat. 73, 92–93.

30. *Id.* § 2, at 73.

31. Act of Sept. 2, 1789, § 4, 1 Stat. 65, 66.

32. Act of July 31, 1789, § 28, 1 Stat. 29, 44. Officers had three months to post the requisite bond.

33. Act of Apr. 14, 1792, § 6, 1 Stat. 254, 256.

34. Act of Apr. 30, 1790, § 21, 1 Stat. 112, 117; Act of Sept. 1, 1789, § 34, 1 Stat. 55, 64–65; Act of July 31, 1789, § 35, 1 Stat. 29, 46.

35. Letter from James Madison to Edmund Randolph (Apr. 10, 1788) *in* 11 The Papers of James Madison: Congressional Series 18, 19 (Robert A. Rutland & Charles F. Hobson eds., 1977).

36. 1 Annals of Congress 571 (1789). Though some denied this power, others claimed that Congress could set qualifications and had done so. *See* David P. Currie, The Constitution in Congress: The Federalist Period 1789–1801, at 43 n.255 (1997).

37. Message to the Senate (Apr. 13, 1822), *in* 2 A Compilation of the Messages and Papers of the Presidents, 1789–1897, at 129, 132–33 (James D. Richardson ed., 1897) [hereinafter 2 Messages and Papers of the Presidents].

38. *See generally* Removal and Tenure in Office, *supra* note 4, at 1787.

39. U.S. Const. art. II, § 2, cl. 2.

40. *Cf. Is Civil Service Reform Constitutional?*, The Nation, Aug. 3, 1871, at 68, 69 (stating that civil service reforms are constitutional: "The final object of the appointing power is certainly not the mere placing a person in office. Its proper execution implies that the individual shall be fit and capable. . . . Any laws which tend to accomplish this design are concerned with the carrying into execution of the power of appointment, and are eminently necessary and proper measures therefor.").

41. Gaillard Hunt, *Office-Seeking During Washington's Administration*, 1 Am. Hist. Rev. 270, 272 n.2 (1896).

42. Leonard D. White, The Federalists: A Study in Administrative History 259 n.19 (1948).

43. *Id.* at 259.

44. Letter from George Washington to James Madison (Sept. 23, 1789), *in* 4 The Papers of George Washington: Presidential Series 67, 67 (Dorothy Twohig ed., 1993).

45. White, *supra* note 42, at 259–60.

46. *See* Mitchel Sollenberger, The President Shall Nominate: How Congress Trumps Executive Power 9–10 (2008).

47. Letter from Thomas Jefferson to James Monroe (Apr. 11, 1792), *in* 23 The Papers of Thomas Jefferson 401 (Charles T. Cullen ed., 1990).

48. Greene, *supra* note 5, at 93, 111.

49. *See id.* at 94, 111–12.

50. *Id.* at 182–83.

51. *See, e.g.*, Del. Const. art. 15 (1776); Mass. Const. pt. II, ch. 1, § 3, art. X (1780); N.C. Const. art. XIII, XIV (1776); N.J. Const. art. X, XII (1776); N.Y. Const. art. XXII (1777); S.C. Const. §§ 19–23 (1776); S.C. Const. §§ 26–30 (1778); Va. Const. (1776).

52. *See* Del. Const. art. 12 (1776) (appointment of justices of the peace).

53. *See id.* (appointment of the attorney general and others); Md. Const. art. XLVIII (1776); N.H. Const. pt. II (1784); N.Y. Const. art. XXIII (1777); S.C. Const. § 25 (1776); S.C. Const. § 32 (1778); Va. Const. (1776); Vt. Const. ch. 2, § 17 (1777); Vt. Const. ch. 2, § XI (1786). In Pennsylvania, the executive council could appoint. Pa. Const. § 20 (1776).

54. Mass. Const. pt. II, ch. 2, § 1, art. IX (1780).

55. 2 Records of the Federal Convention, *supra* note 9, at 41–44, 80–83.

56. *Id.* at 183.

57. *Id.* at 314–15.

58. *Id.* at 538–40.

59. *Id.* at 614.

60. *Id.* at 539 (comments of Gouverneur Morris) ("[A]s the President was to nominate, there would be responsibility, and as the Senate was to concur, there would be security.").

61. *See* The Federalist No. 76, *supra* note 20, at 385 (Alexander Hamilton) (ascribing this complaint to "most intelligent" critics).

62. 2 Records of the Federal Convention, *supra* note 9, at 537, 541–42 (comments of George Mason).

63. Letter from George Washington to Edward Rutledge (May 5, 1789), *in* 2 The Papers of George Washington: Presidential Series 217, 218 (Dorothy Twohig ed., 1987) ("I anticipate that one of the most difficult & delicate parts of the duty of my office will be that which relates to nominations for appointments.").

64. Jack D. Warren, Jr., *"The Line of My Official Conduct": George Washington and Congress, 1789–1797*, *in* Neither Separate Nor Equal: Congress in the 1790s, at 238, 252 (Kenneth R. Bowling & Donald R. Kennon eds., 2000).

65. *Id.* at 252–53.

66. Message to the Senate (Aug. 6, 1789), *in* 2 Messages and Papers of the President, *supra* note 37, at 58–59.

67. White, *supra* note 42, at 85–87.

68. Currie, *supra* note 36, at 23.

69. *See* Conference with a Committee of the United States Senate (Aug. 8, 1789), *in* 3 The Papers of George Washington: Presidential Series 400, 401–2 (Dorothy Twohig ed., 1989).

70. *See* Conference with a Committee of the United States Senate (Aug. 10, 1789), *in id.* at 408, 408–9.

71. *Id.*

72. 1 Annals of Congress 66–67 (1789).

73. U.S. Const. art. II, § 3 ("[H]e may, on extraordinary Occasions, convene both Houses, or either of them."). Under current rules, the president may convene the Senate for executive business. *See* Senate Standing Rules, Rule XXIX (2007). It should be noted that other rules related to nominations suggest more latitude for the modern Senate, including one declaring that nominations may be sent to committees and barring votes on the day of the nomination. *See id.* at Rule XXXI.

74. John McGinnis, Appointments Clause, *in* The Heritage Guide to the Constitution 209, 209–10 (Edwin Meese III et al. eds., 2005).

75. Marbury v. Madison, 5 U.S. (1 Cranch) 137, 157 (1803).

76. *Id.* at 156–59 (discussing the sealing of the commission and delivery of the commission as possible alternative indicators for when an appointment vests).

77. *See* Letter from Thomas Jefferson to George Hay (June 2, 1807), *reprinted in* 10 The Works of Thomas Jefferson 396 n.1 (Paul Leicester Ford ed., 1905); Letter from Thomas Jefferson to William Johnson (June 12, 1823), *in* 12 The Works of Thomas Jefferson 252 n.1, 256–57 (Paul Leicester Ford ed., 1905).

78. *Marbury*, 5 U.S. at 160–62 (noting this possibility).

79. Samuel Johnson, A Dictionary of the English Language (10th ed. 1792) (entry for "To commission").

80. *See, e.g.*, Commission of D. Hartley (Apr. 11. 1783), *in* 1 Memoirs of Benjamin Franklin 532 (1834) (The Crown commission both appointed David Hartley "by these presents" and declared him "appointed."); 12 Journals of the Continental Congress 1774–1789, at 1211–12 (Worthington Chauncey Ford ed., 1908) ("The Board of War reported a new form of commission to officers in the army of the United States, which was agreed to as follows: . . . We, reposing special trust and confidence in your patriotism, valour, conduct and fidelity, do, by these presents, constitute and appoint you to be in the army of the United States."); 28 Journals of the Continental Congress 1774–1789, at 1 (John C. Fitzpatrick ed., 1933) (New Hampshire commissioning its delegate with the words "We do hereby vest in you all the powers, authorities, rights and privileges appertaining . . . to this your appointment.").

81. Letter from George Washington to Robert H. Harrison (Sept. 28, 1789), *in* 4 The Papers of George Washington: Presidential Series, *supra* note 44, at 98, 98–99 & n.1 (the commission arrived on Sept. 30, but Washington told Harrison that he had been "appointed" on the 28th).

82. *See, e.g.*, Commission of Joseph Greenleaf Keeper, *in* 3 Genealogical and Family History of the State of Maine 1370 (George Thomas Little et al. eds., 1909) (noting that President Washington has "appointed" and does "appoint"); Gaillard Hunt, *History of the Department of State VII: Duties of the Department of State*, 5 Am. J. Int'l L. 414, 424–26 (1911) (commissions from President Washington taking the form "I do appoint" the named party to the named office).

83. *See* Letter from George Washington to John Rutledge (Sept. 30, 1789), *in* 1 The Documentary History of the Supreme Court of the United States, 1789–1800, at 21 (Maeva Marcus & James R. Perry eds., 1985).

84. *See* Letter from George Washington to James Iredell (Feb. 13, 1790), *in id.* at 66 (saying that the office of justice was open because of a resignation, even though its previous occupant, Robert Harrison, never functioned as a justice).

85. Opinion on the Powers of the Senate Respecting Diplomatic Appointments (April 24, 1790), *in* 16 The Papers of Thomas Jefferson, *supra* note 19, at 378, 379 (emphasis omitted).

86. U.S. Const. art. II, § 2, cl. 3.

87. The National Intelligencer, and Washington Advertiser, Apr. 3, 1801, at A1 (italics omitted).

88. Act of Sept. 15, 1789, § 4, 1 Stat. 68.

89. *See* United States v. Wilson, 32 U.S. 150, 161 (1833).

90. One might suppose that such an appointment would be stillborn because the president cannot make the appointment without the senator first resigning. But this claim implicitly concedes that the senator must accept the appointment, for the act of resigning in this context is tantamount to accepting the offered post.

91. U.S. Const. art. II, § 2, cl. 3.

92. *See generally* Michael B. Rappaport, *The Original Meaning of the Recess Appointments Clause*, 52 UCLA L. Rev. 1487 (2005). *But see* Edward A. Hartnett, *Recess Appointments of Article III Judge: Three Constitutional Questions*, 26 Cardozo L. Rev. 377 (2005) (arguing that during a Senate recess, the president may recess-appoint to any vacancy that exists, whenever the vacancy first arose). The Rappaport view dates to the Washington administration. *See* Edmund Randolph, Opinion on Recess Appointments (July 7, 1792), *in* 24 The Papers of Thomas Jefferson 165, 165–67 (John Catanzariti ed., 1990). Although I agree with Professor Rappaport and Attorney General Randolph, early administrations may have been less than punctilious about making recess appointments only when the vacancy arose during a recess. *See* Letter from Thomas Jefferson to Wilson Cary Nicholas (Jan. 26, 1802), *in* 36 The Papers of Thomas Jefferson 433 (Barbara B. Oberg ed., 2009) (noting that prior administrations may have appointed to offices that became vacant while Congress was in session).

93. U.S. Const. art. II, § 2 ("[T]he Congress may by Law vest the Appointment of such inferior Officers, as they think proper, in the President alone, in the Courts of Law, or in the Heads of Departments.").

94. *See* 2 Records of the Federal Convention, *supra* note 9, at 627–28.

95. Morrison v. Olson, 487 U.S. 654, 673–76 (1988) (permitting some cross-branch appointments).

96. U.S. Const. art. II, § 3 ("[The President] shall Commission all the Officers of the United States."). Notwithstanding the requirement that the president commission all officers, Congress envisioned "non-commissioned officers" within the military. *See* Act of Sept. 29, 1789, § 3, 1 Stat. 95, 96. Moreover, John Marshall noted that early presidents seem not to have commissioned officers appointed by others. *See Marbury*, 5 U.S. at 156 (admitting that the Commissions Clause "may never have been applied to officers" appointed by others).

97. *See, e.g.*, N.Y. Const., art. XXIV (1777); Pa. Const., § 20 (1776).

98. Commission to Sir Thomas West, Lord La Warr, as Governor of Virginia (1610), *in* Greene, *supra* note 5, at 207, 207–13.

99. *Id.* at 95.

100. *See, e.g.*, 12 Journals of the Continental Congress 1774–1789, *supra* note 80, at 1211–12 (commissions for army officers included the language "we do strictly charge and require all officers and soldiers under your command to be obedient to your orders as [officer's rank]; and you are to observe and follow such orders and directions, from time to time, as you shall receive from this or a future Congress of the United States . . . or commander in

chief."). Delegates from Rhode Island to the Continental Congress received more detailed instructions:

> You are also authorized and empowered to consult and advise with the Delegates . . . upon the most proper Measures for promoting and confirming the strictest Union and Confederation between the said United Colonies, for exerting their whole Strength and Force to annoy the common Enemy, and to secure to the said Colonies their Rights and Liberties, both civil and religious, whether by entering into Treaties with any Prince, State, or Potentate, or by such other prudent and effectual Ways and Means as shall be devised and agreed on; And, in Conjunction with the Delegates from the said United Colonies, or the Major Part of them, to enter into and adopt all such Measures, taking the greatest Care to secure to this Colony, in the strongest and most perfect Manner, its present established Form, and all the Powers of Government, so far as relates to its internal Police and Conduct of our own Affairs, civil and religious. You are also instructed and directed, to exert your utmost Abilities, in carrying on this just and necessary War, in which we are engaged against cruel and unnatural Enemies, in the most vigorous Manner, until Peace shall be restored to the said Colonies, and their Rights and Liberties secured upon a solid and permanent Basis.

4 Journals of the Continental Congress 1774–1789, at 353 (Worthington Chauncey Ford ed., 1906).

101. Opinion on the Powers of the Senate Respecting Diplomatic Appointments (April 24, 1790), *in* 16 The Papers of Thomas Jefferson, *supra* note 19, at 378, 379.

102. *See, e.g.*, Letter from George Washington to John Marshall (Nov. 23, 1789), *excerpted in* 4 The Papers of George Washington: Presidential Series, *supra* note 44, at 192, 192 n.2 ("As some other person must be appointed to fill the Office of Attorney . . . it is proper your Commission should be returned to me.").

103. *See* Ron Chernow, Washington: A Life 455–57 (2010).

104. 1 Blackstone, *supra* note 1, at 319–22.

105. Fragmented Features of the Unitary Executive, *supra* note 4, at 703–4.

106. *See* Embry v. United States, 100 U.S. 680, 685 (1879) ("Wherever the power of removal from office may rest, all agree that Congress has full control of salaries, except those of the President and the judges of the courts of the United States.").

107. U.S. Const. art. I, § 8, cl. 12 (Congress shall have the power "[t]o raise and support Armies, but no Appropriation of Money to that Use shall be for a longer Term than two Years.").

108. *See* Act of Sept. 29, 1789, 1 Stat. 95; Act of Mar. 26, 1790, 1 Stat. 104; Act of Feb. 11, 1791, 1 Stat. 190.

109. *See, e.g.*, Act of Sept. 11, 1789, 1 Stat. 67; Act of Sept. 23, 1789, 1 Stat. 72. For diplomats, Congress ceded a little more flexibility, granting a lump sum for foreign intercourse and imposing statutory ceilings on pay. *See* Act of July 1, 1790, § 1, 1 Stat. 128, 128–29.

110. *See e.g.*, Act of July 31, 1789, § 29, 1 Stat. 29, 44–45 (specifying fees for collectors, naval officers, and surveyors).

111. 1 Blackstone, *supra* note 1, at 243.

112. Antoine Francois Bertrand de Moleville, 3 Private Memoirs Relative to the Last Year of the Reign of Lewis the Sixteenth, Late King of France 342 (1797). *See also* 1 Jacques Necker, An Essay on the True Principles of Executive Power in Great States 303 (1792) (noting that because a prince cannot do everything himself, the unity of executive power is preserved when the monarch can choose, direct, and remove instruments).

113. *See* Saikrishna Prakash, *The Chief Prosecutor*, 73 Geo. Wash. L. Rev. 521, 549–51 (2005) (discussing how governors directed state prosecutors).

114. Articles of Confederation of 1781, art. IX.

115. 2 Records of the Federal Convention, *supra* note 9, at 53–54.

116. *Id.*, vol. 3, at 111. Pinckney's remarks were part of a speech that he likely never gave in full. *Id.* at 106 n.1.

117. *Id.*, vol. 2, at 342–43.

118. Enclosure (June 1, 1787), *in* 5 The Papers of George Washington: Confederation Series 210, 212 (W. W. Abbot ed., 1997).

119. 4 The Debates in the Several State Conventions on the Adoption of the Federal Constitution 106 (Jonathan Elliot ed., 2d ed. 1836) [hereinafter Debates in the Several State Conventions].

120. The Federalist No. 72, *supra* note 20, at 366 (Alexander Hamilton).

121. *Id.*

122. 4 Debates in the Several State Conventions, *supra* note 119, at 47.

123. The Federal Farmer No. 14 (Jan 17, 1788), *in* 20 The Documentary History of the Ratification of the Constitution 1035, 1037 (John P. Kaminski et al. eds., 2004).

124. *Id.* at 1038.

125. James Wilson, Lectures on Law (1790), *in* 1 Collected Works of James Wilson 703 (Kermit L. Hall & Mark David Hall eds., 2007).

126. 3 Annals of Congress 794 (1793).

127. Nathaniel Chipman, Sketches of the Principles of Government 154–55 (1793).

128. Benjamin Franklin Bache, Remarks Occasioned by the Late Conduct of Mr. Washington as President of the United States 37 (1796).

129. The Security of the Rights of Citizens in the State of Connecticut Considered 27 (1792); *see also* Essay on Political Society 54–55 (1799) ("subordinate officers," including those who execute laws and judicial judgments, military officers, the diplomatic corps, and all other executive officers, "are subordinated to" the chief magistrate); *id.* at 110 (the president may direct principal, civil, and military officers).

130. Letter from George Washington to Count de Moustier (May 25, 1789), *in* 2 The Papers of George Washington: Presidential Series, *supra* note 63, at 389, 390 (1993).

131. *See* Letter from Tobias Lear to Woodbury Langdon (July 2, 1792), *excerpted in* 10 The Papers of George Washington: Presidential Series 512–13 n.1 (Robert F. Haggard & Mark

A. Mastromarino eds., 2002); *see also* Letter from George Washington to Thomas Jefferson (Mar. 10, 1793), *in* 12 The Papers of George Washington: Presidential Series 291 (Christine S. Patrick & John C. Pinheiro eds., 2005) (threatening to issue a "peremptory Order" to the governor and judges of the Northwest Territory unless they resumed their functions in the territory).

132. *See* Letter from George Washington to William Stephens Smith (Dec. 7, 1790), *in* 7 The Papers of George Washington: Presidential Series 39, 39 (Jack D. Warren, 1998).

133. *See* Letter from Tobias Lear to Clement Biddle (Nov. 28, 1792), *excerpted in* 11 The Papers of George Washington: Presidential Series 447 n.3 (Christine S. Patrick, 2002).

134. Letter from George Washington to John Taylor Gilman (Sept. 28, 1789), *excerpted in* 4 The Papers of George Washington: Presidential Series, *supra* note 44, at 21 n.1.

135. Letter from George Washington to Alexander Hamilton (May 6, 1794), *in* 16 The Papers of George Washington: Presidential Series 21, 21 (David R. Hoth & Carol S. Ebel eds., 2011).

136. Letter from George Washington to Henry Knox (Oct. 15, 1793), *in* 14 The Papers of George Washington: Presidential Series 215, 215 (David R. Hoth, 2008).

137. Circular to the Heads of Department (Nov. 6, 1801), *in* 35 The Papers of Thomas Jefferson 576, 577 (Barbara B. Oberg ed., 2008).

138. *Id.*

139. Letter from Thomas Jefferson to Destutt de Tracy (Jan. 26, 1811), *in* 3 The Papers of Thomas Jefferson: Retirement Series 334, 336–37 (J. Jefferson Looney ed., 2006).

140. White, *supra* note 42, at 37.

141. *Id.* at 27.

142. Thomas Jefferson once wrote that a statute had granted "the whole executive power" to the capital commissioners and that they stood between Pierre L'Enfant and the president. *See* Observations on L'Enfant's Letter (Dec. 11, 1791), *in* 22 The Papers of Thomas Jefferson 390, 392 (Charles T. Cullen ed., 1986). But this was surely a mistake, for no statute can grant executive power. The Constitution conveys that power to the president and Congress cannot redirect it as it sees fit. Moreover, Washington eventually ousted L'Enfant, notwithstanding Jefferson's claim that Washington could not interfere because L'Enfant was to receive instructions only from the commissioners. All this suggests that Jefferson misspoke. *See infra* text accompanying note 158.

143. *See, e.g.,* Commission, *in* 2 The Papers of John Marshall 41 (Charles T. Cullen & Herbert A. Johnson eds., 1977) (commission from Washington appointing John Marshall as district attorney).

144. Letter from Tobias Lear to Samuel Carleton (Mar. 6, 1790), *excerpted in* 5 The Papers of George Washington: Presidential Series 134 n.2 (Dorothy Twohig et al. eds., 1996).

145. Letter from George Washington to Charlotte S. Hazen (Aug. 31, 1795), *in* 34 The Writings of George Washington 291, 292 (John C. Fitzpatrick ed., 1940).

146. Letter from George Washington to William Tatham (Apr. 14, 1791), *in* 8 The Papers of George Washington: Presidential Series 103 (Mark A. Mastromarino ed., 1999).

147. *See* Letter from George Washington to Mary Katherine Goddard (Jan. 6, 1790), *excerpted in* 4 The Papers of George Washington: Presidential Series, *supra* note 44, at 428.

148. Letter from George Washington to George Walker (Jan. 26, 1797), *in* 35 The Writings of George Washington 375, 375 (John C. Fitzpatrick ed., 1940).

149. Letter from George Washington to Pierre L'Enfant (Dec. 13, 1791), *in* 9 The Papers of George Washington: Presidential Series 281, 282 (Mark A. Mastromarino & Jack D. Warren eds., 2000).

150. Mary S. Austin, Philip Freneau: The Poet of the Revolution: A History of His Life and Times 152–53 (1901).

151. *Id.* at 160–61, 168.

152. Notes of a Conversation with George Washington (May 23, 1793), *in* 26 The Papers of Thomas Jefferson 101, 102 (John Catanzariti ed., 1995).

153. *Id.* at 102.

154. *See* Letter from Thomas Jefferson to Benjamin Latrobe (June 2, 1808), *in* Thomas Jefferson and the National Capital 429, 431 (Saul K. Padover ed., 1946).

155. 1 Op. Att'y Gen. 624–28 (1823).

156. Pacificus No. 1 (June 29, 1793), *in* 15 The Papers of Alexander Hamilton 33, 43 (Harold C. Syrett ed., 1969).

157. *See e.g.*, Letter from Thomas Jefferson to George Hammond (May 15, 1793), *in* 26 The Papers of Thomas Jefferson, *supra* note 152, at 38, 39 (noting that instructions had been given to a "law officer" to prosecute Americans who attacked British interests).

158. Letter from Thomas Jefferson to Pierre Charles L'Enfant (Feb. 27, 1792), *in* 23 The Papers of Thomas Jefferson, *supra* note 47, at 161 (the president regrets "your services must be at an end"); Les Standiford, Washington Burning 145–46 (2008).

159. *See* Letter from George Washington to George Walker (Jan. 26, 1797), *in* 35 The Writings of George Washington, *supra* note 148, at 375, 375; Letter from Washington to the Commissioners of the District of Columbia (Jan. 29, 1797), *in id.* at 378, 379 (giving a copy of Walker's letter to the commissioners and asking them to respond to his charges); Letter from Washington to the Commissioners of the District of Columbia (Feb. 27, 1797), *in id.* at 399, 401 (the president concluding that commissioners had served with merit but also that one commissioner had to move into the district).

160. *See* Letter from George Washington to Henry Knox (Aug. 1, 1792), *in* 10 The Papers of George Washington: Presidential Series, *supra* note 131, at 601, 601–2 (asking Knox to provide information on purchasing, delivering, and accounting for supplies, and noting that he had asked for similar information from Treasury); Letter from George Washington to the Commissioners for the District of Columbia (Mar. 3, 1793), *in* 12 The Papers of George Washington, *supra* note 131, at 250, 251 (advising that commissioners use a "special warrant" procedure as a means of disbursing funds).

161. *See* Letter from Andrew G. Fraunces to George Washington (July 30, 1793), *in* 13 The Papers of George Washington 303, 303–6 (Christine S. Patrick ed., 2007).

162. *See* Letter from Tobias Lear to Andrew G. Fraunces (Aug. 14, 1793), *in id.* at 447.

163. *See* Letter from Alexander Hamilton to George Washington (Aug 9, 1793), *in id.* at 393; Letter from Edmund Randolph to George Washington (Aug. 13, 1793), *in id.* at 442. For a similar presidential intervention, *see* Letter from George Washington to Martha Bland (Aug. 25, 1790), *excerpted in* 6 The Papers of George Washington: Presidential Series 12–13 n.6 (Mark A. Mastromarino ed., 1996) (Washington explaining why a friend's claim against the federal government would not succeed, discussing funds owed Treasury by the friend, and noting that he directed the comptroller to examine issues before spuriously claiming to have acted in his private capacity).

164. Letter from George Washington to Count de Moustier (May 25, 1789), *in* 2 The Papers of George Washington, *supra* note 63, at 389, 390.

165. *See* Letter from Alexander Hamilton to George Washington (Dec. 22, 1790), *in* 7 The Papers of Alexander Hamilton 377, 378 (Harold C. Syrett ed., 1963).

166. *See supra* text accompanying note 130.

167. *See supra* text accompanying note 137.

168. U.S. Const. art. II, § 2 ("The President . . . may require the Opinion, in writing, of the principal Officer in each of the executive Departments, upon any Subject relating to the Duties of their respective Offices.").

169. *See* Lawrence Lessig & Cass R. Sunstein, *The President and the Administration*, 94 Colum. L. Rev. 1, 32–34 (1994).

170. The Federalist No. 74, *supra* note 20, at 377 (Alexander Hamilton).

171. The Federalist No. 72, *supra* note 20, at 366 (Alexander Hamilton).

172. Alexander Hamilton, Opinion on the Constitutionality of an Act to Establish a Bank (Feb. 23, 1791), *in* 7 The Papers of George Washington, *supra* note 132, at 425; Thomas Jefferson, Opinion (Feb. 15, 1791), *in id.* at 348.

173. Henry Barrett Learned, The President's Cabinet: Studies in the Origin, Formation and Structure of an American Institution 382 (1912).

174. *Id.* at 123–24.

175. 4 Debates in the Several State Conventions, *supra* note 119, at 108.

176. *See* Hail to the Chief Administrator, *supra* note 4, at 997.

177. 4 Debates in the Several State Conventions, *supra* note 119, at 110; *see also* Marcus II (Feb. 27, 1788), *in* 16 The Documentary History of the Ratification of the Constitution 242, 246 (John P. Kaminski & Gaspare J. Saladino eds., 1986) ("the President must be *personally responsible* for every thing" and "the President who acts should be responsible for his *conduct*, following advice at his peril").

178. *See* Steven G. Calabresi & Kevin H. Rhodes, *The Structural Constitution: Unitary Executive, Plural Judiciary*, 105 Harv. L. Rev. 1153, 1207 n.262 (1992).

179. James Wilson, Lectures on Law (1790), *in* 1 Collected Works of James Wilson, *supra* note 125, at 730. In The Federalist No. 70, Hamilton also criticizes the use of an executive council. Like Wilson and Iredell, Hamilton recognized that a council often served as a means of concealing faults and avoiding responsibility for executive decisions. *See* The Federalist No. 70, *supra* note 20, at 358–61 (Alexander Hamilton).

180. Akhil Reed Amar, *Some Opinions on the Opinion Clause*, 82 Va. L. Rev. 647, 647 (1996).

181. *See generally, supra* note 4.

182. 1 Annals of Congress 519 (1789).

183. *Id.* at 388, 397, 492–94 (1789) (comments of Vining, Clymer, and Ames, respectively).

184. *Id.* at 481 (1789).

185. *Id.* at 518 (1789).

186. *Id.* at 492 (1789).

187. *Id.* at 493 (1789); *see also id.* at 693 (1789) (another representative saying that officers were necessary to relieve the president of "the inferior duties of his station" so that he could be free of the "minutiae of business" and focus on the "whole machine").

188. *Id.* at 637 (1789).

189. *See New Light on the Decision of 1789, supra* note 4, at 1042, 1049–50.

190. *See, e.g.,* 9 Documentary History of the First Federal Congress, *supra* note 15, at 113 ("I buy a Square Acre of land. I buy the Trees[,] Waters[, and] every thing belonging to it. [T]he executive power belongs to the president. [T]he removing of officers is a Tree on this Acre.") (speech of Oliver Ellsworth).

191. *See, e.g., id.* at 110–12.

192. *New Light on the Decision of 1789, supra* note 4, at 1032–33; Act of July 27, 1789, § 2, 1 Stat. 28, 29.

193. *See* Act of Aug. 7, 1789, § 2, 1 Stat. 49, 50; Act of Sept. 2, 1789, § 7, 1 Stat 65, 67.

194. 10 Annals of Congress 131 (1800); *see also* 2 Annals of Congress 1925 (1791) (Rep. Benson noting that inspectors could be removed at pleasure).

195. *New Light on the Decision of 1789, supra* note 4, at 1065–67. *See also* Letter from Joseph H. Nicholson to Thomas Jefferson (Mar. 27, 1801), *in* 33 The Papers of Thomas Jefferson 469, 470 (Barbara B. Oberg ed., 2006) (noting that "the Executive is authorized to dismiss at Pleasure, all the Officers of Government, Judges excepted").

196. *See* White, *supra* note 42, at 21 n.20 (quoting a 1797 letter from William Smith in which he admits that he was "wrong" during the debates on removal and that Madison was right).

197. In The Federalist No. 77, Hamilton claimed that one advantage of the Senate's role in appointments is that it would have a similar role in the displacing of officers and would thus "contribute to the stability of the administration." The Federalist No. 77, *supra* note 20, at 388 (Alexander Hamilton). This claim was ill considered. First, as noted, Hamilton previously had affirmed that executive officers were to be "superintended" by the president because their statutory functions were constitutionally committed to the executive. They were to be his deputies and assistants. Second, in earlier numbers of The Federalist, Hamilton assumed that officers would be removed when the administration changed. Permitting multiple terms would ensure "the advantage of permanency in a wise system of administration," he said. *Id.*, No. 72, at 367 (Alexander Hamilton). Without such an ability, every new president could "promote a change of men" in the departments and

thereby "occasion a disgraceful and ruinous mutability in the administration." *Id.* If, however, officers could remain in office after the election of a new president because the Senate chose not to remove them (per The Federalist No. 77), the executive's term and reeligibility might little affect the stability of the administration. Hamilton's earlier comments about unstable administration arising from short terms of office are clearly in tension with his terse claim about removal. *Cf.* Jack N. Rakove, Original Meanings: Politics and Ideas in the Making of the Constitution 286 (1996) (labeling Hamilton's removal claim "puzzling").

198. *See* Letter from William Smith to Edward Rutledge (June 21, 1789), *in* 16 Documentary History of the First Federal Congress, Correspondence: First Session 831, 832–33 (Charlene Bangs Bickford et al. eds., 2004) (Hamilton "had informed [Benson] . . . that upon more mature reflection he *had changed his opinion* & was now convinced that the Presidt. alone shod. have the power of removal at pleasure.").

199. *See* Carl Russell Fish, Removal of Officials by the Presidents of the United States, *in* 1 Annual Report of the American Historical Association for the Year 1899, at 65, 69 (1900) (observing that George Washington removed twenty-three officers).

200. Remarks on Monroe's "View of the Conduct of the Executive of the United States" (Mar. 1798), *in* 36 The Writings of George Washington 194, 216 (John C. Fitzpatrick ed., 1941).

201. Myers v. United States, 272 U.S. 52 (1926).

202. Morrison v. Olson, 487 U.S. 654 (1988); Wiener v. United States, 357 U.S. 349 (1958); Humphrey's Ex'r v. United States, 295 U.S. 602 (1935). For a comprehensive history of the removal power, see J. David Alvis, Jeremy D. Bailey, and F. Flagg Taylor IV, The Contested Removal Power, 1789–2010 (2013).

203. Peter L. Strauss, *Overseer, or "The Decider"? The President in Administrative Law*, 75 Geo. Wash. L. Rev. 696, 703–4 (2007).

204. Letter from Thomas Jefferson to George Washington (Mar. 20, 1793), *in* 25 The Papers of Thomas Jefferson 412 (John Catanzariti ed., 1992).

205. Letter from Thomas Jefferson to Destutt de Tracy (Jan. 26, 1811), *in* 3 The Papers of Thomas Jefferson: Retirement Series, *supra* note 139, at 334, 336.

206. Lessig & Sunstein, *supra* note 169, at 34–35, 71–72.

207. *Id.* at 45–46.

208. *Id.* at 71–72.

209. *Id.* at 71.

210. *Id.* at 67–69.

211. *Id.* at 71 & n.289.

212. Jerry L. Mashaw, Creating the Administrative Constitution: The Lost One Hundred Years of American Administrative Law 30 (2012).

213. Id. at 31. Mashaw admits that Washington actually exercised such authority. *Id.* at 55.

214. Steven G. Calabresi & Saikrishna B. Prakash, *The President's Power To Execute the Laws*, 104 Yale L.J. 541, at 566–67 (1994).

215. A Dictionary of the English Language, *supra* note 79 (entry for "Administration").

216. *See, e.g.*, The Federalist No. 72, *supra* note 20, at 366 (Alexander Hamilton) (stating that administration in its most familiar sense involves the activities of executive departments); *Id.*, no. 70, at 354–55 (Alexander Hamilton) (stating that the energy in the executive is necessary for the stable administration of laws); Philadelphiensis IX (Feb. 6, 1788), *in* 16 The Documentary History of the Ratification of the Constitution, *supra* note 177, at 57, 58 (decrying that laws would be administered by a presidential tyrant); 4 Debates in the Several State Conventions, *supra* note 119, at 103 (Davie observing that term limits would ensure that the president would feel the tone of his administration of laws in private life).

217. *E.g.*, Letter from George Washington to John Hawkins Stone (Dec. 23, 1796), *in* 35 The Writings of George Washington, *supra* note 148, at 343, 344.

218. The Essential Meaning of Executive Power, *supra* note 4, at 804–5.

219. Lessig & Sunstein, *supra* note 169, at 27–28.

220. *Id.* at 17.

221. *E.g.*, 18 Journals of the Continental Congress 1774–1789, at 1092 (Gaillard Hunt ed., 1910).

222. *See, e.g.*, 2 Records of the Federal Convention, *supra* note 9, at 53–54 (saying the minister of finance would act in subordination to the president).

223. *See, e.g.*, A Farmer of New Jersey (Nov. 3, 1787), *excerpted in* 13 The Documentary History of the Ratification of the Constitution 558, 559–60 (John P. Kaminski & Gaspare J. Saladino eds., 1981) (proposing to divide the "executive" across three departments, including a "Superintendent of Finance").

224. *See, e.g.*, 1 Annals of Congress 383–84 (1789) (comments of Representatives Boudinot and Benson).

225. *Id.* at 617–18, 624–25.

226. *See* Act of Sept. 11, 1789, § 1, 1 Stat. 67, 67–68.

227. *E.g.*, Expenditures of the Executive Departments (July 5, 1798), *in* 9 Annals of Congress 3597–98 (1798) (report of a committee examining the executive departments' expenditures); 4 Annals of Congress 463–65 (1794) (comments of Rep. Giles on the propriety of Congress examining the operation of the Treasury Department and its "Executive officers").

228. *See* Letter from George Washington to John Jay (June 8, 1789), *in* 30 The Writings of George Washington 344–45 & n.30 (John C. Fitzpatrick ed., 1939) (noting that Washington sought information from the secretary of foreign affairs, secretary of war, and Board of Treasury established by the Continental Congress).

229. *See* Treasury Department Circular to the Collectors of the Customs (Aug. 4, 1793), *in* 15 The Papers of Alexander Hamilton, *supra* note 156, at 178.

230. For a discussion of his actions in the wake of the rebellion, see Chapter 5.

231. *See* Letter from George Washington to Alexander Hamilton (Sept. 24, 1792), *in* 12 The Papers of Alexander Hamilton 424 (Harold C. Syrett ed., 1967).

232. *See* Letter from Alexander Hamilton to George Washington (Dec. 15, 1790), *in* 7 The Papers of Alexander Hamilton, *supra* note 165, at 342 (seeking permission for a Boston collector to take leave to come to the capital).

233. Enclosure from Letter from Alexander Hamilton to George Washington (Mar. 29, 1796), *in* 20 The Papers of Alexander Hamilton 85, 92 (Harold C. Syrett ed., 1974). *See also* The Federalist No. 72, *supra* note 20, at 366 (Alexander Hamilton) (discussing arrangements of financial plans).

234. *See* Letter from Tobias Lear to Alexander Hamilton (Mar. 14, 1793), *in* 12 The Papers of George Washington: Presidential Series, *supra* note 131, at 318 (the president allowing Hamilton to decide whether to remit the penalty).

235. Opinion on the Constitutionality of an Act to Establish a Bank (Feb. 23, 1971), *in* 7 The Papers of George Washington, *supra* note 132, at 425, 425.

236. Lessig & Sunstein, *supra* note 169, at 17.

237. 1 Annals of Congress 635–36 (1789).

238. *Id.* at 636 (1789).

239. *Id.* at 636, 638 (1789).

240. *Id.* at 636 (1789).

241. *Id.* at 639 (1789).

242. *See* Letter from George Washington to Martha Bland (Aug. 25, 1790), *excerpted in* 6 The Papers of George Washington: Presidential Series, *supra* note 163, at 12–13 n.6 (noting that he directed the comptroller to examine a private citizen's claims and accounting issues).

Chapter 9. "Not a Single Privilege Is Annexed to His Character"

1. 1 Annals of Congress 567 (1789).

2. *Id.* at 566 (1789). Smith later changed his mind. *See* Leonard D. White, The Federalists: A Study in Administrative History 21 n.20 (1948) (quoting a 1797 letter from William Smith in which he admits that he was "wrong" during the debates on removal and that James Madison was right).

3. Parts of this chapter draw from Saikrishna Bangalore Prakash, *The Imbecilic Executive*, 99 Va. L. Rev. 1361 (2013) and Saikrishna Bangalore Prakash, *A Critical Comment on the Constitutionality of Executive Privilege*, 83 Minn. L. Rev. 1143 (1999).

4. 1 William Blackstone, Commentaries on the Laws of England 269–70 (University of Chicago 1979) (1765).

5. U.S. Const. amend. I ("Congress shall make no law respecting an establishment of religion.").

6. U.S. Const. art. VI, cl. 3 ("[B]ut no religious Test shall ever be required as a Qualification to any Office or public Trust under the United States.").

7. 1 Blackstone, *supra* note 4, at 261–63.

8. U.S. Const. art. I, § 9, cl. 8 ("No Title of Nobility shall be granted by the United States.").

9. Thomas Jefferson, Third Draft of the Virginia Constitution, art. II (1776), *in* 1 The Papers of Thomas Jefferson 356, 359–60 (Julian P. Boyd ed., 1950).

10. *Id.* at 360.

11. The clause forbidding a statutory bar on the "migration of" persons before 1808, *see* U.S. Const. art. I, § 9, cl. 1 ("The Migration or Importation of such Persons as any of the States now existing shall think proper to admit, shall not be prohibited by the Congress prior to the Year one thousand eight hundred and eight."), suggests that Congress has authority over migration via the Commerce Clause. *See, e.g.*, 3 The Records of the Federal Convention of 1787, at 160–61 (Max Farrand rev. ed., 1966) [hereinafter Records of the Federal Convention] (James Wilson claiming that Congress cannot tax the migration of European whites, indicating that "migration" covered nonslave immigrants); 4 The Debates in the Several State Conventions on the Adoption of the Federal Constitution 102 (Jonathan Elliot ed., 2d ed. 1836) [hereinafter Debates in the Several State Conventions] (James Iredell claiming that the clause covers the migration of free people).

12. The Federalist No. 69, at 354 (Alexander Hamilton) (Garry Wills ed., 1982).

13. *See* N.Y. Const. art. III (1777); Mass. Const. pt. 2, ch. I, § 1, art. II (1780); S.C. Const. art. VII (1776).

14. *See* N.Y. Const. art. XIX (1777); Pa. Const. § 20 (1776); Vt. Const. ch. II, § 18 (1777).

15. Youngstown Sheet & Tube Co. v. Sawyer, 343 U.S. 579, 587 (1952).

16. *See* Del. Const. art. 7 (1776); Md. Const. art. XXXIII (1776); N.C. Const. art. XIX (1776); Pa. Const. § 20 (1776).

17. John Locke, Two Treatises of Government and A Letter Concerning Toleration 172 (Yale University Press, 2003) (1689).

18. *Id.*

19. Message from Abraham Lincoln to Congress in Special Session (July 4, 1861), *in* 4 The Collected Works of Abraham Lincoln 421, 430 (Roy P. Basler ed., 1953).

20. Letter from Abraham Lincoln to Albert G. Hodges (Apr. 4, 1864), *in id.*, vol. 7, at 281.

21. *See* Michael Stokes Paulsen, *The Constitution of Necessity*, 79 Notre Dame L. Rev. 1257, 1257 (2004).

22. 1 Blackstone, *supra* note 4, at 244.

23. *See* Theodore Roosevelt, Theodore Roosevelt: An Autobiography 357 (1920).

24. Akhil Reed Amar & Neal Kumar Katyal, Commentary, *Executive Privileges and Immunities: The Nixon and Clinton Cases*, 108 Harv. L. Rev. 701, 706 n.24 (1995).

25. *See, e.g.*, Akhil Reed Amar, America's Constitution: A Biography 122 (2005) (praising Lincoln's claim of suspension authority and characterizing it as a claim of temporary unilateral authority); William F. Duker, A Constitutional History of Habeas Corpus 144–45 (1980) (arguing that the president has authority to respond to sudden attacks and can suspend the privilege when Congress cannot be consulted); Daniel Farber, Lincoln's Constitution 161–63 (2003) (arguing that the president and Congress had concurrent

power to suspend and that the president's power arises from his power to respond to sudden attacks); Amanda L. Tyler, *Suspension as an Emergency Power*, 118 Yale L.J. 600, 690 (2009).

26. Margaret Burnham MacMillan, The War Governors in the American Revolution 61 (1943).

27. *Id.* at 203–4, 259–60.

28. *Id.* at 76.

29. *Id.* at 73.

30. *Id.* at 86.

31. 1 William Wirt Henry, Patrick Henry: Life, Correspondence and Speeches 506 (1891).

32. MacMillan, *supra* note 26, at 80.

33. 1 Dumas Malone, Jefferson and His Time: Jefferson the Virginian 361 (1948).

34. MacMillan, *supra* note 26, at 82.

35. *Id.* at 92.

36. *Id.*

37. *Id.* at 61.

38. *See* Ga. Const. art. XX (1777); Md. Const. art. XXIX (1776); Mass. Const. pt. 2, ch. II, § 1, art. V (1780); N.H. Const. pt. 2 (1784); N.Y. Const. art. XVIII (1777); Pa. Const. §20 (1776); S.C. Const. art. VIII (1776); Va. Const. (1776); Vt. Const. ch. II, § 18 (1777).

39. *See* Md. Const. art. XXXIII (1776) (the governor may impose thirty-day embargoes during a recess of the general assembly in order to prevent the departure of ships and the export of commodities); S.C. Const. art. XXXV (1778) (the governor may impose thirty-day embargoes during a recess of the legislature); N.C. Const. art. XIX (1776) (the governor, with the consent of the council, may impose thirty-day embargoes during a recess of the legislature); Del. Const. art. 7 (1776) (the president, with the consent of the council, may impose thirty-day embargoes during a recess of the legislature); Pa. Const. § 20 (1776) (the executive council may impose thirty-day embargoes during a recess of the House).

40. MacMillan, *supra* note 26, at 204.

41. Letter from George Clinton to Hugh Hughes (Mar. 12, 1778), *in* 3 Public Papers of George Clinton 28 (Hugh Hastings ed., 1900).

42. Letter from George Clinton to Hugh Hughes (Mar. 17, 1778), *in id.* at 53.

43. MacMillan, *supra* note 26, at 99.

44. *Id.* at 202.

45. 10 The Statutes at Large; Being a Collection of All the Laws of Virginia, 1779–1781, at 478 (William Waller Hening ed., 1822).

46. 6 Journals of the Continental Congress 1774–1789, at 1045–46 (Dec. 27, 1776) (Worthington Chauncey Ford ed., 1906).

47. 8 Journals of the Continental Congress 1774–1789, at 705, 752 (Sept. 17, 1777) (Worthington Chauncey Ford ed., 1907).

48. *Id.*

49. The Federalist No. 23, *supra* note 12, at 112 (Alexander Hamilton) (emphasis omitted).

50. *Id.* No. 30, at 145 (Alexander Hamilton); *id.* No. 31, at 149 (Alexander Hamilton).

51. *Id.* No. 74, at 378 (Alexander Hamilton).

52. U.S. Const. art. II, § 3.

53. Act of May 2, 1792, § 2, 1 Stat. 264, 264.

54. William Hogeland, The Whiskey Rebellion: George Washington, Alexander Hamilton, and the Frontier Rebels Who Challenged America's Newfound Sovereignty 185–86, 196, 206 (2006).

55. Act of May 2, 1792, § 2, 1 Stat. 264.

56. *See* Saikrishna Prakash, *A Two-Front War*, 93 Cornell L. Rev. 197, 213–14 (2007); *see also supra* Chapter 7.

57. 7 John Alexander Carroll & Mary Wells Ashworth, George Washington: First in Peace 132 (1957).

58. U.S. Const. art. II, § 3.

59. Letter from Thomas Jefferson to George Washington (Oct. 17, 1793), *in* 14 The Papers of George Washington: Presidential Series 226, 227 (David R. Hoth ed., 2008); Letter from James Madison to George Washington (Oct. 24, 1793), *in id.* at 278, 279.

60. Letter from Alexander Hamilton to George Washington (Oct. 24, 1793), *in id.* at 270, 271; Letter from Edmund Randolph to George Washington (Nov. 2, 1793), *in id.* at 303, 305–6.

61. Letter from Jonathan Trumbull, Jr. to George Washington (Oct. 3, 1793), *in id.* at 159.

62. During the Revolution, a similar question arose in New Jersey, where it was understood that the governor could not convene the Assembly wherever he wished, despite the danger posed by the British. *See* N.J. Const. art. V (1776) (authorizing the Assembly to empower the Speaker to convene the Assembly). The Assembly ceded the governor statutory authority to change its meeting place. MacMillan, *supra* note 26, at 229.

63. *See* Charles F. Jenkins, Washington in Germantown 88 (1905).

64. Act of Apr. 3, 1794, 1 Stat. 353.

65. 1 Annals of Congress 537 (1789).

66. *Id.*

67. Letter from Thomas Jefferson to John Dickinson (Aug. 9, 1803), *in* 10 The Works of Thomas Jefferson 28, 29 (Paul Leicester Ford ed., 1905).

68. Letter from Thomas Jefferson to John B. Colvin (Sept. 20, 1810), *in* 11 The Works of Thomas Jefferson 146, 148–49 (Paul Leicester Ford ed., 1905) (emphasis omitted).

69. Youngstown Sheet & Tube Co. v. Sawyer, 343 U.S. 579, 650 (1952) (Jackson, J., concurring). To bolster his point, Jackson noted that the German government, using an emergency provision in the Weimar Constitution, had declared an emergency over 250 times over thirteen years. *Id.* at 651.

70. Much of this section is drawn from Saikrishna Bangalore Prakash, *The Great Suspender's Unconstitutional Suspension of the Great Writ*, 3 Alb. Gov't L. Rev. 575 (2010).

71. The judicial writ of habeas corpus requires the custodian of a prisoner to justify to a court the grounds for the detention. If the custodian fails to justify the detention, the court orders the prisoner's release.

72. *See* Ex Parte Merryman, 17 F. Cas. 144, 148–49 (C.C.D. Md. 1861) (No. 9,487).

73. U.S. Const. art. I, § 9, cl. 2 ("The Privilege of the Writ of Habeas Corpus shall not be suspended, unless when in Cases of Rebellion or Invasion the public Safety may require it.").

74. Message from Abraham Lincoln to Congress in Special Session (July 4, 1861), *in* 4 The Collected Works of Abraham Lincoln, *supra* note 19, at 430–31.

75. *Id.* at 431.

76. Letter from Abraham Lincoln to Matthew Birchard and others (June 29, 1863), *in* 6 The Collected Works of Abraham Lincoln, *supra* note 19, at 303.

77. In the summer of 1861, Congress provided that all presidential acts, proclamations, and orders relating to the military, militia, and volunteers were "approved and in all respects legalized and made valid." Act of Aug. 6, 1861, § 3, 12 Stat. 326, 326. But this statute was not generally thought to validate the suspensions.

78. Act of Mar. 3, 1863, 12 Stat. 755.

79. *See* Cong. Globe, 37th Cong., 3d. Sess. 1186 (1863) (comments of Sen. Trumbull) (noting that proponents and opponents of an executive suspension power might vote for the bill because it skirted the constitutional question of who could suspend).

80. Proclamation No. 7, 3 Stat. 734 (Sept. 15, 1863).

81. Mark A. Thomson, A Constitutional History of England, 1642 to 1801, at 286 (1938).

82. *Id.* at 286–87.

83. *Id.* at 415 n.5.

84. 1 Blackstone, *supra* note 4, at 132 (emphasis omitted).

85. Tyler, *supra* note 25, at 622–27.

86. Mass. Const. pt. 2, ch. VI, art. VII (1780). The New Hampshire Constitution contained a similar provision. N.H. Const. pt. 1, art. XXIX (1784) ("The power of suspending the laws, or the execution of them, ought never to be exercised but by the legislature, or by authority derived therefrom, to be exercised in such particular cases only as the legislature shall expressly provide for.").

87. 2 Records of the Federal Convention, *supra* note 11, at 341.

88. 2 Debates in the Several State Conventions, *supra* note 11, at 108–9; *see also id.* at 137 (another representative arguing that section 9 empowered Congress to suspend).

89. *Id.*, vol. 3, at 102, 449, 464.

90. *Id.* at 203.

91. 2 The Documentary History of the Ratification of the Constitution 435 (Merrill Jensen ed., 1976).

92. 1 Debates in the Several State Conventions, *supra* note 11, at 330.

93. *E.g.*, Brutus IX (Jan. 17, 1788), *in* 15 The Documentary History of the Ratification of the Constitution 393, 394 (John P. Kaminski & Gaspare J. Saladino eds., 1984).

94. Editorial, *To the Convention of Massachusetts*, Am. Herald, Jan. 14, 1788, *in* 5 The Documentary History of the Ratification of the Constitution 709, 712 (John P. Kaminski et al. eds., 1998).

95. James F. Johnston, The Suspending Power and the Writ of Habeas Corpus 45–46 (1862).

96. *Id.* at 44–45. After leaving office, Jefferson complained that "[h]abeas corpus was left to the discretion of Congress." Thomas Jefferson, Autobiography (1821), *in* 1 The Works of Thomas Jefferson 3, 119 (Paul Leicester Ford, ed., 1904). It never seems to have occurred to him that the president also might suspend.

97. Amar, *supra* note 25, at 122; Duker, *supra* note 25, at 145–46; Farber, *supra* note 25, at 162–63.

98. *See* 9 Journals of the Continental Congress 1774–1789, at 784 (Worthington Chauncey Ford ed., 1907).

99. *Id.; see also* 5 Journals of the Continental Congress 1774–1789, at 693 (Worthington Chauncey Ford ed., 1906) (all those not owing allegiance to United States and "lurking as spies in or about the fortifications or encampments" of the United States may "suffer death . . . by sentence of a court martial"); 10 Journals of the Continental Congress 1774–1789, at 204–5 (Worthington Chauncey Ford ed., 1908) (providing that murderers and kidnappers of loyal citizens could be tried by court-martial if offense occurred within seventy miles of army encampment).

100. *See, e.g.*, General Orders (Mar. 1, 1778), *in* 11 The Writings of George Washington 8, 11 (John C. Fitzpatrick ed., 1934) (noting several inhabitants were found guilty and given a sentence of lashing or death); Letter from Gen. George Washington to Major Gen. John Armstrong (Mar. 27, 1778), *in id.* at 157, 158 (noting that an inhabitant had been executed for helping sell horses to the enemy).

101. *See* Letter from Gen. George Washington to Brigadier Gen. John Lacey, Jr. (Apr. 11, 1778), *in id.* at 243, 244 (stating that because the law had expired, further apprehensions and courts-martial of inhabitants were not possible); Letter from Gen. George Washington to Brigadier Gen. William Smallwood (May 19, 1778), *in id.* at 420–21 (declaring that because an inhabitant had been caught outside a thirty-mile perimeter around army headquarters, he could not be tried by court-martial for spying, but suggesting that if he was guilty of kidnapping, he might be tried by court-martial under a separate congressional resolve); Letter from Gen. George Washington to Col. Israel Shreve (Apr. 6, 1778), *in id.* at 222 (stating that an inhabitant could not be tried by court-martial because he was outside the congressionally imposed geographic limit).

102. MacMillan, *supra* note 26, at 86.

103. *See* Letter from President Joseph Reed to Gen. George Washington (June 5, 1780), *in* 2 Life and Correspondence of Joseph Reed 209, 211 (William B. Reed ed., 1847) (noting that the statute authorizing the executive council to declare martial law "gives us a power" to do what is necessary, implying that in the absence of a statute, the council could not do what is necessary).

104. *See* MacMillan, *supra* note 26, at 176.

105. *See supra* Chapter 7.

106. Hogeland, *supra* note 54, at 215.

107. Letter from Alexander Hamilton to Henry Lee (Oct. 20, 1794), *in* 17 The Papers of Alexander Hamilton 331, 333 (Harold C. Syrett ed., 1972) (Hamilton conveying Washington's instructions).

108. Letter from Alexander James Dallas to Andrew Jackson (July 1, 1815), *in* 3 The Papers of Andrew Jackson 375, 376–77 (Harold D. Moser et al. eds., 1991).

109. David Frost with Bob Zelnick, Frost/Nixon: Behind the Scenes of the Nixon Interviews 89 (2007).

110. 1 Blackstone, *supra* note 4, at 238.

111. Adam Tomkins, *Crown Privileges, in* The Nature of the Crown: A Legal and Political Analysis 171, 176 (Maurice Sunkin & Sebastian Payne eds., 1999) [hereinafter The Nature of the Crown].

112. Tobin v. R (1864) 143 Eng. Rep. 1148 (C.P.) 1165.

113. Martin Loughlin, *The State, the Crown and the Law, in* The Nature of the Crown, *supra* note 111, at 33, 60.

114. Tobin v. R (1864) 143 Eng. Rep. 1148 (C.P.) 1165.

115. *Id.*

116. 9 The Documentary History of the Ratification of the Constitution 1092, 1126 (John P. Kaminski & et al. eds., 1990).

117. 9 Documentary History of the First Federal Congress: The Diary of William Maclay and Other Notes on Senate Debates 168 (Kenneth R. Bowling & Helen E. Veit eds., 1988) [hereinafter 9 Documentary History of the First Federal Congress].

118. *Id.* at 112 (emphasis omitted).

119. Letter from Thomas Jefferson to George Hay (June 20, 1807), *in* 9 The Writings of Thomas Jefferson 59, 60 (Paul Leicester Ford ed., 1898).

120. The Federalist No. 69, *supra* note 12, at 348 (Alexander Hamilton); *id.* No. 77, at 392 (Alexander Hamilton).

121. 3 Joseph Story, Commentaries on the Constitution of the United States 419 (1833).

122. 2 Records of the Federal Convention, *supra* note 11, at 503.

123. 2 The Documentary History of the Ratification of the Constitution, *supra* note 91, at 495.

124. *Id.* at 579. It should be noted that at the Constitutional Convention, Wilson regarded the enumeration of legislative privileges as unwise because it suggested that the other entities enjoyed none. 2 Records of the Federal Convention, *supra* note 11, at 503 (the enumeration of legislative privileges "might beget doubts as to the power of other public bodies, as Courts &c. Every Court is the judge of its own privileges.").

125. 4 Debates in the Several State Conventions, *supra* note 11, at 109. Iredell held the view that all officers could be prosecuted before impeachment.

126. *Id.* at 47.

127. Cassius VI (Dec. 21, 1787), *in* 5 The Documentary History of the Ratification of the Constitution, *supra* note 94, at 500.

128. An American Citizen I (Sept. 26, 1787), *in* 2 The Documentary History of the Ratification of the Constitution, *supra* note 91, at 138, 141 (emphasis in original).

129. Notes of a Debate in the Senate of the United States (1789), *in* 3 The Works of John Adams 407, 409 (Charles F. Adams ed., 1851).

130. *Id.* at 409–10.

131. 9 Documentary History of the First Federal Congress, *supra* note 117, at 168 (emphasis added, brackets omitted).

132. William Rawle, A View of the Constitution of the United States of America 168–70 (2d ed. 1829).

133. 1 W. Winterbotham, An Historical, Geographical, Commercial, and Philosophical View of the United States of America 235 (1795).

134. Del. Const. art. 13 (1776) (providing that the president could be impeached only when no longer in office, thereby implying that he could not be proceeded against in any way while in office); Va. Const. (1776) (providing the same for its governor). South Carolina provided that the state president (and a few others) enjoyed the protections previously granted to royal officials. S.C. Const. art XXXI (1776). Madison knew of such provisions. *See* The Federalist No. 39, *supra* note 12, at 191 (James Madison).

135. *See* Const. of France, tit. III, ch. II, § 1 (II, VIII) (1791), *in* Benjamin Flower, The French Constitution, With Remarks on Some of its Principal Articles 38–39 (2d ed. 1792) (declaring the king "sacred and inviolable" and providing that he may be proceeded against as an ordinary citizen, even for official acts, if he abdicates); Const. of Poland, art. VII (1791) (declaring the king "sacred and inviolable" and not liable to being held legally responsible for his actions), *in* Stephen Jones, The History of Poland, From its Origin as a Nation to the Commencement of the Year 1795, at 382 (1795).

136. *See, e.g.,* Act of May 2, 1792, § 1, 1 Stat. 264, 264 (making it lawful for the president to summon the militia when the nation is invaded or under imminent threat); Act of Apr. 18, 1796, § 5, 1 Stat. 452, 453 (authorizing the president to pay Indian agents).

137. *See, e.g.,* Amar & Katyal, *supra* note 24, at 714 (arguing for the tolling of suits against the president); *see also* Jones v. Clinton, 869 F. Supp. 690, 698–99 (E.D. Ark. 1994).

138. U.S. Const. art. I, § 8, cl. 17 ("To exercise exclusive Legislation in all Cases whatsoever, over such District (not exceeding ten Miles square) as may, by Cession of particular states, and the Acceptance of Congress, become the Seat of the Government of the United States.").

139. Letter from George Washington to James Mercer (Apr. 4, 1789), *in* 30 The Writings of George Washington 270, 271 (John C. Fitzpatrick ed., 1939).

140. Letter from George Washington to Thomas Smith (Sept. 23, 1789), *in id.* at 410.

141. Letter from George Washington to Reuben Slaughter (Feb. 25, 1792), *in* 31 The Writings of George Washington 485, 485–86 (John C. Fitzpatrick ed., 1939).

142. Letter from George Washington to Bushrod Washington (Jan. 8, 1792), *in id.* at 455.

143. Letter from George Washington to John Marshall (Mar. 17, 1789), *in* 30 The Writings of George Washington, *supra* note 139, at 231, 231–32. Washington surely knew that any suit would continue while he was president.

144. Letter from George Washington to John Francis Mercer (July 23, 1792), *in* 32 The Writings of George Washington 89, 91 (John C. Fitzpatrick ed., 1939). Apparently, Washington had sold the lands as executor of the estate of John Mercer. Frank E. Grizzard, Jr., George Washington: A Biographical Companion 217–18 (2002).

145. Letter from George Washington to John Francis Mercer (July 23, 1792), *in* 32 The Writings of George Washington, *supra* note 144, at 91.

146. Letter from George Washington to Bushrod Washington (Apr. 30, 1794), *in* 33 The Writings of George Washington 347 (John C. Fitzpatrick ed., 1940).

147. Letter from George Washington to James Keith (July 17, 1796), *in* 35 The Writings of George Washington 141 (John C. Fitzpatrick ed., 1940).

148. Notice, London Gazette, Dec. 17, 1796, at 1222.

149. Letter from George Washington to Bushrod Washington (Feb. 10, 1796), *in* 34 The Writings of George Washington 454, 456 (John C. Fitzpatrick ed., 1940).

150. Notice, London Gazette, Dec. 17, 1796, at 1222.

151. Ronan E. Degnan, Livingston v. Jefferson—*A Freestanding Footnote*, 75 Calif. L. Rev. 115, 117 n.10, 123 (1987); *see generally*, Albert J. Beveridge, *The Batture Controversy*, 17 Litig., Spring 1991, at 39.

152. Mark J. Rozell, Executive Privilege: The Dilemma of Secrecy and Democratic Accountability 49–53 (1994).

153. *Id.* at 49.

154. *See* Ralph K. Winter, Jr., Watergate and the Law: Political Campaigns and Presidential Power 55 (1974).

155. Raoul Berger, Executive Privilege: A Constitutional Myth 28 (1974).

156. *See, e.g.*, The Federalist No. 70, *supra* note 12, at 356 (Alexander Hamilton) (arguing that "[d]ecision, activity, secrecy, and dispatch will generally characterise the proceedings of one man, in a much more eminent degree, than the proceedings of any greater number").

157. *See* A Critical Comment on the Constitutionality of Executive Privilege, *supra* note 3, at 1176.

158. *See supra* note 124 and accompanying text.

159. *See supra* note 125 and accompanying text.

160. Daniel N. Hoffman, Governmental Secrecy and the Founding Fathers: A Study in Constitutional Controls 70–71 (1981).

161. *See* Memoranda of Consultations with the President (Mar. 31, 1792), *in* 23 The Papers of Thomas Jefferson 258, 262 (Charles T. Cullen ed., 1990).

162. *Id.* (Apr. 2).

163. *Id.*

164. 3 Annals of Congress 536 (1792).

165. *See* Abraham D. Sofaer, War, Foreign Affairs and Constitutional Power: The Origins 82 (1976).

166. Berger, *supra* note 155, at 168–69; Hoffman, *supra* note 160, at 74–76.

167. Berger, *supra* note 155, at 169 n.34.

168. *See* Louis Fisher, *Congressional Access to Information: Using Legislative Will and Leverage*, 52 Duke L.J. 323, 400–401 (2002).

169. 4 Annals of Congress 34 (1794).

170. Hoffman, *supra* note 160, at 104–5, 112–15.

171. *Id.* at 116.

172. 4 Annals of Congress 38 (1794).

173. Secretary Knox said that none of the correspondence should be provided to the Senate. Attorney General Randolph stated that "all the correspondence proper, from its nature, to be communicated to the Senate, should be sent; but that what the President thinks improper, should not be sent." Hamilton agreed with Knox that the president need not send anything, but that it was fine to send some correspondence. Cabinet Opinion (Jan. 28, 1794), *in* 15 The Papers of George Washington: Presidential Series 141 (Christine S. Patrick ed., 2009).

174. 4 Annals of Congress 56 (1794).

175. Hoffman, *supra* note 160, at 112.

176. Rozell, *supra* note 152, at 35.

177. Sofaer, *supra* note 165, at 81.

178. *Id.* at 84.

179. Letter from William Bradford to George Washington (Jan. 1794), *in* 15 The Papers of George Washington: Presidential Series, *supra* note 173, at 166, 167.

180. 5 Annals of Congress 400–401 (1796).

181. *Id.* at 424 (1796).

182. *Id.* at 759 (1789).

183. *Id.* at 760 (1789).

184. *Id.*

185. *Id.*

186. *Id.*

187. *Id.* at 762 (1789).

188. *Id.* at 761 (1789).

189. *Id.* at 760 (1789).

190. *Id.* at 771 (1789).

191. *Id.* at 771–72 (1789).

192. *Id.* at 782–83 (1789).

193. John C. Yoo, *The First Claim: The Burr Trial*, United States v. Nixon, *and Presidential Power*, 83 Minn. L. Rev. 1435, 1474 (1999).

194. This is not to say that Jefferson was submissive in complying with the subpoena. Though he fully complied with the first subpoena, in response to the second, he redacted

some information from a letter. He was able to do this because Marshall's opinion seemed to contemplate that the executive might make unilateral redactions. These redactions were to stand unless "essential" for the defense. United States v. Burr, 25 F. Cas. 30, 192 (C.C.D. Va. 1807) (No. 14,692D). John Yoo notes that neither Burr nor Marshall objected to the rescissions. Yoo, *supra* note 193, at 1463–64. Burr's failure to object suggests that he did not believe the redacted portions were absolutely necessary.

195. *See* 50 U.S.C. app. §§ 501–96 (2006 & Supp. III 2010).

196. *Cf.* Akhil Reed Amar, *Nixon's Shadow*, 83 Minn. L. Rev. 1405, 1408 (1999) ("The Constitution and laws nowhere demanded that [the defendant] must be prosecuted; they merely required that *if* prosecuted, he be given exculpatory evidence. . . . it was left wholly up to [the president] to choose which was more important to him—getting [the defendant] convicted, or keeping confidential communications secret.").

Chapter 10. The "Combined Authority of Execution and Legislation"

1. 1 Jacques Necker, An Essay on the True Principles of Executive Power in Great States 4 (1792) (emphasis omitted).

2. Cato, Essay IV (Nov. 8, 1787), *in* 19 The Documentary History of the Ratification of the Constitution 195, 198 (John P. Kaminski et al. eds., 2009).

3. 1 William Blackstone, Commentaries on the Laws of England 85, 149 (University of Chicago 1979) (1765).

4. *Id.* at 174.

5. Evarts Boutell Greene, The Provincial Governor in the English Colonies of North America 149–51 (1898); Joseph E. Kallenbach, The American Chief Executive: The Presidency and the Governorship 21–22 (1966).

6. *See e.g.*, Pa. Const. § 20 (1776); N.Y. Const. art. XVIII (1776); Va. Const. (1776). *See* Mass. Const. pt. 2, ch. II, § 1, art. V (1780) and N.H. Const. pt. II (1784) for examples of an executive's power to convene the legislature at a particular location.

7. *But see* Pa. Const. § 20 (1776); Vt. Const. ch. II, § XI (1786). Kallenbach notes that many state executives made legislative recommendations anyway. Kallenbach, *supra* note 5, at 23.

8. Kallenbach, *supra* note 5, at 22. *But see* Mass. Const. pt. 2, ch. II, § 1, arts. V–VI (1780) (granting authority to adjourn and prorogue); N.H. Const. pt. II (1784) (same); N.Y. Const. art. XVIII (1777) (granting authority to prorogue for a limited time).

9. Kallenbach, *supra* note 5, at 24.

10. Mass. Const. pt. 2, ch. I, § 1, art. II (1780).

11. N.Y. Const. art. III (1777).

12. S.C. Const. art. VII (1776).

13. *See* N.H. Const. pt. II (1784) (the executive president served as the Senate's presiding officer, with full voting privileges); N.J. Const. art. VII (1776) (the governor presided over a legislative council, wielding a vote to break ties); Vt. Const. ch. II, §§ X, XVI (1786) (the governor chaired the executive council, which had the right to propose amendments and delay the enactment of legislation).

14. U.S. Const. amend. XX, § 2.

15. The clause seems to have originated in Charles Pinckney's plan. *See* 3 The Records of the Federal Convention of 1787, at 606 (Max Farrand rev. ed., 1966) [hereinafter Records of the Federal Convention]. Pinckney may have borrowed the language from New York's constitution. *See* N.Y. Const. art. XVIII (1777).

16. Letter from Alexander Hamilton to George Washington (Oct. 24, 1793), *in* 14 The Papers of George Washington: Presidential Series 270, 271 (David R. Hoth ed., 2008) (emphasis omitted).

17. Letter from Edmund J. Randolph to George Washington (Nov. 2, 1793), *in id.* at 303, 305.

18. Kallenbach, *supra* note 5, at 325.

19. 1 Journal of the Executive Proceedings of the Senate of the United States of America at 79–80 (1791), 137–38 (1793), 233–34 (1797) [hereinafter Journal of Executive Proceedings].

20. In 1891, Justice Samuel Miller claimed, "The principal exercise of this power has been in proclamations by which the President has called the Senate together at the close of a session of Congress, for the purpose of considering appointments to office, and sometimes treaties." Samuel F. Miller, Lectures on the Constitution of the United States 170 (1891).

21. 1 Journal of Executive Proceedings, *supra* note 19, at 137–38 (1793) (noting that Washington had summoned Senate to a special session to commence on March 4, 1793; that he took the oath of office in front of the Senate; and that they approved of his nominations); *id.* at 233–35 (1797) (noting that on March 1, 1797, Washington summoned Senate to a special session to commence on March 4, 1797, so that it could receive any communications from the president, and that John Adams took the oath of office that day).

22. *See* 2 David K. Watson, The Constitution of the United States 1001–2 (1910) (noting that outgoing presidents often summoned the Senate on the first day of a successor's term so that it could act on the new president's nominations).

23. 1 Journal of Executive Proceedings, *supra* note 19, at 177–78 (1795).

24. *See generally id.* at 177–92 (1795).

25. *See* Cato, Essay VII (Jan. 3, 1788), *in* 20 The Documentary History of the Ratification of the Constitution 572 (John P. Kaminski et al. eds., 2004).

26. Letter from James Madison to George Washington (Oct. 24, 1793), *in* 14 The Papers of George Washington: Presidential Series, *supra* note 16, at 278–79; Letter from Thomas Jefferson to George Washington (Oct. 17, 1793), *in id.* at 226, 227.

27. Letter from Alexander Hamilton to George Washington (Oct. 24, 1793), *in id.* at 270, 271; Letter from Edmund Randolph to George Washington (Oct. 24, 1793), *in id.* at 281–82.

28. Letter from Jonathan Trumbull to George Washington (Oct. 2, 1793), *in id.* at 159.

29. *See* Charles F. Jenkins, Washington in Germantown 88 (1905).

30. *But see* Letter from Edmund J. Randolph to George Washington (Oct. 24, 1793), *in* 14 The Papers of George Washington: Presidential Series, *supra* note 16, at 281, 282 (noting that the 1790 Pennsylvania Constitution had a similar provision and that Pennsylvania's governor was planning to summon the assembly to Germantown).

31. S.C. Const. art. XII (1778).

32. Mass. Const. pt. 2, ch. II, § 1, art. V (1780); N.H. Const. pt. II (1784).

33. *Cf.* Del. Const. art. 8 (1776) ("The president may by summons convene the privy council at any time when the public exigencies may require, and at such place as he shall think most convenient, when and where they are to attend accordingly.").

34. Act of Apr. 3, 1794, 1 Stat. 353.

35. Letter from Edmund J. Randolph to George Washington (Nov. 2, 1793), *in* 14 The Papers of George Washington: Presidential Series, *supra* note 16, at 303, 305.

36. *Id.*

37. *See, e.g.,* Mass. Const. pt. 2, ch. II, § 1, art. V (1780).

38. *See* An American Citizen III (Sept. 29, 1787), *in* 13 The Documentary History of the Ratification of the Constitution 272–73 (John P. Kaminski & Gaspare J. Saladino eds., 1981).

39. U.S. Const. art. II, § 3. This power was apparently borrowed from the Massachusetts Constitution. *See* 10 The Documentary History of the Ratification of the Constitution 1260–61 (John P. Kaminski & Gaspare J. Saladino eds., 1993). The Massachusetts Constitution was a little clearer about the scope of the adjournment power. Mass. Const. pt. 2, ch. II, §1, art. VI ("In cases of disagreement between the two houses, with regard to the necessity, expediency, or time of adjournment or prorogation, the governor, with advice of the council, shall have a right to adjourn or prorogue the general court, not exceeding ninety days, as he shall determine the public good shall require.").

40. *See* 10 The Documentary History of the Ratification of the Constitution, *supra* note 39, at 1296 (Madison describing how if the Senate refused to adjourn for more than three days when the House sought such an adjournment, the president could adjourn both); *see also id.* at 1260 (Madison suggesting that should Senate not agree to an adjournment, the president could intervene). For a similar view after ratification, *see* Jefferson's Opinion on the Constitutionality of the Residence Bill (July 15, 1790), *in* 17 The Papers of Thomas Jefferson 194, 196 (Julian P. Boyd, ed., 1965) (the "right of adjournment" is taken away from Congress when there is "obstinacy or a difference of object" about where to meet or when).

41. Because each chamber has the power to unilaterally adjourn for periods of less than three days, U.S. Const. art. I, § 5, cl. 4, disagreements can arise only if the adjournment is to last longer than three days.

42. 2 Watson, *supra* note 22, at 1003 ("The President has never had occasion to exercise the power conferred upon him by this section, of adjourning Congress to such time as he should think proper, because the two Houses disagreed in regard to the time of adjournment."); *see also* Kallenbach, *supra* note 5, at 332 (claiming that this power has never been used). Since the time when Kallenbach wrote (1965), there does not appear to have been any instance of the president adjourning Congress.

43. *See, e.g.*, 3 Annals of Congress 136 (1792) (the House proposed one day, the Senate another).

44. U.S. Const. art. II, § 3.

45. *See, e.g.*, Letter from George Washington to Congress (Jan. 8, 1790), *in* 4 The Papers of George Washington: Presidential Series 543, 546 (Dorothy Twohig ed., 1993).

46. Letter from Alexander White to George Washington (Mar. 24, 1798), *in* 2 The Papers of George Washington: Retirement Series 155–57 (W. W. Abbot ed., 1998).

47. 3 Joseph Story, Commentaries on the Constitution of the United States 413 n.1 (1833) (observing that presidents give speeches and send messages in order to comply with state of the union obligation).

48. For instance, Washington gave a speech in January 1790 and one that December. Each marked the beginning of a new session of Congress. Adams gave two such speeches in 1797. *See also id.* (Story noting practice of opening each session with a speech).

49. Jeffrey K. Tulis, The Rhetorical Presidency 55 (1987).

50. *Id.* at 55–56.

51. Others may have had a similar view about the inadvisability of personal speeches before the legislature. Under the Georgia Constitution of 1777, messages from the governor to the legislature had to be conveyed by the secretary of the executive council. Ga. Const. art. XXXII (1777). This implied that the governor had no right to address the assembly directly.

52. Kallenbach, *supra* note 5, at 334. Tulis speculates that Jefferson may have discontinued the practice because of his poor public speaking. Tulis, *supra* note 49, at 56.

53. Vasan Kesavan & J. Gregory Sidak, *The Legislator-in-Chief*, 44 Wm. & Mary L. Rev. 1, 19 (2002).

54. *Id.* at 17–20.

55. Letter from George Washington to Congress (Jan. 8, 1790), *in* 4 The Papers of George Washington: Presidential Series, *supra* note 45, at 543, 546 (emphasis added).

56. John Adams confirmed the same when he spoke of fulfilling his state of the union duties by giving an informative speech to a special session of Congress regarding deteriorating relations with France. John Adams, Speech to Both Chambers (May 16, 1797), *in* 9 The Works of John Adams 111, 112 (Charles F. Adams ed., 1854).

57. N.Y. Const. art. XIX (1777).

58. Kesavan and Sidak, *supra* note 53, at 29–33.

59. 2 The Debates in the Several State Conventions on the Adoption of the Federal Constitution 448 (Jonathan Elliot ed., 2d ed. 1836).

60. 1 Blackstone's Commentaries: With Notes of Reference, to the Constitution and Laws, of the Federal Government of the United States; and of the Commonwealth of Virginia app. at 344 (St. George Tucker ed., 1803) [hereinafter Tucker's Commentaries]; *see also* 3 Story, *supra* note 47, at 412–13 (observing that "[f]rom the nature and duties of the executive department, he must possess more extensive sources of information, as well in regard to domestic as foreign affairs, than can belong to congress").

61. *See* Kesavan and Sidak, *supra* note 53, at 54–55.

62. U.S. Const. art. II, § 3. Some state executives also were obliged to propose legislation. *See, e.g.,* N.Y. Const art. XIX (1777) (providing that "it shall be the duty of the governor . . . to recommend such matters to their consideration as shall appear to him to concern its good government, welfare, and prosperity").

63. A Landholder V (Dec. 3, 1787), *in* 3 The Documentary History of the Ratification of the Constitution 483 (Merrill Jensen ed., 1978).

64. 1 Tucker's Commentaries, *supra* note 60, at 344; *see also* 3 Story, *supra* note 47, at 413 (noting that the president "is thus justly made responsible, not merely for a due administration of the existing systems, but for due diligence and examination into the means of improving them").

65. 2 Records of the Federal Convention, *supra* note 15, at 405 (emphasis omitted).

66. *See, e.g.,* Sanford Levinson, Our Undemocratic Constitution 41–43 (2006).

67. Josiah Ober, *Law and Political Theory, in* The Cambridge Companion to Ancient Greek Law 394, 408 (Michael Gagarin & David J. Cohen eds., 2005).

68. William Rawle, A View of the Constitution of the United States 172 (2nd ed. 1829).

69. Notes on Errors of Governments Towards Indians (Feb. 1792), *in* 9 The Papers of George Washington: Presidential Series 558, 559 (Mark A. Mastromarino & Jack D. Warren eds., 2000). Jeffrey Tulis points out that a draft of Washington's inaugural message included seventy-three pages of legislative recommendations, all of which were omitted in the final message. *See* Tulis, *supra* note 49, at 48.

70. Robert J. Spitzer, The Presidential Veto: Touchstone of the American Presidency 109 (1988).

71. 1 William R. Anson, The Law and Custom of the Constitution 64 (1886); *see also* Lindsay Rogers, *The Power of the President to Sign Bills after Congress Has Adjourned,* 30 Yale L.J. 1, 20 (1920) (describing British practice).

72. *See* Rogers, *supra* note 71, at 20 (suggesting that Americans borrowed from Britain).

73. Mass. Const. pt. 2, ch. I, § 1 art. II (1780).

74. Opinion of the Justices of the Supreme Judicial Court on certain questions referred to them by the Senate of Massachusetts, in the year 1791, 3 Mass. (2 Tyng) 567 (1865).

75. *Id.* at 568.

76. Letter from George Washington to Jonathan Trumbull (Mar. 3, 1797), *in* 35 The Writings of George Washington 411, 412 (John C. Fitzpatrick ed., 1940).

77. *Id.* at 411.

78. *See* 1 Stat. xxxi–xxxii (listing bills signed into law on Mar. 2–3, 1797); *see also* 6 Annals of Congress 2351–53 (1797) (noting the passage of a flurry of bills).

79. *See* Max B. May, *Can the President Sign a Bill after the Adjournment of Congress,* 39 Cent. L. J. 68, 70 (1894); *see also* Rogers, *supra* note 71, at 20 (describing the practice).

80. *See* Rogers, *supra* note 71, at 1 (describing how Woodrow Wilson signed more than forty bills at the end of a session).

81. *See* May, *supra* note 79, at 70.

82. *See* E.I. Renick, *The Power of the President to Sign Bills after the Adjournment of Congress*, 32 Am. L. Rev. 208, 208 (1898).

83. *See id.* at 208–9.

84. 7 Memoirs of John Quincy Adams 233–34 (Charles F. Adams ed., 1874).

85. Act of March. 12, 1863, 12 Stat. 820.

86. H.R. Rep. No. 38–108, at 2 (1864).

87. Act of July 2, 1864, 13 Stat. 375.

88. 9 John G. Nicolay & John Hay, Abraham Lincoln: A History 120–21 (1890).

89. *See* Niels H. Debel, The Veto Power of the Governor of Illinois 81–82 (1917).

90. *See* Edwards v. United States, 286 U.S. 482 (1932) (concluding that the president could sign a bill into law after a final adjournment of Congress).

91. Thomas Jefferson might have lodged a similar complaint against royal governors, each of whom had to assent to bills before they became law. *See* Greene, *supra* note 5, at 161–65.

92. Marc W. Kruman, Between Authority and Liberty: State Constitution Making in Revolutionary America 123 (1997).

93. *Id.*

94. *Id.*

95. S.C. Const. art. VII (1776).

96. S.C. Const. art. XVI (1778).

97. Kruman, *supra* note 92, at 124.

98. N.Y. Const. art. III (1777).

99. Mass. Const. pt. 2, ch. I, §1, art. II (1780).

100. Kruman, *supra* note 92, at 126. There was also an absolute veto of sorts in the Vermont Constitution of 1786. The governor and the Executive Council could veto all legislation if they proposed amendments. Vt. Const. ch. II, § XVI (1786).

101. *See* 1 Records of the Federal Convention, *supra* note 15, at 21.

102. *Id.* at 110.

103. *See id.* at 97–98.

104. *See id.* at 98.

105. *See id.* at 100; *see also id.* at 107.

106. *See id.* at 103–4.

107. William Penn, To the Citizens of the United States (Jan. 3, 1788), *in* 3 The Complete Anti-Federalist 171, 172 (Herbert J. Storing ed., 1981).

108. Republicus (Mar. 1, 1788), *in* 8 The Documentary History of the Ratification of the Constitution 446, 449 (John P. Kaminski & Gaspare J. Saladino eds., 1988).

109. U.S. Const. art. I, § 7.

110. Hollingsworth v. Virginia, 3 U.S. 378 (1798).

111. *See* J. Gregory Sidak & Thomas A. Smith, *Four Faces of the Item Veto: A Reply to Tribe and Kurland*, 84 Nw. U. L. Rev. 437, 447 & n.40 (1990).

112. *See generally* Michael B. Rappaport, *Veto Burdens and the Line Item Veto Act*, 91 Nw. U. L. Rev. 771 (1997).

113. Letter from George Washington to Edmund Pendleton (Sept. 23, 1793), *in* 14 The Papers of George Washington: Presidential Series, *supra* note 16, at 124–25.

114. Veto Message, *in* 1 A Compilation of the Messages and Papers of the Presidents, 1789–1897, at 211, 212 (James D. Richardson ed., 1897).

115. *See* Robert Luce, Legislative Problems: Development, Status, and Trend of the Treatment and Exercise of Lawmaking Problems 109 (1935) (noting that President Andrew Jackson vetoed a bill that would have affected the president's power to determine adjournment when the chambers disagreed).

116. *See* Thomas Erskine May, A Treatise on the Law, Privileges, Proceedings and Usage 200–201 (1844).

117. *See* 8 Register of Debates in Congress 1239–40 (Joseph Gales & William Seaton eds., 1833).

118. 1 Records of the Federal Convention, *supra* note 15, at 99.

119. *See* Spitzer, *supra* note 70, at 107.

120. N.Y. Const. art. III (1777).

121. James Madison is said to be the first president to exercise a pocket veto. In fact, he failed to sign a bill that was presented to him at the end of the congressional session. Hence, one might say that Madison relied upon the end-of-session effacement principle rather than upon the Constitution's pocket veto language. Until Andrew Johnson in 1867, twenty-six so-called pocket vetoes actually relied upon the end-of-session effacement principle. *See* Robert J. Spitzer, *The "Protective Return" Pocket Veto: Presidential Aggrandizement of Constitutional Power*, *in* Executing the Constitution: Putting the President Back into the Constitution 109, 113 (Christopher S. Kelley ed., 2006).

122. *See* Wright v. United States, 302 U.S. 583, 588 (1938) ("The reference to the Congress is manifestly to the entire legislative body consisting of both Houses.").

123. *See id.* at 590.

124. N.Y. Const. art. III (1777).

125. Letter from George Washington to Congress (Jan. 21, 1794), *in* 15 The Papers of George Washington: Presidential Series 102, 103 (Christine S. Patrick ed., 2009).

126. Letter from Oliver Wolcott, Jr., to George Washington (June 28, 1796), *in* 35 The Writings of George Washington, *supra* note 76, at 116 n.33; *see also* Act of May 28, 1796, 1 Stat. 477, 477–78.

127. James F. Zimmerman, Impressment of American Seamen 60 (1925).

128. Letter from Oliver Wolcott, Jr., to George Washington, *in* 35 The Writings of George Washington, *supra* note 76, at 116 n.33.

129. *Id.*

130. Letter from Charles Lee to George Washington (July 4, 1796), *available at* http://memory.loc.gov/mss/mgw/mgw4/109/0600/0635.jpg, and http://memory.loc.gov/mss/mgw/mgw4/109/0600/0637.jpg (last checked Oct. 15, 2013).

131. Letter from George Washington to Oliver Wolcott, Jr. (July 4, 1796), *in* 35 The Writings of George Washington, *supra* note 76, at 115, 116 (emphasis in original).

132. *See* Zimmerman, *supra* note 127, at 60–61. The instructions to the collectors were published. *See Federal Gazette & Baltimore Daily Advertiser* 3 (July 28, 1796).

133. This section draws from Saikrishna Prakash, *Regulating Presidential Powers*, 91 Cornell L. Rev. 215 (2005) [hereinafter Regulating Presidential Powers].

134. U.S. Const. art. I, § 8, cl. 18.

135. U.S. Const. art. I, § 4, cl. 1.

136. *Id.* art. III, § 2, cl. 2.

137. *Id.* art. II, § 2, cl. 2.

138. *Id.* art. I, § 8, cls. 14, 16. Perhaps the best way to read these three provisions together is that in the absence of congressional regulation of the armed forces and the militia, the president may establish his own rules of conduct and discipline. When Congress creates regulations, however, they trump whatever rules the president adopted in the absence of congressional regulation.

139. Gary Lawson & Patricia B. Granger, *The "Proper" Scope of Federal Power: A Jurisdictional Interpretation of the Sweeping Clause*, 43 Duke L.J. 267, 333–34 (1993).

140. *See* Act of Settlement, 1701, 12 & 13 W. & M. 3, c. 2 (Eng.); Bill of Rights, 1689, 1 W. & M. 2, c. 2 (Eng.) (imposing numerous constraints on the Crown).

141. The Crown was a third chamber of Parliament and, hence, could thwart legislation that impinged on its powers. Yet there were many occasions when the Crown agreed to a diminution of its powers in exchange for something else from the Parliament. Once a king agreed to some diminution of executive power, future kings and queens had to either accept the regulation or convince Parliament to repeal it.

142. N.C. Const. art. XIX (1776); *see also* Del. Const. art. 7 (1776); Ga. Const. art. XIX (1777); Md. Const. art. XXXIII (1776); Va. Const. (1776).

143. Pa. Const. § 20 (1776).

144. *Cf.* S.C. Const. art. XXXII (1778) (stating that the governor may appoint all other necessary officers unless otherwise directed by law); N.Y. Const. art. XXXVI (1777) (similar); Vt. Const. ch. II, § 18 (1777) (similar).

145. Charles C. Thach, Jr., The Creation of the Presidency 1775–1789: A Study in Constitutional History 32 (1922).

146. For a discussion of these complaints, *see* Saikrishna Prakash, *The Essential Meaning of Executive Power*, 2003 U. Ill. L. Rev. 701, 762–63 & n.337 [hereinafter Essential Meaning of Executive Power].

147. *See* Thach, *supra* note 145, at 42.

148. Thomas Jefferson, Notes on the State of Virginia, *in* 4 The Works of Thomas Jefferson 20–21 (Paul Leicester Ford ed., 1904).

149. Va. Const. (1776) (the governor "shall, with the advice of a Council of State, exercise the executive powers of government, *according to the laws of this Commonwealth*") (emphasis added).

150. *See, e.g.,* The Virginia Plan, *in* 1 Records of the Federal Convention, *supra* note 15, at 20; The New Jersey Plan, *in id.* at 242; The Pinckney Plan, *in id.,* vol. 3, at 595; The Hamilton Plan, *in id.,* vol. 3, at 617.

151. *Id.,* vol. 2, at 74, 299, 300, 407, 551.

152. On September 15, 1787, Gouverneur Morris moved that Congress be given the authority to vest the appointment of inferior officers with the president, the heads of departments, and judges. After initially failing, the provision passed after a claim was made that it was "too necessary, to be omitted." *Id.* at 627–28. I have argued elsewhere that the provision was necessary as a means of circumventing the requirement that all officers of the United States be appointed by the president and confirmed by the Senate. *See* Essential Meaning of Executive Power, *supra* note 146, at 734.

153. *See e.g.,* Regulating Presidential Powers, *supra* note 133, at 244–45.

154. *See* The Federalist Nos. 48–51, at 250–65 (James Madison) (Garry Wills ed., 1982).

155. *See id.* No. 48, at 251, 253 (James Madison) (describing how legislatures can "mask" their "encroachments" and recounting the Pennsylvania assembly's usurpations).

156. Message to the House of Representatives (Mar. 30, 1796), *in* 35 The Writings of George Washington, *supra* note 76, at 2, 5.

157. *See* 5 Annals of Congress 759–60 (1796).

158. I have previously suggested that Washington might have acquiesced had the House made it clear that it sought the papers in relation to a potential impeachment and had the House had statutory authority to request the Jay instructions. *See* Saikrishna Bangalore Prakash, *A Critical Comment on the Constitutionality of Executive Privilege,* 83 Minn. L. Rev. 1143, 1182 (1999). Upon reflection, I very much doubt that Washington would have acquiesced in the request merely had the House and Senate passed a statute, because Washington would have continued to conclude that the House was trespassing upon a power committed to the president and Senate. In other words, the form of the trespass—whether a statute or a formal request—likely would have been immaterial.

159. Memoranda of Consultations with the President (Mar. 12, 1792), *in* 23 The Papers of Thomas Jefferson 258, 261 (Charles T. Cullen ed., 1990).

160. Message to the House of Representatives (Mar. 30, 1796), *in* 35 The Writings of George Washington, *supra* note 76, at 2, 5.

161. Letter from James McHenry to George Washington (July 26, 1796), *available at* http://rotunda.upress.virginia.edu/founders/default.xqy?keys=FOEA-print-01-01-02-0781.

162. 11 Documentary History of the First Federal Congress of the United States of America 1789–1791: Debates in the House of Representatives, First Session, 947 (Charlene Bangs Bickford ed., 1992).

163. *Id.* at 965.

164. Richard Bland Lee drew upon the Necessary and Proper Clause, arguing that the clause permitted Congress to "make every arrangement proper to facilitate the business of every department." *Id.* at 947. Lee's argument did not seem to countenance that

Congress could modify or instruct other branches in the exercise of their constitutionally granted powers.

165. 1 Annals of Congress 481 (1789).

166. *Id.* at 482 (emphasis added).

Chapter 11. Judges as "Shoots from the Executive Stock"

1. W. B. Gwyn, The Meaning of the Separation of Powers 5 (1965).

2. F. W. Maitland, The Constitutional History of England 134 (1908).

3. *Id.*

4. Gwyn, *supra* note 1, at 6–7.

5. Prohibitions del Roy (1607) 77 Eng. Rep. 1342 (K.B.) 1343; *see also* Roland G. Usher, *James I and Sir Edward Coke*, 18 Eng. Hist. Rev. 664, 664–75 (1903) (discussing varying accounts of confrontation).

6. Gwyn, *supra* note 1, at 8.

7. 2 Algernon Sidney, Discourses Concerning Government 223 (1750).

8. C. H. McIlwain, *The Tenure of English Judges*, 7 Am. Pol. Sci. Rev. 217, 224 (1913); *see also* G. E. Aylmer, The King's Servants: The Civil Service of Charles I, at 106–7 (1961). By the end of the seventeenth century, life tenure had come to be regarded as tenure during good behavior, because it was said that good behavior was a requirement of all offices, whether explicitly expressed or not. *See* Harcourt v. Fox (1692) 89 Eng. Rep. 680 (K.B.), *reargued* (1693) 89 Eng. Rep. 720 (K.B.).

9. 1 William Blackstone, Commentaries on the Laws of England 257 (University of Chicago 1979) (1765).

10. *Id.* at 258.

11. 2 Thomas Sheridan, A Complete Dictionary of the English Language (4th ed. 1797) (defining "judge"); *see also* Samuel Johnson, A Dictionary of the English Language (10th ed. 1792) (defining to "judge" as "to pass sentence upon; to examine authoritatively").

12. 3 William Blackstone, Commentaries on the Laws of England 263 (University of Chicago 1979) (1768) (emphasis omitted). A writ of quo warranto was a writ issued to determine whether an entity or person properly exercised some right or power.

13. 1 Blackstone, *supra* note 9, at 257–58.

14. Evarts Boutell Greene, The Provincial Governor in the English Colonies of North America 139–40 (1898).

15. *Id.* at 140.

16. *Id.* at 135–36.

17. *Id.* at 143–44.

18. N.J. Const. art. VIII (1776).

19. Pa. Const. § 20 (1776).

20. Margaret Burnham MacMillan, The War Governors in the American Revolution 175, 177 (1943).

21. *See generally* William Baude, *The Judgment Power*, 96 Geo. L.J. 1807 (2008). The one exception, says Baude, is when the court lacks jurisdiction to issue judgment. In that case, the executive has no obligation to enforce the judgment. *Id.* at 1815–16.

22. James Wilson, Lectures on Law (1790), *in* 1 Collected Works of James Wilson 703 (Kermit L. Hall & Mark David Hall eds., 2007).

23. Philip Hamburger, Law and Judicial Duty 544 (2008). In fact, though a sheriff could not refuse to execute a judgment, chief executives often had authority to remit punishment via a pardon.

24. Theophilus Parsons, The Essex Result (1778), *in* 1 American Political Writing During the Founding Era 1760–1805, at 480, 493–94 (Charles Hyneman & Donald S. Lutz eds., 1983).

25. The Federalist No. 47, at 243, 245 (James Madison) (Garry Wills ed., 1982).

26. 2 The Documentary History of the Ratification of the Constitution 450 (Merrill Jensen ed., 1976) (statement of James Wilson).

27. *See* Thomas Paine, The Rights of Man: Part II (1792), *in* 2 The Writings of Thomas Paine 401, 443 (Moncure D. Conway ed., 1894).

28. Nathaniel Chipman, Sketches of the Principles of Government 119 (1793). Chipman served as a district court judge in Vermont.

29. Michael Stokes Paulsen, *The Most Dangerous Branch: Executive Power to Say What the Law Is*, 83 Geo. L.J. 217, 250–52 (1994).

30. The Federalist No. 78, *supra* note 25, at 392, 394 (Alexander Hamilton).

31. Paulsen, *supra* note 29, at 284.

32. 1 Op. Att'y Gen. 56, 57 (1795).

33. 1 Op. Att'y Gen. 50, 51–52 (1794).

34. Letter from Thomas Jefferson to Edmond Charles Genêt (June 29, 1793), *in* 7 The Works of Thomas Jefferson 422, 422 (Paul Leicester Ford ed., 1904).

35. *See* 1 Op. Att'y Gen. 68, 70 (1797).

36. Letter from Alexander Hamilton to Henry Lee (Oct. 20, 1794), *in* 17 The Papers of Alexander Hamilton 331, 334 (Harold C. Syrett ed., 1972). The army apparently exerted an improper influence on the judge, since the latter felt coerced into approving detentions even when evidence was lacking. *See* William Hogeland, The Whiskey Rebellion: George Washington, Alexander Hamilton, and the Frontier Rebels Who Challenged America's Newfound Sovereignty 222–23 (2006).

37. Letter from George Washington to Peter Trenor (Sept. 6, 1794), *in* 16 The Papers of George Washington: Presidential Series 647, 648 (David R. Hoth & Carol S. Ebel eds., 2011).

38. *Id.* at 649.

39. Hamburger, *supra* note 23, at 545 (quoting "Whether Christianity Is Part of the Common Law?" (c. 1774)).

40. 1 Op. Att'y Gen. 119, 122 (1802).

41. *See* Denis P. Duffey, Jr., *Genre and Authority: The Rise of Case Reporting in the Early United States*, 74 Chi.-Kent L. Rev. 263, 265–71 (1998); William Kent, Memoirs and Letters of James Kent, LL.D. 117 (1898) ("When I came to the Bench there were no reports or State precedents. The opinions from the Bench were delivered *ore tenus* [by mouth]. We had no law of our own, and nobody knew what it was.").

42. Erwin C. Surrency, *Law Reports in the United States*, 25 Am. J. Legal Hist. 48, 48–52 (1981).

43. Act of Sept. 15, 1789, § 2, 1 Stat. 68, 68.

44. Note, *Plurality Decisions and Judicial Decisionmaking*, 94 Harv. L. Rev. 1127, 1127 n.1 (1981).

45. Baude, *supra* note 21, at 1845 n.212.

46. *See id.*

47. Whether Christianity Is Part of the Common Law, *in* 1 The Works of Thomas Jefferson 453, 457 (Paul Leicester Ford ed., 1904).

48. *See* 1 Julius Goebel, Jr., The Oliver Wendell Holmes Devise History of the Supreme Court of the United States: Antecedents and Beginnings to 1801, at 515 (Paul A. Freund ed., 1971).

49. *See id.* at 514–15.

50. *See* Pa. Const. art. V, § 12 (1790); Goebel, *supra* note 48, at 515.

51. 4 The Documentary History of the Supreme Court of the United States 1789–1800, at 112 (Maeva Marcus ed., 1992).

52. *Id.*

53. *Id.*

54. *Id.*

55. 9 Documentary History of the First Federal Congress 1789–1791: The Diary of William Maclay and Other Notes on Senate Debates 168 (Kenneth R. Bowling & Helen E. Veit eds., 1988).

56. *Id.*

57. 1 The Documentary History of the Supreme Court of the United States, 1789–1800, at 566, 571, 573–74 (Maeva Marcus & James R. Perry eds., 1985).

58. Proposals to ban cross-branch appointments between the executive and judicial branches never received a formal vote at the Constitutional Convention. *See* Stewart Jay, Most Humble Servants: The Advisory Role of Early Judges 74 (1997).

59. *See* Steven G. Calabresi & Joan L. Larsen, *One Person, One Office: Separation of Powers or Separation of Personnel?*, 79 Cornell L. Rev. 1045, 1128–31 (1994).

60. John Jay was never properly constituted the secretary of foreign affairs because he was never appointed under the Constitution. He was a holdover officer, having been an appointee of the Continental Congress.

61. Jay, *supra* note 58, at 153.

62. Act of Aug. 12, 1790, § 2, 1 Stat. 186, 186; Act of May 8, 1792, § 6, 1 Stat. 281, 282–83.

63. Act of Apr. 2, 1792, § 18, 1 Stat. 246, 250.

64. The statutory addition of executive duties to a judicial office arguably was an unconstitutional circumvention of the Appointments Clause, for if Congress could change the nature of a judicial office by appending executive functions to it, that statute might force the president to accept an officer whom he abhorred. Yet if the president may direct the executive actions of a judicial officer and also bar the latter's exercise of executive authority (a "removal" of sorts), then the president need not be as troubled by a statute that grants executive functions to a judicial officer. At least some were aware of the related question whether sitting judges could be forced to assume nonjudicial duties. When certain judges concluded that an act had sought to appoint them as commissioners, they claimed that they were "at liberty to accept or decline that office." Excerpt from the opinion of the Circuit Judges for the New York District (Apr. 5, 1792), *in* Jay, *supra* note 58, at 110; *see also* James Iredell, Reasons for acting as a Commissioner on the Invalid Act (Oct. 1792), *in* Maeva Marcus & Emily Field Van Tassel, *Judges and Legislators in the New Federal System, 1789–1800, in* Judges and Legislators: Toward Institutional Comity 31, 40 (Robert A. Katzmann ed., 1988); Letter from Richard Peters to the President of the United States (Jan. 8, 1798), *in* 1 American State Papers: Miscellaneous 162, 162 (Gales & Seaton eds., 1834).

65. Jay, *supra* note 58, at 106–7.

66. Hayburn's Case, 2 U.S. (3 Dall.) 409, 410 n* (1792).

67. *Id.*

68. *See* Letter from James Iredell and John Sitgreaves to the President of the United States (June 8, 1792), *in* 1 American State Papers: Miscellaneous, *supra* note 64, at 52, 52–53.

69. *See, e.g.,* Proclamation of Governor of Massachusetts against Shays, &c (Feb. 9, 1787), *in* 11 Pennsylvania Archives 119 (Samuel Hazard ed., 1855) (ordering judges to discover and apprehend suspects); Proclamation to Arrest John Jenkins &c. (July 8, 1788), *in id.* at 329 (same).

70. *See, e.g.,* Proclamation of George Washington (Sept. 15, 1792), *in* 1 A Compilation of the Messages and Papers of the Presidents: 1789–1897, at 124, 125 (James D. Richardson ed., 1897) (requiring "all courts, magistrates, and officers" to help suppress unlawful combinations opposing the execution of excise laws); Proclamation of George Washington (Mar. 19, 1791), *in id.* at 101, 102 (requiring "all officers" to bring certain offenders to justice).

71. Alexander Hamilton, The Examination, No. 12 (Feb. 23, 1802), *in* 25 The Papers of Alexander Hamilton 529, 531 (Harold C. Syrett ed., 1977).

72. *Id.* at 532 (italics omitted).

73. *See* Sheridan, *supra* note 11 (defining "ministerial").

74. *See* Saikrishna B. Prakash & Michael D. Ramsey, *Foreign Affairs and the Jeffersonian Executive: A Defense,* 89 Minn. L. Rev. 1591, 1678–79 (2005).

75. Act of Aug. 12, 1790, § 2, 1 Stat. 186, 186.

NOTES TO PAGES 280-283

76. Certain extrajudicial duties may not have been subject to presidential control. The Militia Act of 1792 provided that before the president could summon the militia for law enforcement purposes, a federal judge had to first certify that the ordinary means of law execution were inadequate. Act of May 2, 1792, § 2, 1 Stat. 264, 264. It seems likely that in making this determination, federal judges were to reach independent conclusions, free from executive direction. Nonetheless, Washington certainly influenced James Wilson's conclusion that the ordinary means of law execution were inadequate. *See* Robert W. Coakley, The Role of Federal Military Forces in Domestic Disorders 1789–1878, at 36 (1988).

77. Jay, *supra* note 58, at 65–66.

78. *Id.* at 98. Stewart Jay speculates that the chief justice's advice grew more infrequent because he did not reside in Philadelphia. *Id.*

79. Letter from George Washington to the United States Supreme Court (Apr. 3, 1790), *in* 5 The Papers of George Washington: Presidential Series 313, 313–14 (Dorothy Twohig et al. eds., 1996).

80. Jay, *supra* note 58, at 103–5.

81. Maeva Marcus & Robert Teir, Hayburn's Case: *A Misinterpretation of Precedent*, 1988 Wis. L. Rev. 527, 534.

82. Letter from James Iredell to George Washington (Feb. 23, 1792), *in* 9 The Papers of George Washington: Presidential Series 583, 583 (Mark A. Mastromarino & Jack D. Warren eds., 2000).

83. Jay, *supra* note 58, at 73.

84. *Id.* at 135.

85. *Id.* at 136.

86. Letter from Chief Justice John Jay and Associate Justices to President Washington (Aug. 8, 1793), *in* 13 The Papers of George Washington: Presidential Series 392, 392 (Christine S. Patrick ed., 2007).

87. *See* Jay, *supra* note 58, at 159.

88. *See id.* at 161.

89. *See id.* at 152.

90. *See id.* at 152–53.

91. *See* William R. Casto, Foreign Affairs and the Constitution in the Age of Fighting Sail 118–21 (2006).

92. *See* Jay, *supra* note 58, at 152–53.

93. *See* Casto, *supra* note 91, at 55.

94. Letter from Thomas Jefferson to Foreign Ministers in the United States (Nov. 10, 1793), *in* 27 The Papers of Thomas Jefferson 340, 341 (John Catanzariti ed., 1997). For a generic discussion, *see* Charles Marion Thomas, American Neutrality in 1793: A Study in Cabinet Government 114–15 (1931).

95. *See* 1 Op. Att'y Gen. 40, 41 (1794).

96. To the United States Senate and House of Representatives (Dec. 3, 1793), *in* 14 The Papers of George Washington: Presidential Series 462, 464 (David R. Hoth ed., 2008).

97. Charles S. Hyneman, The First American Neutrality: A Study of the American Understanding of Neutral Obligations During the Years 1792 to 1815, at 100 (1934).

98. Glass v. The Sloop Betsey, 3 U.S. (3 Dall.) 6, 16 (1794).

99. *See, e.g.*, 2 The Documentary History of the Ratification of the Constitution, *supra* note 26, at 483 (comments by James Wilson that there would have to be executive and judicial powers to carry the laws "into effect") (italics omitted).

Chapter 12. "Whatever Requisition the President Shall Make" and the Federal Duties of State Executives

1. Art. of Confederation, art. IX.

2. *See id.* art. VIII.

3. Margaret Burnham MacMillan, The War Governors in the American Revolution 132 (1943).

4. *Id.* at 115, 118, 126.

5. *Id.* at 112.

6. *Id.* at 127, 133.

7. 3 The Records of the Federal Convention of 1787, at 616 (Max Farrand rev. ed., 1966).

8. U.S. Const., art. I, § 8, cl. 15.

9. The Federalist No. 16, at 79 (Alexander Hamilton) (Garry Wills ed., 1982).

10. The Federalist No. 27, *supra* note 9, at 133 (Alexander Hamilton) (emphasis omitted).

11. *See* 9 The Documentary History of the Ratification of the Constitution 962 (John P. Kaminski & Gaspere J. Saladino eds., 1990); *see also* 22 The Documentary History of the Ratification of the Constitution 1923 (John P. Kaminski et al. eds., 2008).

12. 22 The Documentary History of the Ratification of the Constitution, *supra* note 11, at 1943–44; *see also* The Federalist No. 45, *supra* note 9, at 235 (James Madison).

13. 4 The Debates in the Several State Conventions on the Adoption of the Federal Constitution 140 (Jonathan Elliot ed., 2d ed. 1836) (statement of William Maclaine).

14. See 9 The Documentary History of the Ratification of the Constitution, *supra* note 11, at 1045.

15. The Federalist No. 16, *supra* note 9, at 79 (Alexander Hamilton).

16. For a defense of the proposition that the federal government may commandeer state executives and an argument that the Constitution implicitly abandoned the commandeering of state legislatures, *see* Saikrishna Bangalore Prakash, *Field Office Federalism*, 79 Va. L. Rev. 1957 (1993).

17. Letter from Thomas Mifflin to George Washington (Aug. 5, 1794), *in* 16 The Papers of George Washington: Presidential Series 516 (David R. Hoth & Carol S. Ebel eds., 2011).

18. Abraham D. Sofaer, War, Foreign Affairs, and Constitutional Power: The Origins 119–120 (1976).

19. *See* Alexander Hamilton to Henry Lee (Oct. 20, 1794), *in* 17 The Papers of Alexander Hamilton 331–36 (Harold C. Syrett ed., 1972).

20. Proclamation of Aug. 7, 1794, *in* 4 Pennsylvania Archives: Second Series 127–29 (John B. Linn & William H. Egle eds., 1876).

21. *See* Circular to the Governors of North Carolina, Pennsylvania, and South Carolina (Sept. 29, 1792), *in* 11 The Papers of George Washington: Presidential Series 165 (Christine S. Patrick ed., 2002).

22. Charles S. Hyneman, The First American Neutrality: A Study of the American Understanding of Neutral Obligations During the Years 1792 to 1815, at 73, 88, 109, 135 (2002).

23. *Id.* at 156–57; Letter from Thomas Jefferson to Isaac Shelby (Nov. 6, 1793), *in* 1 American State Papers: Foreign Relations 455 (Gales & Seaton eds., 1833).

24. Washington's efforts in this regard did not always meet with success, as when he sought to federalize a portion of the Pennsylvania militia and also asked Governor Mifflin to use state authority to deploy the militia to suppress the Whiskey Rebellion. While not doubting the president's ability to order the Pennsylvania militia into service, Mifflin refused Washington's command to use state authority to direct the militia to suppress the rebels. The governor believed that he could use military force only after ordinary means of law execution proved inadequate and that those means had not been shown wanting, at least not yet. *See* Letter from Thomas Mifflin to George Washington (Aug. 5, 1794), *in* 16 The Papers of George Washington: Presidential Series, *supra* note 20, at 514–16; Letter from Thomas Mifflin to George Washington (Aug. 12, 1794), *in id.*, at 553–59.

25. Letter from Thomas Jefferson to Edmond Charles Genet (June 25, 1793), *in* 26 The Papers of Thomas Jefferson 358 (John Catanzariti ed., 1995); Cabinet Opinion on Privateers and Prizes (Aug. 5, 1793), *in id.* at 620–21; Cabinet Opinion on Prizes and Privateers (Aug. 3, 1793), *in id.* at 603–4.

26. Letter from Edmund Randolph to Joseph Fauchet (Oct. 2, 1794), *in* 1 American State Papers: Foreign Relations, *supra* note 23, at 603; *see also* Letter from Edmund Randolph to Joseph Fauchet (Oct. 17, 1794), *in id.* at 589 (noting that because the United States was so immense, governors implemented the president's "rules" on prizes).

27. *E.g.,* Letter from Henry Knox to Governor (May 23, 1793), *in* 6 Calendar of Virginia State Papers 377 (Sherwin McRae ed., 1886).

28. Letter from Henry Knox to Governor (May 24, 1793), *in id.* at 379; *see also* Reasons for the Opinion of the Secretary of the Treasury and the Secretary at War Respecting the Brigantine *Little Sarah*, *in* 15 The Papers of Alexander Hamilton 74, 77 (Harold C. Syrett ed., 1969) (speaking of Washington's "instruction" and "order" to the governors).

29. *See* Notes of a Cabinet Meeting (July 15, 1793), *in* 26 The Papers of Thomas Jefferson, *supra* note 25, at 508 (discussing how orders were given to governors to stop foreign vessels from arming, and saying that governors were to halt arming before any force became necessary).

30. Hyneman, *supra* note 22, at 157.

31. *Id.*

32. *See* Letter from Henry Lee to Vice Consul of Norfolk (Sep. 12, 1794), *in* 1 American State Papers: Foreign Relations, *supra* note 23, at 603; Governor's Instructions (Dec. 5, 1793), *in* 6 Calendar of Virginia State Papers, *supra* note 27, at 671 (speaking of receiving "additional instructions" from the president).

33. Letter from Isaac Shelby to Thomas Jefferson (Jan. 13, 1794), *in* 1 American State Papers: Foreign Relations, *supra* note 23, at 455–56.

34. The Constitution bars states from engaging in war "unless actually invaded, or in such imminent Danger as will not admit of delay." U.S. Const. art. II, § 10, cl. 3. Since some Indian tribes had invaded certain states and others had formally declared war, one might have supposed that the states could wage war without any declaration from Congress. Curiously, no one expressed the view that because some tribes had declared war, the affected states had a constitutional power to unilaterally wage war in response. *But see* Letter from Jared Ingersoll to Alexander Dallas (July 18, 1794), *in* 1 American State Papers: Indian Affairs 518 (Walter Lowrie & Matthew St. Clair Clarke eds., 1832) (observing that the state legislature could unilaterally raise troops because the United States was "at war" with Indian tribes).

35. To the United States Senate and House of Representatives (Dec. 3, 1793), *in* 14 The Papers of George Washington: Presidential Series 465 (David R. Hoth ed., 2008).

36. Letter from Edward Telfair to the Secretary of War (Aug. 13, 1793), *in* 1 American State Papers: Indian Affairs, *supra* note 34, at 370.

37. Letter from Henry Knox to Governor of Georgia (Sept. 5, 1793), *in id.* at 365.

38. Letter from Henry Knox to Governor of Georgia (Aug. 31, 1792), *in id.* at 258–59.

39. Letter from Henry Knox to Governor of Georgia (July 28, 1794), *in id.* at 501.

40. Letter from Alexander Hamilton to Governor of Georgia (Sept. 25, 1794), *in id.* at 502.

41. *See e.g.,* Letter from Governor of Georgia to Henry Knox (Oct. 12, 1794), *in id.* at 499; *see also* Letter from Governor to Georgia to Henry Knox (Aug. 19, 1794), *in id.* at 495 (assuring the president of his "exertions").

42. *See, e.g.,* Letter from Governor of Georgia to Henry Knox (Aug. 30, 1794), *in id.* at 497.

43. William R. Casto, Foreign Affairs and the Constitution in the Age of Fighting Sail 104 (2006).

44. *See* Notes of a Cabinet Meeting (July 15, 1793), *in* 26 The Papers of Thomas Jefferson, *supra* note 25, at 508.

45. Mifflin was better prepared the next time it seemed that a transgressing British privateer was set to depart from Philadelphia. *See* Letter from Thomas Mifflin to George Washington (Aug. 2, 1793), *in* 13 The Papers of George Washington: Presidential Series 321 (Christine S. Patrick ed., 2007).

46. Letter from Henry Knox to Governor Mifflin (May 24, 1794), *in* 6 Pennsylvania State Archives 668 (John B. Linn & William H. Egle eds., 1877).

47. Letter from Governor Mifflin to President Washington (May 25, 1794), *in id.* at 669–71.

48. Some even suggested that Washington's request was unconstitutional. *See* Letter from David Redick to Governor Mifflin (June 5, 1794), *in id.* at 679.

49. *See, e.g.*, Letter from Governor Mifflin to President Washington (June 14, 1794), *in id.* at 701–5; Letter from the Secretary of War to Governor Mifflin (June 19, 1794), *in id.* at 706–7; Letter from Gen. Knox to Governor Mifflin (June 25, 1794), *in id.* at 712–13; Letter from Governor Mifflin to Secretary of War (June 24, 1794), *in id.* at 714–15; Letter from Governor Mifflin to President Washington (July 15, 1794), *in id.* at 742; Letter from Gen. Knox to Governor Mifflin (July 17, 1794), *in id.* at 744–45.

50. As noted earlier, a similar dispute arose over the administration's request that Mifflin use his statutory authority to summon the state militia to suppress the Whiskey Rebellion. Mifflin said that the statutory preconditions for summoning the militia had not been met and that therefore he could not comply. *See supra* note 24.

51. *See* Act of Sept. 23, 1794, 15 The Statutes at Large of Pennsylvania from 1682 to 1801, at 208 (James T. Mitchell & Henry Flanders eds., 1911).

52. Letter from Isaac Shelby to Thomas Jefferson (Jan. 13, 1794), *in* 1 American State Papers: Foreign Relations, *supra* note 23, at 455–56. One author speculated that Shelby would have complied had Washington directly ordered him. *See* Archibald Henderson, *Isaac Shelby and the Genet Mission*, 6 Miss. Valley Hist. Rev. 451, 464–65 (1920).

53. Letter from Edmund Randolph to Thomas Jefferson (Mar. 29, 1794), *in* 1 American State Papers: Foreign Relations, *supra* note 23, at 456–57.

54. Proclamation on Expeditions against Spanish Territory (Mar. 24, 1794), *in* 15 The Papers of George Washington: Presidential Series 446–47 (Christine S. Patrick ed., 2009).

55. Act of June 5, 1794, 1 Stat. 381.

56. *See* Mann Butler, A History of the Commonwealth of Kentucky 228–29 (1834).

57. *See* Letter from Henry Knox to George Washington (Dec. 16, 1793), *in* 1 American State Papers: Indian Affairs, *supra* note 34, at 361–62.

58. *See* Celia Barnes, Native American Power in the United States: 1783–1795, at 167 (2003).

59. Letter from Andrew Pickens to General Clark (Apr. 28, 1793), *in* 1 American State Papers: Indian Affairs, *supra* note 34, at 369.

60. U.S. Const. art. I, § 10, cl. 3. Perhaps Telfair can be charged with having attacked the wrong branch of the Creek tribe, for even if the state had a constitutional right to make war against those who had declared it, the state arguably could not wage war indiscriminately against all Creek tribes.

61. As a legal matter, things stood differently once the president summoned a state governor and his militia. At that point, the governor was subject to the laws of war and could, as a formal matter, be court-martialed. But as the text notes, this legal possibility was fraught with practical difficulties.

62. These early episodes of gubernatorial "insubordination" presaged bitter disputes over James Madison's summoning of the militia in the War of 1812. Several New England

governors rejected the president's orders, arguing that they could independently judge whether the constitutional conditions for summoning the militia had been met. These governors (fortified by some state judicial opinions) denied that the president was the sole judge of whether the militia could be summoned. *See generally* 1 American State Papers: Military Affairs 322–26 (Gales & Seaton eds., 1832). The war was unpopular in New England, suggesting that politics might have spurred the opposition.

63. Martin v. Hunter's Lessee, 14 U.S. (1 Wheat.) 304, 305 (1816).

64. Wesley J. Campbell describes how the federal government increasingly came to rely upon federal (rather than state) officers. *See* Wesley J. Campbell, *Commandeering and Constitutional Change*, 122 Yale L.J. 1104, 1144–45 (2013).

Chapter 13. The President as "Glorious Protector" of the Constitution

1. *See* Cooper v. Aaron, 358 U.S. 1, 18 (1958).

2. *See* U.S. Const. art. VI, cl. 3.

3. U.S. Const. art. II, § 1, cl. 8.

4. *See* Coronation Oath Act, 1688, 1 W. & M., c. 6, § 3 (Eng.).

5. Evarts Boutell Greene, The Provincial Governor in the English Colonies of North America 54–55 (1898).

6. *See, e.g.,* Md. Const. arts. XXXVIII, L (1776).

7. *See* Vt. Const. ch. II, art. XXVI (1786); Pa. Const. § 40 (1776).

8. *See* S.C. Const. art. XXXIII (1776).

9. *See* S.C. Const. art. XXXVI (1778); Mass. Const. pt. 2, ch. VI, art. I (1780).

10. Ga. Const. art. XXIV (1777).

11. 1 The Records of the Federal Convention of 1787, at 22 (Max Farrand rev. ed., 1966) [hereinafter Records of the Federal Convention].

12. *Id.*, vol. 2, at 87.

13. *Id.* at 185.

14. *Id.* at 427.

15. *Id.* At the convention's end, Hamilton, in a document given to James Madison, suggested an oath that apparently was not part of his June plan. *Compare id.*, vol. 1, at 292 (Hamilton's June plan), *with id.*, vol. 3, at 624 (requiring the president to "protect the rights of the people, and preserve the Constitution inviolate").

16. Letter from George Washington to United States House of Representatives (Apr. 5, 1792), *in* 10 The Papers of George Washington: Presidential Series 213–14 (Robert F. Haggard & Mark A. Mastromarino eds., 2002).

17. Editorial Note, *in id.* at 195–96.

18. Letter to House of Representatives of the United States (Mar. 30, 1796), *in* 1 A Compilation of the Messages and Papers of the Presidents: 1789–1897, at 194–96 (James D. Richardson ed., 1897) [hereinafter 1 Messages and Papers of the Presidents].

19. Letter from Thomas Jefferson to Abigail Adams (Sept. 11, 1804), *in* 10 The Works of Thomas Jefferson 89 n.1 (Paul Leicester Ford ed., 1905); *see also* Letter from Thomas

Jefferson to Judge Spencer Roane (Sept. 6, 1819), *in* 12 The Works of Thomas Jefferson 135, 137 (Paul Leicester Ford ed., 1905) ("[E]ach department is truly independent of the others, and has an equal right to decide for itself what is the meaning of the constitution in the cases submitted to its action; and especially, where it is to act ultimately and without appeal."). Perhaps Jefferson's best explanation of interpretive independence comes from a passage omitted from his first annual address. If each branch was to check the others, each "must have a right in cases which arise within the line of it's proper functions" to decide the constitutionality of an act "according to it's own judgment, & uncontrouled by the opinions of any other department." *See* The Paragraph Omitted from the Final Draft of Jefferson's Message to Congress (Dec. 8, 1801), *in* 3 Albert J. Beveridge, The Life of John Marshall 605 (1919). While uniformity of views and public acceptance over time might cement an interpretation, Jefferson also believed that "[s]ucceeding functionaries have the same right to judge of the conformity or non-conformity of an act with the constitution, as their predecessors who past it. [F]or if it be against that instrument it is a perpetual nullity." *Id.*

20. *See* Veto Message (Mar. 3, 1817), *in* 2 A Compilation of the Messages and Papers of the President: 1789–1897, at 576, 582 (James D. Richardson ed., 1897) [hereinafter 2 Messages and Papers of the President].

21. *See* U.S. Const. art. I, § 6, cl. 2.

22. Note from George Washington to Senate (Feb. 28, 1793), *in* 12 The Papers of George Washington: Presidential Series 238 (Christine S. Patrick & John C. Pinheiro eds., 2005).

23. Technically, a violation would have occurred only if the president had appointed the senator. Yet Washington knew that he should not set in motion a chain of events that might culminate in a violation. If the appointment would violate the Constitution, the nomination was problematic.

24. Message from Abraham Lincoln to Congress in Special Session (July 4, 1861), *in* 4 The Collected Works of Abraham Lincoln 421, 430 (Roy P. Basler ed., 1953) (emphasis omitted).

25. Letter from Abraham Lincoln to Albert G. Hodges (Apr. 4, 1864), *in id.*, vol. 7, at 281.

26. After ratification, some states imposed "preserve, protect, and defend" duties on their governors, legislators, and other officers. *See* Fl. Const. art. VI, § 11 (1838); Ga. Const. art. II, § 5 (1789); S.C. Const. art. IV (1790).

27. S.C. Const. art. XXXVI (1778).

28. *Id.*

29. Mass. Const. pt. 2, ch. VI, art. I (1780).

30. The claim here is a relative one, based on the notion that it is generally more difficult to safeguard the Constitution from threats external to, rather than arising from within, the executive branch.

31. *See, e.g.*, Thomas Jefferson, Opinion on the Constitutionality of the Bill for Establishing a National Bank (Feb. 15, 1791), *in* 7 The Papers of George Washington: Presidential Series 348, 353 (Jack D. Warren ed., 1998).

32. The Legal Significance of Presidential Signing Statements, 17 Op. O.L.C. 131 (1993); Curtis A. Bradley & Eric A. Posner, *Presidential Signing Statements and Executive Power*, 23 Const. Comment. 307 (2006) (discussing the practice under President George W. Bush).

33. For an expanded version of the argument contained here, *see* Saikrishna Prakash, *Why the President Must Veto Unconstitutional Bills*, 16 Wm. & Mary Bill Rts. J. 81 (2007). For a contrary view, *see* William Baude, *Signing Unconstitutional Laws*, 86 Ind. L.J. 303 (2011). Baude argues that there sometimes will be a risk of a constitutional violation no matter whether the president vetoes a bill or signs it into law. I believe this is largely a theoretical possibility, because Congress is less likely to include unconstitutional provisions in a world where a veto would automatically issue. In any event, if Baude is right, Congress could induce the judiciary to *uphold* unconstitutional legislation by including a nonseverability clause and including provisions necessary to defend the Constitution that would be eliminated upon a judicial finding that a portion of the law was constitutional. Baude's argument suggests that facing this dilemma, a court could properly decide to uphold the provisions that are unconstitutional. I disagree.

34. That is to say, the president must veto bills when they contain provisions that are incapable of constitutional application. I do not believe that the Constitution ordinarily obliges the president to veto bills containing provisions that are merely capable of unconstitutional applications. Almost any bill's provisions are capable of being executed in an unconstitutional manner. When a bill's provisions are capable of constitutional application, the president may suppose that Congress intended only such applications. But if he concludes that Congress intends its bill to have unconstitutional applications (at least as the president understands the Constitution), then he must veto the bill, because Congress would be demanding that the president take unconstitutional measures.

35. *See* Michael B. Rappaport, *The President's Veto and the Constitution*, 87 Nw. U. L. Rev. 735, 766–83 (1993); Michael B. Rappaport, *The Unconstitutionality of "Signing and Not-Enforcing,"* 16 Wm. & Mary Bill Rts. J. 113 (2007).

36. Letter from George Washington to Alexander Hamilton (Feb. 16, 1791), *in* 7 The Papers of George Washington: Presidential Series, *supra* note 31, at 357.

37. *Id.*

38. *See* Letter from Thomas Jefferson to George Washington (Feb. 15, 1791), *in id.* at 348, 353. To counter Jefferson's statement and President James Madison's view that presidents are obliged to veto unconstitutional bills, the Department of Justice's Office of Legal Counsel notes that Jefferson signed a bill that appropriated funds for the Louisiana Purchase, even though he doubted the constitutionality of the purchase. *See* The Legal Significance of Presidential Signing Statements, 17 Op. O.L.C. 131, 134 (1993). But this argument fails to recognize the possibility that Jefferson viewed himself as *violating* the Constitution when he signed the appropriation. Jefferson believed that it was sometimes appropriate to violate the law in order to serve higher ends: "A strict observance of the written laws is doubtless *one* of the high duties of a good citizen, but it is not the *highest*. The laws of necessity, of self-preservation, of saving our country when in danger, are of

higher obligation." Letter from Thomas Jefferson to John B. Colvin (Sept. 20, 1810), *in* 11 The Works of Thomas Jefferson 146 (Paul Leicester Ford ed., 1905). Having violated the Constitution by ratifying the Louisiana Purchase (at least in his own mind), Jefferson was hardly going to veto an appropriation implementing the treaty. One violation begat another, perhaps justified by a belief that practical considerations occasionally ought to trump constitutional limits. Jefferson never argued that the president lacked a constitutional obligation to defend the Constitution against unconstitutional bills or that his actions with respect to the Louisiana Purchase were legal. In public, he was quiet on the latter question.

39. *See* Letter from Thomas Jefferson to George Washington (Feb. 15, 1791), *in* 7 The Papers of George Washington: Presidential Series, *supra* note 31, at 348; Alexander Hamilton, Enclosure: Opinion on the Constitutionality of an Act to Establish a Bank (Feb. 23, 1791), *in id.* at 425; Edmund Randolph, Enclosure: Opinion on the Constitution of the Bill for Establishing a National Bank (Feb. 12, 1791), *in id.* at 331.

40. *See* Veto Message (Mar. 3, 1817), *in* 1 Messages and Papers of the Presidents, *supra* note 18, at 584, 585.

41. *Id.* at 584.

42. Letter from James Madison to Jesse Jones and Others (June 3, 1811), *in* 3 The Papers of James Madison: Presidential Series 323 (J. C. A. Stagg et al. eds., 1996).

43. Veto Message (May 4, 1822), *in* 2 Messages and Papers of the Presidents, *supra* note 20, at 142.

44. *See* Veto Message (July 10, 1832), *in id.* at 576, 582, 591 (claiming that "[i]t is as much the duty of the House of Representatives, of the Senate, and of the President to decide upon the constitutionality of any bill or resolution which may be presented to them for passage or approval as it is of the supreme judges when it may be brought before them for judicial decision," and noting that by vetoing he had fulfilled his "duty").

45. Bradley & Posner, *supra* note 32, at 335; *see id.* at 323 tbl.1 (citing statistics on presidential signing statements expressing constitutional concerns about statutes).

46. *See, e.g.,* Christopher N. May, Presidential Defiance of "Unconstitutional" Laws: Reviving the Royal Prerogative 16–18 (1998).

47. *See id.* at 127–30.

48. *See id.* at 130.

49. For a defense of a discretionary power to ignore laws that the president believes to be unconstitutional, *see* Presidential Authority to Decline to Execute Unconstitutional Statutes, 18 Op. O.L.C. 199, 200 (1994) (claiming the president has "authority" and "may" disregard unconstitutional statutes).

50. Thomas Jefferson, A Summary View of the Rights of British America, *in* The Essential Jefferson 3, 7 (Jean M. Yarbrough ed., 2006).

51. Tracts of the American Revolution, 1763–1776, at xxxi (Merrill Jensen ed., 1967).

52. Bayard v. Singleton, 1 N.C. (Mart.) 5, 7 (1787).

53. Symsbury Case, 1 Kirby 444, 447 (Conn. Super. Ct. 1785).

54. *See* Commonwealth v. Caton, 8 Va. (4 Call) 5, 20 (1782) (noting that unconstitutional laws were voided by the act in question being found constitutional). *See generally* William Michael Treanor, *The* Case of the Prisoners *and the Origins of Judicial Review*, 143 U. Pa. L. Rev. 491 (1994) (discussing the *Case of the Prisoners* as evidencing early acceptance of judicial review).

55. 2 Records of the Federal Convention, *supra* note 11, at 376.

56. 4 The Debates in the Several State Conventions on the Adoption of the Federal Constitution 188 (Jonathan Elliot ed., 2d ed. 1836).

57. *Id.*, vol. 3, at 540–41.

58. *Id.*, vol. 2, at 446 (emphasis omitted).

59. The Federalist No. 44, at 225, 230 (James Madison) (Garry Wills ed., 1982).

60. If we assume that Madison believed that the president must enforce all unconstitutional laws, his statement is hard to fathom. In that case, the success of the congressional constitutional violation clearly *would not* depend on the executive at all. The success of the usurpation would depend on nothing more than the passage of an unconstitutional law, with enforcement following automatically.

61. Several factors explain why Washington never refused to enforce statutes on the grounds that they were unconstitutional. To begin with, he entered office with a clean slate. Since the Constitution made it clear that preconstitutional statutes were not part of the "supreme Law of the Land," U.S. Const. art. VI, cl. 2, every federal statute that Washington had to enforce was enacted under his watchful eye. If he concluded that a bill was unconstitutional, he vetoed it, as he did with the apportionment bill. Hence, the only way Washington would have faced the possibility of enforcing an unconstitutional statute was if he had had second thoughts about a statute that he had previously permitted to become law. Apparently, this never happened. Similar reasons explain why John Adams never disregarded a law on the grounds that it was unconstitutional.

62. *See e.g.*, Thanksgiving Proclamation (Oct. 3, 1789), *in* 4 The Papers of George Washington: Presidential Series 131, 132 (Dorothy Twohig ed., 1993) (beseeching God to provide a "Government of wise, just, and constitutional laws, discretely and faithfully executed and obeyed"); To the United States Senate and House of Representatives (Oct. 25, 1791), *in* 9 The Papers of George Washington: Presidential Series 110, 113 (Mark A. Mastromarino and Jack D. Warren eds., 2000) (noting that there should be "a steady and firm adherence to constitutional and necessary Acts of Government"); 3 Diary and Autobiography of John Adams 283 (L. H. Butterfield ed., 1961) (agreeing with those who sought to have the governor and council "order the Courts of Justice to proceed without Stamped Papers, upon the principle that the Stamp Act was null because unconstitutional"); Novanglus No. VI (Feb. 27, 1775), *in* 2 The Papers of John Adams 288, 298 (Robert J. Taylor ed., 1977) (arguing that if the Tea Act was unconstitutional, then the "act of parliament is null and void, and it is lawful to oppose and resist it"). *See generally* Saikrishna Bangalore Prakash, *The Executive's Duty to Disregard Unconstitutional Laws*, 96 Geo. L.J. 1613, 1660–64 (2008).

63. Alien and Sedition Act of 1798, § 4, 1 Stat. 596, 597.

64. *Id.*

65. *See* Letter from Thomas Jefferson to William Duane (May 23, 1801), *in* 34 The Papers of Thomas Jefferson 169 (Barbara S. Oberg ed., 2007).

66. *Id.*

67. Letter from Thomas Jefferson to Abigail Adams (July 22, 1804), *in* 10 The Works of Thomas Jefferson, *supra* note 19, at 88 n.I.

68. *Id.* at 87–88 n.I.

69. *Id.* at 88 n.I.

70. *See* Anas (Mar. 12, 1792), *in* 1 The Works of Thomas Jefferson 163, 211–13 (Paul Leicester Ford ed., 1904) (Washington concerned that the Senate might be invading the executive).

71. Letter to House of Representatives of the United States (Mar. 30, 1796), *in* 1 Messages and Papers of the Presidents, *supra* note 18, at 194, 196.

72. *See* Letters from the Secretary of War to the Governors of Georgia, Virginia, South Carolina (Oct. 1792), *in* 1 American State Papers: Indian Affairs 261–62 (Walter Lowrie & Matthew St. Clair Clarke eds., 1832).

73. Protest (Apr. 15, 1834), *in* 3 A Compilation of the Messages and Papers of the Presidents: 1789–1897, at 69, 70 (James D. Richardson ed., 1897).

74. Proclamation (Dec. 10, 1832), *in* 2 Messages and Papers of the President, *supra* note 20, at 643 (emphasis omitted).

75. Act of Mar. 2, 1833, 4 Stat. 632.

76. First Inaugural Address (Mar. 4, 1861), *in* 4 The Collected Works of Abraham Lincoln, *supra* note 24, at 262, 271.

77. *See e.g.,* Address Before a Joint Session of the Congress on the State of the Union, 2010 Daily Comp. Pres. Doc. 55, at 8 (Jan. 27, 2010), *available at* http://www.gpo.gov/ fdsys/pkg/DCPD-201000055/pdf/DCPD-201000055.pdf (criticizing the Supreme Court's decision in Citizens United v. FEC, 558 U.S. 310 (2010)).

78. *See, e.g.,* David Strauss, The Living Constitution (2011).

79. Letter from George Washington to House of Representatives (Mar. 30, 1796), *in* 1 Messages and Papers of the Presidents, *supra* note 18, at 186, 188.

80. *See* U.S. Const. art. II, § 1, cl. 8.

81. *Id.* art. II, § 3.

82. *See* Walter E. Dellinger et al., Principles to Guide the Office of Legal Counsel 1 (2004), *available at* http://www.acslaw.org/files/2004%20programs_OLC%20principles_white%20 paper.pdf (noting that OLC opinions are considered binding on the executive branch).

83. Geoffrey R. Stone, Perilous Times: Free Speech in Wartime: From the Sedition Act of 1798 to the War on Terrorism 71 (2004) (noting that the Sedition Act harmed the electoral prospects of Federalists and helped Republicans).

84. David N. Mayer, The Constitutional Thought of Thomas Jefferson 270 (1994) (quoting Jefferson as declaring that the Constitution may be protected by a "change of the persons" in the departments).

85. *See* Martin K. Gordon, *Militia Controversy, New England, in* The Encyclopedia of the War of 1812, at 471 (Spencer C. Tucker ed., 2012).

86. *See e.g.*, Kentucky and Virginia Resolutions, *in* William J. Watkin, Jr., Reclaiming the American Revolution: The Kentucky and Virginia Resolutions and Their Legacy 165, 170–72 (2004).

87. Letter from Sarah Gardner to George Washington (Nov. 16, 1789), *in* 4 The Papers of George Washington: Presidential Series, *supra* note 62, at 295, 296.

INDEX

Faithful Execution Clause *(Continued)*
judicial review and, 315; pardon
power and, 97; state nullification of,
311; Supremacy Clause confluence
with, 131; suspensions and
dispensations and, 94–95; wartime
statutes and, 161, 162. *See also* law
execution; legislation; Legislative
Power Clause
Farrand, Max, 20
federal courts. *See* judiciary
federal executive. *See* presidency
Federal Farmer, The (pamphlet), 39, 186
Federalists, 20–21, 39, 42, 57, 160, 223, 265;
administrative practices under, 98;
presidency and, 20, 39, 42, 51, 53, 119
Federalist Papers, 47, 96, 143, 193, 205, 210,
265, 308, 358n123, 367n73, 378n60,
388n24, 397n179, 398n197
federal law. *See* Faithful Execution Clause;
law execution; legislation
federal offices. *See* offices and officers
Fifth Amendment, 104
First Congress, 69, 149, 174, 267
Fishbourn, Benjamin, 178
Fisher, Louis, 232
Force Bill, 311
foreign affairs, 1, 2, 3, 8, 11, 64, 66, 82,
110–41, 321, 322; as English Crown
prerogative, 29, 111–12, 113; executive
privilege and, 229, 232–34; formal
diplomatic rules and (*see* diplomats);
judicial advice and, 281–83; letters of
marque and reprisal and, 29, 149,
204–5, 322; neutrality and, 122–24,
126, 139, 201, 282, 283, 290, 291, 293,
294; policy formulation and, 8, 111,
118, 122–26, 131, 135, 140; presidential
limitations and, 111–12, 125–26, 140;
presidential power and, 1, 110–41,
172–74, 283–84; Senate executive

powers and, 83, 110, 116, 117, 118–20,
123–24, 125, 130; shared powers of,
126–31; state executives and, 114, 126,
290–91, 293. *See also* commerce;
Declare War Clause; declare-war
power; Reception Clause; Treaty
Clause; treaty-making power; war
powers
Foreign Affairs, Department of, 120, 121,
124–25, 126, 129, 174, 185, 195, 200,
279
Fourteenth Amendment, 47
France, 44–45, 64–65, 71, 85, 102, 113–14,
122–28, 188, 282–83, 290, 293;
American hostilities with, 147, 240,
243–44; American Quasi-War with,
159; American Treaty of Alliance
with, 122, 124, 125, 127, 130–31, 146;
Constitution of 1791, 13, 14, 23, 52,
114, 265; monarchy and, 13, 14, 15, 23,
52, 130, 184
Franklin, Benjamin, 17, 21, 41, 43, 48, 54,
254
Frederick II (the Great), king of Prussia,
46, 47
French and Indian War, 164
Freneau, Philip, 189–90, 191
Fries's Rebellion, 106

generic grant theory, 68–73, 80, 81, 82,
103, 111, 134, 135; the state
constitutions and, 73–79, 351n69
Genêt, Edmond, 121, 128
George I, king of Great Britain, 46, 107
George II, king of Great Britain, 29, 46
George III, king of Great Britain, 2, 16,
27, 46, 47, 54, 159, 171, 189, 302, 324;
control of ministers, 29–30;
enumerated grievances against, 12, 15,
146, 251; second son of, 18; war
declaration by, 161

state governments, 25, 66, 172; and emergency powers, 208–9; federal laws and, 295–96, 308; federal legislative election regulation by, 261, 285; legislatures and, 37, 48–49, 78–79, 239, 259–61; presidential electors determined by, 49, 50, 285; ratification of U.S. Constitution by, 19–20, 21; Supremacy Clause and, 288, 308; veto power and, 251

state militias. *See* militias

State of the Union Clause, 243–45, 246, 267

statutes of limitations, 225

Stevens, Isaac, 108

Story, Joseph, 161, 218, 222

Strauss, Peter, 197–98

Sunstein, Cass, 199

superintendence, executive power of, 85, 89, 90, 118, 184–92, 193, 194, 196, 323, 398n197

Supremacy Clause, 119, 131, 172, 288, 308

Supreme Court, U.S., 24, 77, 90, 100, 197, 216, 251, 266, 279, 323; appellate jurisdiction of, 261; appointment of justices to, 172, 173, 177, 180, 301; as court of last resort, 282; as defender of the Constitution, 298; and judicial review, 295, 304, 315, 316; opinions and authority of, 274, 275, 276–77, 281, 301; presidential relations with, 48, 277, 281–82, 284, 301; state courts and, 295; and vesting of appointments, 179–81, 182

Suspension Clause, 216

suspension of habeas corpus, 9, 215–18, 236, 237, 301–2, 320

suspensions of statutes, 93–94, 105

Sweden, 14, 20

Taft, William Howard, 4

takings power, 210

Taney, Roger, 216

taxation, 210, 287–88, 290; federal excise tax, 92, 201, 211, 290, 296

Teir, Robert, 281

Telfair, Edward, 292, 293, 294–95

term limits, 43, 52, 53, 174–75, 225, 355n48

Thach, Charles, 32, 33, 81, 82, 83; *The Creation of the Presidency*, 80

title-and-number theory, 72, 81, 82

titles, granting of, 30, 42–45, 65, 83

trade. *See* commerce

treason, 102, 103, 221, 235

Treasury, Department of, 174, 177–78, 185, 188, 196, 199, 200–201, 259, 387n15

Treasury Act, 202

Treaty of Alliance (France-U.S.), 122, 124, 125, 127, 130, 146

Treaty Clause, 136, 140

Treaty of Hopewell, 131

treaty-making power, 14, 71, 94, 127, 148; colonial governors and, 135–36; English Crown and, 29, 112, 135; executive privilege and, 234–35; House encroachment on, 300, 310, 312–13; Indian nations and, 80, 98, 131; judicial advice and, 132, 281–82, 283; of president with Senate advice and consent, 11, 65, 69, 80, 83, 110, 111, 114–19, 130–32, 134, 135–40, 172, 194, 195, 234, 233, 265, 322, 367n23, 371n148; ratification and, 138; withdrawals and violations, 127, 129–32, 371n148

Tripoli, 159

triumvirate executive, 36, 38, 61, 68

Trumbull, Jonathan, 212–13, 241

Tucker, St. George, 218, 246